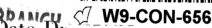
W9-CON-656

HURON COUNTY LIBR

2 008 095999 0

BIBLE BILL

BIBLE BILL

A BIOGRAPHY
OF
WILLIAM
ABERHART

by David R. Elliott and Iris Miller

REIDMORE BOOKS

Canadian Cataloguing in Publication Data
Elliott, David Raymond, 1948 -

Bible Bill

Includes index.
Bibliography
ISBN 0-919091-44-X

1. Aberhart, William, 1878-1943. 2. Prime ministers - Alberta - Biography. 3. Evangelists - Alberta - Biography. 4. Alberta Social Credit League. I. Miller, Iris, 1929- II. Title.
FC3674.1.A24E44 1987   971.23'02'0924   C87-091495-2

Reidmore Books
Suite 012 Lemarchand Mansion
11523 - 100 Ave.
Edmonton, Alberta
Canada

The publishers gratefully acknowledge the financial assistance of the Alberta Foundation for the Literary Arts and Alberta Culture.

Design and typesetting by Pièce de Résistance Ltée., Edmonton
Stripping by Color Graphics (Alberta) Ltd., Edmonton
Printing by Commercial Colour Press, Edmonton

Printed and Bound in Canada.

TABLE OF CONTENTS

■

PREFACE AND ACKNOWLEDGEMENTS

■

I T WAS A *time of drought, dust, Depression, and despair; a time of demagogues and dictators; a time known as the Dirty Thirties, when the world's economic and political scene was a shambles following the stock market crash of 1929.*

Governments rose and fell as they sought to bring stability out of chaos. It was a time when new parties arose and radical programs were tried. The unstable economy gave impetus to the emerging fascist movements in Europe. In the United States, Franklin Delano Roosevelt promised a New Deal to Americans. Others went further: Louisiana's Governor Huey "Kingfish" Long promised to make "every man a king" by redistributing wealth, while the Technocracy movement of Howard Scott sought to turn the government over to a group of economic and scientific experts.

Canada had its own unique responses to the Depression. One of them took place in Alberta where, in the 1935 provincial election, the new Social Credit Party swept the province, securing fifty-six of the sixty-three seats in the Legislature and leaving not one member of the incumbent government in it. For the next thirty-five years the Social Credit Party dominated the politics of Alberta and has had similar success in British Columbia in the last three decades.

The Social Credit victory in Alberta in 1935 was due mostly to the activity of one man, William Aberhart, a Calgary highschool principal and radio evangelist who became interested in Social Credit in 1932 and led his party to victory with a promise of a $25-a-month dividend for every adult citizen. He was unable to fulfil that promise while premier of Alberta from 1935 until his death in 1943, but his attempts at introducing Social Credit economic theory provide one of the most fascinating episodes in Canadian history.

Aberhart had been an authoritarian in his educational and religious activities, and when he entered politics he followed the same pattern, although there was considerable ideological conflict between the theology he had been preaching and the political philosophy he tried to impose. Aberhart's government tried to provide much-needed social and economic reform to alleviate human suffering during the Depression, but a number of his policies verged on fascism. Much of his legislation was quashed by the federal government because of its illegality.

Aberhart was an important figure in Canadian political history because his government dramatically reopened the question of federal and provincial jurisdictions - and he was also the first Canadian politician to use radio and drama effectively, to help win an election. He was a charismatic leader of messianic proportions for some of his followers. Because Aberhart carried on his religious work while premier of Alberta, his political papers reveal much that is new about his religious activities and thought. Now, at a time when fundamentalist religion in North America has allied itself with the radical right in an attempt to reshape public and private life, an examination of Aberhart's religio-political experiment is both interesting and appropriate.

Aberhart was a complex personality; he had many faces. Some readers may object that the Aberhart portrayed here is not the man they knew. This is very possible, for they may have seen only one side of him. We have paid considerable attention to his theological development and his religious activities, because this was the world in which he "lived and moved and had his being." An understanding of his religious thinking is essential to understanding his subsequent behaviour.

William Aberhart has been the subject of many articles and books; however, this is the first complete biography. We have made considerable use of the Premiers' Papers of Alberta, the Aberhart Papers, and the records of various churches and religious organizations with which Aberhart was associated, most of which were closed to earlier scholars. These sources have been supplemented by interviews with Aberhart's family, friends, enemies, colleagues, and students – interviews conducted by the late Professor John

A. Irving from 1946 to 1957, by Iris Miller from 1953 to 1956, and by David R. Elliott from 1972 to 1982. The cartoons produced by Stewart Cameron for the Calgary *Herald* provide important visual documentation of the humour associated with Aberhart's ill-fated attempts at instituting Social Credit. Extensive use has also been made of the transcripts of Aberhart's radio broadcasts, prepared by the United Farmers of Alberta and now on deposit in the Walter Norman Smith Papers of the Glenbow-Alberta Institute, Calgary. As editor of the *United Farmer*, Mr. Smith corresponded with many individuals involved in Social Credit and we have used that correspondence to advantage. The recently-released and much-celebrated diaries of Mackenzie King, deposited in the Public Archives of Canada in Ottawa, provided valuable information on Aberhart's dealings with the federal government.

Many people have made this study possible. We thank the several hundred people who gave us their time and lent us their documents. Helpful academic guidance and criticism were provided by professors J.B. Toews, Henry C. Klassen, Peter C. Craigie, and Harry H. Hiller when much of this book was a M.A. thesis at the University of Calgary. Professor Howard Palmer, also of the University of Calgary, criticized the expanded manuscript at various stages and graciously assisted in applications for funding. The archivists at the Glenbow-Alberta Institute, Calgary, and the Provincial Archives of Alberta, Edmonton, have been of great assistance. Jennifer Shaw edited an early version of this manuscript. The final edit was done by Peter Smith. Financially, the completion of this project was made possible through an Exploration Grant received from the Canada Council and a travel grant from the Canadian Plains Study Center, Regina. A grant from the Alberta Foundation for the Literary Arts assisted in the publication of this book.

David R. Elliott, Edmonton, Alberta
Iris Miller, Ottawa, Ontario

CHAPTER ONE

■

THE FORMATIVE YEARS

I AM *Canadian born,
reared and brought up in Western Ontario; my
parents were pioneers in Ontario. I have gradually
imbibed that Canadian courage that impels us to
stand for right no matter what happens.*

— CFCN Broadcast, William Aberhart, 1935

Having grown up in Egmondville, Ontario, a community named after one of the local heroes of the Rebellion of 1837-38, young William Aberhart had often heard how the rebels had fought against the economic power and political privilege of the Tory "family compact" in Upper Canada. Every day on his way to school he had passed the estate that had once belonged to Colonel Anthony Van Egmond. Van Egmond had died in Toronto's Don Jail for his part in aiding William Lyon Mackenzie's quixotic insurrection, an insurrection that nevertheless and eventually resulted in Britain's granting Canada responsible government. With the actions of such early reformers indelibly imprinted in his mind, Aberhart, years later, rallied the citizens of Alberta to rise in opposition to the "Eastern interests" in Toronto and Montreal.

This childhood experience of an area proud of its rebellious past was not, however, Aberhart's only exposure to non-conformity; reaction against authority had been the main reason why his family had come to Canada in the first place. Aberhart's grandparents, William and Sophia Eberhardt, had lived in the Grand Duchy of Mecklenburg in western Prussia. William died during or shortly after the Revolution of 1848, and the family either fled or were expelled from Germany after refusing to pay taxes to their repressive government.[1]

On the way to North America in 1851, Sophia, her six children, and her newly-acquired second husband Christopher Heffler, a widower some twenty years her senior, were shipwrecked off the coast of Newfoundland. Family tradition claims that most of the passengers carried their entire wealth in money belts and that the ship's crew, knowing this, refused to allow into the lifeboats anyone who would not hand over a considerable amount.[2] After their rescue, and much the poorer, Aberhart's ancestors made their way up the St. Lawrence River and headed for Hamilton, where they took an ox cart to Egmondville in Tuckersmith Township, Huron County, Canada West (now the province of Ontario).

During the 1850s Canada West was still very much part of the frontier. Throughout Huron County, which had been opened up by John Galt and Colonel Van Egmond, pioneers were carving homesteads out of the virgin forests and swamps. Egmondville, which had developed around the estate of Colonel Van Egmond, lost its importance, however, when the railway was put through a mile to the north, in 1858. A new town called Seaforth was created at Guide Board Swamp, and when salt mines brought new industry to Seaforth, most of Egmondville's merchants moved there.

Economic necessity forced the Eberhardt children to begin working at an early age. The fourth child, William (1843-1910), the father of the premier-to-be of Alberta, was seven when they arrived in Canada. Never having attended school, he was illiterate, and his name appeared variously on official documents as Eberhardt, Eberhart, Aberhardt, Aberhart, or other variations thereof, depending on how officials chose to spell it. Eventually he seems to have settled on Aberhart. For the sake of convenience, he is hereafter identified as William Aberhart Sr. In 1861 he appears to have been a blacksmith's helper, and later he worked in the salt mines at Seaforth. On some occasions he and his brother Charles drove the stagecoach between Seaforth and Brussels, Ontario. Another brother, Henry, who carried Christopher Heffler's surname for some time, worked as a teamster for the brewery in Egmondville.[3]

By 1871 William Aberhart Sr. was farming in Tuckersmith Township with his wife Louisa Pepper (1848-1944), who had been born in Fullerton Township, Perth County, Upper Canada.[4] Her English-born parents John and Elizabeth Pepper were also farmers. In 1874 William and Louisa Aberhart purchased a twenty-hectare wheat farm on Concession #8, Hibbert Township, Perth County, approximately fourteen kilometers southeast of Seaforth. William Sr. was a hardworking, successful farmer and steadily acquired more land holdings. About the time of William Jr.'s birth in 1878, William Sr. bought out his brother Henry's twenty adjoining hectares, and then in the 1880s he added yet another twenty hectares to his farm.[5]

The elder Aberhart was tall and powerful, having hardened his muscles in the salt mines, and he could toss barrels of salt into his wagons with little effort. Local merchants knew him as a thrifty man who struck hard bargains.[6] He was also known for his penetrating blue eyes and his flowing blond beard. His beard was worn in Mennonite fashion and blew over his shoulders as he drove his high-spirited horses through the countryside. William Sr. took no active part in the community life of Egmondville and Seaforth, other than occasionally joining his friends for drinks at the local tavern.[7]

Louisa Aberhart worked alongside her husband on the farm. She was short and, in later life, given to stoutness; but she was strong in physique and will. Seven of her eight children were born without medical assistance, and she is said to have left her bed shortly after the most difficult birth to milk an ornery cow.[8] Even compared to her husband she was a solitary person. She believed a woman's place was in the home, and she stuck close to it. The suffrage movement did not interest her; even by 1935 she had never voted, and claimed that if men did not know how to run the country, she did not see how women could be expected to do any better.[9]

On the Hibbert farm the Aberharts lived in a two-story, buff-coloured brick farmhouse at the end of a tree-lined lane. There the fourth of their eight children, and third son, William Jr., was born on 30 December 1878. When he was old enough William Jr. walked to Hibbert School #7, a one-room wooden structure. Then in 1886, when his older sister and brother were ready to attend highschool, the family moved closer to Seaforth; the distance was too great for daily commuting, and they could not afford to board the children in town.[10] They sold the Hibbert property and purchased a new wheat-and-dairy farm located on Mill Road in Tuckersmith Township, approximately two-and-a-half kilometers southwest of Seaforth. William Jr. continued his elementary education at Egmondville.

On the Tuckersmith farm the Aberharts lived better than the average family. Their white, two-story farmhouse, covered with clapboard siding, stood on an open rise of land and could be seen from every direction. The house had a spiral staircase to the second floor, and the parlour boasted a piano and fine furniture. Out behind the house were farm buildings later shaded by the large deciduous trees that the boys planted. A stream flowing through the back of the property provided a ready supply of fish and a source of water for the livestock. A new piggery that William Sr. had constructed along the latest scientific principles, and which was described as a "palatial mansion," was the talk of the community and earned him a reputation as a progressive farmer.[11]

William Sr. encouraged his sons to be hard workers. Years later William Jr. recalled:

My father used to tell us boys on the farm, in our younger days, that we could never plow a straight furrow if we did not focus our attention on a particular post or tree or other landmark away at the end of the field. He warned us again and again not to allow a big stone or clump of bush or a tree to distract us as we passed along.[12]

He heeded his father's words and turned that plowing technique into a philosophy of life; he never allowed distractions to sidetrack him.

William Jr. was also greatly influenced by his mother. Apparently she dominated the family and handled most of the discipline. William Sr. preferred to let the children learn from their own mistakes. On one occasion a hired hand gave William Jr. a plug of chewing tobacco; he became so sick that he never tried tobacco again in any form.[13]

As a boy William Jr. physically resembled his father. He also possessed immense energy and a voracious appetite. His daily routine was full. At four

The Aberhart family. William Aberhart Jr. stands second from the right.

or five a.m. he joined his brothers in milking the family's forty cows. On the way to school they delivered milk to their father's customers in Egmond-ville and Seaforth. One stop was at a hotel where Charles traded glasses of milk for glasses of beer, but William Jr. never acquired a taste for alcohol.[14] After finishing their milk route, the boys left their horse and wagon at the hotel and proceeded to school. Usually there was another milk delivery in the evening because the Aberharts did not have refrigeration facilities.

Life on the farm had many pleasures, but it also had its dangers. Once, while William Jr. was watering his father's high-spirited team, one horse reared and kicked him in the face, knocking him cold. He fell beneath the horses and would have been seriously trampled if his sister Augusta, who had been watching from the kitchen window, had not dragged him to safety. He carried the scars from that accident for the rest of his life.[15]

Louisa demonstrated little affection for her children, but she did desire success for them and considered an education necessary. One day, a local wag, known as "Old Fuzzy" because of his long shaggy whiskers, spoke to Mrs. Aberhart after seeing her sons going to school day after day through all kinds of weather. He felt they were wasting their time and that school would ruin them for the farm. "All they need is 'common old horse sense,'" he argued. But Mrs. Aberhart was certain more was needed to be successful in the modern world. Impressed by Old Fuzzy's logic, William Jr. and his older brother wanted to leave school. After some persuasion from his mother William Jr. agreed to continue, but John quit to become a blacksmith.[16]

At school William Jr. was only an average student, but he shone in some areas. He developed beautiful penmanship, and mathematics was one of his better subjects. He had amazing powers of concentration and retention, and was able to study without effort at the kitchen table, even though the rest of the family or guests were sitting around it talking.[17] But his dependence on his photographic memory had a deleterious effect: he never came to value inductive reasoning. Learning by rote seems to have been fostered by one of his mathematics teachers at Seaforth Collegiate Institute, William Prendergast, who gave his students math problems and their formulae but refused to show them the reasoning behind the formulae. Rather, he emphasized memorization.[18] William Jr. was further intellectually stifled by his father, an opinionated man who became even more so with a few drinks under his belt.[19] Occasionally the elder Aberhart engaged his sons in frivolous discussions and then laughed at their reasoning.[20] Consequently, William Jr. never really acquired an appreciation for inductive intellectual analysis.

There was no pressure for the Aberhart children to stay on the farm. Augusta, the eldest, married and moved to the United States. Charles went to Toronto's School of Pharmacy, and his parents started him in business in Seaforth where he was known as "400% Aberhart" because of his supposed mark-up on goods.[21] John remained a blacksmith and settled at Woodstock, Ontario. Louis, who spelled his last name Eberhart, ran a mill and machinery business in Egmondville. Monetta also married and operated restaurants in Exeter and Grand Bend, Ontario. Henry was the black sheep of the family. He was a horse-dealer with a bad reputation; he abandoned his family, disappeared, and was eventually buried in a pauper's grave in northern Michigan.[22] Wilfrid, the youngest, worked as a barber in Detroit.

As a middle child William Jr. made an extra effort to establish his own identity, and in his quest for achievement, he outshone all of his siblings combined. He often amused himself and learned to play several musical instruments without lessons.[23] Some of his classmates remembered him as someone who did not mix well with the other children at school.[24] He usually went home immediately after school to do his homework, hobbies, and chores.

Since he spent much of his childhood alone, William Jr. had a great amount of time to observe how people functioned socially. He eventually discovered that he, too, could be more socially active, by organizing events and people. Later he said, "I have been organizing all my life. There's nothing I'd rather do than organize. It's a hobby with me."[25] Early in his life he seems to have decided he could work at this hobby by becoming a school teacher, and in the fall of 1896, after completing two years of highschool, he went to attend the model school in nearby Mitchell.[26]

The model schools, created by the province of Ontario to meet the increasing demand for teachers, were usually elementary schools operated by a principal and three teachers. For three months the students received a teaching apprenticeship, along with occasional lectures from the local school inspector. Upon completion of this training, they received a third-class certificate qualifying them to teach in elementary schools. Those who desired higher standing returned to highschool for one or two more years. Educators now characterize this method of teacher training by its cheapness, poor quality, and poor salaries. One scholar has claimed that the "effect of the model schools upon the status of the profession was devastating. They succeeded only in handing over the majority of the schools to the half-trained and immature."[27]

After completing model school William Jr. went to the business college at Chatham.[28] He may have felt that he could make more money as a businessman than as a teacher. One of his instructors reported:

> We found him to be a particularly bright young man, and have every reason to believe that he would make a successful business man. In so far as we have any knowledge of him, he is strictly honest and trustworthy, and his character is above reproach.[29]

Yet, in spite of his success, he withdrew after four months and returned to Seaforth Collegiate Institute to write the summer exams. He then received his second-class teaching certificate,[30] and during the academic year 1897-98 he completed the fourth form.[31] In that final year of school, he established a reputation as an athlete. In the fall track meet he won first place in the running long jump, senior shot put, running high jump, 100-yard dash, and the bicycle race.[32]

He also began to get about socially; he was an unsuccessful candidate for the managing committee of the Collegiate Institute Literary Society,[33] but he did gain recognition as a member of the school football team, where he was considered one of the best players because of his size and weight.[34] It was said that opposing players might as well have run against a stone wall as run against halfback "Whitey" Aberhart, a name he acquired because of his blond, almost white hair. Because of his skill he was selected for the famous Seaforth Hurons, a team that held the Haugh Cup for at least twelve consecutive seasons.[35] Had Aberhart's personality transformation come about from living away from home for a year? Or did his desire to become a minister have something to do with it?

Sometime during his highschool years, William Jr. experienced a religious conversion. William James's classic *Varieties of Religious Experience* notes that conversion can often reorient a person's entire lifestyle;[36] but unfortunately, since Aberhart left few autobiographical comments on the early

William Aberhart at nineteen.

stages of his religious development, the circumstances of his conversion are difficult to establish. When he did refer to his conversion and the development of his theology, in sermons and speeches, his comments appear to have been embellished for homiletical purposes.

As a child William Jr. attended the Presbyterian Sunday school in Seaforth, although neither of his parents attended church. William Sr. had been raised a Lutheran, but was indifferent to religion.[37] Louisa Aberhart's religious background was more obscure. Her parents had declared to census-takers in 1851 that they belonged to no church.[38] Sometime before 1871, however, Louisa Aberhart had established an affiliation with the Presbyterian Church; but William Jr. claimed that while he was a child, she was not much for attending services; her family of eight children kept her too busy. However, he did describe her as a "God fearing woman."[39] What formal religious instruction William Jr. received appears to have been confined to his Sunday school experience.[40]

There is also a story circulated by John A. Irving that William Jr. was influenced by itinerant evangelists, not so much by what they said as by their effect upon people. According to this story (which, it must be noted, comes third-hand from hostile sources), Aberhart gave the following personal reflection during an unguarded moment:

> Excuse my pounding this table. It reminds me of the fact that when I was a boy we had protracted revival meetings in our district. I sat in those meetings night after night and marvelled at the power of the preacher over the people. The preacher was very emphatic and he pounded the pulpit heavily. I was so impressed that I went out into a woodlot, day after day, and practised speaking and pounding a pine stump with my clenched fists. I had discovered the power of words and gestures over people, and I have never forgotten the power of that preacher to dominate those people.[41]

However much the story seems to fit Aberhart's personality, his closest associates do not remember hearing it from *him* and question its authenticity.[42] If William Jr. had contemplated entering the ministry at this time in his life, it was not evident in his actions, for he continued with his education as a school teacher.

After completing fourth form, William Jr. sought further training at the Ontario Normal School at Hamilton; but before leaving for school he broke his leg while picking apples on his father's farm.[43] His departure had to be postponed for several weeks, and the injury prevented him from participating in the sports program. Instead, he threw himself into his studies. One of his fellow-students there was William M. Martin, later premier of Saskatchewan and Supreme Court justice.[44] In the spring, Aberhart again earned his reputation as an athlete, playing centre on the basketball team and continuing to be a formidable halfback in football.

While he was studying at the normal school William Jr. appears to have undergone several spiritual crises, and his new-found religious faith was severely shaken. Either inside or outside of classes he was exposed to modern liberal theology, which emphasized biblical criticism and evolutionary theories. Commenting on this crisis some twenty years later, he said:

> While in my university [*sic*] courses I had listened to the vaporing of modern theology. I heard them say that the first twelve chapters of Genesis was an allegory; that the story of the Flood was an Eastern Exaggeration, for the water had not covered the whole earth; that the crossing of the Red

Sea was Eastern Imagery, and that it was the natural result of an East wind; that the yarn of Joshua and the Sun standing still was merely National legend, and not by any means scientifically accurate; that the story of Jonah and the whale was picturesque and figurative, and not meant to be taken in any literal fashion; that the first chapter of Matthew, which describes the virgin birth, was unscientific and fanciful. I heard them say these things, and for a time I hardly knew where I was at.

I went to a saintly old chap, a Bible teacher, and told him my trouble, and he gave me a little advice that seemed to satisfy, but in reality it kept me back three or four years. He said, "I treat my Bible as I would a nice plate of fish that might be set before me. I eat the meat and leave the bones for the dogs." I thought that was fine, so I went along leaving anything that didn't suit my taste to the dogs. Then one day I came across II Timothy 3:16.... It suddenly dawned on me that there were no husks, no bones, no indigestable matter in the Bible; that ALL Scripture was profitable; and that as long as I assumed the attitude I was [*sic*], I could never receive any correction from it.[45]

For a while he tried to accept the Bible completely and interpret it literally, but he soon became bewildered with the discovery of conflicting dietary regulations in the Old Testament and inconsistencies between the Old and New Testaments.[46] (He solved these difficulties later in Brantford when he adopted a radical system of biblical interpretation called dispensationalism.)

During this time William Jr. also experienced Calvinistic anxiety over whether he was one of the elect, those predestined to eternal salvation. When confronted by a woman who asked him if he had eternal life, he said, "I hope so." "That's no answer!" she replied, and then introduced him to the Arminian interpretation that salvation comes by an act of faith, not divine election.[47] With that new understanding, Aberhart never again appears to have questioned his eternal destination. His adoption of Arminianism also marked the beginning of his digression from Presbyterian doctrines.

Upon graduating from the normal school in 1899, Aberhart received his first teaching post in Huron County at Morris School #7, situated between Belgrave and Wingham, approximately forty-eight kilometers northwest of Seaforth. His salary for the first year was probably $295.[48]

Few details of Aberhart's personal history survive from this time, but as the twentieth century approached, it brought dramatic social changes. It may have been at this time that Aberhart and his old bay mare saw their first automobile. While driving his buggy to town one day he saw an odd-looking contraption chugging and jerking towards them. It could be heard a long distance away. The mare, who was usually such a quiet old creature that she never needed to be tied up, stopped dead still, pricked up her ears, snorted, and then took to the ditch. Aberhart claimed that had he not been able to stop her, he was sure the horse would have cleared the nearby fence – buggy and all.[49]

After Aberhart had taught for two years the public school inspector for East Huron recommended him for a first-class professional teaching certificate. Inspector Robb was especially impressed by the discipline, order, management, and progress of Aberhart's school.[50] Aberhart's personal characteristics – hard work, a strong memory, organizational ability, and determination, instilled in him by his parents and teachers — would become more pronounced during the next phase of his life.

CHAPTER TWO

■

VOCATION OR AVOCATION?

$$\boxed{\text{I}}\ \text{HAVE } known$$

Mr. William Aberhart...intimately...since...
October 1908. He was...actively engaged in Church,
Sunday School and Y.M.C.A. work and he bears an
excellent character.... As a citizen he enjoyed the
confidence and respect of all citizens of Brantford.

— E.E.C Kilmer, Inspector of Schools, 1910

Armed with his professional certification Aberhart moved on in his teaching career. In the fall of 1901 he accepted a teaching post in Brantford, one of the leading commercial and industrial centres of the Niagara Peninsula, known for its manufacture of farm machinery and implements. Because of his training at Chatham Business College, Aberhart was placed in charge of the commercial form at Brantford's Central Public School, at a salary of sixty dollars a month.[1] The school was the pride of the community, with its neogothic architecture, sculptured hedges, and manicured lawns, and it was to be Aberhart's place of employment for the next ten years. However, his involvement in religious activities soon rivalled his career as an educator.

While Aberhart was living in Brantford, and after he adopted dispensationalism, his theology underwent radical changes. Dispensationalism was a sectarian system of theology alien to Aberhart's background in the Presbyterian Church, and at odds with his role as an educator. It included a pessimistic cyclical philosophy, dividing human history into seven unequal periods of time, called dispensations. In each dispensation God made a covenant with man, man broke the covenant, and judgment followed. Each time, man's failure to keep the covenant was of increased magnitude. In each period the regulations were somewhat different; therefore the key to understanding the Bible was to know which verses applied to which dispensation.[2]

Aberhart seems to have been led to dispensationalism by his interest in biblical prophecies concerning the future.[3] Aberhart said of prophecy:

> It is a fact that many have been led to believe in Christ through its study, and scores of others have been edified in the Christian faith through its acceptance. I personally bear my testimony to the truth of this last statement. It was through its study that I became interested in the Bible.[4]

The prophetic movement with which Aberhart became associated was loosely linked to the Plymouth Brethren sect formed in the mid-1820s, after John Nelson Darby (1800-1882) and others left the Church of England because they believed that the Christian church in general had become secular and corrupt.[5] The Brethren rejected an ordained ministry and invented dispensationalism, which reflected their anti-clerical and anti-ecclesiastical attitudes.[6] Dispensationalism then spread from England and Ireland to North America through Brethren literature and through visits by Brethren missionaries, who established a Bible conference in Boston in 1868. There, and at other conferences throughout the United States and Ontario, a frequent theme was the expected imminent return of Christ and the establishment of the Millennium, a thousand-year reign of peace on earth. Because they expected Christ to return *before* the Millennium, they were called premillennialists. They claimed that theirs was an orthodox, if neglected, doctrine. However, theological critics charged that the idea of an earthly millennium was not an orthodox Christian idea at all, but a heresy derived from apocryphal and pseudepigraphical writings.[7] The premillennialists were naturally outspoken in their opposition to post-millennialists, who believed that through man's progress and social reform, the Millennium could be established, and that only *after* its thousand-year fulfillment would Christ return. Post-millennialism had been the standard eschatology of nineteenth-century American revivalists who had fathered the social gospel. However, as the social gospel became more secularized, its adherents had dropped belief in the *physical* return of Christ.

From 1883 to 1897 the premillennialists held conferences during the summers at Niagara-on-the-Lake, and these subsequently became known as the Niagara Bible Conferences. Because many Canadians attended these meetings, premillennialism and dispensationalism became quite prominent in Southern Ontario.[8] Although premillennialism and dispensationalism were not synonymous, the dispensational form of premillennialism was the dominant theme. It was accepted by many laymen and ministers although it contained theological concepts at variance with Protestant creeds in general and Presbyterian doctrines in particular.[9] A surprisingly high number of delegates to the conferences were from Presbyterian backgrounds.[10] It has been suggested that the Calvinists joined with the dispensationalists because they saw them as an ally in their struggle for the doctrine of biblical inerrancy and against the theology of the social gospel.[11]

The Niagara Bible Conferences continued until 1900, when they were discontinued because of a drop in attendance largely caused by growing dissatisfaction with the emphasis on dispensationalism.[12] For those who were classical premillennialists, dispensationalism marked a radical theological departure, with its sharp dichotomy between faith and works, differentiation between Jew and Gentile, separation of the church from the Kingdom of God, making the Millennium an earthly Jewish kingdom, its claim that the Lord's Prayer and most of the contents of the Gospels had no relevance for the Christian, and its division of the Second Coming of Christ into two phases – the imminent Rapture (or divine "evacuation" of all Christians from the earth) before the terrible Tribulation (a period of unprecedented world chaos), followed by the return of Christ after seven years.[13]

Even though dispensationalism has been described as a modern heresy,[14] it is not surprising that Aberhart adopted it. A number of prominent Ontario clergymen had been active participants in the Niagara Bible Conferences, among them the Reverend Henry M. Parsons (1828-1913) of Toronto's Knox Presbyterian Church, who was known for his dispensational theology; the Right Reverend Maurice Baldwin (1836-1904), Anglican Bishop of Huron, who was a frequent speaker at the Conferences; and the Reverend Robert Cameron, whose Park Baptist Church in Brantford was across the street from Zion Presbyterian Church, which Aberhart attended. Another Baptist minister from Brantford, the Reverend Elmer Harris (1854-1911), son of John Harris of Massey-Harris fame, founded Toronto Bible College. He later served as one of the consulting editors of the *Scofield Reference Bible*, an annotated version that became the standard source for dispensational teaching.[15]

Just how Aberhart was first introduced to prophecy and dispensationalism is not known; but he did credit Cyrus Ingersol Scofield (1843-1921), the well-known American dispensationalist, with influencing his theological development:

> It was Dr. Scofield who started me on my Bible study. He advertised a Correspondence Course of some fourteen lessons for $5.00. I sent for it and his first four lessons started me off so that I knew how to study. I owe a great deal to Dr. Scofield. He placed me on a path that has proved more bright as the days go by.[16]

Such a correspondence course would have appealed to Aberhart: it reduced difficult theological problems to a matter of memorizing questions and answers.

Aberhart learned more of dispensationalism when Zion Presbyterian Church hosted a Bible conference in 1902.[17] Guest-speakers included Elmer Harris and A.C. Dixon, who later edited *The Fundamentals*, a series of paperback books defending conservative Christianity from the advances of modern theology. The following year Aberhart met and heard his theological mentor Scofield when the latter spoke at the church.[18]

Not all of Aberhart's time, however, was spent in theological speculation. During this period he married Jessie Flatt (1878-1966) of Galt, Ontario,

Jessie Aberhart, c. 1902.

whom he had met at a football game in the fall of 1901. Little is known of her background. Their romance appears to have been a little one-sided at first: somewhat of a social butterfly, Jessie considered the young teacher a good catch.[19] As the feelings became mutual, William's main concern was whether or not he could afford to be married. In the spring of 1902 he applied for a raise of $100 a year. He and Jesse were married on 29 July 1902 in North Dumfries, near Galt, with William's brother John as best man.[20]

It is unlikely even at this time that Jessie shared William's religious and moralistic attitudes. Along with dispensationalism William had acquired those personal beliefs and behavioural patterns that were associated with a fundamentalistic outlook. He disapproved of theatre-attendance, card-playing, drinking, and smoking. It was about this time that he wrote his parents a letter in which he criticized their religious attitudes and, in particular, castigated them for dishonouring the Sabbath.[21] Needless to say, his comments were not appreciated.

While Aberhart's theology was developing, he continued to advance in his teaching career. In a letter of recommendation his principal, William Wilkinson, noted Aberhart's personal qualities, his teaching methods, and especially his disciplinary powers. His discipline was stressed again the following year by the public school inspector.[22]

Aberhart recorded his own thoughts on school discipline in an essay he wrote in the winter of 1903, around the time of the birth of his first child Khona Louise. In that essay he discussed the tension between the creativity and individuality of a student on the one hand and group discipline on the other. He chose the latter. His essay revealed a certain amount of personal insecurity; he viewed the classroom as a battlefield in which he had to be the victor, and he frequently used military terminology. He also expressed admiration for Oliver Cromwell and his organization of the New Model Army.[23]

Aberhart's classroom operated much like an army camp. He assigned each of his students a three-digit number by which he addressed them rather than by name,[24] and stamped their assignments with a rubber stamp that read "Checked by Wm. Aberhart."[25] Some students appreciated Aberhart's teaching methods, but others hated them. With recalcitrant students he had no patience; for slight misdemeanors he is said to have doled out strappings on Monday, Wednesday, and Friday, and for more serious offences he recommended suspension or expulsion. One former student claimed that Aberhart did everything he could to break the spirit of a child.[26] But whatever one may now think of Aberhart's pedagogical techniques, they were apparently accepted by his educational peers and superiors.

In 1905 the principal of Central Public School died suddenly and Aberhart became the interim principal. At the end of the school term, he was appointed to the position for the next year. He was considered a good candidate because of his experience and the commercial specialist's certificate with honours that he had earned from the Ontario Department of Education.[27] His new position as principal brought his salary up to $1,000 per year. The extra income came in handy, for in August the Aberhart's second child Ola Janet was born.

About this time Aberhart began preaching as a layman. On many Sundays he rode his bicycle out to a semi-rural school at Tranquility, near Brantford, where Zion Presbyterian Church operated a Sunday school that drew forty to fifty children and adults of various denominations.[28]

Aberhart's theology had been developing through contacts with visiting evangelists, and he had established a friendship with Norman Camp, from Moody Bible Institute in Chicago, who taught a course at the Y.M.C.A. that sought to reconcile the Bible and modern geology. Camp used as his text George H. Pember's *Earth's Earliest Ages*. Pember, a dispensationalist, argued that there was a gap between Genesis 1:1 and 1:2, during which time, after the rebellion of Lucifer, God had turned off the sun. This, Pember said, resulted in the ice ages, and caused the destruction of life and created the fossil record. Then, after possibly millions of years, God re-created the earth, along with plant and animal life, including man. Aberhart found Pember's book convincing, and it became one of his standard theological texts.[29] He was also present when the Reverend William Bell Riley of Minneapolis spoke in Brantford in 1904. Riley was one of the major leaders of the fundamentalist movement and would cross Aberhart's path again in the future.[30]

During the next two years Aberhart had further opportunities to listen to dispensational speakers. In October 1905 Arno C. Gaebelein, editor of the dispensational magazine *Our Hope*, and one of the editors of the *Scofield Reference Bible*, spoke at Park Baptist Church in Brantford.[31] In January 1906 Reuben A. Torrey, first superintendent of Moody Bible Institute and later founder of the Bible Institute of Los Angeles, whose books were widely advertised in Brantford, held meetings in Toronto. A special train was hired by those in Brantford who wanted to go to the meetings. Aberhart also heard J. Wilbur Chapman, D.L. Moody's colleague, when Chapman spoke in Brantford.[32]

Since many of the above-mentioned men who had an influence on Aberhart's theology had been associates of Moody (especially Camp, Torrey, and Chapman), it was not surprising that Aberhart developed a great admiration for that evangelist. Dwight L. Moody (1837-1899) was not an ordained minister; he had been a shoe salesman who began a transdenominational Sunday school in Chicago and later worked as an itinerant evangelist whose influence was felt internationally. Moody had also promoted a Bible institute in Chicago for the training of lay ministers and missionaries. Aberhart admired Moody's energy and fame, described in a biography published in Brantford in 1901.[33]

Probably as a result of these influences Aberhart decided to study for the ministry and enrolled in a correspondence program from Queen's University at Kingston, Ontario, writing on his application "minister" as his intended profession. His university education was rather unusual; he took his entire degree by correspondence, had no time for extensive research, and was never able to interact with his teachers and other students and thereby refine his thinking. That he was able to complete his degree at all shows a tremendous amount of ambition and initiative, for he had to carry his studies along with his duties as principal, husband, father, and lay preacher. Other than first-class honours in mathematics, his marks were very poor, reflecting the little time he was able to devote to his studies. He failed Greek twice, Hebrew once, and received only 35 per cent in Honours Political Science. He finally completed his B.A. degree in 1911.[34]

As Aberhart was preparing for the ministry he quickly became involved in the administration of Zion Presbyterian Church. In 1906 he became an elder of the church, having won the highest number of votes in the election.[35] As an elder he was responsible for visiting members of the congregation, assisting the minister in conducting worship, and serving on the decision-making board of the church.

In 1907 he began listing in a ledger his sermons and the places he preached them, revealing that he was supply-preaching in Presbyterian, Methodist, Baptist, and Congregational churches in Brantford, Hamilton, and the surrounding area. One of his most common and favourite themes was the Second Coming of Christ.[36]

In his earliest extant sermon, "The Second Coming of Christ," Aberhart sought support from the writings of Luther, Calvin, Latimer, Milton, Wesley, and Whitefield to show that belief in the return of Christ was a standard Christian doctrine.[37] However, he seems to have failed to realize that his interpretation of this doctrine differed considerably from that of the sources he cited.

The concept of the Rapture, as taught by Aberhart, had been popularized around 1830 by Darby of the Plymouth Brethren, and by Edward Irving (1792-1834), a defrocked Presbyterian minister who had founded the Catholic Apostolic Church in England. Samuel P. Tregelles, a biblical scholar who had been associated with both Darby and Irving, claimed that the Rapture idea had originated during one of Irving's pentecostal meetings.[38] Whatever its origin, the idea of the Rapture as a divine "evacuation" had never been part of the creeds of Christendom, but was an idea based on scattered biblical verses taken out of context.

Whether he realized it or not, Aberhart was teaching a complex system of biblical interpretation with a distinctive ecclesiology derived from the Plymouth Brethren, whose anti-clerical rejection of the established churches underlay their dispensationalism and their Rapture concepts. They believed that most church members were not Christians, and they sought to gather people from the "world" and the churches to await the Rapture. A correspondent to the editor of the Methodist *Christian Guardian* noted that advocates of Brethren ideas often "wormed" their way into congregations, disrupting church life and withdrawing with their supporters.[39] Aberhart followed a similar pattern later in Calgary.

Most dispensationalists rejected the social gospel that taught that Christians had to minister to their neighbours' physical needs as well as their spiritual ones. Not only did dispensationalists reject man's ability to ameliorate social conditions but also they insisted that to interfere with the status quo would be against the will of God, since the Bible (they claimed) had prophesied bad social conditions in the last days.[40] They also believed that since Christ could appear at any moment, there was no time for social action, and all effort had to be devoted to evangelism.[41] The arch-dispensationalists, the Plymouth Brethren, refused to vote or to hold public office, and some even refused to read newspapers.[42] Aberhart expressed some of the same sentiments when he stated in 1907:

God never intended us to reform the world. The world will never be fit for the everlasting habitation of the just. We are to seek and save the lost, pointing them to Jesus....[43]

Although Aberhart denounced the Brethren for their rejection of the established church,[44] he retained their theology even though it was very contrary to the goals that he, as a Presbyterian elder, was supposed to adhere to: those of extending the Kingdom of God in the world by both sacred and secular means. As a dispensationalist Aberhart believed that the Kingdom of God would only be realized in the Millennium. At the same time, his position as principal of Central Public School was also contrary to his dispensational theology, for he was very much involved in the affairs of the "world" in preparing boys and girls to be its citizens. These conflicts of thought and behaviour reflect the impracticability of his theology, his eclecticism, his leadership ambitions, and his need to make a living. The contradictory aspects might also be explained by his compartmentalized thinking, characterized by memorization instead of inductive thought.

In this same sermon of 1907, "The Second Coming of Christ," Aberhart also broke with Scofield, who taught that the seven churches listed in the Book of Revelation were a panorama of church history. Aberhart rejected that idea, and instead followed an interpretation advocated by some of the more extreme Plymouth Brethren: the seven churches were future apostate churches that would exist during the Tribulation, after the "true" Christians had been "raptured."[45]

Aberhart taught these dispensational concepts in many places. He organized a Bible Class for the teachers of his school, supervised the Young People's Guild at Zion Presbyterian Church, taught a training class for Bible study leaders at the Y.M.C.A., and another for students at the Brantford Collegiate Institute. He also conducted evangelistic services at the Massey-Harris factory, as well as supply-preaching, and conducting a Bible class at Zion Presbyterian Church.[46]

In spite of his dispensationalism Aberhart continued in his plans to enter the Presbyterian ministry, perhaps feeling that this would be the best means for spreading dispensational "truth." He submitted a letter to the local Presbytery requesting that he be recognized as a candidate for the ministry and, in the event that he received his B.A. that year, that he be permitted to complete the theology courses for a B.D. degree at Knox College, Toronto, in two years rather than three. His application was supported by letters of recommendation from the ministers of Zion Presbyterian Church and St. Andrew's Presbyterian Church in Brantford.[47] The following month Aberhart addressed the ecclesiastical court, and after hearing his request and questioning him, they forwarded his request to the General Assembly, which granted it the following year. (By that time Aberhart had moved to Calgary, so it was suggested that he be transferred to the supervision of the Presbytery of Calgary.)[48]

In 1910 a headline in the Brantford *Daily Courier* read: "Popular Principal Receives an Offer from Calgary. Mr. Aberhart of Central School

Wanted."[49] Aberhart would soon become part of the human drift to western Canada.

After the new provinces of Saskatchewan and Alberta had been created in 1905 there was a massive immigration into this "last best west," where

Aberhart and his young daughters Ola and Khona.

homesteads were available to those who wished to escape the crowded urban centres of Central Canada, the United States, and Europe. Between 1906 and 1911 Alberta's population doubled. Among those who were part of the exodus from central Canada were two of Aberhart's teaching colleagues who had gone to Calgary, and as Caleb and Joshua, they had sent him favourable reports from the frontier.[50]

Because Aberhart's friends had spoken very highly of him in their conversations with Calgary school officials when they were building a new school, the Calgary School Board sent him an unsolicited offer to be its principal – with the offer of an annual salary of $1,400, $200 more than he was currently receiving. For a while Aberhart was undecided. He was firmly entrenched in the educational and religious life of Brantford, but the offer was tempting. As president of the Brantford City Teachers' Association Aberhart knew that the Brantford School Board was not likely to give him a raise to match Calgary's offer.

But when the public heard of the offer to Aberhart they raised a clamour. His staff and fifty of his commercial students petitioned the School Board asking that Aberhart be retained. To test the waters Aberhart offered his resignation, prompting the School Board to offer him a one-hundred-dollar raise because they, too, were anxious to have his services.[51] Another motion was put forward suggesting that Calgary's offer be matched, but it was opposed by one Board member, Tom Ryerson, a local fruit merchant with a reputation for parsimoniousness, who had a personal dislike for Aberhart.[52] The raise was set at $100. Taking this to be a divine sign that he should accept Calgary's offer, Aberhart asked the Board to accept his resignation and allow him to leave by the first of April.[53]

Aberhart quickly made plans for his move to Calgary; he put his two-story frame house on Nelson Street up for sale and began completing his other business. When he submitted his resignation as president of the Teachers' Association he expressed the hope that he would be able to invite some if not all of his fellow-teachers to join him in Alberta.[54] His resignation was accepted with regret, and one school teacher, a Mr. Parks, added that it was unfortunate Toronto and the West could steal the best teachers from smaller centres by offering them larger salaries. In one of his rare letters to the editor, Aberhart responded to Mr. Parks by stating his philosophy of education, blaming school boards for the present problems in education. Teachers, he said, had to be treated as professionals, and their salaries should reflect their training and place in the community.[55]

Aberhart carried with him to Calgary letters of appreciation and best wishes from his students, teachers, and some public officials. The mayor spoke for many of Brantford's citizens when he wrote to Aberhart:

> I am more sorry than I can express that you have decided to leave Brantford. Everyone admits that you have done first class work as Principal of our Central Public School and you have surrounded yourself with a large number of friends who esteem you very highly for your moral worth and Christian character. I know that you have been the instrument through which God has spoke to many a heart and no greater honour than that can come to any man in this world. No one can blame you for seizing the wider opportunities of our growing West. I sincerely hope that your fondest hopes may be fully realized and that Mrs. Aberhart, yourself, and the children may enjoy life in your new home.[56]

Aberhart seems to have considered that his "ministry" in Brantford was complete; he was being called to a new mission field in the West. The new school in Calgary seems to have been only a secondary consideration.

CHAPTER THREE

■

PREACHER ON THE PRAIRIES

WE HAVE *assembled here today to express to you our deep gratitude for the solicitude with which you have watched over this little flock during the too brief period of your Pastorate....*
Yes, we shall try to show forth in our lives, the doctrine you have so eloquently preached, striving to imitate from afar, your all embracing benevolence and charity.
— Members, Westbourne Baptist Church, 1916

When Aberhart arrived in Calgary during the Easter holidays of 1910, he was met at the train station by a delegation consisting of clergymen, and of children and teachers from Alexandra Public School.[1] That night he was shown the sights of the city. His wife Jessie and their two daughters had remained in Brantford so that Khona could finish her school year and he could find a place for them to live. Although he had been appointed to the new Mount Royal School, it was not yet ready, and in the meantime he was to be principal of Alexandra School,[2] which was situated not far from the original site of Fort Calgary.

Not long after his arrival in Calgary, Aberhart received word that his father had died as a result of a drinking accident. At this time Huron County was "dry," and alcohol could be obtained legally only for medicinal purposes. Charles Aberhart operated the drugstore in Seaforth and kept a bottle of whiskey handy on a certain shelf so his father could get a drink whenever he was in the store. One day, a new clerk rearranged the bottles on the shelf, not knowing of the tacit agreement. Being illiterate William Sr. accidently reached down a bottle of carbolic acid and took a swig. Realizing his mistake, he ran across the street to the doctor's office but died within minutes.[3] Aberhart did not attend his father's funeral; the distance was too great and he was awaiting the arrival of his wife and children. The incident no doubt strengthened his aversion to alcohol and propelled him into the temperance movement.

Jessie Aberhart and the girls at last joined William, who met them at the train in Calgary and lifted the girls through the open window of the coach. From the station they made their way to the upper portion of a house that he had rented across the street from Alexandra School, in the east end of the city.

It was a new experience for Mrs. Aberhart to encounter the raw atmosphere of a town that, thirty years before, had been almost non-existent. Here there was nothing of the sedate predictability that they had left behind in the tree-lined streets of Brantford. The "Sandstone City" in which they found themselves was still a cowtown. The wooden railings outside the hotel bars were gnawed thin by the bored horses of cowboys in town for the cattle market, supplies, and relaxation. The smell of horse manure permeated the air. (Another visitor to Calgary in 1910 remarked that it was the "horse-smellingest town" he could remember.[4]) Drunkenness was common; Ninth Avenue, which ran in front of the C.P.R. station, was called "Whiskey Row." One day Mrs. Aberhart was appalled to see a lurching, muttering, drunken Indian on a downtown sidewalk and hurriedly conducted her daughter Ola into the middle of the street to avoid encountering him face to face.[5] Frontier culture provided the Aberharts with other surprises. On the first Sunday after his arrival, Aberhart went to church wearing a silk top hat and frock coat, as had been his custom in Brantford. To his embarrassment he discovered that he was the only one attired in this manner, and when he returned home he put these clothes into storage.[6]

Calgary was, however, rapidly changing. Many public buildings constructed of sandstone or travertine, with neoclassical façades, began to replace the wooden structures. Opulent mansions owned by Calgary's business élite were making their appearance in the fashionable districts of Mount Royal, Elbow Park, and around Central Park. The number of automobiles was steadily increasing, and a street-railway system had been inaugurated only a few months before Aberhart's arrival. The population of Calgary in 1910 was about fifty thousand, and the city was bursting at the seams. As the building of homes, roads, schools, and stores continued, the city limits were extended in 1910 – and again in 1911.

In the fall of 1910 Mount Royal School, to which Aberhart had been appointed, was still not completed, so he was made principal of Victoria School.[7] At about the same time the Aberharts moved to their newly-purchased two-story woodframe house at 1216 Thirteenth Avenue S.W. – then on the outskirts of the city. This house would be their home for the next seventeen years.

One of Aberhart's early friends in Calgary was the Reverend George W. Kerby, minister of Central Methodist Church and founder-principal of Mount Royal College. It was not long before Aberhart started appearing as a guest-preacher at Kerby's "Men's Own" meetings.[8]

Aberhart plunged into the religious life of the community, and within a short time he was supply-preacher at Trinity Methodist Church and in other Methodist, Presbyterian, and Baptist churches in and around Calgary.[9] Lines between Protestants, particularly between Presbyterians, Methodists, and Baptists, were rather fluid. Ministers of these denominations exchanged pulpits, held joint services, and talked of church union. This ecumenical spirit had developed partly as a result of frontier conditions. In the early days of Calgary's history the cost of heating two churches of different denominations in the same vicinity had caused congregations to unite for the winter months.[10] As well, ministers and congregations of most Protestant denominations had cooperated in the temperance movement, the Lord's Day Alliance, and the fight against prostitution. Their joint involvement in social reform had also been reflected in the establishment of the local Y.M.C.A. and Y.W.C.A.[11] Such interdenominational activities had created a religious atmosphere in which people could move from church to church with little difficulty. Aberhart had lived and worked in a similar religious atmosphere in Brantford, and the premillennial movement that he represented had adherents in most denominations.

During the first months that the Aberharts lived near Alexandra School they worshipped at nearby St. Andrew's Presbyterian Church, where Aberhart established a Bible class that was very well attended. He made an immediate impact on his audience and gathered a group of fascinated adherents, some of whom followed him for many years. However, he soon discovered resistance to his theology. The minister of St. Andrew's, the Reverend A. Mahaffy, was lukewarm in his appreciation of certain aspects of Aberhart's teaching concerning the Second Coming of Christ, and the resultant rift was the first of many in Aberhart's evangelistic career in Calgary. Aberhart made a hasty exit from St. Andrew's, followed by a considerable number of his Bible students, who moved to Trinity Methodist Church two blocks away.[12]

Aberhart and his family remained Presbyterians, however, and joined the affluent Grace Presbyterian Church in November 1910. Immediately after morning services at Grace Church, and after lunch, Aberhart hurried over to Trinity Methodist to conduct his afternoon class, which had over seventy-five members.

Aberhart brought dispensationalism to most of his audience for the first time. The teaching that God had divided the history of the world into seven dispensations, or periods of time, appealed to them as being orderly and logical. It gave Aberhart the concrete framework within which he felt impelled to organize any subject he was teaching. "How he could sub-divide the work!" said one admiring student from those far-off days of 1910.[13]

The apparent contradictions in the Bible were at once stripped of their difficulty when Aberhart suggested that in each dispensation God followed a different plan for the salvation of man. The teaching of the imminence of the Rapture indicated that the present dispensation might end at any moment. Aberhart's emphasis on the imminent Rapture worked a certain magic on his audience, who dreamed that they themselves might be allowed to take part in that event and escape the experience of death. It lent a feeling of urgency to Aberhart's already eager audience and explains the sense of mission that caused him and other dispensationalists to float from church to church, spreading their evangelistic message, hoping to gain converts before the Rapture closed the door of salvation forever.

Aberhart's Bible students were stimulated by his enthusiasm, his personality, and the freshness of his approach. Many were unwilling to leave when the class was over. He often walked home with a group of class-members and stood at their gateways in lively debate. They plied him with questions, and sometimes the discussions went on in one or other of their homes. The lesson was examined again, and was followed by discussions of the lives of the great evangelists whose biographies and memoirs most of them had read. On these occasions it would sometimes be two o'clock in the morning before Aberhart walked home through the chilly streets. "We had never seen anything like it," one student said forty-five years later. "We thought him to be the 'pearl of great price.'"[14]

However, a few Bible classes and the occasional sermon were not enough to fill Aberhart's spare time. He played soccer for the Young Men's Club at Trinity, and his Bible class had several picnics during the summer months. It was at one of these picnics that the subject of Aberhart's baldness came up, and he recalled an episode in Ontario in which he and a number of other young men had dared each other to shave their heads. "Mine was one that didn't grow in again," he said, with a wry smile. Someone replied that he could not expect to have brains and hair too.[15] In these moments of relaxation Aberhart was entirely charming, "a big man with a big smile and a big laugh." He could relax and enjoy a joke and entered into social evenings with almost as much enthusiasm as he brought to his teaching.

The audience that Aberhart had at Trinity Methodist Church was mainly working-class; its needs were not being met by formal, conventional churches whose academically-trained ministers were far removed in experience and sympathy from the lives of most parishioners. Aberhart gave working-class people the opportunity to participate in religious life actively.

While Aberhart's Bible class at Trinity Methodist Church flourished, he was also becoming very active in the affairs of Grace Presbyterian Church. He had been inducted into the eldership and was responsible for ministering to the spiritual life of Presbyterians living in the district bounded by Ninth and Twelfth streets and Ninth and Fifteenth avenues S.W. He was also involved in church finances, auditing the treasurer's report and the financial statement of the Missionary Committee. Jessie Aberhart served the church as secretary-treasurer of the Home Mission Society.[16]

Aberhart appears to have been very popular at Grace Church, and was elected president of the men's fellowship, The Brotherhood of St. Andrew and Philip.[17] His Advanced Bible Class, which met on Monday evenings, received special billing in the church's newspaper advertisement.[18] He kept the class occupied with many special features, for example preparing and producing a play in which the doctrines of the Presbyterian Church were put on trial in courtroom fashion. Sports teams were also part of that Bible class, and they played against the teams of other churches. Aberhart enjoyed playing soccer, baseball, and tennis, and the class used the sports facilities at Mount Royal School where he was now principal.[19]

In spite of his popularity, Aberhart experienced some emotional difficulty when he preached during regular services at Grace Church. In his sermon ledger he recorded his own feelings when delivering his sermons, and the responses he received. On three of the occasions that he preached there, he recorded that he had "laboured" during his sermon delivery.[20] At no other time did he record this phenomenon. The members of Grace Presbyterian Church represented a higher social, economic, and educational level than that of the people to whom he usually preached. Calgary's business élites were very conscious of their social position and controlled the political life of the community through rigidly-imposed property qualifications for civic office. They also belonged to exclusive clubs similar to those in Toronto and Montreal,[21] and it is probable that Aberhart felt insecure in their presence. His membership at Grace Presbyterian may have had more to do with the wishes of his wife, who was a social-climber.

In the spring of 1912 Aberhart's popular Bible class at Grace Church came to a sudden halt and he eventually disassociated himself from that church. The incident that led to this break was quite common in church politics, yet the real reasons ran deep and stemmed from his authoritarian personality. The rift occured when one of the class members, Hugh Fraser, was in the hospital and the class sent him a small gift costing one or two dollars, purchased with offerings that had been collected in the Bible class. One of the elders, Thomas Humphries, objected, stating that all offerings belonged to the church. Aberhart insisted that the class could use its offerings any way it pleased.[22] A heated row developed between the two men. One night the minister, the Reverend Alexander Esler, slipped a note under Aberhart's door suggesting that he resign as elder because of the conflict,[23] an action performed without the knowledge or permission of the rest of the Session, the church's governing body. As a result of the note Aberhart resigned his position and withdrew from the church.

Aberhart's class was very upset and sought to have a congregational meeting without the Session's authorization, and when the Session sought to have a meeting with the Bible class, the class refused, whereupon the Session charged the class with insubordination and cancelled it. The class then took its grievances to the Presbytery and appealed for an investigation. After examining the Session Minutes, the correspondence between the parties, and after meeting with the class, the Session, and Aberhart and Humphries, the committee formed by the Presbytery presented its report. It ruled that the class had been insubordinate in going against the directives of the Session which, in turn, had been negligent in its duty towards the class by not allowing a congregational meeting. The committee also ruled that Aberhart's withdrawal from the church had been voluntary, but it still considered him a Presbyterian in good standing.[24]

Some have suggested that Aberhart's conflict with Humphries and Esler was theological,[25] but the Presbytery Minutes made no mention of this. Esler himself was very close to Aberhart in theology, being described as a fundamentalist,[26] and possibly a dispensationalist. He had such well-known dispensationalists as James Martin Gray of Moody Bible Institute and R.A. Torrey of the Bible Institute of Los Angeles preach at Grace Church.[27] Aberhart's conflict appears to have been largely over issues of personality and polity.

Aberhart's own plans to enter the Presbyterian ministry had by now faded. The biblical languages, the plague of many a divinity student, had been a problem for him. By the time he had earned his B.A. degree he was well established in Calgary, both his children were in school, and he could not afford to take off two or three years to study theology in Toronto. At the same time his own temperament was growing unsuited to the Presbyterian denomination, whose churches were run with little room for the personal freedom he desired. He preached at St. Paul's Presbyterian Church in June 1913; it was not until 1922 that he again gave a sermon in a Presbyterian church.[28]

After leaving Grace Presbyterian Church in 1912, Aberhart kept himself busy by preaching at Trinity Methodist Church during that summer and establishing another Bible class for those who had attended his class at Grace Church. Called the "West End Bible Class," the transplanted class from Grace Church met in the old Wesley Methodist Church building.[29] This was in addition to the class already at Trinity Methodist Church.

The Aberhart family started attending Wesley Methodist Church. By September 1913 Aberhart had become a member of its official board and was busy on banquet and financial committees, serving as offering-envelope steward, and teaching a boy's Sunday school class on Sunday mornings.[30]

Among Aberhart's fellow-church-members at Wesley Church were other famous Albertans. John E. Brownlee, a young lawyer from Sarnia, Ontario, who taught a literary class at Wesley, later became premier of Alberta. He also was a lay preacher, and he and Aberhart shared the preaching tasks at Trinity Methodist Church.[31] Another of Aberhart's acquaintances at Wesley

Church was Nellie McClung, the famous suffragist writer and temperance worker, who became a frequent guest-speaker at Aberhart's schools and worked with him when he became chairman of the Prohibition campaign sponsored by all of Calgary's Sunday schools.[32]

Meanwhile, Aberhart's Bible class at Trinity Methodist Church was becoming one of the largest in the city,[33] but it was not without its difficulties. As a result of an unknown dispute, Aberhart resigned in the fall of 1913, and it was only after a delegation asked him to return that he did so.[34] In the spring of 1915 he sought to extend his activities by offering an additional class on a week-night evening, but his request for the use of the church did not meet with wholehearted enthusiasm from one member of the church's board, who felt that since most of the members of Aberhart's class were not members of Trinity Church, the class was not really a church function.[35] Aberhart's "floating Bible class" had been drawing people from all the churches where he had preached and previously held classes. Also, the West End Bible Class had now shifted its venue to Trinity Methodist. But after the main dissenting board member resigned, Aberhart's request for a weeknight class was granted.[36]

As a result of this extra activity Aberhart began to withdraw from activities at Wesley Church and was last mentioned in the Minutes of Wesley Methodist Church for April 1916.[37] His departure seems to have been occasioned by greater opportunities elsewhere.

In October 1915 Aberhart had begun a series of lectures on the Book of Revelation on Monday evenings at the Baptist Young People's Society at First Baptist Church, and later at Heath Baptist Church.[38] Soon he learned that Westbourne Baptist Church, a small mission related to First Baptist Church, needed someone to preach for them since their minister had resigned.

On 5 December 1915 Aberhart preached his first sermon at Westbourne, which was near the Stampede Grounds, and after 2 January 1916, he was preaching there usually twice on Sundays.[39] The deacons reported that "although the church has not made any great strides in the matter of members, yet the little flock has so far been well supplied by lay preachers who had willingly come over and helped us."[40]

Sometime in April 1916 Aberhart indicated that he was planning to leave Westbourne. Whether his intention was real is not certain, but in all probability he was testing his popularity. The church responded to his intended resignation by giving a social night in his honour and presenting him with an illuminated address that expressed their appreciation.[41]

With this show of support and loyalty Aberhart stated that he would continue at Westbourne. Now that he had ascertained their loyalty, he felt confident that he could ask for the use of the church for his Bible class. The latter was facing problems at Trinity Methodist Church.

Trinity Methodist Church had been having financial difficulties for some time. The parishioners were not wealthy and, during the First World War, they had had problems paying the minister's salary. Aberhart's Bible class had attracted many people from all over the city, but they were not contributing anything towards the support or upkeep of the church. In February

1916 the church board requested that Aberhart's class help support the work of the church. There was a promise of support; but, since many of the class's members were not members of the church and hesitated to contribute, the class decided to move over to Westbourne, where Aberhart was preaching and holding another class.[42] In this way they could get free use of the Westbourne building. The Trinity class then dispersed its funds, donating $10 to Trinity Methodist Church and the balance to relief work in Belgium. Then, without informing the board of Trinity Church, the class left and took with them twenty-nine Bibles, twenty-nine prayer books, and five song books that the class had purchased during the past six years. Trinity's board objected to both Aberhart's withdrawal of the class from the church and the class's removal of the Bibles and books they considered church property.[43] Thus, Aberhart's class "floated" to the new site of Westbourne, the third move in the class's short history, and under less than auspicious circumstances.

The enlarged Bible class at Westbourne was very popular and grew in size. One woman who attended wrote to Aberhart:

> Your teaching has been so wonderfully beneficial to me. I've wanted to learn more about the Bible, but never have had the opportunity of studying with one who made it so plain and interesting as you do.[44]

Gradually Aberhart extended his influence throughout every phase of Westbourne's church life, until he was virtually in control of the church – all this without becoming an ordained minister, or even a deacon or member of the church; he was not even a Baptist. His influence over the congregation was so great that these issues did not seem to matter. Eventually Aberhart held more power than a minister, and confidently directed the operations of the board of deacons – that elected body whose word, within its own church, was law. The deacons, like the church membership, gave him implicit loyalty almost without exception, and Aberhart found in the Baptist practice of complete autonomy within each church the scope he needed. Here members were free to manage their own affairs, and they chose to call upon Aberhart for guidance, a call he expected. What seemed presumptuous high-handedness in Presbyterian or Methodist precincts was to these Baptists inspired leadership. The democratic norms and forms were, of course, observed.

Yet, in spite of his high position of authority at Westbourne, Aberhart had a reluctance to perform certain aspects of the ministry there. He had a "high church" attitude towards the sacraments and did not feel that he, as an unordained person, could administer them. He insisted that the church find some Baptist ministers who would administer communion, perform baptisms, and also handle some of the preaching duties.[45]

In April 1917 Aberhart discontinued his practice of recording his sermons, and since Westbourne had ceased advertising its services in the newspapers, it is rather difficult to trace his activities until the beginning of 1918. It is possible that during this time he became involved with another Bible class taught by Professor William Tucker Broad, LL.B.

Professor Broad (c. 1860-1923) was born in Cornwall, England, and may have been associated with Cliff College, a Methodist institution. After being involved in educational work in England he became a superintendent of schools in Pennsylvania.[46] He was a specialist in biblical languages and had served on the translation committee of the *Twentieth Century New Testament*. In 1910 he moved to Calgary and was one of the first organizers of Mount Royal College, where he taught math and English on a part-time basis. Denominationally, Broad was a Methodist and worshipped at Central Methodist Church. He also organized a Sunday-evening Bible class that met in various halls and was known as either the Calgary Bible Study Class or the Calgary Bible Institute.[47]

Broad was a dispensationalist and appears to have been a British-Israelite. British-Israelism is a chauvinistic belief system that teaches that the British peoples are descendants of the Ten Lost Tribes of Israel, and thus have a manifest destiny prophetically foretold in the Scriptures.

Several sources indicate that Aberhart and Broad worked together in religious pursuits for a short period of time, but since Aberhart's name never appeared in any of Broad's newspaper ads, their relationship is unclear. Oral sources indicate divergent opinions from Broad – reportedly everything from "Hear William Aberhart – the greatest man in Western Canada" to "Mr. Aberhart's doctrine is absolutely sound, but he simply doesn't know how to work, or cooperate with others, and he doesn't know the meaning of the word 'love.'"[48]

When Broad eventually moved to the Okanagan in 1918, Aberhart's class at Westbourne received an additional influx of members. T.S. Hughes, a rancher who was the president of Broad's Bible class, joined Westbourne, became a deacon and became president of Aberhart's class.[49]

Because Aberhart had expressed a wish to Westbourne Baptist Church that he be relieved of excessive preaching duties, the congregation, which was financially unable to keep a minister, applied to the Baptist Home Missions Board, asking that institution to support a pastor for six months, hoping that by the end of that time Westbourne Church would be in a position to pay part of his salary.[50] Meanwhile, Aberhart's class had grown larger, and he sought to expand its activities into another evening of the week. He was granted use of the church for that purpose.[51] Shortly afterward, however, the church was plunged into crisis. The congregation was stunned by a letter they now received from the Home Missions Board. Aberhart, it had said, would have to go; he would have to withdraw his Bible class from Westbourne.[52]

It was evident that Aberhart's sway over the life of Westbourne Church had been observed with some apprehension by the Baptist Union of Western Canada, of which Westbourne was a member. Though the Union had no direct power over any of its member-churches, it understandably preferred to see its churches under dependably orthodox management. A freelance leader like Aberhart could not be relied upon to remain bounded by even the slight restrictions of Union membership. He had already earned a reputation in Calgary. News of his activities had no doubt spread to Westbourne's trustees, and one of these was Thomas Underwood, a prominent businessman and former mayor of Calgary, who moved in the same social circles as Presbyterian and Methodist leaders with whom Aberhart first had come into conflict. The Home Missions Board, backed by the trustees from First Baptist Church, therefore stipulated that Westbourne should first offer some assurance of loyalty to the Union by removing the uncertainty implicit in the presence of Aberhart before expecting financial assistance.

While some close to Aberhart have claimed that Thomas Underwood's actions against Westbourne Church were not directed against Aberhart's theology, but only against his personality,[53] there is evidence that Aberhart's non-Baptist status, his dispensationalism, his eschatology, and his unusual preoccupation with the Devil were important reasons for the suspicions Baptist officials had of him.

Thomas Underwood was a staunch Baptist – so much so that he earned the nickname "Mr. Baptist." In Baptist polity there was no central Baptist Church, no hierarchy; each church was autonomous and had a loosely-defined creed. Yet there were certain beliefs that were held to be traditional. Membership in the Churches was generally restricted to those believers who, as adults, had been baptized by complete immersion. Aberhart had not been baptized in this manner, and this in itself would have been a touchy point with Underwood.[54] Baptism was not even discussed in Aberhart's sermons until 1920, and then in a context completely different from traditional Baptist beliefs.

The members of Westbourne were being called upon to decide their loyalty. Would they dispense with Aberhart, who had served them without remuneration, or would they repudiate his assistance and favour the Home Missions Board? Feelings ran high. The affair reached a climax when the congregation, arriving at Westbourne for their Sunday service, found the church doors locked against them. A notice on the doors stated that this was the action of the trustees from First Baptist Church.[55] Aberhart, however, had won the allegiance of the Westbourne membership. His destiny was theirs; working with him was a privilege of which no Home Mission Board or trustees were going to deprive them. They would, they said, keep Aberhart and his Bible class, and forget about the Home Missions Board.[56] The church was forced open and services resumed. Aberhart's followers were loyal and his foothold was revealed to be firm; but the affair constituted an indignity that Aberhart never forgot, and set off a feud with the Baptist Union that continued until his death.

Aberhart's Bible class, which met on Thursday evenings, had attracted so many people that Westbourne Church could no longer hold it. It was soon decided to move the class outside the church in order to attract a larger interdenominational following. For some time they met at the Calgary Public Library and changed the name of the class to the Calgary Prophetic Bible Conference. Aberhart had inserted "Prophetic" because it was a catchy word, and in a title would attract more people than the plain "Calgary Bible Conference." However, Aberhart found to his dismay that members of other sects had begun to attend his meetings. They kept asking questions that disrupted his discourse, so he moved the Prophetic Conference back to Westbourne Church, where the class paid a rental of $5.00 a night.[57] There, on his home base, Aberhart had more control over his audience.

Soon Westbourne was again plunged into crisis. It was discovered that the trustees had allowed the mortgage on the parsonage to default; the mortgage company seized it along with some other church property. The church also owned a cottage that it rented out, but the trustees who collected the rent had not paid taxes on the cottage, and the City seized it, too.[58] The congregation then sought to have the trustees inform them of the financial and legal status of the church.[59] The ensuing affair was to loom large in the lives of the church members – who came to consider it one of the darkest episodes in their church's history – and this incident had far-reaching effects upon Aberhart's association with Westbourne.

On 6 May 1919 the trustees met the church membership and stated that they considered themselves trustees of a church that had gone out of existence when the present congregation had rebelled against the Home Missions Board by keeping Aberhart. Underwood claimed that the present congregation was in reality only a tenant, a tenant who had not been paying rent for the building, or its taxes. The congregation sought legal advice and then demanded that the trustees give a written statement of their stewardship. The situation was embarrassing to the trustees, but they agreed to comply.[60] Underwood redeemed the church's cottage from the city, but when the trustees were slow to provide a financial statement, the congregation asked them to resign and to turn over all books, accounts, and funds to new trustees who had been elected from among Westbourne's membership. The original trustees replied that they would do so only if the congregation would agree to let them transfer the church's property in trust to the Baptist Union of Western Canada. The trustees seemed to want to remove themselves from an embarrassing situation and still prevent the property's falling into Aberhart's hands. The congregation agreed to the proposal, possibly feeling that they would have peace once Underwood was no longer meddling in their affairs.[61]

Westbourne's problems with the former trustees, however, had not yet come to a close. The eventual financial statement showed that the trustees' calculations did not match Westbourne's. Underwood had also charged the congregation for a piano that he had given as a gift to the church many years earlier. Nor did Underwood turn over Westbourne's funds. In desperation the deacons appealed to the executive board of the Alberta Provincial Baptist Convention for intervention.[62]

Although the Minutes neither prove nor disprove the fact, it was generally assumed that Aberhart took a leading part in Westbourne's struggle for independence. Very seldom did Aberhart himself put a motion on the floor, but one member claimed that Aberhart arranged that members make motions. Aberhart would talk with them and influence them to think and feel as he did, making it clear that if they wanted a certain item, they would have to do something about it. He would remind them, ''Remember that at the next meeting.''[63]

During the next four years the dispute with Underwood dragged on, causing bitterness and regret to both factions. Aberhart came to be recognized by the Baptist Union as Westbourne's lay minister; but his powerful personality, his obsessive drive to preach, his refusal to become ordained and submit to ecclesiastical authority, and the unusual beliefs he had been teaching were of continued concern to Baptist officials. He had developed a theology peculiar to himself.

CHAPTER FOUR

■

ABERHART'S THEOLOGY

T HE TROUBLE *is that people do not know about the Antichrist. Many of those in the pulpits of our land, who are supposed to be Specialists in Scripture Knowledge, do not tell us anything about this fearful opponent of Christ. The Devil has seen to it that the great bulk of the people know absolutely nothing of it. Thank GOD for the number of earnest people, here and there, the world over, who are opening their Bibles and reading for themselves what men have failed to tell them.*

— William Aberhart from *God's Great Prophecies* c. 1918

Aberhart's theology had been taking its own course over the past few years. It had become ultra-dispensational, and he had added his own twists. Certain aspects of his own personality seemed to be exerting a questionable influence on the direction his theology was taking.

Whenever he preached or lectured Aberhart held the Bible in his hand as he simplified, enlarged, divided and sub-divided, explained, and dramatized it. He tackled its difficulties fearlessly, sweepingly, and dramatically. Most of his listeners were familiar with the Bible, some had spent many a lonely hour over its obscurities. Their ministers often dispensed only its ethical message, but here was a man who took the Bible for his text. "Mr. Aberhart gave us the Gospel," recalled one of his early followers. "With some ministers you get the message, but where is the Gospel?"[1]

Aberhart held that every word of the Bible was significant, and that the more difficult portions should not be neglected for the ones in everyday language. He emphasized this principle when he dealt with the prophecies. Aberhart's orderly mind abhorred the idea of any confusion or obscurity hindering the efficient functioning of Holy Writ, and he gloried in the triumph of the fulfilled prophecies concerning Christ's first coming,[2] while claiming to understand with equal facility those that he believed were yet to be fulfilled. The prophecies had always taken pride of place in dispensational teaching, an emphasis Aberhart continued, thus neglecting the ethical aspects of Christianity and speaking derogatively of ministers whose main concerns were the social applications of Christianity.

During this time, the use of the Bible was a controversial matter between modernists and fundamentalists.[3] The archaeologist and the student of oriental languages modified modernists' interpretations of the Bible, as they took into consideration new historical and scientific facts that had a bearing on their subject. The fundamentalists also looked to the archaeologists and scientists for support for their position, but when there was a disagreement in interpretation, they gave the greater weight to the Bible. Fundamentalists held that no knowledge or skill, other than the ability to read simple English, was necessary to understand the past, present, and future of our universe, our bodies, and our souls. As a result, many people with limited academic education were easily led to dispensationalism by teachers like Aberhart. The theories of the dispensationalists were, however, no simpler than those of the modernists, who found it necessary to extend the categories of allegory and symbolism to include many matters in the Bible that were not in accord with newly discovered scientific "facts." The dispensationalists eschewed such compromises and insisted on literal accuracy - which led to ingenious and even more complicated theories designed to explain away the various contradictions that presented themselves to the careful reader.[4]

All dispensational teaching revolted against the abstract. Aberhart did not ask his followers to grasp difficult philosophical theories or understand abstract ideas. Instead, he plunged into discovering, for instance, the exact schedule of the soul's experiences after death in each dispensation, and whether or not the soul had bodily properties. All the information that he unearthed was cast in a tangible and prosaic form. He taught, for example, that just as human history had seven divisions, Heaven and Hell, too, could be subdivided.[5]

The practice of dispensationalism that drew sharp divisions between the Old and New Testaments, the law of God and the grace of God, and faith and works had ethical implications. The result was that Aberhart relegated the ethics of the synoptic Gospels, the epistles of Peter and James, and the Book of Revelation to Jews of the future. He did this on the assumption that while those passages that spoke of "works" referred to Jews, those that spoke of "faith" related to Christians.[6] For all practical purposes, the sources of Aberhart's ethics were restricted to the Gospel of John, the Book of Acts, and the Pauline epistles (which, according to Aberhart, included those known as the Pastoral Epistles). He had been influenced by the writings of Scofield, Bullinger, and some of the more radical Plymouth Brethren dispensationalists.

Aberhart's rallying cry, however, was still "The Bible, the whole Bible, and nothing but the Bible!" He held that the King James Bible of 1611 embodied the literal, unabridged, and undiluted Word of God. This version had, according to his belief, been contrived by divine intervention so that no problems of authenticity or translation arose. By interpreting Matthew 5:18 out of context, he could claim that the original text had been providentially preserved even to the punctuation.[7] The only modifications that he would tolerate were in cases where the meaning of the English had changed since the translation was made. He admitted, for instance, that the word "let" should be replaced where it carried the meaning "hinder."[8]

Aberhart deplored the confusion and disagreement among those making new translations, his *bête noire* being the Revised Version of 1884, in which, he believed, cardinal doctrines like the Virgin Birth of Christ and the Trinity had been diluted through spurious translation. He cast aspersions on the scholarship and honesty of the translators of the Revised Version, and accused them of Unitarianism.[9] He claimed that the translators of the King James Version were superior scholars. In so doing, he brushed aside all the developments in textual criticism and archaeology, and the nineteenth-century decipherment of Near Eastern languages that had shed new light on biblical studies. He also claimed that the manuscripts on which the King James Version was based were superior, and that they had been preserved in the Alps by faithful Christians who had not come under the influence of Rome. But he provided no real evidence to support his statements.[10]

Aberhart cried out against those scholars who claimed that a knowledge of Greek and Hebrew was necessary to study the Bible properly. "Take a warning, my friend!" cautioned Aberhart. "These men know that the majority of people cannot contradict their statements, for the common people do not know the Greek or Hebrew. They therefore hope to make themselves into a kind of priestcraft to whom the common people must come for the truth of GOD'S WORD."[11] The way in which he repeatedly castigated such scholars, and distorted the issue, suggests that his objections were more than doctrinal; they may have been a reaction to his own failures in those languages. Aberhart wanted to be thought of as a biblical scholar, and appears to have rationalized away the need for Greek and Hebrew by insisting on an infallible English version. He could then show his own scholarship by emphasizing the study of English verb-tenses, upon which he built fine theological distinctions.

His emphasis on the King James Version was somewhat unique among dispensationalists and fundamentalists. None of his theological mentors (like Scofield, R.A. Torrey, or William Bell Riley) shared his position. They frequently found fault with the King James Version, in fact, and advocated the Revised.[12]

Aberhart's eschatological doctrines of death, the afterlife, heaven, hell, the end of the world, prophecies, the final judgement, and so on were of concern to the Baptist Union. Around Calgary, those who had not investigated his ideas thought he was a Russellite or Jehovah's Witness.[13] The then-minister of First Baptist Church the Reverend H.H. Bingham described Aberhart's prophetic lectures as "pathetic" rather than "prophetic."[14] Aberhart had turned religious science fiction into dogma. A simplified portrayal of his complicated eschatology, and the purpose it served in his preaching, follows.[15]

Central to Aberhart's eschatology was the idea of the Rapture, the supposed "divine evacuation" of the Christians from this world. Speaking of the Rapture, Aberhart said, "This glorious event is just at hand. It may happen at any moment...."[16] On another occasion he stressed: "Understand me, please! The Rapture of the Church may happen tonight. You may never see another sunrise...."[17]

Aberhart believed that at the Rapture, God's prophetic clock would once more begin to tick,[18] and that following the Rapture the world would be thrown into unprecedented confusion. Thousands of non-Christians would die as a result of train- and car-crashes, after Christian engineers and drivers disappeared from the controls. Christian doctors would disappear while performing operations, leaving their patients to die on the operating table. Crime and violence would abound as men's passions would run unchecked without the influence of the Christians – or the Holy Spirit, which had also departed with the "raptured" Christians.

Aberhart also believed that immediately following the Rapture, the world would be plunged into war, since Japan and China would attack the western world.[19] During this war, an important figure would arise on the international scene who would be considered a "superman" on account of his vast knowledge, diplomatic skills, charismatic personality, and economic expertise. Aberhart claimed that this person, called the Antichrist, would be the Devil incarnate, having been born to an occult-practising Jewess living in Turkey.[20] Possibly through his participation in the peace negotiations at the end of this "Yellow Race War," the Antichrist, as yet incognito, would gain international fame as a diplomat.

The concept of the Antichrist as an apostate Jew, a persecutor antithetical to Christ, was a composite idea arrived at by combining Daniel's "Little Horn," Paul's "man of sin," Revelation's "beast," and certain hints in John's epistles.[21] But none of those sources by themselves could substantiate the broader picture that Aberhart and others painted. Many of the details were borrowed from apocryphal and pseudepigraphical writings that had been influenced by the dualism of Persian mythology. The idea of a future apostate Jewish "superman" had been expounded in the anti-Semitic writings associated with the spurious *Protocols of the Elders of Zion*, and found expression in *The Coming Prince*, by dispensationalist Sir Robert Anderson, sometime director of Scotland Yard,[22] and later popularized by Sydney Watson's apocalyptic novel *Mark of the Beast*. The latter's works highly influenced Aberhart's thinking, and Aberhart advertised Watson's novels in his publications.[23]

Aberhart believed that during the so-called "Yellow Race War" there would be a large migration of Jews to Palestine, where they would rebuild Solomon's Temple – parts of which, he said, had already been constructed by wealthy Jews living in other countries and were waiting to be shipped to Palestine when the right moment came.[24] The focus of history would then move to the Middle East. A ruler of a northern kingdom comprising Russia and Germany would eye the quantities of wealth pouring into Palestine, and would attempt to seize it. Great Britain, France, and Italy would intervene, and war would again break out. For a time, the allies would succeed in hindering the Russian-German forces, but they would eventually fail, and Palestine would be taken by the Russians.[25] Soon afterwards the King of Russia would die (Aberhart seemingly believed that Russian autocracy would be restored first), and the Antichrist, ruling as a prince of Turkey, would make a claim to the throne of Russia:

> His claim shall appear in vain at first, but he will cleverly make a covenant with the Jews to give them their temple worship for seven years if they will support him and immediately he will obtain the kingdom peaceably.[26]

This would take place 250 days after the Rapture.[27]

As a result of the league with the Antichrist, the Jews would be allowed to build their temple in Jerusalem and resume the daily sacrificial system. However, after several years, Great Britain would perceive that the Jews were being used by the Antichrist and would launch an attack on Russia – but it would fail. The Antichrist would then stop the daily sacrifices in Jerusalem and desecrate the temple – whereupon 144,000 loyal Jews, 12,000 from each of the twelve tribes, would oppose him and be killed in battle.[28]

Meanwhile, the Antichrist, through his military might, would gain control of a ten-kingdom confederacy comprising the countries of Europe, and would establish a Fifth World Empire.[29] With his "United States of Europe" the Antichrist would gain control of the world's economy,[30] rebuild the ancient city of Babylon, and establish that city as the centre of the world's commerce and government.[31] He would then attempt to gain military control over other parts of the world and would attack Britain and her colonies. Japan would come to the aid of Britain, and during the battle the Antichrist would be fatally wounded; but, in mockery of Christ's resurrection, the Antichrist would come back to life and receive the worship of many.[32]

A religious leader known as the False Prophet would then emerge from the apostate Christian denominations and lead mankind in the worship of the Antichrist. A statue of the Antichrist would be erected in the temple at Jerusalem, and the False Prophet, through his miraculous powers, would make it speak. All would be forced to bow in obeisance and have branded into their forehead, or into the palm of their hand, the number 666. Without that brand, no one would be permitted to buy or sell; those who refused the brand would be killed.[33]

Aberhart claimed that many Jews would refuse to worship the Antichrist, and that the Antichrist would then march on Jerusalem:

> The armies shall besiege Jerusalem and then the immediate signs in the Heavens shall occur which precede the Lord's Coming. The stars will fall. The moon shall be turned into blood and the sun shall be darkened. On the earth a terrific earthquake shall shake its very foundations and men's hearts shall fail through fear. They shall call upon the mountains to fall on them and hide them from the wrath to come.[34]

Aberhart believed that a tremendous earthquake would then destroy Babylon; Constantinople would sink into the sea; and Jerusalem would be sacked by the Antichrist.[35]

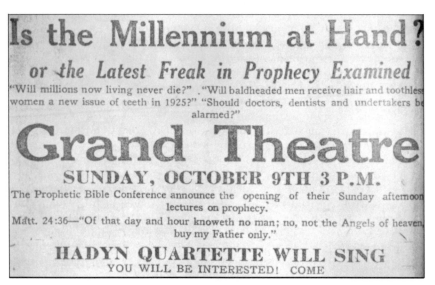

Biblical prophecy was Aberhart's central theme. Another successful "teaser" (Calgary Herald, *8 October 1920, p. 6) that must have given Aberhart's employers, the Calgary School Board, pause.*

The climax would occur when Christ came from heaven with the Christians and angelic hosts. They would alight on the Mount of Olives overlooking Jerusalem, and then proceed to the Valley of Megiddo north of Jerusalem to meet the Antichrist and his forces in the battle of Armageddon. Aberhart believed that the battle would be of such magnitude that blood would flow to the height of the horses' bridles, and that it would take seven months to bury the dead and seven years to burn the weapons.[36] The outcome would be a decisive victory for Christ and the Christians.

Aberhart claimed that all these events would occur within a period of seven years after the Rapture. Following the Battle of Armaggedon, Christ would establish his Millennium, bringing all remaining Jews to Palestine, where King David, now resurrected, would once more reign for a thousand years. During that theocratic monarchy, the twelve apostles of Christ (Matthias replacing Judas) would judge the twelve tribes of Israel. After the Millennium, Satan would again lead a rebellion and be defeated; the unrighteous dead would be resurrected and judged, then thrown with Satan into a Lake of Fire; the world would be destroyed, and a new heaven and a new earth would be created.[37]

Aberhart defended this grandiose fantasy of the future by implying that some of its unique features, which differed from those suggested by other dispensationalists, had come to him by divine illumination.[38] While maintaining that he interpreted the Bible literally, he claimed that biblical references to "Media" and "Persia" meant China and Japan, and that "Tyre" meant Constantinople.[39] When pressed to give evidence, he stated that the Devil had changed the names of those ancient nations and locations in order to confuse students of the Bible.[40] Some of Aberhart's notions had no doubt been borrowed from British-Israelism.

During the First World War and afterward, Aberhart baited his audiences with comparisons of his prophetic interpretations with current events. He suggested that a knowledge of prophecy would make the reading of newspapers more interesting; but at the same time he repeatedly criticized all attempts at setting dates for the Rapture.[41] He claimed the Rapture could occur at any moment and that no definite "signs" would precede it, although certain social and religious conditions would be "prophetic shadows" of events that would follow the Rapture, because history was a process of cause and effect. But he made the "shadows" so general that they could apply anywhere from St. Paul's day to the present.[42] However, at the same time, he emphasized that the Antichrist had already been born, but was still incognito,[43] to be revealed after the Rapture and other definite "signs" had occurred,[44] – "signs" that were beyond present verification and could be of no use to Christians as an apologetic tool. Aberhart's eschatology did give Christians hope; since the Rapture could occur at any moment, their present problems could be over "in the twinkling of an eye." In a negative way his eschatology also helped them understand history. He told them that Kaiser Wilhelm was not the Antichrist and the First World War was not the Tribulation.[45]

Aberhart's use of prophecy should be understood more as a vehicle of evangelism than anything else. If people would become Christians, they could look forward to the Rapture and thus avoid the terrors of the Tribulation. In his printed lectures Aberhart said little about other aspects of eschatology like the doctrines of heaven and hell, but emphasized more the dangers of falling into the hands of the Antichrist. In one of his sermons he stated:

> Yes, they may find fault with you and me as followers of Christ, but they cannot find fault with the Captain of our Salvation. I say it will serve them right when that vile person, that Man of Sin, the Antichrist, sets up his image and forces them to crawl upon their hands and knees before it, to bow down and say prayers to an Image of the Beast while his ambassadors take cognizance of it and brand them like cattle, so that they may go and buy their daily bread. Read it for yourself in Revelation 13:14-17. Hear me, my brother, don't be a fool! Give your homage and love to the Saviour who died for you and not that Beast, the Antichrist, who will make merchandise of you.[46]

At most of his meetings Aberhart invited people to become Christians and thus avoid the Tribulation.[47] His audiences were greatly affected by his

Aberhart's followers were mostly working-class people, and his eye-catching advertisements were pitched to them. This one is from the Calgary Herald *(13 November 1920, p. 20.)*

dramatic descriptions of the future. Around 1920 some of the fundamentalists in the district of Three Hills, Alberta, had been trying to convert some of the local businessmen, but without success. When Aberhart preached there on the Rapture and the Tribulation, some of those businessmen came to hear him out of curiosity, and by the end of the meetings, a number of them were up at the front of the hall on their knees, confessing their sins.[48]

Finally, Aberhart's eschatology served as a method of social control. Since Christ could "appear" at any moment, Christians should be living circumspect and serious lives, for they would not want to be found in dance halls, theatres, and cinemas when the Rapture occurred.[49]

Aberhart's sermons and lectures reveal a preoccupation with the negative aspects of eschatology: the Devil, Antichrist, demons, spiritism, and so on – a constellation of ideas very real to him. There was also a curious sexual aspect to his eschatology. He praised Innocent VIII, the medieval pope, for promoting the *Malleus Maleficarum*, the manual on fighting witchcraft. Aberhart personally believed in the existence of *incubi* and *succubi*, sexually active demons that attacked people as they slept.[50] "Wet dreams" were explained as the result of such attacks. Women in Aberhart's congregation were required to wear hats in church to ward off attacks by "fallen angels."[51] Besides the bizarre sexual aspects one detects elements of anger and sadism in his thought, particularly in the fate of sinners at the hands of the Antichrist, and in the suffering of the unrepentant in Hell.

Even though most of Aberhart's ideas about the Devil and the Antichrist were not *sui generis*, it is significant that he held them: it appears that some of the characteristics he attributed to the Devil and the Antichrist – rebellion and totalitarianism, for example – were projections of traits that he denied in his own personality, but which were very much a part of it. His life was characterized by reaction against anyone, including school boards and ecclesiastical bodies, who challenged his authority.

While assessing Aberhart's preaching, the same minister who described his prophetic lectures as "pathetic" also admitted that when Aberhart presented the essentials of the Gospel, the matter of justification by faith, he was superb, and few could match him.[52] It may have been this gift that discouraged the Baptist officials from taking more drastic action against Aberhart. Yet, while they were disturbed by his eschatology, they would have even more grounds for concern when he added aspects of pentecostalism to his theology after 1920.

CHAPTER FIVE

■

THE PRINCIPAL OF CRESCENT HEIGHTS HIGH SCHOOL

A CROWBAR *does not pull an object. It gets under it and pushes. All life is a pushing thing. Press down a sapling, torture it in any conceivable way, and instead of giving up it will proceed to push its way around or over the obstacle. Remember, where one man succeeds through Pull, there are ninety-nine who succeed through PUSH.*

— William Aberhart, to his students at
Crescent Heights High School, 1922

While Aberhart roused the ranks of fundamentalism on weekday evenings and weekends, it would have been hard to find a more exemplary public servant than the portly principal of Crescent Heights High School. Aberhart's teaching career in Calgary had seen many promotions, yet the Minutes of the Calgary School Board until 1919 reveal little more about him. From Mount Royal School he had been transferred to King Edward School in 1913. Then, in 1915, Aberhart was made principal of the new Crescent Heights High School housed in the Balmoral School on Sixteenth Ave. N.W., a "temporary" arrangement that lasted until 1928.

At Crescent Heights, Aberhart played the sort of successful schoolmaster, genial and fatherly, whom parents would wish to see in charge of their children, under whose guidance children would do well. He had somewhat lessened the harshness of his disciplinary measures, and therefore his contacts with his students there were happier than they had been in Ontario. But his students were still in awe of him. It was said that Aberhart could still clear the corridors with his voice, while on other days his hearty laugh would reverberate through the halls.[1]

Aberhart still adhered to the old-fashioned teaching method of analysis and repetition, and taught his pupils the value of an orderly mind. He taught them to absorb facts, but not the value of independent reasoning. One teacher under Aberhart described him as a dog-trainer and the school as a factory.[2] His staff learned to respect his passion for efficiency, but they also found him approachable when they had some constructive suggestion to contribute. Although it was not easy to persuade Aberhart to change his mind, a good argument, eloquently presented, would sometimes move him – and then he would cling to the new idea as fiercely as he had to the old.

Aberhart's sense of fun was one attribute that made him approachable, and his positive personality made a vivid impression on his fellow-teachers. Since his hobbies differed from their own, he became known as an eccentric; they liked to "kid him along," and were relieved to find he took teasing in good part. On one occasion, when the highschool teachers had challenged the public school teachers to a hockey game at the Central High School rink, Aberhart, who was to play goalie, arrived in his usual headdress – a black bowler – which he tried to wear throughout the game. However, it frequently fell off, and the players used it as a puck. Aberhart's booming laughter echoed over the fence into Twelfth Avenue to the amusement of passersby, as he defended the goal against his own bowler hat.[3]

As principal, Aberhart prided himself on being a good organizer. He even found time personally to prepare each student's timetable.[4] He also organized and supervised the orchestra, glee club, operettas, productions of Shakespeare's plays, the debating society, contests, student companies, and sports. When two members of the debating society were called to Edmonton to compete, it was Aberhart himself who accompanied them on the train, returning with them the following day.[5]

Besides administering his school, Aberhart also taught English in the classroom. He worked hard for the success of his students, often spending time before and after school helping those who were slow students. When a student was willing to learn, Aberhart was willing to extend himself; but when a student refused to cooperate Aberhart had no patience.

Aberhart's students, in spite of his rigid disciplining[6] and rather inflexible teaching methods, were allowed some freedom of thought. Sometimes during "spares" books were pushed aside and discussions became eager and heated. One such topic was "Was the beheading of Charles I justified?" The murmur of debate floated through the transom and was plainly heard in the echoing corridor at one time or another by members of the staff, including Aberhart, who apparently decided, however, that the activity was assisting their education. Such discussions were allowed to continue regularly, without interruption.[7]

On another occasion, a difficult question was taken to Aberhart himself for judgment. The group had begun arguing about the correct form that baptism should take. A student who was a member of Westbourne Baptist Church evidently thought that here was an opportunity to gain her point, for she felt certain that her view was shared by the principal. Accordingly, she went to Aberhart and requested his support for the theory she had put forward that complete immersion was the only acceptable form of baptism. But Aberhart explained to the student that other people had viewpoints different from hers, that all had their reasons for what they believed, and that she must practise toleration.[8]

Aberhart was acutely conscious of critical scrutiny, and was most careful to give no opportunity to those who were ready to leap on him for neglecting any aspect of the duties for which the public paid his salary. This was why he took scrupulous care never to introduce his religious doctrines into the school. This was a change from his practice in Brantford. He was now well aware that such a violation of the principle of religious freedom would be an opportunity the School Board would not hesitate to use to dismiss him.

His life was very compartmentalized. His colleagues in one field knew about his activities in another only by hearsay. Yet, he did bring his religious bias into the school in a negative way. According to his dispensational theology, the Lord's Prayer was not intended for Christians but for Jews living during the Millennium, and therefore he did not have it repeated in his classes.[9] He also tried to have the Calgary School Board ban school dances as he felt that they contributed to immorality; but he may have been successful in stopping them only in his own school.[10]

Through Aberhart's influence, Crescent Heights High School was one of the first schools in the city to establish a parent-teachers' association, and it soon became the largest, with an average attendance of two hundred parents. Every month, one or two days before the meeting, each student would take home a notice informing parents of the subject of the meeting, the name of the speaker, and other topics under discussion. Aberhart won the goodwill of the parents by giving them the opportunity to ask questions and gauge their children's work. Every so often he showed slides of scholarship- and contest-winners. When the *Albertan* ran a contest on the lives and works of outstanding musical composers, Aberhart encouraged his students to participate, and one won the city-wide contest with 99.5 per cent.[11] Aberhart made sure his school received press coverage, and he gave parents the impression that if it was not the best in the province, it took first place in Calgary at least. Some observers did not share his confidence, in particular members of the Calgary School Board, some of whom claimed that Aberhart's school was able to obtain very high per-student percentage on the departmental examinations because he eliminated inferior students ahead of time by giving them a qualifying examination.[12]

An annual event among members of Alberta's teaching fraternity was a short stay in Edmonton marking departmental examination papers for the Board of Education. The fact that Aberhart was one of the teachers who regularly accepted the Board's invitation to do this provided some of his critics an opportunity to accuse him of being mercenary. There is, however, reason to believe that Aberhart had other profits in mind when he met in Edmonton with teachers from all parts of the province. The paper-marking sessions tended to become conventions, at which new ideas in education, current affairs, economics, and many other subjects were circulated and discussed with stimulating effect.[13] The lunchroom was a forum for the free exchange of ideas, in which Aberhart's powerful voice could be heard expressing opinions on every subject that arose. Those listening in the background would smile at the persistence with which he took on all comers, his earnestness and resourcefulness in discussion, and he became something of a "character." More than anything Aberhart used his visits to Edmonton to look for new teaching talent. When he saw a particularly sharp teacher he would say, "There's a teacher who ought to be at Crescent Heights" – and soon he or she was.[14]

As in his religious life, and later in his political life, Aberhart inspired extreme reactions – from trusting, almost loving devotion among student and staff, to outright contempt. Several of his students came back and worked as teachers under him for many years, but his relationships with some of his staff, particularly men, were not the best. In 1919 Aberhart received one of the greatest challenges to his authority when eight teachers at Crescent Heights appealed to the School Board, asking that there be a full investigation of conditions at the school. The school inspector discovered that Aberhart and his staff were out of harmony, and that the problem was not only with the teachers. Most of them were unhappy about the extent to which Aberhart organized the school: it left them with little initiative. The School Board transferred three of the male teachers to other schools, and stated that if there were any more staff problems at Crescent Heights, resignations would be asked for, including the principal's.[15]

This crisis arose while Aberhart was involved in the turmoil with the trustees of Westbourne Baptist Church described in the previous chapter. There does not appear to have been any direct connection between the two incidents; but this would have been little comfort to Aberhart, who was deeply hurt by both challenges to his authority.

After the teachers' revolt Aberhart gave his teachers a little more leeway, but overall his relationship with them was poor. He never entered the staffroom except to issue an order[16] and spent most of his lunch hours supervising student activities. Some felt that he was afraid to be around intellectual people who could pick holes in his schemes and arguments. At school Aberhart seemed to be a different man from the Aberhart they saw in Edmonton marking exams. On his own turf he had to be the boss. His teachers had more respect for him as a principal than as a man. They found him personally parsimonious, uncharitable, and hypocritical.[17] Nevertheless, he experienced no more staff revolts, and the school inspector noted in 1921 that there was a "much better spirit of cooperation among the members of the staff than existed when this school was last inspected." He added: "We were impressed with Mr. Aberhart's administrative and executive ability. He is a capable organizer."[18]

These years, though filled to overflowing by most people's standards, while Aberhart was running his school, preaching at Westbourne Baptist Church, and teaching his Bible classes, were more leisurely than any he was to enjoy in the future. He still had time for long discussions on odd subjects that interested him, and also spent many evenings playing chess, one of the few forms of real relaxation he genuinely enjoyed. Like everything else Aberhart touched, chess was something serious; he even wrote a manual on it.[19] One of his favorite opponents was Abe Shnitka, a Jewish printer who printed some of Aberhart's religious booklets. Aberhart enjoyed a fast game of chess, and usually won; but if his opponent was slow to make a move, he would lose interest; his mind would wander and he would make mistakes.[20] His friends from Westbourne would drop in during these events and many a pleasant hour was passed with the game and in lively discussion.

Among his more active hobbies Aberhart still enjoyed participating in sports. Though his football days were waning, he arranged for the Crescent Heights gymnasium to be available to the teachers for badminton on certain evenings, frequently joining the game himself.

At home he spent many hours reading. On the second floor of the house he had his study, which was lined with shelves containing works on education, religion, philosophy, law, biography, and poetry. He particularly liked Dickens.[21] It was in this room that Aberhart "burned the candle at both ends," never sleeping before 2 a.m., and sometimes managing with as little as four hours of sleep each night.[22]

In his study Aberhart prepared lectures and lessons, and wrote his letters, himself taking care of family correspondence with his relatives in Ontario. Since moving from Ontario he had no other contact with any of them, except for a short period when his brother John, who had been Aberhart's best man, worked as a blacksmith in Calgary in 1912. However, the two Aberharts did not get along well and John, who had no education, resented William's education and position.[23] At a later date, Aberhart conducted a regular correspondence with his niece Irene in Seaforth, writing in his neat, flowing, and decorative hand many warm letters containing family news and, often, sound advice coated with affectionate teasing.[24]

Aberhart did not usually include membership in clubs or other social organizations among his pastimes. Two exceptions at this time were his memberships in the Masonic Lodge and the Alberta Teachers' Association

(A.T.A.). His membership in the Lodge had been transferred from Brantford to Calgary in 1911,[25] and it says much for Aberhart's fierce individualism that he retained this membership until 1926, since many fundamentalists frowned upon membership in secret societies.[26] Westbourne's congregation, however, may not have known of his Masonic membership, again because of the compartmentalized nature of his life.

Aberhart joined the A.T.A. when it was formed in 1919, but he allowed his membership to lapse in 1923. In spite of many flattering advances, including an invitation to him to become their president in 1927, he never rejoined.[27] It seems strange behaviour for a man who later elevated the A.T.A. to a status of unprecedented importance in the province; but it is fully understandable when one considers the stormy history of his associations with other organizations. He was always more of a founder than a joiner.

Aberhart's spare time, if not taken up by one big project, was divided among several small ones, all of equal urgency, to judge by the restless energy he devoted to them. It was even said that he started his large Buick in second gear because starting in first took more time.[28] In his very early days in Calgary, he kept the books for one or two small companies to supplement his income.[29] Later, however, as his financial position improved, he gave most of his spare time to his religious activities.

For some time in 1918 Aberhart retired regularly to his garage where an astonished visitor would find one wall festooned with a gigantic canvas, measuring 1.8 by 6.3 metres, on which was painted the dispensational history of mankind. Aberhart possessed a natural skill in drawing and a strong visual imagination, so that he could represent his ideas in diagrammatic form. This huge canvas, which he entitled *God's Blueprint of the Ages*, was painted in subdued colours, with off-beat perspective and inconsistent scale.[30] The canvas was used for many years in his Bible lectures and was reproduced thousands of times in miniature for use by his students. He was always aware of the effectiveness of colour, music, and drama when imprinting his ideas upon the mind of his audience.

Aberhart had a keen ear for music. As a child he had learned to play the mandolin and piano by ear and, though self-taught, he could get a tune out of a violin. His daughters inherited his musical bent, and when Ola developed a fine singing voice, Aberhart saw to it that she was provided with lessons. Musical evenings were not uncommon, especially on Sundays when the family gathered to sing hymns.

In his personal habits Aberhart was neat and orderly. He brought to odd jobs around the house, such as building a fence, the same methodological approach he took to any other problem, breaking them down theoretically into simple steps and then following up in practice with neat and delicate workmanship.

In spite of his farm upbringing, or perhaps because of it, Aberhart was not drawn to the outdoor life. He showed no interest in gardening or in animals. He was observed to pat dogs on the head in much the same way as one raises a hat to a nodding acquaintance – not so much to solicit closer friendship as simply from habitual good manners.

Although the Aberharts gave the impression of being a markedly happy and united family, close friends claimed otherwise. Aberhart is said to have had very little say in his own home. There Jessie had her own way except in matters affecting her husband's career.[31] There was also some tension regarding their religious values. Family hymn-sings were the only form of communal devotion in the household. Family prayers were not part of the daily routine: Aberhart's strong evangelical urge was not shared by his family, and he did not press the issue. His forbearance was returned by cooperation on the part of his family, who willingly complied with convention when a minister was a guest in the house.

Jessie Aberhart had very little to do with William's extracurricular activities. She did teach in the primary department of Westbourne's Sunday school, and sometimes catered at his social functions; but she did not share his circle of friends. She was regarded, because of her attitude, furs, and jewels as something of a "blue blood." Generally her pursuits were more urbane than his. She held memberships in the Woman's Canadian Club, the Red Cross Society, and served as social convener for the Y.M.C.A. and Y.W.C.A.[32]

Inside the Prophetic Bible Institute. Note Aberhart's dispensation chart.

Up until 1920 Aberhart still had time to spend at home with his family, who enjoyed his company. He was quite demonstrative in his affection for his children, but he did not spoil them with overindulgence and was always concerned about their correct upbringing, ensuring obedience and discipline. When his daughters were small, Aberhart enjoyed telling them Bible stories. Their favorite was "Daniel in the Lions' Den," and he delighted them by augmenting the narration with lusty roars.[33] However, as they grew older and he became more occupied, he had less personal involvement with them, spending more time in his study without sharing his ideas with his family.[34] Jessie is said to have encouraged her daughters to disregard their father's wishes – by dancing, playing cards, and attending movies.[35] Because of their values and fashions, Aberhart's wife and daughters were somewhat of a scandal to Westbourne's members.

Beginning in 1918, the Aberharts began spending their vacations in Vancouver. The girls liked the ocean, and Aberhart had an opportunity to preach in some of Vancouver's churches.

Much of the energy that Aberhart began putting into religious pursuits may have been either the cause or the result of a disintegrating relationship with his family. Some of his critics suggested that his religious overzealousness was a sublimation of strong sexual needs that were not being met by his wife. Even if this assumption were wrong, Aberhart's busy life certainly did not allow for much of a marital relationship. Some of the bizarre sexual ideas we have already seen in his theology suggest a distorted sexuality.[36]

That Aberhart's family did not share his beliefs was a strong reason for his not seeking ordination and assuming the ministry of Westbourne Baptist Church when it was repeatedly offered to him. Also, Jessie did not want to be a minister's wife, and the low salary would not be adequate for her lifestyle.[37] Aberhart's salary as a principal in 1920 was a healthy $3,200, and his job was secure. He had refused the pastorate of Westbourne by saying, "What would I do if people got tired of me?"[38] He had correctly judged that his success depended on his popularity and that congregations could be fickle. He also found one aspect of pastoral duties impossible: he had an aversion to hospitals, the smell of which made him faint. On those occasions when he visited a patient his unconcealed haste in leaving the hospital caused much family amusement. On one occasion he tried to conquer this aversion. His daughter Ola was confined to hospital. Unable to bear his own helplessness, Aberhart suddenly declared his intention of going into the dreaded building to sit with her. "I think I can communicate some strength to her," he said, "if I hold her hand." He sat beside her bedside, her hand in his, but could stand the ordeal no longer than five or ten minutes, after which, to everyone's relief, he went home.[39] As a minister he would have been faced with regular hospital visitation, but with his school responsibilities he could plead that he did not have time, and could get other people in the church to do it.

A final reason for Aberhart's steering clear of ordination may, as hinted before, have been theological. Aberhart had become friendly with W.P. Harvey, who had been the School Board's dentist before going into private practice. Harvey had been a member of the Plymouth Brethren and brought local Brethren together with Aberhart at the Harvey home, where they had some stimulating discussions. As dispensationalists they had much in common. Sometime before 1920 Aberhart had tried to join their small group, but they had been very wary of his leadership ambitions.[40] However, he incorporated some of the Brethren's anti-clerical rhetoric and emphasis on lay ministry into his own style of ministry. Although he had been influenced by the Brethren, there were differences of opinion over their principle of separating themselves completely from all other groups. Aberhart assured them that this was a mistaken policy. He returned to this point again and again in his preaching, always reproving those who were responsible for disunity among the churches, especially those who broke away to form their own splinter groups. It was a strange condemnation to come from Aberhart, who soon was to follow that same course of action himself.

Like his heroes D.L. Moody and Sydney Watson, who were unordained evangelists and pastors, Aberhart continued to preach and teach as a layman, keeping his position as principal of Crescent Heights High School in order to provide a stable income and keep peace in his family.

CHAPTER SIX

■

THE BIRTH OF A SECT

T HE *Methodist or Presbyterian or Baptist Churches have no grounds for pointing the finger at the Roman Catholic Church in regard to Apostasy. "Let him who is without sin cast the first stone."*

— William Aberhart from *God's Great Prophecies* c. 1922

The year 1920 marked a transition in Aberhart's theology and religious behaviour. His adoption of certain doctrines associated with Pentecostalism assisted his rise to power at Westbourne Baptist Church and turned it, and his Calgary Prophetic Bible Conference, into a theological sect with peculiar doctrines, a separatist stance, and an élitist self-awareness. Yet, Aberhart, like so many other sect leaders, did not consider himself the leader of a sect.

Although Aberhart had been preaching at Westbourne Baptist Church, he was not a Baptist since he had not been baptized by immersion as an adult believer. So far as it is known from his sermon ledger and his newspaper ads, he had never preached on the topic of baptism. But then, in the spring of 1920, he began a series of sermons on baptism and related topics, and he had himself baptized on 9 May 1920. Aberhart's interest in baptism seems to have been inspired by his contact with Pastor Harvey McAlister, a member of Canada's original Pentecostal family. His brother Robert McAlister had gone to Los Angeles, where he had experienced "speaking in tongues" in 1906, and brought Pentecostalism back to Ontario.

Along with "speaking in tongues" and faith healing, which Pentecostals regarded as divinely given, the sect introduced other doctrinal innovations, one being that baptism by immersion should be done in the "name of the Lord Jesus" and not with the standard Trinitarian formula. Robert McAlister was one of the first to proclaim this new "truth."[1] A number of Pentecostals, including Robert and Harvey McAlister, were rebaptized "in the name of the Lord Jesus," and it became the standard formula for Canadian Pentecostals until 1921.

Another theological development was associated with the new baptismal formula. Denying the traditional doctrine of the Trinity, some Pentecostals, including the McAlisters,[2] claimed that there was only one God, Jesus, who had three manifestations as the Father, Son, and Holy Spirit. That claim was considered heretical by other Pentecostals, but the "oneness of God" theory became the platform of the Pentecostal Assemblies of Canada. However, in 1921, when the Pentecostal Assemblies of Canada joined the Assemblies of God of the United States, the new doctrine was dropped and the Trinitarian formula was reinstated. A group of dissidents, including Harvey McAlister, did not join the American group and instead established the Apostolic Church of Pentecost of Canada (Full Gospel Church) and continued to propagate the anti-Trinitarian position and the "Jesus only" baptismal formula.[3]

McAlister's first sermons in Calgary involved apocalyptic and dispensational themes.[4] Soon he switched to themes concerning water baptism, its mode and formula, the Holy Spirit, spiritual gifts, apostolic succession, and divine healing. On 2 May 1920 he held a baptismal service at Westbourne Baptist Church.[5]

McAlister's use of Westbourne suggests a connection with Aberhart, who would have had to give his approval or at least be consulted. However, there is stronger evidence for Aberhart's association with McAlister. The Sunday of the week following McAlister's Friday-night sermon on baptism was the occasion of Aberhart's first sermon on this topic.[6] Then, the Sunday following McAlister's baptismal service, Westbourne Baptist Church held its own. The following week Aberhart preached on how the Christian graces were bestowed, a topic similar to one preached by McAlister one week previously.[7] This parallelism of their sermon topics was more than coincidental. Since some of McAlister's meetings were held on Friday evenings, Aberhart would have had the opportunity of attending; he made a practice of following what other prophetic lecturers were discussing. A final factor suggesting Aberhart's attendance at McAlister's meetings was his adoption of many of McAlister's ideas.

Aberhart, who had probably been baptized as an infant by means of sprinkling in the Presbyterian Church, now sought to be baptized as an adult by immersion, with the "Jesus only" formula – not because he was anti-Trinitarian, but because he believed the new formula to be dispensationally correct.[8] Aberhart was not baptized by McAlister, but by the Reverend James Desson of Heath Baptist Church,[9] probably because he knew that the Baptists would not accept his being baptized by a Pentecostal who was regarded as heretical. When Aberhart had approached Desson asking to be baptized by the "Jesus only" formula, Desson had hesitated to depart from the standard Trinitarian one; but Aberhart was able to persuade him to do so after saying that he would bear the divine consequences, if any.

Desson was a small man of about 57 kilos, while Aberhart weighed about 118. Consequently, in the baptismal tank, Desson had difficulty handling the larger Aberhart, and the congregation worried that he would not be able to raise him up out of the water.[10] Another version of the event, possible apocryphal, possibly malicious, reported that in the confusion, when Desson was having difficulty handling Aberhart, Desson forgot his previous agreement with Aberhart and baptized him with the standard formula.[11]

Aberhart's desire to be baptized by the "Jesus only" formula was connected with his belief that it was necessary for receiving "the baptism of the Holy Spirit." He differed from the Pentecostals in that he did not equate this with "speaking in tongues";[12] his definition corresponded more with the belief of the Holiness movement out of which Pentecostalism grew. The Holiness movement taught that there was, subsequent to conversion, a second work of grace by which the power of the Holy Spirit was given to Christians. Aberhart's hero Dwight L. Moody claimed to have had experienced a "second blessing," and Moody's successor R.A. Torrey devoted a book to the subject.[13] Considering Aberhart's previous exposure to such ideas, it is not surprising that after his contact with McAlister, he sought a further blessing from the Holy Spirit. Aberhart's own baptism brought him some immediate results, not so much in the way of added spiritual power as in the way of political power over Westbourne's congregation. Now he officially became a Baptist and assumed the position of deacon.

When Aberhart began to introduce these new doctrines among the people at Westbourne Baptist Church, he was met by a certain amount of opposition.[14] In the meantime baptisms were conducted by the minister of Crescent Heights Baptist Church the Reverend Christopher Burnett, who used the Trinitarian formula.[15] Burnett was also an active proponent of British-Israelism.

During the five years or so following 1919, when he had founded the Calgary Prophetic Bible Conference, Aberhart became acquainted with a number of people who were to be his firm friends and loyal workers for many years to come. His name was becoming more and more widely known, and those who thought his particular approach to the Bible would interest them made it their business to seek his acquaintance. One such family, destined to give many years of assistance, was that of Ernest Hutchinson, newly arrived in Calgary from an Okanagan fruit farm. One Sunday afternoon in 1920, while walking down First Street S.W., Hutchinson noticed a sign over the entrance of the Grand Theatre announcing Aberhart's Prophetic Conference lectures, which had been moved there because Westbourne Church could not hold the crowds. The sign caught Hutchinson's eye and he went in, having heard of Aberhart from Professor Broad, who had continued his Bible class at Summerland, B.C. after moving there from Calgary.[16]

Hutchinson found two or three hundred people sitting in the theatre. Music and prayer opened the meeting and Aberhart's Bible lecture followed. For most of the audience the lecture was the highlight of the program: they could expect a solid hour of Bible teaching. Afterward, the meeting was thrown open for questions. Aberhart would jot down the questions and, during the musical interlude that followed, he would thumb through his Bible before answering. When Aberhart had first confronted public audiences at the Public Library meetings, his experiences at "question time" had not been very happy; he was embarrassed several times by questions to which he did not have ready replies. However, by the time of the Grand Theatre meetings "question time" was no longer a problem, and he could lightheartedly set aside his Bible and take on all comers, speaking extemporaneously and with assurance, his replies liberally garnished with Biblical quotations, and delivered in a manner that showed his questioners up to such disadvantage that many never ventured more than one question. Aberhart had by then mastered the King James Bible so well that he could identify almost any quotation by chapter and verse.

Ernest Hutchinson was impressed with Aberhart and the work he was doing; and since he himself was a competent musician, it was not long before he was acting as violinist and organist, and taking charge of all the music for the Conference meetings. Music was always an important part of Aberhart's meetings; he would never accept any performer whom he had not auditioned himself. Occasionally a worker with a special talent would be assisted by the Conference, and an item of nine dollars appeared in the Minutes for voice-training for a young worker, with the proviso that he "use his voice to the glory of God."[17]

There was no trained choir at this stage. The singers were soloists who sometimes combined in duets or trios while the audience participated in congregational singing. As might be expected from the informal and evangelical nature of the meetings, Aberhart chose music that was derived from the type of religious music known as "Gospel songs." He exercised sufficient discretion to avoid the use of the more shallow examples of that popular genre and mixed the better sort with some well-known hymns of the mainline churches.

Although Aberhart was not the only freelance evangelist in town, he attracted the biggest audiences. He commanded attention the moment he stepped on the platform. The vitality that radiated from him gave his great bulk an appearance of tremendous power. He was now in his early forties, and obesity had begun to overlay his muscular physique. No suggestion of lethargy was in evidence, however, as he paced the platform lightly while he spoke, and brought down his fist every now and then on a stout-legged table. He seemed to get great satisfaction from public speaking, beginning his lectures in a quiet voice that gradually became more passionate as he lunged forward at his audience to make his points. His oration developed into a roaring crescendo, after which climax his voice became very quiet again, as if he had experienced an emotional release.[18] His voice was pleasing, richly toned, well modulated, and with occasional idiosyncrasies of pronunciation that endeared themselves to those who hung on his words but irritated those who did not – and he could display depths of emotion like a trained actor. He seemed to have come by this talent naturally, and his lectures were, indeed, a "performance."

When Aberhart was speaking on his favorite subject, the Book of Revelation, his graphic presentation thrilled his audience. When lecturing on the "Book of the Seven Seals" he appeared on the platform holding a replica of an ancient book in the form of a large scroll, which he had made and sealed with seven wax seals. As Ernest Hutchinson provided background music on the theatre organ, Aberhart repeated the appropriate passage from the Book of Revelation. As he broke the first seal, the organ rolled forth "as if it were the noise of thunder" and continued until the breaking of the seventh seal when, as Aberhart read the words "there was silence in heaven," the music suddenly ceased. Aberhart allowed an impressive silence to permeate the auditorium before he spoke again.[19] There were few who did not feel the dramatic impact of his technique.

Aberhart organized the activities of the Prophetic Conference just as he did the affairs of Westbourne Baptist Church. Each department was under the care of a member of the executive – music, finance, pamphlets, library, etc. – each member of the executive having a particular job assigned to him. Although he delegated the work of the Bible Conference, Aberhart kept the control to himself, going as far as he could to guide matters toward the goal that had been agreed upon. He knew that the best way to be effective was to persuade those who differed from him to think as he did *before* a meeting began: known dissenters were reasoned with in telephone conversations and drawn aside before meetings. When he wished to, Aberhart dominated a conversation, and if he pleased, he could change the subject with confounding suddenness. When he knew an opponent would be in the audience, Aberhart would discuss beforehand with a follower the line of argument he proposed to take, asking anxiously if it was convincing enough to move his antagonist.[20]

Aberhart was a master of manipulating people, and this skill was crucial to his style of leadership. When all devices of argument failed and the decision looked likely to go against him around the conference table, he was still prepared. If Aberhart was uncertain which way the discussion would go, he would go into the conference room with two written motions, one in each breast pocket, so that he was armed for either advance or retreat. He used the parliamentary system in a masterly manner, until even *that* seemed a weapon in his hand and his opponents were quite overawed by his skill. If all these measures failed, and Aberhart saw his opinions put aside to make way for ideas he considered mistaken or harmful to the progress of the organization, he would resort to his last weapon, which seems to have paralyzed his companions, supporters, and non-supporters alike. He would resign. He resigned from chairmanships. He resigned from moderatorships. He resigned until the element of surprise was no longer a factor. But still the device seemed effective, for always the rebels would ask themselves the one unanswerable question "Who would take his place?"

The deacons of Westbourne Baptist Church and the executive of the Prophetic Conference were deeply indebted to Aberhart. His formidable Sunday schedule began with the morning worship service at 11 a.m., to be followed by Sunday school at noon, with its adult class taught by Aberhart. The Bible Conference was held at the Grand Theatre at 3 p.m. The evening service was again held at the church, and was sometimes followed by a deacon's meeting at which he presided. The fact that he did all this entirely without remuneration put the church and the Prophetic Conference in Aberhart's debt to an embarrassing extent. Even had he allowed them to ease the burden from his shoulders, they knew that only one man had the breadth of vision that could take in the whole sweep of their field of activity, and even more important, that only one man could draw the crowds. The deacons of Westbourne could well remember the fruitless struggle of the first ten years of the church, when it was as much as they could do to attract thirty or forty people to Sunday services. The church was now packed, and a glance at the attendance figures for the Bible Conference now showed a rapid increase to six and seven hundred people every Sunday.

Brother Aberhart was considered essential to the success of both the church and the Bible Conference. Usually his letter of resignation was tactfully dropped into the nearest waste-paper basket, and the subject was not mentioned again. The resignations of his opponents, however, might be slipped quietly in at the next meeting, and there would be a discreet shuffle of executive personnel. Aberhart would still be in the chair, and the measures would be either his or put forward by one of a few who were his never-failing supporters.

One incident clearly illustrates how Aberhart exercised his power. Two of the Conference executive members were Presbyterians who had followed Aberhart from Grace Church. When he was rebaptized in 1920 they were offended and voiced their displeasure. To disarm their opposition he recommended that the Conference should officially come under the control of the Deacons' Board of Westbourne and that all executive members had to be Baptists. After this motion was passed, the two Presbyterians withdrew, claiming that the Conference was no longer interdenominational, as it claimed to be.[21]

For those who stood with Aberhart there was a strong feeling of camaraderie. He was their hero. Conference members remembered one particular incident when Aberhart devastated an opposing preacher. During the early twenties a Seventh-Day Adventist evangelist, F.W. Johnston, came to Beiseker, about sixty-four kilometers northeast of Calgary. He got the local population there quite stirred up by telling them that they had to close their businesses on Saturday, and challenged all comers to a debate on the question. Finally, a group of Beiseker Presbyterians came to Calgary and invited the minister of Grace Church to participate in the debate. He refused, but as the delegation was leaving, the church secretary suggested that they contact Aberhart. They did and he consented to go.

The debate was arranged for the town hall at Beiseker on Saturday evening after sundown. People came from eighty kilometers around. When Aberhart, the Scrimgeour brothers, and Lem Fowler arrived, the hall had been packed for an hour. Each speaker had an hour to present his subject, and then ten minutes for rebuttal. Johnston spoke first, Aberhart followed. The crowd responded more to Aberhart, and he was considered the winner. He then offered to lecture against another Seventh-Day Adventist doctrine, soul-sleep. Johnston left, claiming that he had to prepare for his lectures the next day. Aberhart stayed to answer questions and discuss the Bible with the crowds until midnight. Then, with the members of the Prophetic Conference's executive who had accompanied him, he went to a friend's place for supper, where they talked until 3 a.m. On the way home the roads were iced-over and full of snow. They arrived back in Calgary at 7 a.m. with Aberhart saying, "Boys, I've got to get my Sunday school lesson ready and I haven't yet prepared my afternoon lecture."[22]

Aberhart's seemingly boundless energy, which was devoted night and day to the "work of the Lord," caused his supporters to overlook some of his more obvious faults. Now he needed only the official surrender of the title deeds of the church in order to hold the future of Westbourne firmly in his hand – or so it seemed. Distrusted as Aberhart may have been by officialdom, in the form of the Baptist Union of Western Canada, the people of Westbourne were his.

Aberhart advertised his lectures at the Prophetic Conference as "inter-denominational, non-sectarian, and orthodox,"[23] as he did not want to be identified as a leader of a sect, even though he was moving in that direction. As noted before, to Aberhart the word "sect" had odious theological connotations, and he himself used the term to describe those religious groups whose beliefs he considered unorthodox.[24]

At its inception, the Calgary Prophetic Bible Conference was an interdenominational organization. For several years it remained at a stage that sociologist Bryan Wilson has described as "pre-sectarian":

> It is common for sects to begin with a strong affirmation of their hostility to sectarianism. They frequently arise to unite all Christians, and there is strong expression of indifference to denominational boundaries. Thus Alexander Campbell, leader of the American movement which eventually split into the Disciples and the Churches of Christ, rejected all the divisions of Christendom. So too did the early Plymouth Brethren, who were intent on providing a simple form of worship for all who lived the Christian life. At this stage, a movement is being called out, and its leaders have not yet worked out the implications of their activity. Strictly, we may be justified in calling this stage "pre-sectarian," a period of incipient crystallization, when commitment is still somewhat equivocal. As hostility is met and as followers need to know who are reliable associates, who are Christians to be accepted at worship or for social intercourse – so boundaries come to be drawn and the sect acquires real shape.[25]

Aberhart transformed Westbourne Baptist Church and the Calgary Prophetic Bible Conference into an élitist and separatist sect. However, these two organizations had different levels of sectarian behaviour. Westbourne Baptist Church became a sect much more quickly, as Aberhart was able to introduce and enforce his doctrinal innovations there more easily.

At first the Calgary Prophetic Bible Conference did not appear to be in competition with other churches. For example, when Grace Presbyterian Church held some special meetings, Aberhart cancelled his own meetings so that his audience could attend.[26] When First Baptist Church held special revival meetings, Aberhart offered that church the use of the facilities of his Prophetic Conference at the Grand Theatre.[27] He himself continued to preach at the Methodist "Men's Own" meetings directed by his friend Dr. Kerby,[28] and was also a frequent speaker at Crescent Heights, Hillhurst, and Heath Baptist churches. During 1922 and 1923, on behalf of the Prophetic Conference, he conducted two-week-long evangelistic campaigns at the North Hill Presbyterian Church, Pleasant Heights Presbyterian Church, and Hillhurst Baptist Church.[29] These churches were happy to have him present his lectures because he drew people into their churches and it did not cost them anything. Much of his support for the Prophetic Conference came from the Hillhurst Church and Crescent Heights Baptist Church, as the minister of the latter, the Reverend Christopher Burnett, was a frequent speaker at the Prophetic Conference.[30] The interdenominational nature of the Conference began to change, however, after Aberhart placed it under the control of the deacons of Westbourne and insisted that members of the Conference executive be Baptists.

Aberhart's influence in the wider religious community is a difficult matter to assess. In his study of the religious milieu in Alberta, sociologist W.E. Mann has listed a number of sects and cults that flourished there, implying that the members of these groups were part of Aberhart's religious audience and also later supported him in his political career.[31] This implication is somewhat misleading, since some of the groups that Mann listed were separatist sects opposed by Aberhart, and opposed to him. In his lectures and sermons Aberhart denounced the doctrines of Spiritism, Christian Science, Theosophy, Mormonism, the Jehovah's Witnesses, and the Seventh-Day Adventists as heretical.[32] He made a special point of disassociating himself from some of those groups. Thus he once advertised: "These lectures are NOT Adventist nor Millennial Dawnist (Jehovah's Witness) propaganda."[33] Because of Aberhart's denunciations and their own separatist leanings, active members of these groups would not have been likely supporters. However, he may have influenced some members of these groups to change their allegiance.

Aberhart's supporters appear to have come from the major Protestant denominations and from sects such as the Christian and Missionary Alliance, Evangelical Free Church, Baptists, Nazarenes, Pentecostals, British-Israelites, Prairie Bible Institute students, and the Open Brethren. However, his support from those groups fluctuated as he developed new doctrines. For example, some people at Prairie Bible Institute at Three Hills objected to his mixing British-Israelism with his prophetic interpretations.[34]

As long as Aberhart taught doctrines common to fundamentalism, he had a wide audience, for there were many fundamentalists within the major denominations. But once he began to advocate new doctrines, the nature of his audience changed, beginning late in 1922 when he introduced his "pentecostal" doctrines to the public meetings of the Prophetic Conference. Rather than remaining interdenominational, the Prophetic Conference began to mirror the theological shifts that had occurred at Westbourne Baptist Church. As Aberhart became more sectarian, active members of other sects and churches had to make a decision either to join him or to break with him. Sects do not very often allow for theological latitudinarianism; once Aberhart became identified as a sectarian, his audience began to be limited to merely nominal adherents of other churches and sects, and to those with no previous religious commitment at all.[35]

By 1922, the increasing crowds that Aberhart had drawn into Westbourne Baptist Church caused the deacons to consider hiring a minister, since Aberhart still had neither the time nor the desire to undertake the necessary pastoral duties. Because of Aberhart's wish that baptisms be performed with the "Jesus only" formula, a minister was needed who would abide by the decisions of the deacons' board that Aberhart dominated. Aberhart suggested the Reverend Ernest G. Hansell (1895-1965) as a suitable minister for Westbourne. Born in England, Hansell had moved to Calgary, where he had worked for a time as a cartoonist for one of Calgary's newspapers. He was a Baptist by upbringing. His first, somewhat inauspicious contact with Aberhart had been during the First World War, when Aberhart had brought a special speaker up from the United States whom Hansell had gone to hear because of his reputation. When the speaker could not appear because of illness, Aberhart substituted for him. Hearing of the change in plans, Hansell said to his companion, "Let's leave, we don't want to hear that man."[36] So they left. Apparently Hansell thought that Aberhart held certain doctrines of the Jehovah's Witnesses.

Hansell's next contact with Aberhart came a couple of years later. He had gone to the fundamentalist Bible Institute of Los Angeles to study for the ministry, and on one of his visits home he was invited to give some sermons at Crescent Heights Baptist Church. His hostess Mrs. G.W. Gallagher asked him if he had ever met Aberhart. On replying that he had never met him personally, he was told that Aberhart had attended one of his own meetings. When Hansell commented on Aberhart's supposed unorthodoxy, Mrs. Gallagher replied that she had attended Aberhart's lectures and was sure that Hansell was incorrect. She then set about arranging a meeting between them over the noon meal at her home, which was only a few blocks from Aberhart's school. Aberhart arrived in good time for the luncheon, and was sitting in the living room when Hansell arrived. With the disconcerting directness of youth, Hansell immediately began to question Aberhart on his doctrinal beliefs. Aberhart was momentarily thrown off balance. When he recovered, however, he threw back his head and laughed heartily. Then he goodhumouredly joined battle. "What does the Bible say?" he demanded. Judging by later events, the debate must have raised each man considerably in the other's esteem. After that meeting Hansell left to continue his studies in Los Angeles, and the two saw nothing more of each other for some time.

After graduating, Hansell conducted evangelistic campaigns in the Okanagan Valley and used his talent as a cartoonist to spread the gospel message there. During the summer of 1922 he met Aberhart again in Vancouver, and was soon recommended for the position at Westbourne. Hansell was entirely unknown to any of the Westbourne deacons, but they were willing to rely on Aberhart's judgment. Hansell was hired in the fall of 1922 to do some of the preaching and perform all of the pastoral duties.[37]

Aberhart, however, still remained the real leader of the church. In describing the hiring of Hansell, one of the deacons of the church stated:

> Aberhart said to the executive committee, "Let us get Hansell in and guarantee him a salary. We'll create a pastor's salary fund. I'll write to him and tell him we have six month's salary ahead." (We had already raised $750.) The pastor came and Aberhart said to him, "Now Mr. Hansell, if we have to break into this fund, you'll realize you're not wanted."[38]

This arrangement, which placed the minister subordinate to Aberhart and made the minister's tenure a matter of dollars and cents, became a characteristic of Aberhart's religious organization from then on. Such an arrangement caused endless problems and was one of the factors leading to the organization's eventual undoing.

After Hansell's arrival Aberhart gave up his title of "Moderator," and though he now had more time to spend on the affairs of the Bible Conference, no detail of church affairs escaped his notice and members were constantly under his scrutiny. Nothing was done without his approval.

In January 1923 Aberhart, now relieved of some of the duties at Westbourne, was able to channel his energies into the development of a Bible institute, a dream that seems to have been in the back of his mind for some time. He called his new endeavour the Calgary Bible Institute.[39]

Interdenominational Bible institutes had become a regular feature on the North American scene since the upsurge of fundamentalism at the end of the First World War. There were several reasons for their existence: sometimes they were part of a church's or denomination's department of Christian education; more often they became a substitute for regular theological education for fundamentalist ministers, who feared modernism in the existing seminaries. The theological basis of Bible institutes was usually dispensationalism. The academic requirements for entrants were low, and courses were provided in most branches of religious work – theology, Bible study, public speaking, and business administration. Graduates became ministers, missionaries, Bible teachers, youth workers, or Sunday-school teachers. By insisting with one accord on the inerrancy of the Bible, such institutes advanced the fundamentalist cause, and they ranged in ambition from short courses carried on in temporary, makeshift accomodations to full degree-courses in large organizations with far-reaching activities, centered on extensive, modern premises. The Moody Bible Institute in Chicago and the Bible Institute of Los Angeles were the best known, the latter in fact being Hansell's *alma mater*. Aberhart had visited this school when he had spent a previous summer preaching in Los Angeles, and no doubt he was encouraged in his plans by what he saw there.

Aberhart's institution was not the first to be established in Alberta. In 1920 the Nazarenes had started one in Calgary,[40] and in 1922 Prairie Bible Institute was founded at Three Hills and became one of the largest of its kind in North America.[41]

Bible institutes seemed to fill a need in Alberta, where churches were few and far between in the rural areas, and where one minister was usually responsible for several charges. Native-born ministers were a rarity, since farm boys who may have wanted to enter the ministry usually did not have the educational prerequisites nor the money to attend university and seminary. As a result, most ministers had to be imported from urban centres. The Methodists and Presbyterians had theological colleges in Edmonton, but most ministers came from central Canada, England, and the United States, and most were far more educated than their rural parishioners. As well as educational barriers, these imported ministers also met social and cultural ones. Many imported ministers were products of middle-class urban homes and found it difficult to adjust to the hardships of rural prairie life. The Baptist Home Mission Board Report for 1922, for example, reported that young Baptist ministers preferred becoming missionaries in India or South America to ministering in rural Alberta.[42]

Aberhart began his Calgary Bible Institute with the religious needs of rural Alberta in mind. His institute, housed in Westbourne Church, was held on week-nights, beginning with three courses, each lasting ten weeks. On Wednesday night there was a class for Christian workers, which dealt with Bible teaching, preaching, and effective Christian organization. Thursday evenings began with a class for Sunday school teachers in which they studied, under his guidance, the *International Sunday School Lessons*. It was feared that these lessons were tainted with modernism, so this influence had to be countered: following the class Aberhart gave lectures on "how we got the Bible."

Later, Aberhart expanded the curriculum of the Bible Institute and added correspondence courses.[43] This was the sort of thing he loved doing most, and this new enterprise was part of the dream that was to be fully realized within the next four years.

When Hansell had been hired by Westbourne Baptist Church he was unaware of the doctrinal innovations on baptism and the Holy Spirit that Aberhart had been introducing slowly into the church.[44] How Hansell initially responded to Aberhart's interpretations is not known, but later he said, "Aberhart had such a forceful way of interpreting Scripture that it was impossible to argue with him."[45] Hansell soon became convinced of Aberhart's doctrines.

Some time after Hansell's arrival, Aberhart began propagating his new doctrines with more vigour. On 29 April 1923 a baptismal service was held at the church, with the sermon topic being "The Baptism of the Holy Spirit according to Scripture."[46] It is likely that Hansell was now using the "Jesus only" formula, since in June it was part of a new church creed stated in Westbourne's "Declaration of Incorporation" that was registered with the provincial government. Besides the article dealing with baptism by immersion "in the name of the Lord Jesus Christ... for the receiving of the Holy Spirit in power,"[47] the new creed included Aberhart's doctrines concerning the Rapture. Other doctrines were spelled out in quite some detail and acceptance was obligatory for membership in the church. Although Westbourne still remained within the Baptist Union of Western Canada and participated in its affairs,[48] the rigidity of this creed and its special emphasis on the Holy Spirit were taking the church outside Baptist tradition, which stressed the doctrinal autonomy of each believer.

In the fall of 1923 Aberhart's theology underwent another development as a result of another contact with Pentecostalism. Charles S. Price, a faith healer from the United States, came to Calgary on his cross-Canada healing campaign. He was a recent convert of Aimee Semple McPherson, the famous Canadian-born faith healer in Los Angeles.[49] Night after night for over two weeks, crowds reaching eight thousand people packed Price's meetings at the Victoria Pavilion, Calgary's livestock exhibition hall. As Price, dressed in a frock coat, annointed people with oil and laid his hands on their heads, most of them fell to the floor in a faint. They were "slain in the Spirit," claimed Price. Some began "speaking in tongues" when they revived. One night seven people claimed instant healings.[50] Price taught that divine healing was part of the atonement of Christ.

Reaction to Price was mixed. Even before Price commenced his campaign, the Reverend Christopher Burnett of Crescent Heights Baptist Church preached a sermon entitled "Why I Do Not Expect to Co-operate with Dr. Price." Burnett was particularly critical of Price's doctrine of divine healing.[51] Some others were more favourable; several Presbyterian and Methodist ministers in fact gave Price strong support.[52] However, harsh criticism came from the medical profession. Dr. Dunlop, addressing the Alberta Medical Association, claimed that Price's "healings" were a matter of psychosomatic suggestibility, and that Price was hypnotizing his audience. In the midst of Price's campaign the Calgary Medical Association had a court summons issued, charging Price with practising medicine without a license; but the case was dismissed on a technicality.[53] There was also a claim by a medical-clerical investigation team in Vancouver that some people had to be hospitalized as a result of becoming severely depressed when they were not healed.[54]

The press, which had given Price considerable publicity, also turned on him, after there were rumours of financial irregularities during his previous meetings in British Columbia. Dr. Price refused to disclose his financial "take" and refused to have anything to do with the Vancouver medical committee investigating his "cures." He also claimed that he was being treated unfairly by a hostile press. The Calgary *Herald* described his meetings as "hysterical," as some people were muttering and groaning and others became comatose after Price laid his hands on them.[55]

At the close of the campaign, the Reverend Christopher Burnett attacked Price in another sermon entitled "Why I am Glad I Didn't Co-operate in the

Price Campaign.'' He stated that Price advertised himself too much, and that his doctrine that healing is part of the atonement was wrong. In a subsequent sermon Burnett claimed that divine healing was not part of the present dispensation; miraculous powers had passed away with the early church.[56]

Because of the widespread interest in the subject, Aberhart spoke of it at the fall opening of the Prophetic Conference. Following his habit of riding the waves of other speakers' popularity, Aberhart advertised his lecture as a follow-up of Price's meetings, and said that he took the same stand as Price, that the Bible was the inspired Word of God.[57] Such advertising was misleading, however, because the Bible's inerrancy was only a minor part of Price's message and the two men were not in accord on other, more important points of doctrine.

On 7 October 1923, when Aberhart lectured on the subject "Is Healing In The Atonement?'' he drew a vast crowd, and the Grand Theatre was full an hour before the lecture began. Starting with a question of divine healing, Aberhart soon switched the emphasis to eschatology and warned that the Devil would ape the miraculous during the Last Days. That evening Westbourne also held its evening service at the Grand Theatre because of the expected crowd. Hansell came more to the point than Aberhart, and attacked Price's financial dealings in a sermon entitled "Making a Saint Out of a Grafter.''[58]

In spite of their criticism of Price's methods, Aberhart and Hansell's doctrine of the Holy Spirit was modified as a result of their exposure to Price, who taught that the Holy Spirit was imparted by the "laying on of hands.'' During Price's meetings they had seen dramatic results following that practice, and Aberhart found biblical support for it in the New Testament.[59] Aberhart came to believe that the Holy Spirit was received by the laying on of hands by "apostles.'' Several modern groups who rejected the doctrine of apostolic succession taught by the Roman Catholics and Anglicans had created their own "apostles.'' The Catholic Apostolic Church, or Irvingites, established a council of twelve apostles in the 1830s.[60] So did the Mormons, later. Several Pentecostal groups have had apostles in their organizations.[61] Harvey McAlister, who introduced Aberhart to the "Jesus only'' baptismal formula, taught a restored order of apostles.[62]

Within several weeks of Price's campaign, Aberhart launched into a series of sermons on the Holy Spirit, healing, and apostleship.[63] The latter subject created quite a controversy, and at a November meeting of the executive of the Prophetic Conference, Hansell expressed the opinion that there should be agreement on doctrinal belief among the executive members - in spite of the fact that the Conference was still ostensibly interdenominational. He added that he now believed that the laying on of hands was the normal way for baptized people to receive the "baptism of the Holy Ghost,'' and that this should be among the beliefs upon which the executive members should agree. Some members balked at accepting this dictate, and after a tussle, Aberhart gave notice of motion that he would resign. The only event that would prevent this would be the resignation of the dissenting members. This meeting saw the withdrawal of two more from the Conference executive.[64]

One of those who left was Louis H. Fowler, who later became a Presbyterian minister. He disagreed with Aberhart on the question of healing and had reservations about Aberhart's slavish dependence on the King James or Authorized Version and his views on baptism.[65] Fowler's cousin Lem Fowler, who was Aberhart's song leader, had personal as well as doctrinal reasons for leaving. Following one of Aberhart's lectures, Lem expressed his feelings to Aberhart and said that he could not agree with him, but after some discussion, he was prepared to accept Aberhart's views. That night, however, during the evening service, while Lem Fowler was sitting on the platform in his capacity as song leader, Aberhart told his audience of a certain misguided young man who had come to see him about a doctrinal disagreement, and of how he had reasoned the young man out of his errors. Aberhart drank in the crowd's adulation as they laughed at the young man's "foolishness." Meanwhile, Lem was becoming more and more embarrassed and, at the close of the meeting, he told Aberhart he felt that he had been used and that he was resigning.[66] Thus left the young man who three years before had been given voice lessons so he could "use his voice to the glory of God."

With the opposition gone, "baptism of the Holy Ghost" by the "laying on of hands" by an "apostle" was accepted in principle by the Conference executive, the personnel of which were the same as that of the deacons' board of Westbourne. Aberhart's next task was to convince the church members. It would be no easy matter, for the innovation constituted not only the introduction of an entirely new point of doctrinal belief, which Baptist churches had so far got on very well without, but also the creation of a new post of authority higher than any so far existing in a Baptist church. Aberhart did not stop at suggesting that his new doctrine was desirable and should be adopted by Westbourne; he went so far as to say that those who did not accept the doctrine should be refused membership in the church. This would have been abhorrent to the Baptists, who allowed church members a great deal of discretion where beliefs were concerned. It seems that Aberhart recognized these difficulties, and bearing in mind the hostile reception his ideas had received from some of the Conference executive, he began a series of indoctrination classes in which he could prepare the church membership for the innovation. He held the classes on Thursday evenings in the church.[67] They were well attended, and Aberhart, never happier than when discussing some biblical problem, stood before them Bible in hand, advocating his new doctrine.

Aberhart convinced church members that apostles were necessary in the modern church. He speciously equated the office of apostle with that of a bishop. The next question was how apostles were to be acquired. Aberhart maintained that each church could appoint its own apostle. After he had primed the congregation with the idea, it was not long before someone nominated him to the position. He, however, insisted that since the New Testament frequently spoke of apostles in the plural, there should be two apostles in each church. Hansell was soon nominated, and shortly thereafter the deacons of the church ordained Aberhart and Hansell co-apostles, after anointing them with oil and laying their hands on them.[68]

Sometime within the first half of 1924 Aberhart and Hansell commenced their duties as apostles, and Westbourne went through a "holy roller" phase. (If the Minutes of the church for that period were available, the matter could be dated more exactly.[69]) Hansell claimed that on more than one occasion people passed out cold after he and Aberhart had laid hands on them.[70] Others reported some individuals "speaking in tongues" and others having associated "charismatic" manifestations.[71] One source stated that a woman went berserk after going into a trance following "the laying on of hands." After this, Aberhart and Hansell warned the congregation against expecting such results, and it is said never to have happened again.[72]

Instead, Aberhart emphasized the seeking of the less spectacular "gifts of the Spirit," one of which was the "gift of prophecy." Aberhart always insisted that he used the infinitive "to prophesy" in the sense of "to explain the Scriptures," but this "gift of prophecy" conferred by the "laying on of hands" did not imply that any fortune-telling powers were acquired by the recipient, even though the biblical sense also contained the idea of foretelling the future.[73] Aberhart's definition of prophecy was rather restricted, for in practice it came to mean the ability to expound the eschatology that Aberhart taught. At least one church member had his membership revoked for disagreeing with a minor point of Aberhart's eschatology.[74]

Aberhart's insistence upon the acceptance of the quasi-pentecostal doctrines of apostleship and spiritual gifts caused further disruption within Westbourne Baptist Church, and the number of those walking out the door for the last time was on the rise.

CHAPTER SEVEN

■

AN EXPANDING INFLUENCE

T HE HOLIER-*than-thou*

attitude may be caused by virtue,

but usually it is the result of a poor memory.

— From an advertisement in the *Calgary Herald*,

by William Aberhart, 1925

In spite of the increasing sectarianism of Aberhart's theology the meetings of the Prophetic Conference still proved very popular. During the 1923-1924 season the average attendance was about six hundred. Aberhart's name was becoming better known across Alberta, and through his published writings and personal appearances, his influence extended as far as California. In 1925 his influence was even further extended by his effective use of a new communication medium, radio broadcasting.

Throughout the 1923-1924 season the Prophetic Conference had given away twenty thousand pieces of religious literature that had been purchased or printed on its own press. Also, some two thousand copies of Aberhart's lectures, printed in a series called "God's Great Prophecies," had been circulated.[1] These booklets formed the corpus of Aberhart's theological thought. At the end of each was a series of questions, and for one dollar Aberhart would personally mark responses and provide answers to three other biblical questions a student might wish to ask.

During the summer of 1924 Aberhart gave special prophetic lectures in Vancouver and then travelled to Los Angeles, where he held more meetings.[2] The meetings of the Prophetic Conference commenced again in the fall, running between October and May to coincide with the slow time of the agricultural year, so farmers could come to the meetings. Because of the expected crowds, it was decided to move the Conference to the much larger Palace Theatre on Eighth Avenue.

Another venture of the Prophetic Conference was the beginning of its own religious journal called *The Prophetic Voice*. This magazine included reprints of Aberhart's lectures, comments on current events, and articles by other executive members of the Conference. *The Prophetic Voice* was intended as a monthly publication, but only three issues appeared from October 1924 to January 1926 (when it was discontinued until 1942). It seems as if Aberhart was a better public speaker than he was a writer, or perhaps he did not have the time required to keep the magazine going.

Those among Aberhart's audiences who did not participate in the frivolities of secular pleasure expected nevertheless to find a certain amount of sober entertainment and emotional outlet in their religion. Those who attended his lectures purely for their entertainment value were prospective converts. Satisfying the constant demand for new and interesting material was therefore one of Aberhart's biggest problems. The biblical prophecies provided him with subject-matter for most of his lectures, but on occasion he had to go outside the Bible for material. One such subject was a little-known theory that claimed that the original names of the signs of the Zodiac were given by divine inspiration, and that when aberrations (caused when Greek and other ideas were superimposed on the originals) were removed, the story of the Bible could be seen in the constellations. Thus, according to the theory, God provided, for people who lived before the books of the Bible were written, prophecies that foretold events of biblical history.

Aberhart discovered this theory set out in a book belonging to his friend Harry Scrimgeour. *Witness of the Stars* had been written by an Anglican ultra-dispensationalist, Ethelbert W. Bullinger. Aberhart is reported to have asked, "Do you mind if I borrow this? I would like to give a lecture on it." Apparently he could read a book one night and lecture on it the next; but great as Aberhart's talents were, such hasty assimilation must often have precluded his thorough understanding of the material. However, his gift for vivid presentation and his photographic memory concealed any imperfections in the matter he was propounding, or in his understanding of it. *Witness of the Stars*, skirting astrology as closely as it did, was a popular idea in British-Israelism and associated theories, which claimed that the Great Pyramid of Egypt contained in its design a prophetic depiction of biblical history and Britain's role

SEDUCING SPIRIT & ITCHING EARS

THE PLACE OF WOMEN IN RELIGION

DO YOU KNOW—

1.—That there are a number of Religious Sects in our city that have been commenced by women?

2.—That the Bible warns us distinctly about certain disorders that are to come through this?

YOU WILL WANT TO HEAR THIS

PALACE THEATRE

SUNDAY, FEB. 1st

Organ Recital 2:30 p.m. — Lecture at 3 p.m.

Topic:
THE PRESENT DAY RELIGIOUS TREND TO APOSTASY

The great need of the hour is for people to know the false from the True. The Bible has given certain earmarks by which to tell. DO YOU CARE?

Aberhart was antagonistic to women preachers; he believed they were more easily deceived by the Devil than men were. Another of his eye-catching ads in the Calgary Herald *(31 January 1925, p. 14).*

in the future. Aberhart held his audiences spellbound with these discussions and similarly unconventional speculations. Two other books on the subject assisted him: Joseph A. Seiss's *Gospel in the Stars* and Sydney Watson's novel *What the Stars Held? or the Secret of the Sphinx*.[3] For some months, star-study became the subject-matter of Aberhart's Bible class at Westbourne. Often, to illustrate his topic, he took the class on nightly field trips to Riley Park, where they could observe the stars undimmed by the city's lights.[4] To the uncritical, Aberhart was a genius; not only was he a student of the Bible, he was also an astronomer.

The rising attendance at Westbourne Baptist Church caused the deacons, in January 1925, to seek an architect to draw up plans for expanding the existing facilities of the church.[5] The congregation now had legal control over the building and property. Two years previously Dr. M.L. Orchard, secretary of the Baptist Union of Western Canada, had been a special speaker at Westbourne, and the deacons had talked with him about their past problems with the trustees.[6] Orchard smoothed things over, and in 1924 the deeds to the property were turned over to the congregation, with an unwritten understanding that the church would remain within the Baptist Union and support its projects.[7]

The expansion plans for the church became very dear to the hearts of both church members and Conference personnel. Suggestions flowed freely while the building fund reflected a steady increase in church membership during the next year. The modest plans were transformed into a bold new proposal. Undoubtedly the changes in the current theological scene spurred them on to more ambitious visions.

On 10 June 1925 the United Church of Canada came into being, an amalgamation of a great number of the country's Methodist, Presbyterian, and Congregational churches.[8] Aberhart feared that this union would result in a creedless church, that it was a forerunner of the apostate ecclesiastical structure of the End Times. In his sermons around the time of church union Aberhart presented an idea that seems to have been unique to him. He gave identifications to the seven churches of Revelation, chapters 2 and 3: Ephesus (Baptist), Smyrna (Presbyterian), Pergamos (Church of England), Thyatira (Roman Catholic), Sardis (Methodist and United Church of Canada), Philadelphia (Lutheran), and Laodicea (Christian Science),[9] such identifications reflecting his own theological preferences. The church with the least faults (Ephesus — Baptist) was the one he was associated with, the second-rate church (Smyrna — Presbyterian) was the one he next preferred. Aberhart was very much opposed to Presbyterians' joining the United Church, and he sided with those who stayed out. During the months of May and June 1925, he and Hansell supplied the pulpit at Pleasant Heights Presbyterian Church while its congregation was waiting for a new minister.[10]

The unrest over the formation of the United Church of Canada occurred at the peak of the fundamentalist-modernist controversy that was raging in the United States, and which had its counterpart in Canada. Many of those Presbyterians who stayed out of church union were fundamentalists. Central to the fundamentalist-modernist controversy was the way in which the

Bible was to be interpreted. The fundamentalists saw the Bible as divinely inspired and infallible, while the modernists viewed it as the record of man's evolving comprehension of God and ethics.[11]

During the summer of 1925 Aberhart would have been quite aware of current theological controversy while he was lecturing in Los Angeles. At that time two of America's famous lawyers, William Jennings Bryan, thrice-defeated presidential candidate and former secretary of state under Woodrow Wilson, and Clarence Darrow, the brilliant criminal defence attorney, made daily headlines in the famous Scopes Trial. John T. Scopes was being tried for violating Tennessee's Butler Act, which forbade the teaching of evolution in the schools in that state. Scopes's conviction gave strength to the fundamentalist movement, despite the embarassments suffered by the fundamentalist Bryan during the trial, despite the fact that the bulk of public opinion was not with Bryan on the issue.[12] Modernist thought had become so widely accepted that it was surprising to many observers that fundamentalism could match it in strength. Ever since the First World War, however, fundamentalists had put aside denominational differences and fought single-mindedly against the liberalizing of Christian belief. The Scopes Trial was a spectacular climax to the then-current phase of the ever-present conflict between liberals and conservatives in religion. Bryan looked upon the Scopes Trial as one of the greatest in all history, an event for all the ages, comparable only to the trials of Socrates and Jesus. At the very least, the trial certainly did excite widespread interest and demonstrated the vitality and pugnacity of the fundamentalist movement.

When Aberhart returned to Calgary at the end of the summer, he was more than ever resolved to fight modernism and became personally involved in a controversy that was upsetting religious life in Canada, particularly in Baptist circles. In 1922, certain Baptist ministers in British Columbia had charged that some of the professors at the Baptist college in Brandon were modernists and that they were undermining the faith of their students.[13] The same charges had been levelled against some of the professors at McMaster University, another Baptist institution, then still in Toronto. Throughout most of its history McMaster had been troubled by charges against the orthodoxy of its staff.[14] The current attack on McMaster was led by the Reverend T.T. Shields, minister of Jarvis Street Baptist Church in Toronto, the largest Baptist Church in Canada, who was also a member of McMaster's board of governors.[15]

During September and October 1925 the Prophetic Conference, Westbourne Baptist, Grace Presbyterian, and another Baptist church sponsored a series of meetings featuring T.T. Shields and the Reverend P.W. Philpott. Aberhart had known both men when he lived in Ontario. Philpott had founded an Associated Gospel Church in Hamilton and was currently pastor of Moody Memorial Church in Chicago. Shields and Philpott drew crowds to Victoria Pavilion nightly with such topics as "The Source of Modernism and its Symptoms; or the Cesspool of Religious Malaria." Daytime meetings were conducted by Shields at Grace Presbyterian Church, which had not joined the United Church of Canada.[16]

Following the Shields-Philpott meetings Aberhart commenced another season of his midweek Bible Institute at Westbourne, but he felt it was not enough to counter the influence of modernism. Something on a grander scale

"30,000 Years Ago"

Science declares that the great Coal Areas were formed and pre-historic animals lived thirty millenniums ago. What saith the Scriptures?

OPENING LECTURE

The Calgary Prophetic Bible Conference Announces the Opening of the Sunday Afternoon Lectures in the

PALACE THEATRE

SUNDAY, OCTOBER 11th, 3 p.m.

Organ Recital and Song Service, 2:30 p.m.

Topic--"30,000 YEARS AGO, or

Is the Bible Story of Creation Scientific?"

Speaker: WILLIAM ABERHART, B.A.

Do you believe in British fair play? Then should everyone not know what the Bible says before they doubt its scientific accuracy? The modernist theory of Evolution needs to be examined.

Why not enrol as a student in our Bible Institute, which opens November 1st? Ask for bulletin or phone W4245. Of interest to Sunday School Teachers, Prospective Missionaries, Young People preparing for the ministry, and others.

Aberhart actively campaigned against the theory of evolution. This ad in the Calgary Herald *(10 October 1925, p. 20) has the now-familiar pitch for "fair play" for Creationism.*

was necessary. He had again visited the Bible Institute of Los Angeles during the summer, and he must also have known of T.T. Shields's plans for building a seminary in Toronto.[17] After a discussion, the executive of the Prophetic Conference passed a motion that a "Bible Institute be established with Mr. Aberhart as Dean and the Prophetic Conference committee being the Board of Governors."[18] How to obtain funds for this project was still an unsolved problem; but before the year was out Aberhart and his followers embarked on an entirely new enterprise that provided the means of implementing their plans on a grand scale.

Radio had come to Alberta in 1922, and by 1925 the small transmitter of radio station CFCN was already a familiar sight perched on the North Hill. The crystal set was becoming more and more a part of home furnishings in town and country alike. It is probable that the suggestion that the Bible Conference go on the air first came from W.W. Grant, a pioneer in Canadian radio broadcasting who was also the proprietor of CFCN (which was known as "Voice of the Prairies Ltd."). Grant approached Robert Scrimgeour, one of the Conference's executive members, who worked as a bookkeeper for the Northern Electric Company. Scrimgeour brought the subject up at a Conference executive meeting, and it at once occasioned animated discussion. The general feeling was in favour of the idea, but a few, of whom Aberhart seems to have been one, needed some persuasion before they could accept it wholeheartedly.

Grant did not find it easy to sell air time. The great machinery of commercial radio had not yet been developed, and it was not as yet generally recognized that air time was a commodity worth buying. No one on the Committee had realized radio's potential value as a publicity vehicle, and Aberhart, according to his normal practice, must have considered carefully whether the Conference could support the cost of such an enterprise.

Aberhart's qualms were, however, soon overcome, and with characteristic energy, the group organized their new venture and secured a five month contract from Grant. A committee was set up to arrange the details of the Radio Club, the membership fee being two dollars.[19] The club was to help finance the undertaking. By November 1925 a microphone stood on Aberhart's rostrum in the Palace Theatre, while wires, strung from wall to wall, suspended other microphones above the stage and audience. For the first time the Prophetic Bible Conference could be carried into all those Alberta homes that were equipped with receivers. Aberhart, stimulated by the unseen addition to his audience, delivered his Bible lecture as enthusiastically as ever, now and then taking a few restless paces to and fro — as was his habit while he spoke — but returning hastily to the microphone as he recalled Grant's instructions.

That day in November 1925 was also probably the most important in Aberhart's career. He did not then know, but was soon to discover, that in radio he had found his greatest single means of influencing the public. It was indeed his own medium. He was to use it to the full, and without it his career might have developed very differently. While his great skill always had been, and was to remain, his ability on the public platform, he was also able to project his personality through the microphone. Through the medium of radio he rose above his competitors in the field of religious leadership, and was to use this power later in the field of politics.

The immediate importance of the *Back-to-the-Bible* broadcast was the vastly greater number of people he was able to reach – which meant that the effectiveness of his work was increased many times over. He was also reaching an audience different to that which had hitherto walked into the Palace Theatre from the sidewalks of Calgary. Aberhart's arresting voice could now be heard in the kitchens of many farmhouses far out on the prairie and on ranches in the foothills.

Into the quiet Sunday afternoons of many of those people now came Aberhart's voice, discussing the very biblical problems that had long interested many of them. Thus, in some isolated homes, from which churches might be far distant, it became the custom on Sunday afternoons for the family to gather around the radio with open Bible, to listen to the voice of William Aberhart. Neighbours who had no radios dropped in to listen, and sometimes decided to buy a set on their next trip to town. Aberhart even encouraged the formation of small groups of listeners, and the Conference supplied them with crystal sets. Radio receivers were also distributed in the hospitals, to those who desired to listen. The Conference executive went so far as to purchase a horse and buggy for one of their members whose task it was to deliver the radio sets locally.[20]

Week by week people gathered to hear Aberhart, and soon the morning and evening services of Westbourne were also broadcast. For some, Aberhart's radio broadcasts took the place of going to church, one listener noting that he no longer had to get dressed and shaved in order to worship; he could listen to Aberhart, smoke his pipe at the same time, and bypass the offering plate.[21]

However, not all were happy with Aberhart's radio activities, because he was using the *Back-to-the-Bible* broadcast to further the fundamentalist position in the fundamentalist-modernist controversy. One of the leaders at First Baptist Church in Calgary wrote to Dr. H.P. Whidden, Chancellor of McMaster University:

> Aberhart is broadcasting every Sunday afternoon and has made some very bitter remarks... and is stirring up all the trouble he can, Burnett and Harber lining up with him, and they don't stick to facts anymore here than Dr. Farmer has found them do in Toronto. Now that you have made a break and have gone after them I hope you keep it up as I am convinced that is the only way to keep them from hindering the progress of the Baptist Denomination and evangelization of the world. Their attitude and methods are mighty proof that the "Devil is not Dead."[22]

There were now three broadcasts on the air each Sunday from one or another of Aberhart's enterprises.[23] In September 1926 the Radio Sunday School was formed.[24] Aberhart devoted a portion of his afternoon broadcast to children and sent them out religious literature that the Conference had purchased from the American Baptist headquarters in Philadelphia. Later, he wrote his own lessons because he feared modernism was creeping into the literature he had been using. What he prepared was especially designed for each age-group, and there were enough lessons so that a child could move up to the next stage without duplication of subject-matter.

Aberhart placed the operation of this new ministry in the hands of one of the Conference executives, Charles R. Pearce, who was a wholesale grocery salesman. A printing press was purchased so that Pearce and his wife could print the Radio Sunday School lessons. Each child who was a member received an individually-addressed lesson each month, regardless of how many children there were in a family that belonged. Each lesson came with an examination, and handsome prizes were awarded to conscientious scholars. Volunteers assisted in marking and mailing the lessons. The considerable expense of this scheme was carried entirely by subscription - not from the children who were instructed but from the general radio audience of the *Back-to-the-Bible* broadcast. Fifty cents would support one student's lessons for one year. At its height, the Radio Sunday School had over 9,141 children enrolled in its lessons.[25] The many children whom Aberhart influenced from 1926 to 1935 would later be important in his political career. He was influencing a new generation of voters.

The radio had not only increased Aberhart's audience but also widened the financial base from which he could draw funds for his new Bible Institute. His radio audience proved to be more important to his religious career than his local supporters, who were always embroiled in church politics.

The affairs of the Calgary Prophetic Bible Conference and Westbourne Baptist Church had become closely connected over the past few years because they had interlocking boards. In March 1926 the executive of the Bible Conference formally approached the congregation of Westbourne Church with a scheme that would make the new Bible Institute a joint undertaking. The building project had reached its final ambitious form in the minds of the Conference executive. Contributions had continually risen as Aberhart spoke on the radio. As Aberhart looked over the figures showing the number of Radio Club memberships sold and the estimated number of his listeners, he was confident that he could raise $15,000 from the citizens of Calgary and $25,000 from people in the rural areas. Adding to that the $10,000 Westbourne could contribute, they could build a $50,000 Bible Institute and Church, a fine building large enough to house classrooms, offices, a library, dormitories, and a beautiful church auditorium. The deacons' report recommending the new building scheme was read to the church members, and after some discussion, the plan was adopted enthusiastically.[26]

Westbourne's official participation was, however, short-lived. In June, the Bible Conference was formally disassociated from Westbourne Church, and the Institute became once more the project of the Conference, with Westbourne being given first preference in renting the auditorium it would contain. Under the original plan, the pastor was to be the head of the Institute and Church; but by this time Hansell and Aberhart had begun to drift apart. Aberhart took a warning from other recent defections and argued that in any future split the Bible Conference executive might lose control of the Bible Institute. Under Baptist democratic voting methods, 51 per cent of those voting could take over the new Institute if they wished. Having a realistic awareness of the fickleness of the public, Aberhart considered this a real threat to the people who were mainly responsible for the creation of the Institute. He convinced the Conference executive of the desirability of having the

Institute firmly in their *own* hands, and accordingly the people who had already contributed towards the building fund through the church were circularized with the proposed change in ownership and advised that if they were dissatisfied with the new arrangement, their money would be refunded. There were, apparently, no requests that money be returned, and the fund remained available for the building of the Institute.[27]

The building fund then stood at about $6,000, which sum was still not enough. There were varying opinions about how the deficiency should be remedied now that Westbourne was officially not a part of the project. One suggestion was received from a newcomer to the streets of Calgary who played havoc for a few days with the future of the Bible Conference venture, then disappeared as suddenly as he had come.

The newcomer, carrying a large carpet bag, first passed Harry Scrimgeour, one the Conference executives, as he walked down Eighth Avenue. There was something about him that caused Aberhart's colleague to pause a moment, to look after him and speculate on his destination, his calling, and his background. His destination was soon to be discovered. The revelation of the other two was to take place in due course.

Back in his accounting office, Harry Scrimgeour answered his telephone and heard Aberhart's voice: "I have had a man here from Bristol, England. He has got a most wonderful scheme by which we can build our Institute. I want to have a meeting in the basement of the church." Two or three of Aberhart's teachers, members of the church, and some outsiders made up the substantial crowd that attended the meeting. William Taverner, the man with the carpet bag, was introduced to the audience, and using the Bible class blackboard to illustrate his points, he explained his business, which he called Quarterly Dividends Ltd. and House Purchase Ltd. He added that he represented a mutual benefit society in England, and that his scheme, having become popular there, was now being extended to all parts of the Empire. His skill with figures was evident when he began to expound his theory. The scheme was of the "pyramid" type, and the unorthodoxy of his ideas bred suspicion in the minds of some of his audience.

Aberhart, never alarmed by the prospect of throwing over the prosaic for the exotic, was favourably impressed by both the man and his scheme. During the next few days Aberhart sounded out the others who had been at the meeting, expressing his own enthusiasm; but he encountered in several quarters a coolness that astonished him. When Mabel Giles, one of his staff-members at Crescent Heights and also member of Westbourne, stated that she felt Taverner could not be trusted, Aberhart said, "You shouldn't make up your mind about people so quickly."[28] Jessie Aberhart had also voiced her suspicions. However, the Conference executive passed a motion "to entertain favorably the propositions submitted by Mr. Tavendor [*sic*]." A finance committee, consisting of the Scrimgeour brothers and Aberhart, was appointed to investigate,[29] but soon the Scrimgeour brothers had second thoughts. Both were accountants by training, and they felt that the scheme was a confidence scam, whereby dividends were paid out of capital so that when new subscribers ceased, the bubble burst. They felt that they had to stop Aberhart before he invested Conference funds in the scheme. A wire they sent to a Toronto newspaper for a report on Taverner received the immediate reply "Taverner ex-jail bird. Just released from serving time in penitentiary in England for having absconded with Mutual Club's money. Have nothing to do with his scheme."[30] Aberhart was still not convinced. "That doesn't upset the theory, though," he replied. The Conference funds were not, however, invested in the scheme.

Taverner left Calgary shortly afterwards, claiming to be on his way to Ottawa to incorporate the Calgary branches of his two companies, in which Aberhart, some of the Conference executives, and some of Aberhart's school teachers had invested. During the summer of 1926, while supplying the pulpit of West Broadway Baptist Church in Vancouver, Aberhart held special meetings to promote Quarterly Dividends Ltd. and House Purchase Ltd., and in August he reported his activities pertaining to those companies to the Conference executive.[31] Both schemes came to a quick end when those who invested lost their money.[32] Although Aberhart refused to believe the charges against Taverner, he was a little angry that Taverner later used his name as a reference in his British promotional literature.[33] It was not long afterwards that the Scrimgeours learned that Taverner was again receiving free room and board at His Majesty's expense. As late as 1929, Aberhart was still convinced that the Quarterly Dividends scheme was workable; the only thing hindering it, he thought, was lack of subscriptions.[34]

Aberhart's involvement with Taverner was only one of many of his participations in fly-by-night schemes. When it came to economics the Scrimgeours felt that Aberhart was "chuckle-headed."

In spite of Aberhart's new ventures – the plans for the Bible Institute, and the operation of the Radio Sunday School – all was not well in his life or at Westbourne. The organizational structure that made Hansell, the minister, subordinate to Aberhart had been creating tensions at Westbourne. One group rallied around Hansell, while another supported Aberhart. That situation had been exacerbated in January 1926, when the format of the morning service had been changed so that Hansell ran a worship service for those who desired it, while Aberhart taught a class on dispensationalism in another part of the building.[35] Also, the Taverner affair had caused some hard feelings, and Aberhart had lost face with some of the inner core of the Prophetic Conference when they would not allow him to invest the building fund in the scheme.

On 10 October 1926 Hansell announced his resignation.[36] Besides the tensions between him and Aberhart, Hansell could no longer abide by the quasi-pentecostal doctrines that Aberhart had introduced into the church. Hansell had been finding that new families seeking to join the church refused to do so after hearing of apostleship, "laying on of hands," and "spiritual gifts." Hansell's resignation was accepted and made effective immediately. With him went a number of his supporters.

While feuding with Hansell, Aberhart had also been fighting the First Baptist Church. Its minister, the Reverend H.H. Bingham, had applied for a position at the large Hinson Memorial Church in Portland, Oregon. Aberhart joined T.T. Shields in writing letters to the Portland Church trying to prevent Bingham's hiring.[37]

With Hansell's departure, Westbourne no longer had any ties with the Baptist Union of Western Canada — something the former trustees had feared might happen. Aberhart preached a series of sermons to reinforce the doctrines that had been rejected by Hansell. He was also made moderator again, and given the power to conduct baptisms and communion. Now that he was an "apostle," he did not hesitate to perform these ordinances. The deacons were busy arranging for the purchase of books on the "baptism of the Holy Spirit," and Aberhart was asked to prepare a new Creed, Covenant, and Confession of Faith for the church.[38]

The new creed, known as the "Red Book," differed considerably from that of 1923. In the new book there was no mention of the duties of the minister whatsoever, but the position and duties of the "apostle" were spelled out in detail. Two classes of church membership were also elaborated: general and active. The latter were those who had been baptized "in the name of the Lord Jesus," had had hands laid on them, and were practising their "spiritual gifts." Only they could hold church offices and teach in the Sunday School. The Creed did mention, however, that certain people could receive the gifts of the Holy Spirit directly, without the laying on of hands.[39]

The new creed also outlined rigid behavioural rules. It was laid down that only unleavened bread could be used in the communion service at Westbourne, and Aberhart personally checked up on those who did not attend communion regularly.[40]

Members now came and went to and from Westbourne with bewildering rapidity. Those who could not bring themselves to agree with Aberhart had but one alternative, for as he often said later in his political career, "He who is not with me is against me." It is interesting to note, however, that he stayed on speaking terms with many of the people who parted company with him, almost as though he was too busy to remember those with whom he had fallen out.

There were, of course, many who weathered the storms of those days. Some were ambitious for their church and saw in Aberhart an unequalled instrument for "winning souls." Others admired his skill in administration and counted themselves fortunate in having their efforts used to such good advantage. Still others were attracted by the magnetism and the good humour that had made him so acceptable to his early students. Even some of those who could not agree with him, and who deplored his increasing highhandedness, still liked him for his better qualities and his humour.

In the midst of these hectic days Aberhart was studying law by correspondence from the American Extension University in Los Angeles.[41] For some time his reading hours, which lasted as usual until 2 a.m., were devoted to this subject.

As if he had not enough enterprises to fill his hours, in November 1926 Aberhart organized a series of revival meetings conducted by the Reverend R.E. Neighbour from the United States. While arranging Neighbour's timetable, hiring halls, organizing publicity, not to mention his own radio programs, Aberhart was conducting a pulpit battle with Hansell over the doctrinal beliefs at Westbourne. Their sallies against each other were receiving press coverage, and it must have been an exasperated School Board chairman who opened his Saturday newspaper, for example, to find Aberhart's extracurricular activities receiving treatment in triplicate. There would be a report on Neighbour's meetings, from which "as many people were turned away as found seats in the theatre." Hansell, on the other hand, who was explaining from the pulpit of Crescent Heights Baptist Church why he had resigned from Westbourne, was quoted as saying he felt it "impossible to work successfully where teaching and practices contrary to general Baptist principles were countenanced."[42] Side by side with this article was the regular Westbourne advertisement, with Aberhart's name appearing prominently since the departure of Hansell.

The pace at which events were now moving, and the number of responsibilities that Aberhart had heaped upon himself, far from tiring him, seemed to stimulate him to further activity. "You couldn't keep up with him," said one of his followers. "He was a dynamo!" Publicity ideas for the new Institute campaign flowed unabated from Aberhart. Their success again showed his appreciation of the workings of the public mind. His ideas seem hackneyed to us today only because they have been used so often in the past years. Aberhart for example promoted the idea of "selling" parts of the building: sods, bricks, mortar, and rafters. One hundred dollars would buy a "sod," two would buy a "brick." In a printed leaflet he invited people to "lay a brick for us." Children under sixteen could purchase a "brick" for one dollar. Attached to the leaflet was a "mortar" coupon, representing the price of the mortar needed to set each "brick" sold (25 cents). The leaflet announced:

> We wish to make known the fact, far and near, that in Calgary, Alberta, this prosperous city of the Middle West, a NON-DENOMINATIONAL BIBLE INSTITUTE is about to be established, where young men and women, and any others who may so desire it, may secure a careful training in Bible Knowledge, Personal Evangelism, Homiletics, Public Speaking, History of Literature, and other kindred subjects, without fear of atheistic or modernistic theories, which undermine and destroy faith.[43]

Aberhart's unsophisticated excitement shone through the printed word. "It will be," he declared triumphantly, "a school where the fundamentals of the Bible will be taught in all their simplicity and power.... We have already received enough money to turn the sods and lay the foundation... and now [one can almost hear the rubbing together of his hands] we must prepare for the superstructure." He even organized an inexpensive form of competition among the members of the Conference executive, in which he who sold the most bricks would be treated to a supper by the other members. Aberhart often exploited the competitive spirit, knowing that, small as the prestige to be gained might be, it added an extra spice of excitement to keep morale high among the participants.[44]

Aberhart was able to raise another $30,000, mainly through his radio appeals. This was a tremendous achievement, but $35,000 more was still needed to complete the Institute. He therefore worked out another plan for completing the financing of the project. He issued bonds bearing 8 per cent interest to the general public. He announced the issue on his Sunday-afternoon broadcasts, saying, "The banks will give you five percent, but I will give you eight!" At the same time, he said, purchasers would be assisting a worthy cause. The scheme was an unbounded success, and the bonds were over-subscribed. (Yet, knowing that the success of the project depended on Aberhart, the Conference executive took out an insurance policy on his life, so that in the event of his death they would not be left with an empty, debt-bound building.[45]) Many people donated their interest, as it became due, to the cause of the Institute's work, and many even donated their bonds. Having skillfully engineered the financing of the Institute, Aberhart found himself in the strongest position he had ever occupied for arranging matters to suit his own taste.

The Board Members of the Calgary Prophetic Bible Institute, 1927.

As time went on, his religious views became more and more sectarian. In October 1926 he had dropped his Masonic membership, and in March 1927, he preached against Christians holding membership in lodges.[46] In February 1927 Westbourne hired as its new pastor the Reverend W.W. Silverthorne, who had been a member of T.T. Shields' church in Toronto.[47] Westbourne's leaders began advertising themselves as "extreme fundamentalists."[48]

In March 1927, six months after the fund-raising campaign had begun, the land on which the Calgary Prophetic Bible Institute was to be built was purchased. They were the lots at 516 Eighth Avenue S.W., purchased at a price of $5,300.[49] That location, on Calgary's main street, was on the edge of the business district; but since the business section gradually spread westward and engulfed it, a better location could hardly have been chosen.

There was some discussion over the incorporation of the venture. If it were incorporated as a Bible institute, taxes would have to be paid, taxes the Conference knew they could not really afford. It was therefore decided to incorporate the building under the Church Holdings Act – which action would render it exempt from taxes. The name under which it was registered was the Calgary Prophetic Bible Institute Church Incorporated. Most of Westbourne's congregation and the radio audience knew nothing of this fictitious "church," its membership consisting solely of executive members

The Calgary Prophetic Bible Institute at 516 Eight Avenue West, opened in 1927.

of the Prophetic Conference, their tenure of office depending on the will of the president, Aberhart.[50]

As soon as the old bookstore that occupied the site on Eighth Avenue had been pulled down and building operations begun, the Aberhart household had a foretaste of the future as it saw less and less of the head of the household. After school was over for the day Aberhart appeared instead on the Institute building site. He wandered from one building operation to another, enquiring into progress and seeing that all was to his liking. The building could not go up fast enough for him. He had worked out the syllabus of courses and was mustering voluntary teachers to give daytime classes. (His own teaching would have to be done in the evenings.) He was also registering students, for he wanted the Institute to be in operation at the commencement of the school year in September.

Aberhart's delight knew no bounds as he puttered around the building, which smelled of fresh mortar and wet paint, but construction delays postponed the opening. The two-story building was less elaborate than had been originally planned; the architecture was simpler, and there were no dormitories for the students. In the meantime, services continued at Westbourne until 2 October 1927, when services began in the new building. The official opening of the Calgary Prophetic Bible Institute was delayed until 30 October 1927. William Bell Riley, a leading fundamentalist from Minneapolis, was the guest-speaker. Earlier that year he had opened T.T. Shields' new seminary in Toronto.

Among the small company of students who reported to the Institute on the first November morning of 1927 was a slim lad of about eighteen who stood silent, cap in hand, waiting for the first class to begin. The shy composure of the frail figure, as out of place on that first morning as the other lads who came in from country places to study in the fresh new building, concealed a keen brain and resilient strength of character that marked him for high office. He had been the first to enroll in the new Institute and his name appeared at the top of the list of students: Ernest Charles Manning.

Ernest C. Manning fresh off the farm in 1927.

Ernest Manning had been born on a farm near Carnduff, Saskatchewan, in 1908, and had attended school in nearby Rosetown. In the fall of 1925, Manning accidently heard Aberhart's voice on CFCN, which was then the most powerful station in western Canada. Young Manning listened with interest to Aberhart's Bible lecture. Shortly afterwards he made a religious commitment, and hearing of Aberhart's announcement of the building of a Bible institute, he determined to go to Calgary. Early in 1926 Manning came to talk with Aberhart about the educational opportunities the new institute would offer, and before Manning's return to Rosetown, Aberhart baptized him at Westbourne. A firm friendship and long and close association had been founded.

When Manning returned in November to begin studies, he was invited to live with the Aberharts in their new house, which had been built that year in the fashionable district of Elbow Park. Aberhart's daughters had by then left home. Manning gladly accepted the opportunity of closer association with the man he so much admired – and with his unassuming manner, quiet ways of helping with whatever jobs needed to be done, his receptive and serious mind, and eagerness for learning, he began to creep into a place in Aberhart's heart that had, perhaps, been reserved for a son.

The teachers who saw Manning sitting day after day in their classes were deceived by the fact that his extraordinary gifts received no advertisement from his manner. Here was no showcase for brilliance, no ready tongue to demonstrate a quick mind, no dashing figure craving attention and assuming leadership. On the contrary, he was extremely reserved, a quiet, serious boy who gave no trouble. "A good student," was their verdict. "A good prospect for the ministry." Perhaps not surprisingly he was the first to complete the course of studies offered by the Institute.

Manning soon came to occupy places of responsibility and affection in Aberhart's organization that had been recently vacated by two promising young men who had fallen out of Aberhart's good graces. Noel and Cyril Hutchinson had studied under Aberhart at the mid-week Bible Institute at Westbourne from 1923 onwards, and both were slated to be instructors in the new Bible Institute. Noel was a member of the executive of the Prophetic Conference and was the choir leader at Westbourne. On 16 October 1927, several weeks after Westbourne had moved into the Bible Institute, an altercation broke out between Noel and Aberhart over a minor issue, and Noel, Cyril, and their wives were then expelled from the church and from Aberhart's organization.[51]

As Aberhart walked into the Institute for his first evening of teaching, he felt that at the age of forty-nine he had finally reached a point at which there was no longer any material impediment to the realization of his life's dreams. In the well-equipped, spacious, well-placed, and well-advertised establishment that he virtually controlled, he was now free to use his teaching powers to the full in the subjects that interested him most and, without checks or supervision, to mold young minds for religious work.

For Aberhart there were now two sets of lessons to prepare and deliver, a double quantity of work to correct and assess, two sets of end-of-term examinations to prepare, two timetables to organize, two staffs of teachers and two schools of students to guide and govern. He usually taught three or four nights of the week. Classes lasted till 10 p.m. If he was not teaching on some nights, he was still involved in activities every night of the week. The Young People's Society, which included everyone from the ages of nine to ninety, met every Monday evening; prayer meeting was on Wednesday evening. Classes were also held on Saturday. On Saturday night Jessie Aberhart dutifully prepared a roast beef supper in the Institute basement for the staff and students, after which the students went out street-preaching.[52] There were also Institute board meetings and deacons' meetings over which to preside. When Westbourne was without a minister, Aberhart often worked until 4 or 5 a.m. on Sunday, preparing his sermons for the morning and evening services, and his lecture for the afternoon broadcast. During the school term Jessie saw little of him. He would gather the news of the day from the paper when he arrived home from school, join his wife for dinner, and then leave for the Institute. On arriving home after his classes, he would read until the small hours. He was getting less sleep than ever, but appeared to thrive.

It was hard to understand, even for those closest to Aberhart, how he could take in his stride the double life that he had chosen. They did not understand how the circumspect servant of the Board of Education in the well-pressed business suit and round-lensed pince-nez, could preserve the static propriety of scholastic routine and at the same time be the tempestuous rouser of the multitude to revolt against the mainline churches.

Believing his heart to be completely in his religious work, some of his followers suggested to him after the Institute was opened that he give up his school and devote himself full-time to the Bible Institute. He refused, however, displaying cautious shrewdness. Again he replied, "What would I do if people turned against me? What about my pension?" Here again was his insight into the collective mind and behaviour of the people, for his fears were soon to be realized.

CHAPTER EIGHT

■

HE WAS LOVED
HE WAS HATED

N OTHING *is interfering*
with my work as principal. I am devoting all
my time to the school. Someone has been
carrying tales and doing me an injustice.
— William Aberhart before Calgary School Board,
as quoted in the *Calgary Herald*, January 1929

Within a few months Westbourne was again plunged into a crisis. As had happened in the Aberhart-Hansell case, members of the congregation had polarized themselves around the personalities of Aberhart and Silverthorne, and Silverthorne was not strong enough to handle the problems that this created. In June 1928 Silverthorne submitted his resignation, little more than one year after having been hired.[1] That same night Aberhart also resigned as moderator, perhaps trying to force his own position on some point. His threat of resignation was effective, for it was tabled. Silverthorne's resignation, however, was accepted. The following Sunday evening the deacons showed their support of Aberhart by presenting him with an illuminated address filled with laudatory remarks.[2]

The conditions at Westbourne and in the Bible Institute, however, were not as idyllic as the testimonial suggested. As president of the Calgary Prophetic Bible Institute "Church," Aberhart had ultimate authority and exercised it ruthlessly. All correspondence had to pass through his hands, and there was a provision written into the "Declaration of Incorporation" stating that the vice-president had to report on any of the executive members who were in any way disloyal to the organization or creed.[3] Anyone who disagreed with Aberhart could be immediately voted out of the executive. The same spy system operated within Westbourne Baptist Church.[4] Aberhart had a suspicious nature and frequently imagined slights where they were never intended. On more than one occasion those critical of Aberhart had their church membership rescinded, and a number of young men who, like Silverthorne, were leaders within the church and Bible Institute left as a result of this policy.[5]

With Silverthorne gone Westbourne required another minister. During July 1928 Aberhart had invited a former acquaintance, the Reverend W.J.H. Brown of Toronto, to preach at Westbourne while he was on vacation. Recently Brown had been associated with T.T. Shields in Baptist battles in Ontario.[6] After Brown's ministry was completed at Westbourne the pulpit was supplied by other fundamentalists from across Canada and the United States.[7] The effect of these speakers was to heighten the fundamentalist-modernist controversy in the minds of Westbourne's members and cause them to take an even stronger isolationist position.

In October 1928 the members of the church decided that they wanted the Reverend W.J.H. Brown, whom they had listened to that summer, to be their minister. He eventually turned down their invitation, probably because of issues of doctrine, financial arrangements, and Aberhart's overriding authority.[8]

Westbourne was still without a pastor. In the meantime Aberhart continued to conduct the baptisms and communion services, while some of the Sunday preaching duties were assigned to visiting ministers and missionaries. The problems of Westbourne and its need of a pastor, however, were soon overshadowed by a larger crisis in which Aberhart found himself involved.

During his second year of operating the Calgary Prophetic Bible Institute, Aberhart locked horns with the Calgary School Board. No citizen, no matter how unobservant, could possibly have avoided seeing the Calgary Prophetic Bible Institute, situated as it was on a main street; and no pains were taken to hide the fact that the dean of the Calgary Prophetic Bible Institute was none other than William Aberhart, B.A. When the School Board superintendent paid a visit to one of the Westbourne deacons at his place of business, the deacon assured him that Mr. Aberhart would be devoting his allotted time to Crescent Heights High School and that the Institute would occupy only his off-duty hours. An outline of Aberhart's new schedule was carried back to the School Board.

The efficiency with which Aberhart ran his highschool was a source of constant amazement to the School Board, as they could not conceive how he could possibly devote enough time and interest to his school when they saw how his leisure hours were strained to the bursting point to contain his unbelievable burden of outside activities. Occasionally they heard rumours of Aberhart having students employed in stuffing envelopes with religious material, and of his secretaries typing his religious correspondence. When they were informed that he was using the school telephone for prolonged periods while making long-distance calls involving his religious business, they investigated the complaint and ordered him to stop.[9]

Aberhart's name would catch Board members' eyes as they scanned the Calgary *Herald*. If he had been opening a school sports day or addressing a meeting of the Alberta Teachers' Association, all would have been well; but these were no such mundane announcements. On the contrary, here was William Aberhart, B.A., holding an evangelistic meeting, the subject of the address being "The Shadows of the Beast, or the Latest News Regarding the Anti-Christ."[10] Sometimes they would see six-inch-square advertisements in the Calgary *Herald* leaping out from among the sedate notices of the liturgical churches, announcing a forthcoming lecture by William Aberhart, B.A., and headed by the jarring question "Will U.B. There?"[11]

The members of the School Board were shocked by the lower-class appeal of Aberhart's preaching, and were amazed by the occasional slips of grammar he made on the public platform. Though supposedly an educated and well-spoken man, and admired as such by his followers, Aberhart knew that any socially superior airs he might put on would remove him at once to the same distance from his followers as hampered the mainline clergy in their work. He was therefore careful not to lose altogether the warm informality and earthy, folksy language of his farm background.

Not only did Aberhart do too much of the wrong thing in the wrong way to suit the School Board, but he seemingly arranged matters so that they were unable to penalize him. It was interesting to observe how the man could, over the weekend, prepare his sermons, hold public meetings, preach several times on Sunday, sandwich in a Bible class, administer and teach in the Bible Institute – and still arrive at school Monday morning, not just on time but bouncing with energy and good humour, eager to get on with the day's work.

In 1929 Aberhart wrote complacently to his pupils at Crescent Heights High School:

> In order to utilize our odd moments to best advantage, we should not have to decide each time what we shall do during the moment, or we shall spend most of our time deciding. The remedy for this is the possession of a hobby which we may mount instantly and be off without hesitation.[12]

The School Board, however, held a different view of hobbyhorses. By that time Aberhart was principal of the largest highschool in Calgary, having moved his staff and students into the new Crescent Heights High School building after a thirteen-year sojourn in Balmoral School. Eighteen of the twenty-one classrooms were occupied at once, and Aberhart was the proud master of the handsome new red-brick building he was to govern for the rest of his teaching days. The new school brought new responsibilities, and the School Board felt that Aberhart's "hobbies" were interfering. Fred Spooner, the Board's chairman, also charged that Aberhart's broadcasts, in which he denounced other churches, were slandering the people of Calgary who employed him.[13] A motion was passed by the Board, stating:

> that, in view of the amount of work necessary for the proper organiza-
> tion and conduct of the Crescent Heights High School, this Board request
> Mr. Aberhart, Principal of that school, to devote his full time to the work
> of the Calgary School Board, and that, while not wishing to interfere with
> his work as a Sunday School teacher, or his activities as a layman in con-
> nection with his own church, we are of the opinion that what is practically
> the charge of a church and the conducting of services over the radio and
> the amount of correspondence entailed thereby is such that it interferes
> with his work as Principal of Crescent Heights School.[14]

Aberhart saw immediately that another campaign was called for and set about organizing one. He assembled a band of his teachers who prepared a letter claiming that he did full justice to his position as principal, and that he did not allow any of his side-interests to interfere with his duties.[15] Then, appearing before the School Board, Aberhart stated the same things and argued that he considered himself free to do anything he desired on his own time.

Although the Minutes of the Calgary School Board do not record the event, Fred Spooner claimed that Aberhart was ordered to resign as leader of Westbourne Church if he wished to keep his position at Crescent Heights High. Aberhart therefore immediately resigned as moderator and as chairman of the deacons at Westbourne and submitted a copy of that resignation to Spooner.[16] Because of his apparent obedience and the support of his teachers, it was difficult for the School Board to argue with him. Consequently the motion of censure was dropped.[17]

The Calgary School Board would have had a difficult time proving that Aberhart was not perfectly capable of running Crescent Heights just a little better than most people. With his inborn ability to grasp the essentials of organization, he ran his school with scrupulous efficiency. The academic standard there was consistently high. For his work he received one of the highest salaries in the system: $4,200, with a yearly increment of $100.[18]

The rap on the knuckles that Aberhart had received from his employers may have had a momentarily sobering effect on him; but the even greater crisis that soon befell him gave him hardly any time to dwell on those reproaches.

During this period of Aberhart's latest crisis with the School Board, the members of Westbourne Church had begun to evaluate their situation. Because Aberhart was no longer preaching for the church, the church had the added expense of temporary preachers like the Reverend L.E. Maxwell, a Southern Baptist minister from Kansas, who was then the principal of Prairie Bible

Institute at Three Hills.[19] As the weeks passed, it became more and more obvious that it would be difficult to hire any minister while Aberhart held any position of authority in the church. Even though he had now resigned from some positions, he was still a deacon and the apostle of the church. Then again, it was also becoming obvious that very few ministers would ascribe to the doctrinal position that Aberhart had imposed on the church. Nor could the church even afford to hire a minister.

According to the original arrangement the members of Westbourne were to occupy the Institute building, the church contributing "not less than $600 per month" to the Institute, that sum to be made up from the offerings from three Sundays in each month.[20] Apparently the uncongenial atmosphere was already encouraging the withholding of contributions, and after the first year, it was obvious that the offerings were not sufficient to cover the amount agreed upon. Aberhart recommended that something be done, but the rest of the deacons protested that they were helpless. The affair was thrashed out at meetings, and for days there was much visiting and telephoning among church members. Mabel Giles, one of Aberhart's teachers and a member of the church, felt such rent was outrageous. Aberhart tried to excuse it by saying that it was all part of the same organization.[21]

On 20 March 1929, at a meeting from which Aberhart was absent because he was appearing before the Calgary School Board, the congregation decided to reduce its payment of rent to the Institute to $350 a month, and that the Bible Institute had to pay for its own radio broadcasts. It was further agreed that the financial structure of the church be revised. In the past, as noted before, Aberhart structured the finances so that each department of the church had a different account and members could allocate their offerings to whichever department they wished. Aberhart had usually supported the pastor's salary account, but as soon as he disagreed with the minister or vice versa, he directed his offerings elsewhere and the minister's salary account dwindled. Since each department had to carry itself financially, funds were seldom transferred to other accounts, other than to the Bible Institute, which usually absorbed any surplus. When the pastor's salary could not be paid he was therefore forced to resign. The church members now decided to have one general fund out of which all obligations would be paid.[22]

Aberhart was angry with the new arrangements proposed, but this time even his resignation would not cause the mutineers to throw down their arms. His demands had always been great, but this time they were too great. Aberhart's influence, which had enabled him to lead them through the strange evolution that the spiritual and temporal life of Westbourne had followed, was now broken. He tried to gain the upper hand by leading his bewildered opponents into a tangle of procedural points of order and leaving them to disentangle themselves with the aid of legal advice; but he gradually came to realize that the church members were this time displaying a determination equal to his own.

Finally, a majority of the church membership reluctantly acknowledged the only possible solution: they would return to the old Westbourne Baptist Church building. The old building had been vacant since January, except for some services that students from the Bible Institute were holding there.[23] Aberhart agreed that the dissidents should return to the old church building, but suggested by way of amendment that he be given authority to establish a new church from among those who supported him. The motion was lost.[24]

Aberhart's request for authorization to start a new congregation rested on his idea of church succession; no new chuch was legitimate in his eyes unless it had been duly authorized by another legitimate church. Aberhart contended that that chain of succession extended from Westbourne back to the original apostles – even though some of the links were extremely fuzzy.[25]

On 10 April 1929 the dissidents decided that they would grant Aberhart's request, possibly fearing more controversy if they refused. They would allow him to start a new congregation, and they would ordain a new set of deacons for him. The property was also to be divided: the Westbourne congregation would have full possession of the old church building and the adjacent cottage, while those people remaining with Aberhart would get the Institute building. Even though the members of Westbourne had contributed heavily to the Institute's financing, there was no attempt to wrest it from Aberhart. The rest of the chattels were divided evenly between the two groups, even down to the cups and saucers in the kitchen.[26]

It was a disappointed group that returned to Westbourne and its ghosts. But the little church had had its hopes dashed before and had recovered. The members set to work to build themselves a church life. For the next few months the pulpit of Westbourne was supplied by L.E. Maxwell and his staff from Prairie Bible Institute.[27] After returning to their old creed the congregation was again able to hire a minister, the Reverend Morley Hall, and shortly afterwards the church allied itself with the Regular Baptists founded by T.T. Shields[28] after he had been expelled from the Baptist Convention of Ontario and Quebec. During the 1930s and 1940s Westbourne's congregation was able to operate Western Baptist Bible College, staffed mainly by those who had left Aberhart.[29] The last personal contact that most of Westbourne's congregation ever had with Aberhart was on 18 April 1929, when the deacons of Westbourne ordained deacons for Aberhart's new church.[30]

Those who remained with Aberhart to form a new church were mainly younger people who had been converted through his ministry and who did not have Baptist roots. In some ways the recent split had strengthened Aberhart's personal power, for his supporters' religious loyalty was mainly to himself; he was not likely to face much opposition because most of his supporters were experienced only with his form of church government.

As the new congregation was being organized, it was suggested that the church be called "Spurgeon's Tabernacle" after a famous London Baptist preacher, Charles Haddon Spurgeon (1834-1892). However, they settled for the more prosaic title "Bible Institute Baptist Church."[31] The arrangements by which the new church occupied the Calgary Prophetic Bible Institute were very much like those that had existed for Westbourne's tenancy; the new church had to carry a great part of the expenses of the Bible Institute, its broadcasts, and activities. The finances of the church were again divided into individual departments, and each theoretically had to carry itself. One of the consequences of Aberhart's having lost 60 per cent of the Westbourne congregation was that he had less money to spend on advertising; his newspaper ads accordingly became smaller and less elaborate for the time being.

Another consequence of Westbourne's defection was that the teaching staff of the Bible Institute was severely reduced because many of the teachers were among the group that went back to Westbourne. Aberhart replaced them with housewives and several school teachers who taught part-time.

Changes also had to be made in the leadership of the Calgary Prophetic Bible Institute "Church," the organization that served as a tax dodge for the Bible Institute. Only three of the original executive members remained with Aberhart: his friend Harvey, the dentist; Fred Battisto, a hot-tempered Corsican who operated Hunt's Bone Yard, an auto wrecking firm; and Charles R. Pearce, the grocery salesman who managed the Radio Sunday School. From among his loyal supporters Aberhart added four more men to an executive now with a lower educational and occupational level than that of the original executive that had grown out of the Calgary Prophetic Bible Conference.

As before with Westbourne, most of the members of the new Bible Institute Baptist Church were not aware of the nature of the hidden board that held legal title to all of the property. This would cause problems again in the future.

The School Board still had cause to worry about Aberhart. Not only was he president of the Calgary Prophetic Bible Institute Church, dean of the Calgary Prophetic Bible Institute, apostle of the Bible Institute Baptist Church, superintendent of the Sunday School, and chairman of the church board, but he also sometimes preached up to four times on Sunday and was still involved in other religious activities occupying almost every night of the week. To alleviate some of this pressure Aberhart did bring in guest-speakers, among them the Australian evangelist L. Sale-Harrison, who was internationally known for his fundamentalism and interest in eschatology.[32]

During the summer of 1929 Aberhart had his old friend the Reverend Dr. Andrew S. Imrie supply the pulpit. They had both lived at the Commercial Hotel in Brantford before Aberhart was married, and Imrie most likely had been a strong influence in Aberhart's early theological development. Imrie had earned a doctorate from a seminary in Texas and was a member of the senate of McMaster University. Although a theological conservative, Imrie was a moderate in the fundamentalist-modernist controversy and highly regarded by both camps for his pastoral skills. Aberhart and the congregation of the Bible Institute Baptist Church sought to have him become their minister. His own commitments, however, were to delay that decision.

For the next year the pulpit of the church was supplied by fundamentalists from across the United States and Canada. One of the special speakers was the Reverend Harry Rimmer, an amateur scientist who fought the theory of evolution and whose message was that true science and the Scriptures did not conflict.[33]

When Dr. Imrie finally accepted the call to the Bible Institute Baptist Church pulpit in 1930, he probably did so on the strength of his past friendship with Aberhart. He came to the church with thirty years of pastoral experience, and in terms of personality, was very different from Aberhart, being more methodical, gracious, and dignified. In the pulpit he always wore a Prince Albert coat, his sermons were a new experience in worship, and pastoral visitation was his forte. With Dr. Imrie's arrival, Aberhart's church became more like other churches; although it remained isolationist, it seems to have lost its excessive pugnacity.

The heavy responsibilities of the Bible Institute came to be shared with Aberhart by Aberhart's protégé Ernest Manning, who became a teacher on the Institute staff, acted as secretary of the Institute, and assisted in countless other ways.[34] There is no doubt that without such a willing and competent assistant, even Aberhart would have been unable to get through the unbelievable quantities of work he undertook, and the even greater burden that lay ahead for him.

It was in many ways an ideal and unique relationship. Manning's mind delighted Aberhart with its skill and quickness. It was a mind on which he could sharpen his own wits and clarify his own thinking.[35] Manning could give him a good argument on the subjects that interested them both; he debated as vigorously as Aberhart, and could match his power of prolonged concentration.

There were other students in the Institute whom Aberhart considered had great promise and in whose future he took a personal interest. Most of these, however, failed to retain his solicitude in one of two ways. Some could not keep up with his untiring energy, and once they lagged behind in interest or effort, Aberhart dropped them. Others gradually assumed their own independence and made the break themselves.

Manning was therefore unique in being able to satisfy Aberhart's intellectual requirements without allowing this success to force him into self-assertiveness. When he and Aberhart turned to getting the work of the Institute done, Manning cast off the independence of thought he had assumed during their academic arguments and Aberhart's word was again law. Aberhart could leave the routine work of the Institute and the spadework for his lectures to Manning with the certainty that they would be thoroughly and efficiently carried out. But to the public, Manning was indistinguishable from the other followers whom Aberhart so completely eclipsed.[36]

Aberhart's dealings with church affairs became more peremptory. The Bible Institute Baptist Church membership was merely a tiny portion of his real congregation, his radio audience. Many of these people, especially those in rural areas, did not attend church, but considered themselves instead members of Aberhart's radio church, sending him the financial support they would normally have given to their pastors. Aberhart, with characteristic insight into human nature, provided "booster" and "associate" memberships, depending on their amount of contributions, and made effective exertions to convey over the air the feeling of fellowship his listeners would have expected to experience, had they been sitting in the pews in front of him. These were the people who supported the educational work of the Institute financially, and Aberhart knew as always that its essential income depended on his delivering an interesting Bible lecture over the air on Sundays from 3 to 5 p.m.

The operation of the Bible Institute remained his chief interest, however. Besides the full-time program, which not more than half the students took, the Institute offered many part-time courses that many students pursued while they worked at regular jobs in Calgary.

Even in the work of the Bible Institute, Aberhart tended to limit, by his quirk of individuality, the field of its effectiveness. The expression "he was a founder, not a joiner" was still true. In spite of his long-ago reproofs of his Plymouth Brethren friends, and the constant reiteration of his disapproval of splinter sects and their uncooperative attitude, Aberhart's conviction was not as strong as the individuality that had driven him to form what amounted to a new sect, a sect which he was loath to contaminate by even the most tenuous connection with other organizations. His doctrinal stance prevented cooperation even with nearby Bible institutes, and he had also written off the denominational missionary societies. The reason he gave was that modernism, which he was pledged to resist, was now woven into the fabric of these organizations. There were also fundamentalist missionary societies, but they would not readily accept his graduates because of the peculiarities of the doctrines he had taught them. The result was that none of his students at that time went to foreign mission fields, unlike those graduates from Prairie Bible Institute at Three Hills who were encouraged to go. Few of Aberhart's graduates moved much farther than the provinces of Alberta, Saskatchewan, and British Columbia. However, this fact alone strengthened his influence, for members of churches in those provinces were close enough to attend his lectures occasionally or at least to listen to his broadcasts.

"He was loved. He was hated. He was never ignored" – thus, with unusual accuracy, his obituaries were much later to sum up Aberhart. This state of affairs had developed more and more after he had begun broadcasting. In contrast to its earlier limited range, his voice fell not only on ears eager to hear, minds where his ideas found ideal germinating conditions, but also on stoney places. Many orthodox churchgoers, and some with other or no religious affiliation, came to question the sincerity of Aberhart's own convictions. On more than one occasion his denunciations of the other denominations offended people, and there were pressures applied to CFCN to take him off the air.[37] Fortunately for Aberhart, such attempts at censure could not touch him, for CFCN was financially indebted to him. In 1928 the Bible Institute had loaned CFCN a large amount of money when the company had got into financial difficulties. The chattel mortage held on the company was to be paid off in weekly air time, thus ensuring the continuity of Aberhart's broadcasts.[38] (Like so many of Aberhart's "good ideas at the time" this one would return to haunt him.)

Every petty squabble in Aberhart's organization served to throw him into harsher outline in the eyes of those who disapproved of him. He did not conform to the accepted pattern of godliness. "He does not practice what he preaches" was a frequent accusation. He seemed to some to be lacking all those gentle and saintly qualities that should be found in a shepherd of men. Where, they asked, was the soul-searching caution that would have moderated his actions, cooled his impatience? Where was the Christian charity that should have protected those who worked for him to the limit of human conscience and endurance? Had he himself dispensed with religion in his struggle to bring religion to others? If not, asked his critics, how did he justify the apparently unchristian means he often used to gain religious power?

In trying to understand this seeming paradox, one must first of all realize that Aberhart had a genius for leadership. Many saints have brought fewer souls to God for lack of it, and many leaders have used their talents to worse effect.

Some, who watched this leadership manifest itself during Aberhart's platform performances, thought he believed himself set aside for special work – a modern-day prophet of the Lord. Indeed, he shared this feeling, but the power that enabled him to sway the multitude and the strength that led him to persist beyond the endurance of most men were unquestionably drawn from deep within himself. He was a character of extraordinary strength, driven by unsuppressable inner fires. Wherever he was among men, he would sooner or later become either their leader or their rival. Though he could not suppress this inner energy, he harnessed it as best he could, using it to develop the strongest elements of his character – courage, single-mindedness, and industriousness – qualities that aided and accentuated his ambition and his capacity for leadership. He derived great pleasure from tackling the hardest problems of a project, and was never so happy as when getting his teeth into seemingly impossible academic or organizational difficulties. Once the hurdles were surmounted, he lost interest and was anxious to be off to some other challenge.

Aberhart's photographic memory, his imperturbable orderliness of mind, and the confidence that went with a schoolteacher's habitual assumption of intellectual superiority enabled him to attack intellectual problems that would have awed most men. He was not naturally endowed with any extraordinary powers of independent reasoning, or of deep, abstract thinking, and this was a serious handicap to him. As a result, his technique in dealing with the complicated economic and social problems that were soon to face him was no more complex than the techniques he brought to the somewhat arbitrary principles of dispensationalism, the literalness of fundamentalism, or the unquestionable facts of the eight-times table.

Aberhart's academic inadequacy did not denote an inferior mentality, but rather an above-average one, the training of which had been too hasty and scanty for the tasks his ambition and courage drove him to take on. Aberhart never, throughout his whole life, allowed himself enough time and energy for his own education. In his childhood, his studies had been sheared to a minimum by his duties on the family farm. Later, as a teacher, he crammed facts in his spare time from a university correspondence course. His theology had also come from a correspondence course. Aberhart seemed to be aware of his own academic shortcomings and overcompensated for them by stressing his B.A. degree in most of his advertisements and printed materials.[39]

Aberhart was always trying to instill habits of self-discipline into his students at Crescent Heights. Since he was unable, under the stern gaze of the School Board, to give them any moral training that might savour of religion, he did what he could to pass on to them his own recipe for success. Though he himself was capable of far more flexibility than he advocated to his students in the school annual *The Bugle*, his writings described forcefully his confidence in the qualities of courage and persistence to attain the seemingly impossible. He considered thrift and hard work fitting companions for courage, and told his students every one of them had at hand the requirements for success. Aberhart's unlimited confidence in the capabilities of the creatures God had made, was not the least important of his attitudes. His words do not reveal a man who blindly put himself into the hands of a higher power: he wrote, for example, "If you fall back upon yourself, believe in yourself, and be loyal to your highest interests you must inevitably succeed."[40] This humanistic emphasis would not have been shared by most fundamentalists, but it reflected the intellectual schizophrenia that characterized Aberhart's life.

In explaining the Bible to others Aberhart found a truly noble cause – a worthy channel for his talents, his emotions, his energies, his ambition – in which he felt every achievement would be a contribution to the welfare of his fellows. This was important to him. His ambition did not lie in personal gain in the form of the idleness and luxury wealth can buy. What he enjoyed was power over people. Perhaps the greatest tragedy of his life was that the reward he desired most – the gratitude and affection of those who benefitted from his work – was so often denied him because his drive and ideas alienated many of those he tried to help.

Aberhart's involvement with dispensationalism and fundamentalism was congenial to his own mental and emotional makeup. A review of the nature of fundamentalist Christianity may explain further the strange aspect Aberhart's behaviour presented to Alberta's orthodox churchgoers. Fundamentalism was an evangelical and authoritarian religion. The authority on which fundamentalism rested was, of course, the Bible, and fundamentalists accepted the spreading of the Word as their primary duty and the salvation of souls as the first purpose of that work. Since these duties took first place in their religion, the social applications of Christianity had to take second place. Among dispensationalists the latter generally had no place at all. The Christian way of life, its ethical rules, its ability to make the day-to-day existence of a community more pleasant and civilized were less highly regarded by the fundamentalists than by the modernists. There was a general repudiation by fundamentalists of any thought or expression that was not somehow contained in the Bible – the study and broadcasting of which was their main concern, for they felt that the Bible was their main link with the mind of God.

Had Aberhart continued focusing on fundamentalism, with its emphasis on isolationism, sectarianism, élitist self-awareness, and peculiar doctrines, his religious work could easily have stabilized or even died, for these elements limited his influence and were involved when 60 per cent of Westbourne's congregation left him in 1929. If the decreasing revenues of the Calgary Prophetic Bible Institute are any indication,[41] it appears that his radio audience was also dwindling. Fortunately for the success of his work, the economic, emotional, and physical suffering caused by the Great Depression caused him to modify his thinking and behaviour, and his subsequent involvement in politics brought him an even greater audience and influence.

CHAPTER NINE

■

BACKGROUND TO SOCIAL CREDIT

P OWER *to execute plans of any description, designed to implement any policy is* monopolised *by a small minority of individuals, of all countries and of none, not inaccurately identified as those in control of International Finance.*

— Major C.H. Douglas, from his booklet *Reconstruction*, 1932

The New York stock market crashed on 29 October 1929. This catastrophe, which echoed across the continent, leaving its grim trail of bankruptcy and suicide, ushered in a period of suffering such as Canada had never before experienced. Diverse economic panaceas were advocated to deal with the crisis; one of them was called Social Credit.[1]

Various people had been toying with Social Credit for more than a decade. During the early twenties, in a weekly newspaper called *The Alberta Non-Partisan*, published in Calgary, the editor William Irvine (1885-1962) advanced the theory that lack of purchasing power and resultant underconsumption were prime causes of the country's monetary ills. This was one of the theories that Major C.H. Douglas had begun to circulate in Great Britain within the previous two or three years. Douglas had called his theories of monetary reform "Social Credit."

The financial instability from which the farmer suffered naturally led many to suspect that the monetary system of the country was at fault. They examined the whole question of credit particularly closely. Social Credit, Socialism, and Populism were some of the theories advanced by newcomers from the United States and Great Britain who were disappointed in their hope of finding in a younger society freedom from the oppression of money interests, monopoly, and protection that had, at least partly, driven them from their homelands.

George Bevington, who had been active in populist politics in the United States, became prominent in the United Farmers of Alberta (U.F.A.) and promoted certain principles of Social Credit within that organization.[2] However, U.F.A. leader Henry Wise Wood did not share Bevington's opinions, and therefore Social Credit had no place in the politics of the U.F.A. in the provincial election of 1921, when it swept out the Liberals, winning thirty-eight of what were then sixty-one seats in the Legislature. The U.F.A. consigned the two mainline parties to semi-oblivion for a long time. (The provincial Liberal party has not yet recovered to this very day.)

The table talk in Calgary in 1921 had been concerned with what effect "group government" would have on town-dwellers, and how extreme the legislation of the new radical party would be. Similar questions were abroad in other parts of Canada. Ontario had its first farm-labour government. In Ottawa, sixty-five Progressives, representatives of the various farmer movements across the country, sat for the first time as a result of the 1921 federal election.[3] The first labour group also sat there, represented by two men. One was William Irvine, M.P. for Calgary East; the other, J.S. Woodsworth, M.P. for Winnipeg Centre.

J.S. Woodsworth (1874-1942) had given up his work as a Methodist minister because of theological doubts, and had taken up the difficult task of fighting in politics for the cause of the underprivileged.[4] Woodsworth and Irvine, who had found themselves thrown together as the only representatives of labour in the federal House, were acquainted with each other. Years before, the Reverend James Woodsworth (the father of J.S. Woodsworth) had brought Irvine from the Shetland Islands to train as a Methodist minister in Canada. Irvine later joined the Presbyterians, but left them after being acquitted in a heresy trial. He then became a Unitarian minister for a short time, before establishing a Labour church in Calgary.[5]

It was impossible for these two men to merge inconspicuously into Ottawa routine. Indeed, Woodsworth found himself so out of patience with the ceremonies at the opening of Parliament that he wrote in disgust that he had used to think that Parliament was "a very serious affair – its members to be prayed for in churches," but had discovered that "so far it has been a series of foolish formalities and ostentatious display."[6] Woodsworth and Irvine were obsessed with a feeling of urgency. The miseries endured by their fellows harrowed their imaginations; their feelings drove them to attack mercilessly the lethargy and caution they found in government.

The Progressives, representing the largest occupational group in Canada, the farmers, harboured among them many who, like Woodsworth and Irvine, felt themselves to be crusaders against the centrally-controlled machinery of politics. They were determined to carry out what they considered to be their true function: each M.P. should represent the people of his own constituency, not the policies of his party.

These two groups, Progressives and Labour, came into the House like a fresh west wind. They ruffled the ranks of the old-line parties and broke up the two-party system. The cobwebs of complacency that had accumulated during the years of prosperity were swept aside, and the fresh air of reappraisal and reform were inhaled involuntarily by all parties. It was on this invigorating breeze that the concept of wider governmental responsibility and the seeds of Canadian socialism and Social Credit were sown.

The Alberta Progressives were well to the fore of these radicals in the federal House. This is not to say, however, that their spirit was matched in the U.F.A. provincial government. As often happens, the responsibilities and realities of office somewhat tempered the radicalism of at least the provincial section of the party. The U.F.A. won the provincial elections of 1925 and 1930, but became increasingly conservative in practice, though it continued to speak highly of reform and raise questions about federal-provincial jurisdictions.

With his history of interest in monetary reform, it is not surprising that William Irvine visited Major C.H. Douglas, a fellow Scot, in London in 1922.[7] Largely through Irvine's efforts, when the Standing Committee on Banking and Commerce sat the next year in Ottawa, one of its duties was "to investigate the basis, the function and the control of credit, and relation of credit to industrial problems." A number of critics of the orthodox financial system appeared before the committee, including Major Douglas, George Bevington from Alberta, and Professor Irving Fisher of Yale University.[8]

Clifford Hugh Douglas (1879-1952), a reserve officer of the Royal Air Force and a mechanical engineer by profession, claimed he had first begun to question the efficiency of the economic system during the First World War. He noted that the money received from a factory's products was greater than the sum paid out in wages to the workers. Since the sale price included not only the cost of labour, but also that of raw materials, interest charges, depreciation, profits, and other external costs, workers could never consume all that they made. That was the idea expressed in his famous A + B Theorem (see chapter XIII for a more detailed discussion). He concluded that a more efficient system had to be devised if the economy were to be prevented from slipping into a depression.

Douglas claimed that he arrived at this concept while he was assistant superintendent of the Royal Aircraft Factory at Farnborough. There seems to be evidence that his analysis was *ex post facto* — and at best a very poor example upon which to base an economic theorem. (Douglas was known to have embellished his past on a number of occasions.[9]) It is doubtful that his

Major C.H. Douglas and his wife on their visit to Alberta in 1934.

example arose out of his work at the factory; it seems more likely to have been created later to bolster the anti-Semitic theories that dominated Douglas's thought.[10] A government aircraft factory in an artificial wartime economy is not exactly an example of an open-market situation. Credit costs would not be an issue, neither would profits and dividends. Finally, few workers would want to buy a fighter aircraft.

Douglas's radical criticism of the existing monetary system was not altogether new; much of what he said had already been said by others: Sismondi, Marx, Bellamy, Proudhon, Kropotkin, and Veblen. The conclusions Douglas drew from his observations, and his own remedial theories, did not, however, emerge in sharp and simple outlines from the books in which he expounded them. These involved works did not provide a thorough examination of all aspects of the subject, nor were they written in a style that was easily comprehensible.[11] Trained economists dismissed Douglas's theory as inexact, incomplete, and based on false premises. Besides the natural conservatism of the orthodox economists, the main difficulty Douglas had to face in the promotion of his ideas was the resistance of vested interests whose financial power would, he believed, be ended by the introduction of his remedies. Douglas believed that there was an international Jewish conspiracy to control the economy of the world. In later years this conviction would come to obsess Douglas, and it became a clanking ball-and-chain that dragged ominously at the heels of the movement.

By 1923 Douglas had embarked on a program of public education, and was aided from time to time by the vagaries of economic conditions. He had a deep life-long conviction that politics inevitably bred corruption and impotence, and he steadfastly refused to promote his theories by entering politics. Having decided upon this long-term policy of influencing public opinion, Douglas, while continuing to write and speak wherever he could get a hearing, pursued with almost equal enthusiasm his hobbies of fishing and sailing, while operating his own small boat yard on the green banks of the Solent, out of Southhampton Water.

John Mitchell, for many years a close associate of Douglas in his Social Credit work, stated in a 1955 interview that Douglas brought his attitude of realistic pessimism to Ottawa when he appeared before the Standing Committee on Banking and Commerce in 1923. Douglas was well aware that to hope for an imminent adoption of his theories was out of the question; but he was pleased to have his ideas recorded for reference in official and permanent form, and hoped that the publicity his visit received would arouse interest in his theories.[12] When he left Ottawa, his only achievement, apart from this personal satisfaction, was in having taken part in an inquiry that had brought to parliamentary and public notice the facts that credit and banking ought to be controlled by a national agency, and that the banking system did not satisfactorily supply the credit needs of agriculture.

These faults of the Canadian banking system, though largely ignored during the economic recovery in the years following 1923, were to be taken up again and remedied during the next period of depression. The most perceptive observer would have been unable to gain a hint of Aberhart's future concern in the matter, as Aberhart put aside the newspaper accounts of the committee's hearings and turned with keener interest to the serious business of his prophetic lecture research.

In November 1929 the World Engineering Conference was to be held in Japan. One of the delegates from Britain, crossing Canada in early October on his way to the conference, was Major Douglas. In Ottawa he was entertained by some of the acquaintances he had made during his previous visit. In the course of dinnertable conversation he was reminded laughingly of the words he had said during the hearings of 1923:

> If you go along the lines you are following at present, and if you continue along those lines for any considerable period of time... I am perfectly certain that you are heading for the most terrific disaster that the mind of man can conceive.[13]

An acquaintance asked jocularly whether Douglas would now care to put a date on that prediction. Encouraged, he afterwards admitted, by the fact that he would by then be out of Canada, Douglas declared that he would not be surprised if it happened within a month.[14] On 29 October 1929 the New York stock market experienced "Black Tuesday."

With the onset of the Depression caused by the collapse of the stock market, Alberta was plunged into economic crisis: foreign markets for Alberta's wheat and cattle were now restricted, and prices of agricultural produce dropped drastically. Since agriculture was Alberta's major source of income, the province and its inhabitants were left in a precarious position. When farmers shipped their produce to markets in central and eastern Canada they received small returns; sometimes the sale price of the goods did not pay for even the shipping costs. It was not uncommon for some farmers to destroy their animals and burn their grain in an attempt to keep prices up.

Alberta farmers were adventurers. When the price of wheat grown in Canada had dropped from an average of $1.05 per bushel in 1929 to 49 cents in 1930,[15] the farmers had joined the rest of the world in its economic distress, not uncomplaining but still optimistic. They had experienced such depressions before and looked forward to the improvement that always came. This time it did not come. In 1931 the price of wheat dropped to 38 cents. Even a rise in prices would not have solved their problems, for by this time the climate had suddenly turned against them. In spite of an extreme and unpredictable climate, these enormous plains seemed always to provide the few simple conditions necessary for growing wheat: regular rainfall during the growing season, long hours of sunshine with cool nights, and a rich soil as yet undepleted by cultivation and laid out in millions of level hectares. The only serious problem had been the development of grains with short growing seasons so that agriculture could push forward into the shorter summers of the north. Great advances were being made in that endeavour when the inexplicable chain of catastrophes began to cripple the wheat industry.

In 1930, the year of the first drastic drop in the price of wheat, the rain did not come. The winds that blew perpetually and unhindered over the featureless prairies, licking the resilient wheat until it shone, suddenly took on a malign character. Among the thin dry wheat stalks of that drought year the soil lay unprotected. The wind whipped it up into little eddies and let it fall again in a different place. The soil drifted onto the roads; the whole prairie seemed to be moving and there was no moisture to bind the soil. The hardy prairie grasses whose roots would have bound the soil together had been ploughed under to nourish the more delicate wheat. The wind increased in force, whipping the dust higher and higher, until the farmer saw the precious topsoil of his farm rise in great turbulent clouds and travel away across the prairie. This was the "black blizzard," erosion by wind.

The cattlemen were also suffering. In 1931 the Annual Report of the Alberta Department of Agriculture recorded sadly:

> The year 1931 will go down in history in Alberta as recording the lowest prices of livestock and livestock products for the past thirty years. They are, however, in line with prices of other farm commodities....[16]

Alberta farmers managed to harvest a fair grain crop in 1931 in spite of drought, drifting soil, and sudden increase in damage by wireworm in the north – the first of a series of disasters by insect pests. The following year, 1932, was another drought year for many parts of the province. Wireworms and cutworms increased again in the north. In some districts where there had been good crop yields the farmers had to stand idle while rain and snow delayed the harvest. A considerable percentage of the crop between Calgary and Red Deer was not worth harvesting. The wheat that was salvaged from 1932 was of high quality, but those fortunate farmers who harvested it saw the price of wheat drop to 35 cents. As well as the problems of closed markets and falling prices, the prairie provinces were plagued with hail, frost, and grasshoppers. In a matter of minutes a year's work could be destroyed. It was often reported that in some areas the need for food forced some people to pickle gophers. These conditions were to last for ten years.[17]

While Alberta did not experience the same severity of dust storms as Saskatchewan did, it faced perhaps greater financial difficulties. The last-settled of the prairie provinces, Alberta was relatively newer and had larger debts. Shortly before the Depression, Alberta's farmers had started to convert to power machinery, but since the province was furthest from eastern manufacturing centres, its farmers had to pay the highest prices. Banks, mortgage companies, and machinery dealers had offered easy credit with high interest rates, and many farmers had borrowed beyond their means, even mortgaging their farms, hoping that the next year would provide them with a bumper crop.[18] As crops failed, credit institutions began to refuse the further credit the farmers desperately needed. Often crop yields were not enough for farmers to pay anything on their debts, let alone their interest charges, and credit-granting institutions began foreclosing on those who were in default on their payments.

With no extra money, farmers were forced to improvise. Children's clothes were often made out of flour bags and gunny sacks. With no money to buy gasoline, some farmers converted their cars into "Bennett Buggies" by removing the engines and pulling them with horses. The pneumatic tires, springs, and cushioned seats offered a smoother ride than the conventional buggy. These "Bennett Buggies" were named after R.B. Bennett, the Calgary lawyer and acquaintance of Aberhart who had become Canada's Conservative Prime Minister in 1930.

As economic conditions became more difficult, the failures of industry led to mass unemployment in urban centres. Compounding this problem were the masses of young men from the farms who came seeking work in the already unemployment-ridden towns and cities. Bread lines, soup kitchens, and "riding the rods" became the order of the day. Governments seemed incapable of dealing with the economic and social problems.

When plagues of drought, dust, hail, and grasshoppers assailed Alberta, biblical analogies easily suggested themselves. One of the leaders of Prairie Bible Institute at Three Hills suggested that the Depression was a visitation of God's wrath upon the civilized world because modern man had forsaken him.[19] Indeed, some fundamentalists interpreted the Depression in apocalyptic terms: the desperate conditions indicated that the End Times were at hand. The rise of fascist movements in Europe added to their fears. Since the late nineteenth century, some fundamentalists had believed that the Antichrist would revive the ancient Roman Empire.[20] When Mussolini announced his intention of doing just that, some preachers suggested that he was the Antichrist, or at least his forerunner.[21]

Aberhart's theology was affected by the Depression in several ways. According to his principles of eschatological interpretation, no definite

A sign of the times: confrontation between the unemployed and the RCMP in Edmonton in 1930.

prophecy would be fulfilled before the Rapture, but there would be "foreshadows" of things to come.[22] For some time he had been baiting his audiences with comparisons of current events and prophecy. Indeed, he had claimed that the Antichrist was already alive, but incognito.[23] During the past few years his sermon titles had reflected his increasing preoccupation with the negative aspects of eschatology: the Devil, demons, witchcraft, spiritism, *incubi, succubi,* the Antichrist, and so on. His theology had become very Manichean; everywhere he saw a cosmic battle between two opposing forces, God and Satan. The Depression reinforced this belief in Aberhart's mind. When climatic disturbances and plagues of pestilence attacked Alberta's crops, Aberhart claimed that they were not punishments from God, but rather attacks from the Devil.[24]

Aberhart became fascinated with Mussolini and he preached a number of sermons on Mussolini and prophecy.[25] It is unfortunate that no copies of these sermons are extant, for Aberhart's newspaper advertisements give no indication of his own position on Mussolini. However, Aberhart had several special speakers at the Bible Institute who interpreted Mussolini as the

Antichrist, or at least as his forerunner.[26] Aberhart used this idea as an attention-getter, even if he did not himself believe it.

The apocalyptic expectancy during the Depression is further illustrated by a play that Aberhart and Ernest Manning wrote and produced in 1931.[27] The play was an adaptation of Sydney Watson's *Mark of the Beast*. Entitled *The Branding Irons of the Antichrist*, it depicted the terrors and persecutions experienced by a brother and sister during the Tribulation; they had not listened to the Gospel message before the Rapture. Following their mother's disappearance in the Rapture, they decided to believe in Christ at any cost. After refusing to accept the brand of the Antichrist they were executed. The moral of the play was that the audience should accept Christ then and there, and avoid the terrors of the Tribulation by being taken up in the Rapture, which Aberhart called "the overhead route."[28]

The play was performed by members of the Bible Institute Baptist Church's Young People's Society and was taken to other towns in Alberta. Those who witnessed the performance were terrified.[29] One young lady who was a member of the church discovered that the terror stayed with her for some time. Afterward, when visiting a Christian friend and finding no one home, although the doors were open, she feared that the Rapture had occurred and she had been left behind to face the Antichrist.[30]

The play illustrates the state of Aberhart's thinking during the early part of the Depression. He had not yet fully realized the Depression's impact upon people. On those occasions when he touched on it during his sermons, it appears that he used it only as an illustration; the Depression was but a taste, a "foreshadow" of the problems to be experienced by the non-Christian during the coming Tribulation. The general financial catastrophe had not yet affected Aberhart's way of life, although attendance at and income from his religious activities were dropping. In 1931 he wrote to a former student who had been involved in unemployment demonstrations in Vancouver, dismissing the demonstrators as Bolsheviks. He suggested that the student should quit complaining and stay away from the radical element and instead aid society by joining the police force.[31]

However, Aberhart himself soon rejected the status quo. He received many letters from people on the farms telling of the desperate conditions and asking him to pray for them. Crescent Heights graduates came to him asking that he give them direction in fighting the Depression, and he found some of his current students suffering from malnutrition because their unemployed fathers had no money to buy better food. When one of his grade-twelve graduates committed suicide after wandering for some time through the hobo jungles,[32] Aberhart was shocked out of his complacency. With his deep care for young people, the sincerity of which is revealed in his letters,[33] Aberhart could not sit by and do nothing. This suicide launched him into what became a political campaign.

CHAPTER TEN

■

THE DIVIDING OF THE WATERS

I COULD *have remained in the schoolroom and could have hardened my ear to the unhappy, unfortunate plight of the rising generation who are graduating from our schools and universities. I could have turned my religion into that formal type that is good on Sunday but is never applied during the week.*

— William Aberhart, CFCN Broadcast, 5 May 1935

Aberhart was as bewildered as the next man by the staggering misfortune under which his society was collapsing. Discussions were going on all over the country, and it is not surprising that the 1932 summer session of exam-marking in Edmonton, where Aberhart again spent part of his vacation, was a booming exchange where ideas were traded more actively than ever before. On his arrival in Edmonton he renewed acquaintance with Charles Scarborough, an Edmonton highschool chemistry teacher whom he had known since 1929. Aberhart knew that Scarborough, a personable man with much vitality, had long been a proponent of Social Credit, which he had first learned about in England. Though dearly loving a debate with Scarborough, a man who knew his own mind and spoke up with a challenging conviction Aberhart could not resist, Aberhart had never taken a serious interest in the theories he had put forward – and even Major Douglas's books, when Aberhart had glanced over Scarborough's copies, had never made any impression on him.

It is interesting to observe that a minor decision by the Alberta Department of Education was instrumental in making the exam-marking session the birthplace of an idea that altered the whole course of the history of Alberta and British Columbia. Among the rules laid down for teachers marking exams was one that limited their lunch periods to one hour, instead of the one-and-one-half hours they were usually allowed during the school year. Charles Scarborough, a man who never lost an opportunity to escape from the confines of the city to his home just outside Edmonton, had always managed to get home for lunch and take a refreshing nap before returning for his afternoon classes. Given the curtailed lunch periods of the exam-marking session, however, Scarborough was unable to continue this practice and was reluctantly confined to the lunchroom with the other teachers.[1]

As another year had passed and the Depression still dragged on, Scarborough, more convinced than ever that the Social Credit theories of Major Douglas embodied the principles upon which a new and stable economic structure could be built, plied Aberhart over and over again with his arguments. He was not a religious follower of Aberhart, but of all the people with whom he came into contact in Alberta he could think of none better to promote an idea and organize a movement. Given Aberhart's gift for organization and his vast radio audience ripe for the assimilation of new ideas, Scarborough felt he could not allow Aberhart to return to Calgary without using every device in his power to make him realize that Social Credit needed only the proper promotion and application to bring an end to the evils that were destroying the world around them. During the preceeding years Scarborough had discussed with another teacher, J.M. Swain, ways of getting Aberhart's support. Scarborough believed that with Aberhart's help in promoting Social Credit, coupled with the development of the tar sands, Alberta would soon experience economic recovery.[2]

As the lunch period came around each day, sly nudges and smiles passed among the other teachers when Aberhart and Scarborough took up their positions for their daily verbal duel. Scarborough was making little progress, but he had been advocating the same ideas without success for fourteen years and was not easily disheartened. One day he brought a book, said to have been borrowed from the normal school library, into the lunchroom. "I have a book here I think will interest you," he said to Aberhart. Aberhart pocketed the book without much enthusiasm.

That night in the room he occupied in St. Stephen's College at the University of Alberta, Aberhart took up the book. It was called *Unemployment or War*,[3] and its author was Maurice Dale Colbourne, an English actor who frequently appeared in the plays of George Bernard Shaw. Aberhart intended to read only a few pages before retiring for the night. He found, however, that he could not put the book down. He was carried from page to page, finding himself in complete accord with its strikingly simplified analysis of the world's economic problems. Colbourne declared that the Social Credit principles of Major Douglas were the only logical and certain remedy that could save civilization. The book was neither technical nor exhaustive. The first part was a simply-worded indictment of an economic order that caused the injustices and misfortunes that had fallen on the masses. The second half pointed out the obvious justice and, indeed, absolute necessity of the initial reforms advocated by Douglas, and described in general terms some of the principles Douglas would apply in constructing a new economic order.

Colbourne's book made easy and rapid reading. Aberhart finished it in one sitting. When he closed the book in the early hours of the next day and stared thoughtfully at the wall of the small room in St. Stephen's College, Aberhart believed he held in his hand the means of ending the tribulations of his generation. Colbourne's analysis seemed to fit Depression-ridden Alberta. Later that morning Aberhart remarked to one of his staff from Crescent Heights High School, "I read the most fascinating book last night on Social Credit. It seems to me that it has got a solution which could be applied."[4]

After the exam-marking session was over, Aberhart departed for Vancouver for the wedding of his daughter Khona to James Cooper. While there he studied more works on Social Credit. He was remarkably thoughtful for some time and spoke of Social Credit in terms that were unusually moderate for an Aberhart in the throes of a new enthusiasm. This was not surprising when we consider the various aspects of the business of advocating Social Credit that Aberhart had to consider. He had strayed from strictly biblical subjects before (though not so far as radical economics), in order to keep up listener interest. Was it possible that by incorporating economics, the subject that obsessed every mind, into his Bible lectures he could gather a greater number of listeners? The task of integrating the Bible and Social Credit would not be altogether easy, though one of the aspects of Douglas's approach to economics that caught Aberhart's attention was that the basis of Douglas's motivation *appeared* to be the ethics of Christianity. Offsetting the arguments for throwing caution to the wind was the fact that many people felt that a religious leader should confine himself to religion and would consider economics with a political flavour an unsavoury companion to the Bible. Aberhart thought he might lose as many listeners as he might gain. He hesitated to use air time for which the Institute paid in order to promote an idea that might alienate some of the Institute's financial support.

As Aberhart turned these various considerations over in his mind, the apparent soundness of Douglas's opinions added an eloquent argument, and Aberhart decided to try out the new subject cautiously, preparing at the same time to withdraw it if the results were undesirable. Aberhart's second recorded mention of his discovery came after a meeting of the Institute's executive board. Sometimes these meetings were followed by the members adjourning to a restaurant for dinner and informal conversation, and it was at these friendly gatherings that Aberhart often tried out his new ideas. At this particular dinner, which took place at the Tea Kettle Inn, Aberhart, in restrained terms and without mentioning the phrase "Social Credit," asked whether in view of the national situation the executive would consider economics a proper subject for inclusion in his Sunday lectures. Politics did not, of course, enter into the proposals in any way. Aberhart's approach, like Douglas's, was to be purely educational. The board agreed without one dissenting vote.[5]

Before going on the air Aberhart re-read Douglas's books with new interest. It is unlikely that such a reading gave him a mastery of Douglas's involved theories, for Douglas had baffled many who had more technical knowledge than Aberhart's commercial teaching diploma, extramural B.A. degree, and correspondence law courses represented, and had devoted many more hours of study to Social Credit and related subjects. Aberhart's knowledge of the strengths and weaknesses of his new lecture-subject was limited; but whatever disadvantage he had on that score, and doubtful of the reactions he might receive from his audience, Aberhart stepped up to the microphone on 21 August 1932 and (perhaps unfairly to Edmonton and C.M. Scarborough) spoke on "What I Learned in Vancouver." Two weeks later his advertisement read:

> Time to do Some Thinking! Every citizen of Canada should do some serious thinking regarding the present economic situation. To encourage this a series of lectures on the Bible and modern economics will be given at the Calgary Prophetic Bible Institute.[6]

Aberhart had embarked on his last and most far-reaching project, in the course of which he would come to believe that if the people were willing to follow, he had found the means of dividing the waters and leading them out of the Egypt of Depression.

Aberhart was not the only one in western Canada prepared to tackle the Depression. Another political movement began in Calgary in August of 1932: the Co-operative Commonwealth Federation (C.C.F.). The C.C.F. was an amalgamation of the socialistic League for Social Reconstruction directed by intellectuals from eastern Canada,[7] various labour groups including those represented by J.S. Woodsworth and William Irvine, and various farmers' groups. Their aim was to defeat the Depression by nationalization and socialism. J.S. Woodsworth became leader of the new movement.[8] Both the C.C.F. and Aberhart's Social Credit would share some of Major Douglas's ideas spread by William Irvine, and Aberhart and the C.C.F. would cross paths often in the next few years.

With such ideas in the wind Aberhart found a ready response from his radio audience. Some of those who formerly considered his prophetic lectures the ranting of a madman, began listening to him with interest. Aberhart had spoken of economics without incurring the reproaches he had feared.

He had explained that the God of his religion was no more indifferent to men's sufferings than he was to their spiritual needs. Aberhart spoke in religious anger of the injustices that were being suffered by the people as a result of a faulty monetary system. Encouraged by the attentive response that his new subject received in the autumn of 1932, he let fall the words "Social Credit" and "Douglas."

Aberhart's discussions of Social Credit stimulated a series of letters between him and members of his audience. One set of letters was particularly illuminating: those between Aberhart and a C.C.F. advocate, J.H. Coldwell, a station agent for the C.N.R. at Kathryn, about thirty-two kilometers northeast of Calgary. These are the earliest and fullest of the extant letters in which Aberhart discussed his economic and political thought.

In Aberhart's first letter to Coldwell on 14 September 1932 he claimed that nationalization of actual wealth was needed.[9] In a later letter he stated "that the money system must be banished entirely before the masses will be freed from the power of the financiers."[10] Such comments sounded very leftist. Three years later, when addressing an audience in Seaforth, Ontario, Aberhart stated that the bad conditions had distressed him.

> And when [the Depression] continued I became "pink" and by that I mean tingeing close to "red."[11] Conditions in [Alberta] almost made me a Communist, although I have no use for Communism. Instead I turn [*sic*] to Social Credit.[12]

Towards the end of 1932, overjoyed at the favourable reception that had greeted his new subject, Aberhart began throwing his whole being into the movement. During the Christmas holidays of 1932, which he spent in Vancouver, he organized two lectures on Christmas Day dealing with prophecy and economics, and a lecture every night of the following week.[13]

Major Douglas had declared that the education of the public was the only way to bring about the acceptance of his ideas. If it was done well, it was all that would be needed to implement Social Credit and usher in a new economic order. At least this was the way Aberhart understood Douglas. Education was his forte; he could do it, and do it well.

Aberhart's method of educating the public in the principles of Social Credit took several stages. He began by mixing Social Credit into his Sunday-afternoon religious broadcasts, a mixture that was deliberate since he had been warned that many would turn off their radios when he started talking about prophecy. Commenting on this later Aberhart laughed, "But I fooled them. I mixed it so they couldn't tune me out."[14]

As Aberhart's listeners caught his enthusiasm for Social Credit, they suggested that he should put out a booklet on the subject. He mentioned this to Mrs. Lettie Hill, his school librarian. She said, "Why don't you talk to my husband? He has read all that stuff." Aberhart requested an interview with H.B. ("Hilly") Hill and brought along his notes for the pamphlet. And what notes they were! As Hill describes them, they were written on every size, shape, and kind of paper: on the backs of envelopes, school board stationery, letter paper, and so on. The writing was clear, concise, and legible, but grammatically awful. Hill was shocked that Aberhart, being a highschool principal, was so illiterate.

During the course of the enjoyable evenings that Aberhart and the Hills spent revising his notes, the Hills took him to task for his grammar. "Hilly" also had serious doubts whether Social Credit could be applied provincially without Dominion acceptance. He was a disabled veteran of the First World War and had read most of the radical literature on economics while he was recuperating in Colonel Belcher Military Hospital in Calgary. Whether Aberhart knew it or not, Hill was also a professed communist.

When they had completed the sifting of the gist of Aberhart's ideas into pamphlet form, Aberhart asked, "Now do you think that this is all right and what Douglas means?"

"Yes, in my opinion, that is what Douglas means, but it won't work!" Aberhart replied, "You're crazy, Hill! Of course it will work!"

"All right," said Hill, "then when you become Premier of Alberta, you make me provincial treasurer and we'll both have a swell time."

They both laughed heartily at his humour. As Aberhart was leaving the Hill's residence, "Hilly" said to him, "For God's sake, don't publish that thing! No matter how insistent the demand is, don't publish it! You'll get into a jack-pot of a fight and the school board will fire you for sure."

Aberhart replied, "Well, I never ran way from a fight in my life and I won't now. I'm going to print it and sell it to whomever wants it for ten cents a copy."[15]

Aberhart did publish the pamphlet, anonymously. It became known as the "Yellow Pamphlet" because of its cover and was entitled *The Douglas System of Economics*. The pamphlet suggested that dividends be given every month to every bona fide citizen in the form of credit (not money, but non-negotiable certificates) amounting to about $20 in value. (Soon the figure would be changed to $25). This credit would provide for the bare necessities of food, clothing, and shelter.

The proposed changes to the economic system were very radical. All hoarding of wealth or credit was to be banned. Credit had to have continuous flow. An automatic price-control system would be necessary to equalize production and consumption and prevent the hoarding of foodstuffs. All citizens having money in banks, trust companies, or other financial institutions would have to turn it over to the government in exchange for government bonds bearing 4 per cent interest, payable in credit. The government would use the money gained to liquidate all provincial debts and facilitate out-of-province business. Because basic dividends would pay for food, shelter, and clothing, life insurance would no longer be needed, and policies would have to be cashed in for government bonds. Owners of real estate, industrial plants, and stores could transfer their property to the government in exchange for bonds, or retain it and bequeath it to their heirs - or to the government, which would also take over mortgages on farms, private houses, and businesses, and ask individuals to make their payments in credit to the government. This way, Aberhart declared, the government could entirely eliminate provincial and private debt.

The provincial government was portrayed as an independent State that would be viewed by its citizens "as a gigantic joint stock company with the resources of the province behind its credit." Each bona fide citizen would be a shareholder entitled to the bare necessities. The qualifications of citizenship would "be clearly defined and rigidly enforced." No citizen would "be allowed to barter away or otherwise dispose of his dividends beyond the... then current year and thereby become a vagabond or tramp." Salaries or wages for work would be paid in State Credit, while those who were handicapped or mentally ill would "be given bonus dividend protection."

Aberhart suggested that individual enterprise would be encouraged in every possible way, but to prevent exploitation, citizenship would be denied to unworthy individuals. All residents of the province who would not cooperate would "be assessed heavy taxes for the privilege of doing business in the province."

In summary, the economics of the system would work thus: all basic dividends would have to be used during the current year; all salaries or wages from whatever source would likewise have to be spent by the end of the year. Any unused credit would be retained by the government, unless it had been used by the citizen to purchase, for himself or others, government bonds maturing later. All such bonds would become the property of the government at the death of the person in whose name they stood. If a person wanted to leave the province permanently, his bonds could be redeemed for Canadian currency when they came due.

Aberhart's proposed state-controlled bureaucracy had social ramifications. Since men would now only have to work eight to sixteen hours a week, citizens would be taught profitable occupations, and special provision would be made for direction in the use of leisure time.[16]

Some of the authoritarian overtones of the Yellow Pamphlet may have come from "Hilly" Hill's communistic views. Other aspects appear to have been borrowed from Edward Bellamy's utopian novels *Looking Backwards, 2000-1887* and *Equality*, to which Harry Scrimgeour had introduced Aberhart before 1929.[17]

As Aberhart expounded the ideas contained in his pamphlet he soon moved outside of his usual bailiwick. In February 1933 he addressed a receptive audience of fifteen hundred people at a meeting sponsored by the League for Social Reconstruction, the Canadian Labour Party, and the Calgary local of the U.F.A., these groups being the mainstay of the C.C.F.[18]

The next stage in Aberhart's program was the commencement of a series of Thursday-night lectures on Social Credit in the basement of the Bible Institute.[19] Those lectures were well attended, and after a few meetings, Aberhart invited those of the audience who were interested in studying Social Credit further, and in working for it personally, to stay behind. Aberhart told those who remained that he intended to start a study group for people who wished to spread the idea of Social Credit. The first meeting was announced on the radio. He assured those who intended to come that hard work was ahead of them, and aroused interest by warning the curious to stay away. "I don't want everyone to come down," he said. "Only those who will work."

PUBLIC
MEETING

PLACE • • • • Al Azhar Temple
506 – 17th Avenue West

DATE • • • • Monday, June 26th
at 8 p.m.

CHAIRMAN • • Dr. R. G. Williams

SPEAKER • • • Wm. Aberhart, B. A.

Male Voice Quartette
Harold De Caux, Tenor Soloist

• • SUBJECT • •

The
Douglas System
of Economics

Aberhart comes out in the open: Social Credit handbill, 1933.

It was a recapitulation of Aberhart's success in religious instruction. So many people crowded into the Institute basement for those meetings that they had to be moved to the main church auditorium. Week after week almost eight hundred people attended Aberhart's Social Credit instruction. Printed pamphlets containing a résumé of the particular part of Douglas's writings to be studied that evening had been prepared by Aberhart and were handed out at the doors. Giant charts comparing the proposed Social Credit program to the human blood-circulation system were prominently displayed at the front of the auditorium – as charts of the seven dispensations once had been. After Aberhart's lecture came the inevitable question period. Sometimes the crowd questioned Aberhart, sometimes Aberhart asked the questions. The earnestness of the group was unmistakable. They had come to learn, and from among them Aberhart drew some of his earliest and hardest-working helpers. He made public speakers of them. "You notice a sympathetic face down there," he said, "a kindly one over there, an interested one in the gallery – those are the three people you talk to all evening." He made his audience into Social Credit "experts" and organized them. He also conducted Social Credit lectures by invitation at U.F.A. locals throughout southern Alberta.[20]

On more than one occasion, after hearing Aberhart speak, people tried to copy his oratorical skills. One farmer climbed onto the top of his outhouse and, using it for his speaking platform, sought to emulate his master. He lost his balance and sustained a nasty facial gash when he fell to the ground. Years later he referred to the scar as his "Aberhart scar."[21]

Aberhart began devoting more and more air time to Social Credit. Soon the first hour of his Sunday-afternoon broadcasts was devoted to explaining to his listeners why the current economic system had resulted in their present predicament and appealed to them to read Douglas's books, preferably in the company of others, thus organizing study groups around the province.

The temper of the times added to Aberhart's following. Unemployment and hardship were everywhere. Revolution was in the air. The federal government feared an internal overthrow by communist groups. In an attempt to avoid political unrest, the federal government, in 1932, had established relief work camps directed by the Department of National Defense. Unemployed single young men were sent to these "concentration camps" located in isolated places, where they earned $7.50 a month plus room and board.[22]

The cities, too, were filled with tension. A riot on Mission Hill in Calgary between the employed, unemployed, and the police occurred in April 1933.[23] Two weeks later a riot in Regina caused the death of a R.C.M.P. inspector.[24] The leftist rhetoric in Aberhart's broadcasts appealed to many of the unemployed who felt the federal government was unsympathetic to their needs.

Shortly after publishing the Yellow Pamphlet, Aberhart wrote to Coldwell, the C.C.F. advocate: "I have no brief for our present capitalistic system and am fully convinced that there is no hope of recovery until it is abolished and a new system of economics introduced."[25] At times, various local representatives of the C.C.F. were featured on Aberhart's platform.[26] In his private correspondence, he claimed not to be a socialist,[27] viewing Social

Credit as quite distinct from socialism – which he equated with "Red Radicalism, which would prove, if anything, a greater disaster than even our present system.... The Douglas System embodies all the advantages of socialism, but eliminates its drawbacks."[28] Aberhart suggested that one of the drawbacks of socialism was that there were no rewards for individual enterprise, another that it did not go far enough in destroying the present financial system. Coldwell responded by stating that Aberhart was misrepresenting the C.C.F. and was a socialist without knowing it.[29]

Coldwell's appraisal of Aberhart was shared by others in the C.C.F. William Irvine, after receiving a copy of the Yellow Pamphlet wrote a personal letter to W. Norman Smith, who had promoted Social Credit ideas in the *United Farmer*, and said:

> but unless Douglas has changed his System Aberhart is not expounding it correctly, although most of what he is advocating seems O.K..... It seems to me that most of what is in Aberhart's pamphlet is what we are preaching. Why not let him go to it?[30]

Because of "Hilly" Hill's input into the Yellow Pamphlet, it is not surprising that it was so radical and advocated measures that would have resulted in a socialist state. Aberhart's reluctance to side with the C.C.F., however, seems to have been motivated by several technical differences. Aberhart's program was more radical when it came to the elimination of money and banks. He also sensed a difference between the C.C.F and himself regarding employment levels. One C.C.F. advocate, writing to Aberhart prior to publication of the *Regina Manifesto*, had implied that the C.C.F. planned to have full employment; Aberhart did not.[31] Major Douglas claimed that unemployment was a sign of economic progress;[32] that modern technology had eliminated the need for full employment. Reduced individual working hours, redistribution of existing wealth, and the dividend system would provide the bare essentials for everyone.

After school closed in June 1933, Aberhart and Ernest Manning made a tour around the province, covering roughly that part of Alberta lying south of an east-west line through Red Deer (a town midway between Calgary and Edmonton). They met for the first time many of those who had become interested in Social Credit through the radio broadcasts. For these people 1933 was the worst year yet, as every disaster of previous years visited the province again. A promising spring had deteriorated into a hot, dry, dusty summer in the south; crops wilted and cattlemen were at their wit's end to find feed for their stock. To drought and erosion was added a grasshopper plague. Swarms of insects descended upon large areas of the land. When they left, not an ear of wheat nor a leaf was anywhere to be seen. In the north crops were poor because of frost damage. Even though market conditions had improved, the total yield of wheat for Alberta in 1933 was only slightly more than half the 1932 yield.

The tour doubtless brought home to Aberhart how much influence he could wield if he chose. He was stimulated by the experience. On 31 July 1933 he wrote to his niece in Seaforth: "Some people here tell me I should run for the Premier [*sic*] of Alberta – ha-ha! I have no ambition along that line but the Radio Broadcast has made me well-known all over the province."[33] One can hear the gears moving in Aberhart's brain, in spite of his denial of political ambition.

During the second half of the summer Aberhart vacationed in Vancouver with his married daughters. While there he had several conversations with A.J.E. Liesemer, a member of his staff at Crescent Heights High School who was also an active member of the C.C.F. It was agreed that Aberhart should meet with some provincial leaders of the U.F.A., and with federal U.F.A. members of Parliament who were leading the C.C.F. W. Norman Smith, editor of the *United Farmer*, was contacted to arrange the meeting. Since both William Irvine and Aberhart were on the Coast, Smith wrote to them and suggested that they begin preliminary talks.[34] Aberhart attended one of Irvine's meetings in Vancouver, and they had an interview the following day. A conference between members of Aberhart's group was agreed upon, and Irvine informed Aberhart that the C.C.F.'s provincial platform would include Social Credit proposals.[35]

On his return to Calgary, Aberhart was immensely pleased with the way his hand-picked students had handled the Social Credit meetings at the Institute while he had been away. He found that in spite of the absence of the holidayers from Calgary, large crowds had regularly attended the meetings.

While Social Credit activities at the Bible Institute were thriving, however, there were serious problems developing within the congregation of the Bible Institute Baptist Church. In September 1933 Dr. Andrew Imrie resigned as pastor. Although he was well liked by the congregation, difficulties had been developing between him and Aberhart for some time. Their personalities were antagonistic; Dr. Imrie was a methodical thinker, while Aberhart was impulsive; they could not work together. Aberhart's position as "apostle" created divided loyalties in the church, and Dr. Imrie had difficulty defining his role while also disagreeing with Aberhart's doctrinal position.[36] Financial matters were involved as well. When Imrie had been hired he was promised a salary of $4,000 per year; but as the Depression grew worse the offerings were not enough to provide his salary, and Aberhart had not seen fit to transfer surplus funds to the pastor's salary account.[37] Another issue at stake was Aberhart's use of the pulpit for political purposes. Initially, Dr. Imrie had been in favour of the Social Credit study groups at the Bible Institute, but when Aberhart's sermons became so devoted to Social Credit, Imrie objected.[38] Dr. Imrie visited with Robert W. Scrimgeour, who had broken with Aberhart in 1929, and on Scrimgeour's suggestion, he submitted his resignation.[39] At the church board meeting at which Imrie's resignation was considered, the discussions became so heated that Aberhart ordered several pages of the minutes removed.[40]

After Imrie's departure Ernest Manning and Cyril Hutchinson were hired by the church to perform the pastoral duties and some of the preaching.[41] Cyril Hutchinson had recently returned to the church after having been expelled by Aberhart in 1927. For some time he had drifted between various churches, and having found none that would satisfy him, he asked Aberhart if he could return. Aberhart said he could, provided that he toe the line.[42]

Dr. Imrie was not the only one at the church disturbed by Aberhart's mixture of Christianity and Social Credit. Several members of the church complained that "when Social Credit entered the front door of the church, the Holy Spirit left by the back door."[43] Aberhart cared little for their objections and immediately preached a series of sermons denouncing the "so-called scriptural objections to Social Credit."[44]

At this time Aberhart's theology was in a state of flux. When he first took up Social Credit he seems to have used it as a springboard for evangelism. To one of his correspondents he wrote that Christianity and economics "went hand-in-hand." He added that religious conversion was the first step in being able to apply economics properly:

> It is the transformation of the individual's life and attitude of mind from this personal relationship with the living Christ, that I am convinced is essential to the proper application of economics in order that the desired results may be realized.[45]

Aberhart drew analogies between Christianity and his understanding of Social Credit:

> The appeal of God today is for the individual to understand that God's policy is to provide man with a salvation full and free, without money and without price, and then to offer him future rewards for his individual enterprise in the service of God. I am convinced that this is the basic principle of a practical economic system. Government credit, such as advocated by Major Douglas, gives to the individual, who is a bona fide citizen of the Province, the essentials of physical life, such as food, clothing, and shelter, and then offers him additional reward for his individual enterprise.[46]

In another letter Aberhart wrote:

> One thing that appeals to me and I believe will appeal to every thinking Christian, in the Douglas system of Economics, is the fact that from beginning to end it was based on the principles of God's great economy.[47]

Here Aberhart was venturing beyond the usual theological concerns of fundamentalism; most fundamentalists accepted the economic status quo. Aberhart appeared to be giving *carte blanche* approval to Douglas's radical ideas.

Both Douglas and his expositor Maurice Colbourne had used religious terminology in their writings, but in a manner quite foreign, if not directly antithetical to Aberhart's dispensational and fundamentalistic theology. They repudiated the idea of original sin and accepted the theory of evolution.[48] Douglas's 1933 edition of *Social Credit* was extremely anti-Semitic and he considered the Old Testament a "repulsive tribal rag-bag."[49] He viewed man's ultimate aim as a life of leisure.

In the past Aberhart had disassociated himself from those who held liberal theological views; now he was adopting a system of thought based in certain respects on liberal premises. He did not seem to be aware of his inconsistency. By a kind of ultra-dispensationalism he adopted Colbourne's attitude that Genesis 3:19 and II Thessalonians 3:10 were no longer applicable in a technological world.[50] However, he had not totally divorced himself from his previous dispensational theology; he continued to reject the Sermon on the Mount, which had been used by Douglas as a basis for Social Credit "theology," as not being applicable to the present age.[51] These were only some of the many inconsistencies that characterized Aberhart's amalgam of ideas.

While Aberhart's preaching still contained strong elements of apocalypticism, he gradually began focusing more on the issue of the social justice that was the main thrust of the biblical prophets. In a sermon entitled "The Prophetic Significance of the Republican Defeat," Aberhart compared the current political situation in the United States to that prevailing at the time of Christ. He chose as his text a statement by John the Baptist: "And now also the axe is laid unto the root of the trees: and therefore every tree which bringeth not forth good fruit is hewn down and cast into the fire." The tree, suggested Aberhart, was the government of John's day, while the root of the tree was the Jewish nation. That nation had been judged because of its sinfulness – the sins of selfishness, hypocrisy, usury, violence, injustice, and discontent with wages. Aberhart implied that for similar waywardness the American Republican government had been removed from office, and that if Canadians did not bring forth "fruits worthy of repentance," they would also be judged.[52]

As time passed Aberhart's statements against the government became more intense. In another sermon he used as his text:

> Or what man is there of you, whom if his son ask bread, will give him a stone? Or if he ask a fish, will give him a serpent? If ye then, being evil, know how to give good gifts unto your children, how much more shall your Father which is in heaven give good things to them that ask him? (Matt. 7:9-11, K.J.V.).

The church reporter for the Calgary *Herald*, who was beginning to take notice of Aberhart's sermons, made the following comments on his interpretation of the passage:

> The speaker likened the state to the father and the citizens to the children and applied Christ's statement to existing economic conditions throughout the world. Boldly he declared that in a world where its Creator had planned all things for the service of man in such an abundance that never would there be cause for physical or material need on the part of anyone, governments had been so mismanaged as to bring about an era of dire physical and material poverty for millions. Citizens as children of the state were pleading with the state, their father, for bread and in response to their appeals were being given what was in effect nothing but stones.[53]

Besides becoming very allegorical, Aberhart's preaching was becoming more secular. Writers to the editor of the Calgary *Herald* noted the confusion in Aberhart's preaching. N.J. Noble, a Calgary lawyer, claimed that Aberhart was overlooking God's role in the matter and wondered if Douglas had taken God's place in Aberhart's theology.[54] Another writer pointed out that when Aberhart had preached on the Book of Daniel, he had given the impression that Daniel had introduced Social Credit into the court of King Nebuchadnezzar. He went on to say that Aberhart's descriptions of the Antichrist and his totalitarian program seemed, ironically, to fit Major Douglas and Social Credit economics.[55]

Aberhart's involvement with Social Credit was, therefore, a radical departure from his previous theology, a theology that can best be described as highly sectarian, separatist, apolitical, other-worldly, and eschatologically-oriented. We are reminded of a comment from one of his sermons of 1907:

> God never intended us to reform the world. This world will never be fit for the everlasting habitations of the just. We are to seek and save the lost, pointing them to Jesus....[56]

Aberhart's sermons during the twenties had reflected the same attitude:

> I would rather ten times over hear about some of GOD'S GREAT PRO-PHECIES than some of the non-essential stuff we hear from the platforms and pulpits of today. If it is a matter of time [before Christ's return] why not eliminate some of the Socialistic, Political, and Economic arguments and give us more of GOD'S OWN WORD.
> Oh, yes, my political friend, put this down in your little note book. The very best form of Government, democratic or otherwise, that man could ever establish upon this earth will not be sufficient to recover mankind, but will ultimately end in anarchy.[57]

When speaking specifically about the social-gospellers, Aberhart claimed that their efforts were as futile as a farmer trying to purify a polluted well by painting the pump handle.[58] Now Aberhart was preaching social reform, and he soon received criticism from other fundamentalists. The Reverend L.E. Maxwell, principal of Prairie Bible Institute at Three Hills, wrote an editorial in *The Prairie Pastor* stating that while Christians had the responsibility of casting an intelligent vote, they had no business becoming involved in the world's affairs by trying to bring about social reform.[59]

With his adoption of Social Credit Aberhart departed from a long-apolitical tradition that had characterized the adherents of dispensationalism. Separation from the "world" permeated their theology.[60] Even fundamentalism, which had been an offspring of dispensationalism, but generally more conservative in its method of biblical interpretation, inherited much of the same worldview. On various occasions (before and after Aberhart), fundamentalists became involved in quasi-political movements: campaigns for anti-evolution laws, Prohibition, anti-communist crusades, opposition to the World Council of Churches and the United Nations, support for anti-Semitism and anti-Catholicism, and opposition to racial integration. By and large fundamentalism has been characterized by negativism, with little or no positive political and social thrust.[61] It would appear that Aberhart may have been the first active fundamentalist to have organized a political movement with a "socialistic" character.

Aberhart's ideological shift was not, however, unusual for him; previously he had not allowed his dispensational theology completely to dominate his behaviour. Politically he had identified himself as a Liberal and had voted that way until he developed a friendship with the Conservative R.B. Bennett, who was the Member of Parliament for the riding in which Aberhart lived. After that, Aberhart began voting for Bennett, and even persuaded his dentist friend Harvey to do likewise.[62] Jessie Aberhart claimed that her husband's voting for Bennett was based on his principle of voting for the man rather than the party.[63]

The closest Aberhart had come to political activity before the Depression was his involvement in the Calgary branch of the League of Nations Society. In 1923 he became its first secretary.[64] R.B. Bennett was the honourary president. Yet, Aberhart's involvement was quite out of keeping with his own theological pronouncements and one correspondent to the Calgary *Herald* wondered aloud how a man who had been prophesying the next war could now be working to defeat the inevitable.[65]

After 1927 Aberhart seems to have dropped his involvement with the League of Nations Society; his theology became more sectarian and separatist, reaching its height between 1927 and 1932. When he threw his support behind Social Credit, he was identifying himself more with his earlier experience in the Presbyterian and Methodist churches: the Calvinist-Presbyterian ideal of the church and state united in a Holy Commonwealth, and the Methodist ideal of social reform mixed with revivalism.[66]

To some of Aberhart's contemporaries, the antithetical elements in his theology and his behaviour were just another example of his "chuckle-headedness" when it came to economics. Harry Scrimgeour, his former friend from Westbourne days, later saw certain parallels between Social Credit and the Quarterly Dividends scheme that Aberhart had promoted for Taverner, the confidence man:

> Both schemes were entirely unorthodox to accepted financial principles and had at their foundation the setting of the masses against existing financial authority; both called for the payment of a dividend; both paid this dividend out of Capital, thus reducing or debasing the equity and were thus inflationary and both appealed to those who had a grudge against conditions which deprived them of the privileges of the monied classes.[67]

Aberhart seemed to be susceptible to get-rich-quick schemes. In the early twenties he had also invested in a pecan-nut orchard in Georgia, but as late as 1937 he still had not received any dividend from his investment – not even a bag of nuts.[68]

CHAPTER ELEVEN

■

THE MUSHROOMING MOVEMENT

E VERY *citizen should be able to secure food, clothing and shelter from the country he lives in,...and the present economic situation under which we are now living is unable to provide British fair play to those living here.*

— William Aberhart quoted in the *Calgary Herald*, 1933

Aberhart's copious mail began to contain letters that asked what the next step was after one had learned and approved of Social Credit. He gave his simple answer over the air: "Tell your legislative representative." To put pressure on the U.F.A. government he now organized the Douglas Social Credit League, with an executive that would share in the work of organizing the educational campaign. At the same time, other Social Credit groups arose to object to Aberhart's interpretation of Douglas. The controversies between the groups merely added to public interest in Social Credit, so much so that the U.F.A. government decided to hold a public inquiry on Social Credit and invited both Aberhart and Douglas to appear, with the intention of exposing their differences and discrediting Aberhart, whose potential as a political rival had become very obvious.

The Central Council of the Douglas Social Credit League was, of course, under the direct authority of the Calgary Prophetic Bible Institute. During the fall of 1933, Aberhart's new organizers spoke in schools, halls, private homes – wherever they could get a hearing – and study groups were initiated. These meetings occupied the first four nights of each week, while on Friday nights meetings were held in the Institute. Week by week, many men and women who had been sitting idle by their radios, driven to a state of hopelessness by the fruitless search for work, heard Aberhart's call to arms; and the next week they flocked to the Institute. A typical Social Credit worker related that he sold a good set of golf clubs for far less than its value, and bought a new pair of pants to go with his coat, so that he could speak in public.[1] Soon there were sixty-three study groups operating in Calgary alone. One of the largest was organized at the C.P.R.'s Ogden Shops; this demonstrated the strong urban working class support that Aberhart attracted. Country districts were just as active, and eventually sixteen hundred study groups dotted the province.

Aberhart's study groups represented only a portion of those people across Canada who were interested in Social Credit. Across Canada other Social Credit enthusiasts had organized associations to cooperate with Douglas's Social Credit Secretariat in the work of spreading information about his theories. Douglas considered these organizations the essential propaganda nuclei that would marshal public opinion in support of Social Credit. Douglas had, therefore, kept in close touch with these scattered pockets of people, gathering, through personal correspondence with them, news of the spread of his ideas.

During his 1923 visit to Ottawa, Douglas had made a number of personal friends who furnished him with contacts and ready advocates when general interest began to be shown in the opinions of unorthodox economists. Among the most influential of those contacts were two members of the Southam newspaper publishing family. Harry Southam, publisher of the Ottawa *Citizen*, and his brother Wilson Southam, publisher of the Calgary *Herald*, were both enthusiastic advocates of Douglas's brand of Social Credit. Several times since 1923 they had visited Douglas in London, and they are said to have helped finance his visit to Alberta in 1934.[2] Their editor at the Ottawa *Citizen*, Charles A. Bowman, was also an outspoken advocate of Douglas's Social Credit theories.

In 1933 Clifford Hugh Douglas claimed to have active Social Credit groups in "every great city in Great Britain," two in Paris, one each in Norway and Switzerland, several in Ireland, and several on the West Coast of the United States, and in New York and Washington. But the greatest strides had been made in Australia, New Zealand, and Alberta.[3] Douglas was not uninformed about events in Alberta, but his information must have left him with the impression that a personal inspection would be the only way to get a reasonably clear idea of what the actual situation was.

Very early in Aberhart's Social Credit activities, correspondence among the various Canadian Social Credit organizations and Douglas's Secretariat brought up the issue that was to cause more discussion and dissension during the next few years than any other of the many vexing questions about Social Credit. Aberhart stated that he was fighting for Social Credit for Alberta only. Trying to get the federal government to adopt Social Credit would be such an enormous task that he thought attempting it a waste of time. He saw an advantage in the compactness and international insignificance of Alberta and therefore concentrated on the provincial field - feeling that if it were made to work there, Social Credit would be immeasurably stronger elsewhere in Canada.[4] This decision, however, called forth immediate protests from other students of Social Credit, including C.M. Scarborough, who had introduced Aberhart to Social Credit theories and who felt that they could work only if applied federally.[5] The same thought was shared by J. Larkham Collins, a chartered accountant in Calgary.

Collins was a member of the Group of the Open Mind, a gathering of about eight professional men in Calgary who met for the purpose of discussing topics of the day. Among their members were well-known barristers, a doctor, and W. Norman Smith, editor of the *United Farmer*, who was an active socialist. Each week a member of the group took a topic on which to speak, his address followed by discussion among the other members. The fact that the group's meetings were broadcast by radio gave them considerable influence on current thought in Alberta.[6] The speaker who caused the greatest stir was Collins, when he said that Social Credit could not work provincially.

Collins was not a convinced Social Crediter, but was interested in examining Social Credit as a possible solution to the economic troubles of the world. In his discussions with Aberhart, Collins detected considerable deviation from Douglas's position.[7] Therefore, he submitted copies of Aberhart's Yellow Pamphlet and a list of questions both to Major Douglas and to C.V. Kerslake of Toronto, a musician who was the self-appointed secretary of the Douglas Credit League of Canada. Both Douglas and Kerslake informed Collins that Aberhart's ideas about the abolition of money, banks, life insurance, the cancellation of unused credit at the end of the month, and dividends having to be spent only on necessities were not part of the Douglas plan.[8]

Douglas and Kerslake differed, however, on the question of whether Social Credit could be applied at the provincial level. Douglas believed that it was technically possible, but that national (if not international) financial interests would fight it. However, according to Douglas, the fight would have to take place anyway, so it might as well start in Alberta, which could probably survive because it was an agriculturally self-supporting province. Kerslake, on the contrary, felt that the British North America Act, which laid down the spheres of influence of the provincial and federal governments, withheld from the provinces the power to introduce Social Credit without the consent of the federal government. Even though Kerslake's view was firm, he wished to get a further opinion on the subject, and therefore submitted Aberhart's Yellow Pamphlet to the Social Credit Secretariat in London for further appraisal.

Although Douglas had apparently concurred with Aberhart's position, Collins sided with Kerslake, believing that Kerslake was better informed on Canada's constitutional situation. Section 92 of the British North America Act listed the "subjects of exclusive Provincial Legislation." Those items that dealt with financial matters were the approval of direct taxation within the Province in order to raise revenue for provincial purposes, and the approval of the Province's borrowing money on its own sole credit. All powers other than those listed in Section 92 rested with the federal government, which also had the power to disallow many kinds of provincial legislation.[9] Aberhart, for his part, believed that because the influence of the federal government in provincial affairs had been diminishing, any legislation the Alberta Legislature might enact to put theories of Social Credit into practice within the province would not be challenged.

Aberhart's critics noted, however, that even if provincial legislation escaped federal disallowance, its constitutionality could still be challenged in the courts. This would be the final test. Kerslake and Collins pointed out that monetary powers other than those mentioned in Section 92 were specifically reserved to the federal government. Social Credit legislation as envisaged by Douglas would, therefore, if passed by a province, certainly be judged unconstitutional if tested in the courts.

In arguing with Kerslake and Collins, Aberhart concentrated not on constitutional questions, but on the political argument. In his pamphlet, "The B.N.A. Act and Social Credit," Aberhart commented:

> Whether the people of this province would consent to have the will of the majority rendered inoperative by loosely-jointed constitutional machinery, overstepping its proper functioning through influences of a sordid nature brought to bear upon our good governments remains to be seen.
>
> One thing is certain. The people will not much longer bear up under the present unsatisfactory conditions, when Social Credit offers them a solution.
>
> Especially will this be the case when the only objection is one of constitutional authority, being intruded into a realm of unnecessary interference.

Aberhart also found little support from the older students of Social Credit in Alberta. W. Norman Smith, who had corresponded with Douglas since the early twenties, wrote in a letter to William Irvine:

> Some of Mr. Aberhart's fanatical but ill-informed supporters regard any expression of difference from his views on "economics" as sacrilegious. I don't think he should be allowed to get away indefinitely with the idea that he has patent rights in Douglas, or in ideas on financial or economic reconstruction in any sense.[10]

Even William Irvine's promise to Aberhart to promote Social Credit principles in the C.C.F. came not because Irvine was in favour of Aberhart's view that it could be provincially applied, but rather because it would embarrass the federal government:

> as we are convinced that such proposals imply Dominion legislation, it might be possible for us to agree to advocate the Douglas sytem for the province of Alberta and when the implementation of that program is held up in the province for lack of Dominion support, then to place the responsibility for failure to proceed further on the Dominion Government.[11]

Sometime during the summer of 1933 Aberhart had written to Douglas complaining of Kerslake's opposition. Major Douglas replied that he would have the problem rectified. "Soon after," claimed Aberhart, "I received a letter from Mr. Kerslake telling me he had received a letter from Major Douglas, informing him Major Douglas was of the opinion it could be done in Alberta, but he, Kerslake, was still of the opinion it could not be done."[12]

Aberhart, happy he could still claim the blessing of Douglas on his proposition, was further pleased by a gesture of friendliness that Douglas made a month later. Mr. Munger, a member of Aberhart's study group, had visited Major Douglas in London and presented him with a copy of the Yellow Pamphlet, suggesting that Aberhart would be very gratified if Douglas would autograph it. Douglas signed it, "With kindest regards from C.H. Douglas."[13] Soon afterward Douglas sent Aberhart a copy of his latest book with a short message: "In recognition of outstanding labour."[14] Aberhart's own delight ran away with his imagination, and he took these gestures as a personal endorsement by the founder of Social Credit of his own interpretation of the doctrines as they applied to Alberta. At his public meetings Aberhart made much of Douglas's autograph,[15] and his enthusiasm was again heightened when Douglas wrote to a Social Credit group at Provost, Alberta, and supported Aberhart's contention that Social Credit could be applied provincially:

> Although I am reasonably familiar with Canadian conditions, I should not like to put forward a definite scheme without considerable consultation with practical men on the spot, but I am entirely of the opinion that a community of the type represented by the province of Alberta could quite easily develop its own credit system without reference to the rest of Canada.[16]

Were Douglas's signatures official endorsements of the pamphlet and Aberhart, or merely autographs? No one yet seemed to know.

Besides his religious following, some of whom worked for him as vigorously in the new venture as in the old, Aberhart's widening field of interest began to bring into his orbit people of more widely varying types than those with whom he had associated before. As a belated justification of his fears that he might be censured for introducing politics into his religion, there were now people who resented his attempt to bring religion into their politics.

Charles Palmer, formerly a mine promoter, now first vice-president of the Central Council of Aberhart's Douglas Social Credit League, a sincere and impatient worker for Social Credit, was one who suffered acute discomfort in the Bible Institute atmosphere. Aberhart, however, made no concessions. "What are you going to open with, Palmer?" he asked, as the latter organized a meeting.

"O Canada!" Palmer replied.

"I think you should have 'O God Our Help in Ages Past,' "[17] said Aberhart, in a pronouncement that became part of Alberta Social Credit rules of procedure for meetings.

Besides his position on the Central Council, Palmer was secretary of a group known as the New Age Club, which was originally one of the Social Credit study groups that Aberhart had established. This club, which had a membership of two hundred, operated in a somewhat bohemian but effective manner from an office over a store on Eighth Avenue. To Palmer's office gravitated many of those advocates of Social Credit who found the Bible Institute uncongenial, preferring a more Simon-pure version of economics, unmixed with religion.

In spite of their differences the New Age Club worked closely with Aberhart in promoting Social Credit, and it was from the club's office that signatures were collected on a petition that had been drafted by Aberhart. The petition stated that despite the poverty of the people, despite surpluses so great "that much of our products are being wantonly destroyed or wasted," despite the fact that no "prospect of deliverance" was in sight, the Douglas Social Credit League now resolved

> that we petition our provincial Government Representative to take into careful consideration the method of solution known as the Douglas system and after investigation, if he finds this system feasible, that he presses for action to inaugurate it at as early a date as possible so that it may be given a fair trial.[18]

The names and addresses of about twelve thousand citizens of Alberta, mostly in Calgary, were eventually affixed to the petition, which was addressed to the six Calgary members of the Provincial Legislature.

The political cycle that had swept the U.F.A. into power had now come full circle. The farmers who had put the U.F.A. in power in Edmonton were indignant once again. The U.F.A. government had become little different from the old-line parties. Most of its decisions were made in caucus, and the farmers felt that they no longer had a direct say in government: more and more U.F.A. leadership positions were being taken by non-farmers. The farmers demanded that the provincial government implement monetary reform to ease their burdens.

The spectre of a provincial election, which could not be delayed beyond the summer of 1935, loomed at the government's elbow as it read the Social Credit petition, and listened to constituency representatives who reported the threats of their constituents to vote only for a candidate who pledged to fight for the implementation of Social Credit. Aberhart's name had been suggested already as one to whom the government could go for advice in investigating Douglas' scheme.[19] Opposition parties were taking advantage of the pressure on the government by calling for a legislative investigation of a Social Credit scheme for Alberta. Some of the U.F.A. members felt that the best way to handle the situation would be an inquiry by the Agricultural Committee of the Legislature. They felt that the clamour could be stilled by the government's willingness to have an investigation.[20] On 13 November 1933, Premier John E. Brownlee announced the probability of a committee being formed to consider the Douglas proposals to see whether they were practicable for the province.[21]

Two months before, Brownlee had been in Toronto as a member of the Royal Commission on Banking and Currency; while there, he had had discussions about Social Credit with Kerslake, who expressed his doubts about Aberhart's views, but was still waiting for an opinion from the Secretariat. Brownlee, who was anxious to receive a copy of this opinion, continued corresponding with Kerslake.[22]

So far, no one in Alberta had received a definite analysis of Aberhart's pamphlet by Major Douglas or the Secretariat. However, several letters from Douglas to his correspondents in Alberta suggested that he was somewhat equivocal about Aberhart's plan for Alberta. J. Larkham Collins had not been satisfied with Douglas's reply to him on 17 August 1933. Feeling that Douglas was misinformed about the situation in Alberta, Collins wrote him a lengthy letter outlining the legal and constitutional problems involved.[23] Douglas's reply to Collins was more than Collins expected, for Douglas suggested how Social Credit could be applied provincially - by military *coup*:

> In regard to the question as to the possibility or otherwise of instituting a Social Credit regime in Alberta, I think the shortest practical answer that I can give you is the one which I give to such questions everywhere, and that is, that the inauguration of a Social Credit system anywhere is *really neither a theoretical nor an economic problem, but in the last resort, is a military problem* [authors' italics]. The present financial monopoly has devoted at least 100 years, if not more, to obtaining control of the ultimate sanctions of civilization, such as police and military forces, and so long as this control is maintained, the question as to whether it is legal to take certain steps for the breaking of the monopoly of credit is quite academic, since if it did happen to be legal, the law would unquestionably be altered to make it illegal.... The real task of the Social Credit army is not, I need hardly say, to raise a new military army, but to detach the existing forces from the possibility of use in such a situation. It is not an insoluble problem, but it is a very difficult one, and I should not like to give an off hand decision as to what extent a unit of the size of Alberta could act alone.[24]

In another letter Douglas commented on Aberhart's pamphlet:

> Mr. Aberhart's pamphlet is issued entirely upon his own authority, and I have regarded it merely as preliminary progaganda, for which purpose it appears to have been effective... In view of your remarks, I have passed it on to the Publications Committee of the Social Credit Secretariat for analysis, as you will realise that it is physically impossible for me to deal personally with all the pamphlets which are reaching me from all quarters of the world.[25]

Douglas, in referring to the Secretariat, was overrating its size and importance; it was composed of a small group of his loyal followers. Surely Douglas must have known of the contents of Aberhart's pamphlet, but he refused to comment on it publicly because he needed the publicity for his ideas. Although Douglas had not denounced Aberhart, neither did Aberhart have Douglas's full endorsement for his pamphlet.

Shortly before Brownlee had announced the probability of an investigation into the Douglas scheme, Kerslake had changed his mind on the constitutionality of provincial Social Credit. Kerslake wrote to Brownlee suggesting what while Aberhart's plan was a departure from Douglas, there was a possibility that the Douglas plan might work in the province:

> Douglas has pointed out that *technically* it is possible to operate the Douglas plan in any area but it would need constant vigilance to prevent sabotage from opposing interests that would seek to discredit it in the eyes of the people. My personal thought is that if you (convinced of the soundness and efficiency of the Douglas plan) should inaugurate it in your province, I should unhesitatingly credit you with more moral courage than any other man in the public life of Canada.[26]

Kerslake also suggested that should the Alberta government seriously consider the Douglas Plan, Brownlee should invite Major Douglas to Alberta as an adviser.

However, Brownlee had no such plans to implement Social Credit in Alberta. In a letter to the secretary of the U.F.A. local at Balzac, Alberta, Brownlee stated that Aberhart's plan was a departure from Douglas and was unworkable from an administrative standpoint. The B.N.A. Act, he said, also prevented a provincial program of Social Credit. Brownlee cast serious doubts even on Douglas's theories:

> I should probably inform you that Major Douglas appeared before the MacMillan Commission in England during the investigation of that body.... The personnel of that Commission included some of the most radical students of political economy such as Mr. J.R. Keens [*sic*; J.M. Keynes]. The proposals were rejected by the entire Commission as being impracticable. Major Douglas also appeared before the Select Committee on Banking and Finance of the Dominion Parliament some time ago and excepting for a very few members his proposals were not seriously considered.[27]

By publicly agreeing to an inquiry on Social Credit, Brownlee seemed to hope that both Aberhart and Douglas would be discredited, thus taking much of the pressure off the government. With such widespread public interest in Social Credit as there was, the government would only have added to its troubles if it did not appear to regard the interests of its citizens.

At that time the U.F.A. government was on shaky ground. Besides the alienation of the U.F.A. locals from the government, there were clouds hanging over the moral reputations of senior cabinet ministers. O.L. Mcpherson, minister of Public Works, had recently been involved in a spectacular divorce case that resulted in a virtual wife-swap,[28] and now Premier Brownlee himself had been accused in court of having seduced and carried on an affair with the daughter of the mayor of Edson.[29] (Brownlee, we may recall, had been a fellow-lay-preacher with Aberhart many years before at Wesley Methodist Church.) Rumours were also circulating that George Hoadley, minister of Agriculture, might also be charged with moral turpitude.[30] When Mcpherson and Brownlee's court cases were dragged through daily newspapers the credibility and integrity of the Alberta government were irreparably damaged.

While the Alberta government was preparing for the investigation of Social Credit, the Social Credit Secretariat in England finally commented on Aberhart's Yellow Pamphlet. Sometime in December 1933 Kerslake and Collins received the following message from W.L. Bardsley, secretary of Douglas's London office:

> This pamphlet is fallacious from start to finish; it would take too long to comment on each error, so only a few of the more glaring are selected.... The pamphlet should be withdrawn at once, or at least all references to Douglas and Social Credit should be deleted.[31]

Outside of Kerslake, Collins, Brownlee, W. Norman Smith, and some of the other leaders of the U.F.A., however, no one knew of the Secretariat's denunciation of Aberhart's pamphlet. Their hesitancy to make this information public may have been motivated by a hope that an even stronger denunciation could be delivered by Douglas himself.

In an attempt to further discredit Aberhart, Brownlee turned for help to Collins, who was preparing a major rebuttal to Aberhart's views. Collins felt that although Aberhart had been discredited by the Secretariat, he might still proceed with his own plan without Douglas's endorsement. What was needed now was a complete exposure of the fallacies of Aberhart's ideas. Collins suggested that Aberhart be thoroughly cross-examined at the forthcoming investigation in the spring of 1934. Brownlee agreed and planned on having Collins appear as an expert witness before the Committee.[32]

In the meantime Aberhart's Yellow Pamphlet was causing great concern among writers to the editor of the Calgary *Herald*. Some saw the proposals as communistic, while others saw them as fascistic.[33] Another writer, James Gaule, a C.C.F. advocate, detected in Aberhart's scheme a gigantic confiscation program, with the little man being hurt far more than the rich man.[34] In one of his rare letters to the editor Aberhart denied this charge, and shifted the responsibility from himself by suggesting that "an intelligent person like Major Douglas would not make such a glaring suggestion of inconsistency."[35] Gaule replied that Aberhart had not answered the questions he raised, and that there was a contradiction between what Aberhart wrote in the pamphlet and what he was now saying.[36] In another letter, Gaule pointed out that Aberhart's scheme did not appear to allow producers and merchants any profits, and that the entire scheme would probably result in public ownership – something that Douglas and Aberhart claimed to decry.[37]

In spite of the variety of opinion being expressed on Aberhart's ideas, his movement was becoming a reality on the political scene. That became quite apparent in January 1934, when a by-election was held in Calgary to fill a vacancy in the Provincial Legislature. Aberhart had the four candidates appear before the Central Council of the Douglas Social Credit League to give their opinions of Social Credit.[38] He was particularly interested in the comments of Amelia Turner, a member of the Calgary School Board, who was running on the C.C.F.-Labour ticket. Miss Turner called for the development of Social Credit at the expense of the banks and financial interests, but she was not yet pledged to any particular system of Social Credit. She was, however, in favour of having Major Douglas brought before the Agricultural Committee for investigation. In another speech she claimed that she would advocate the use of Social Credit to embark on a program of public works.[39] In commenting on the election campaign, Aberhart said that he did not consider it his duty to tell people how to vote; but he added that he felt the existing political structure had failed to supply the answers to the problems facing society. He hoped that people would vote only for those candidates who were serious about Social Credit.[40] His own preference for Miss Turner seemed to have been demonstrated when he allowed her to use the Calgary Prophetic Bible Institute auditorium for a campaign meeting that was too large for the Grand Theatre.[41]

Over the past months since his meeting with William Irvine, Aberhart had been warming to the C.C.F. On 30 October 1933, he and some of his executive had held a secret meeting in the office of W. Norman Smith with three of the federal U.F.A.-C.C.F. members of Parliament: E. J. Garland, Henry E. Spencer, and George C. Coote. Some of the provincial U.F.A. executive were also in attendance.[42] It was agreed that Aberhart and the C.C.F. would not hinder each other's work, and that they would advertise each other's activities. After the meeting Aberhart and Mr. and Mrs. Garland went for a drive. Garland was favourable to uniting Aberhart's movement with the C.C.F., and later, at some of his meetings, he spoke in praise of Aberhart's work. Within Aberhart's group there was some talk that should they win political power in Alberta, William Irvine would make a good candidate for premier.[43]

During the latter part of January 1934, the nervous U.F.A. held its annual convention in Edmonton. While the convention itself took no official stand on the Social Credit question, other than officially announcing the upcoming investigation, it turned the matter over to its C.C.F. wing for study.[44] Meeting in separate session were the United Farm Women of Alberta, who received a telegram from seven hundred women studying the Douglas System at the Calgary Prophetic Bible Institute, asking them to add their support to the investigation of Social Credit.[45] Shortly after the convention the twelve-thousand-name petition asking for the government investigation of Social Credit was formally presented to the government.

Aberhart's invitation to the inquiry came not from the government, but rather from the opposition. The Honourable J.J. Bowlen, later lieutenant-governor of Alberta but in 1934 Liberal member for Calgary, did not escape Aberhart's mission of Social Credit education for all. Mr. Bowlen recalled being buttonholed by Aberhart one day while he was passing the Bible

Institute. Aberhart drew Bowlen aside, plying him with arguments for the adoption of Social Credit by the Liberal Party. Hardly in a position to make a pronouncement on the subject then and there, Bowlen suggested that Aberhart should appear before the Legislature. Aberhart replied that he doubted they would let him in, but Bowlen assured him that it could be arranged.[46] Not too long afterwards W.R. Howson, leader of the Liberal opposition, made a motion in the Legislature that the government fully investigate the Douglas system, with Aberhart and other interested persons called to furnish evidence.[47] This action on the part of the Liberals was not due to any love for the principles of Social Credit, but to a desire to embarrass the U.F.A. government even further and to create more disunity among the Social Crediters.

Aberhart seemed to be happy with the way his educational work for Social Credit was going. It *appeared* to him that his efforts were being taken seriously. Little did he know that almost every faction advocating the investigation (other than his own) was doing so for the purpose of discrediting him.[48]

When Douglas learned of the inquiry, he expressed his interest in coming to Alberta upon his return trip from Australia and New Zealand.[49] Besides appearing before the inquiry Douglas had hopes of being appointed as a consulting engineer to the government, for the purpose of implementing Social Credit. To Collins he wrote:

> I regard it as essential, in view of the extreme subtlety both of the subject and the situation that someone, and preferably myself if it can be arranged, should be in a position to exercise a directive influence backed by formal authority.[50]

When Aberhart heard that Douglas was coming to Alberta, he had hopes he would be able to host Douglas's visit,[51] but that was an idle dream. Collins had already been corresponding with Douglas on this matter. On 15 February 1934 Premier Brownlee formally invited Douglas to appear before the Legislature. Douglas replied that he could appear in April and his fee would be $1,250.[52] Because the inquiry was to be held in March, and because Douglas requested payment for his services, it was decided to hold the inquiry without him. Brownlee then wired Kerslake, asking for names of persons who could properly present the Douglas System. Kerslake replied that Herbert Boyd, a lawyer at Edgerton, Alberta, and J. Larkham Collins could do the job.[53]

The activities of Collins were becoming a thorn in Aberhart's side. Sometime in February 1934, while in Vancouver, Collins had been interviewed by W.A. Tutte of the Vancouver *Sun* who was also an ardent Douglasite. In this published interview Collins revealed that the Secretariat had repudiated Aberhart's Yellow Pamphlet. When news of this repudiation reached Aberhart, he was furious and promptly announced that on Monday 26 February 1934 he would give his last lecture on Social Credit in Calgary.[54] At this meeting Aberhart followed the pattern that had worked so well in his religious sphere of activities: he resigned as president of the Douglas Social Credit League. He claimed he was doing so because of criticism from Kerslake and others, but he would not elaborate. He was going to step aside until things could be clarified by Major Douglas's visit. Yet he maintained that he had Douglas's support, and allowed his followers to think that his pamphlet had had Douglas's approval before going to press. A motion of censure was also sent to the Vancouver *Sun*, complaining of its reporting.[55]

Aberhart's resignation had a profound effect upon his audience. One of Aberhart's young followers is reported to have rushed madly to the stage of the Bible Institute and implored Aberhart to reconsider.[56] But Aberhart let his resignation stand.

In an interview published by the *Albertan*, Palmer, who continued to be vice-president of the Central Council of the Douglas Social Credit League at the Bible Institute, said he would continue to circulate Aberhart's pamphlet.[57] However, that same day Palmer, whose New Age Club had recently become affiliated with the Secretariat in London, enclosed a copy of the Yellow Pamphlet with a letter to Bardsley, secretary of the Secretariat. Palmer asked for clarification of Douglas's attitude toward Kerslake's Douglas Credit League and Aberhart's Social Credit League. (Douglas himself was in Australia when the Secretariat received Palmer's letter.) In his reply, Bardsley, a close associate of Douglas, commented on Aberhart's pamphlet:

> It is an expression of views of Mr. Aberhart which cannot by any stretch of imagination be described as Douglas Social Credit.... His views should not be put forth as being those of Major Douglas, or as being based on Major Douglas's writings.[58]

Bardsley sent a copy of his letter to Kerslake, who released it to the press – an action that further angered Aberhart. Losing none of his shrewdness in the heat of the moment, however, Aberhart chose to see a bitter personal enemy in Bardsley, whose name became poison to him. In public at least, Aberhart did not associate Douglas personally with this uncompromising rejection of his interpretation of Social Credit, though in private it no doubt cooled his enthusiasm for Douglas's visit.

Aberhart's position on the Central Council of the Douglas Social Credit League would normally have been taken by Palmer, but recent developments had prevented that. Aberhart wanted Palmer to sign a temperance pledge, but Palmer refused. Aberhart had been seeking the support of the Women's Christian Temperance Union,[59] and apparently he had promised that in return his movement would "take the pledge." Because of the Central Council's stand on alcohol Palmer was bypassed, and Gilbert McGregor, a proofreader for the *Albertan*, was made president.

Besides the temperance question, other factors were putting Palmer in disfavour with Aberhart. The affiliation of the New Age Club with the Secretariat was a point of contention. A spy working for Aberhart reportedly searched the files of the club, seeking details of correspondence between the club and the Secretariat.[60] After Bardsley's letter was released, Palmer found himself and the New Age Club promptly ejected from Aberhart's Social Credit League.

From that time on the New Age Club became predominantly a "Douglas" rather than an "Aberhart" organization, though its members adhered more closely than most Douglasites to the belief inculcated by Aberhart that the operation of Social Credit in a single province was possible.[61]

Palmer's position as vice-president of the Central Council was taken by Ernest C. Manning. Although on the surface it appeared that Aberhart had resigned from his position in the Social Credit movement, he was still very much in control. Gilbert McGregor was president of the Central Council, but the Council was under the control of the Calgary Prophetic Bible Institute. McGregor's speeches had to be cleared by Aberhart. Aberhart's "resignation" had been effective. He had been able to test his popularity and get rid of opposition within his movement, getting his wind while a figurehead leader, McGregor, took his place.

Contributions from the sixteen hundred Social Credit study groups flowed into the Bible Institute. Its financial records reveal that Aberhart's introduction of economics into his radio broadcasts had boosted the income of his organization considerably.[62]

The public hiatus in Social Credit leadership was short-lived. On 1 March 1934 the Alberta Legislature adopted W.R. Howson's motion that Aberhart be called to give evidence at the inquiry into Social Credit; but there was still a question of whether the government could afford to pay Douglas's fee.[63] Within a few days William Irvine asked the House of Commons to call both Aberhart and Douglas to present their ideas in Ottawa. Aberhart thanked Irvine for his efforts and hoped that he could count on Irvine's assistance in the establishment of Social Credit in the province of Alberta.[64] However, Aberhart did not realize that Irvine was not being honest with him, for Irvine had also written to W. Norman Smith of his plans to discredit Aberhart or force him to follow Douglas:

> You did not make any comment on the fact that I had moved to call Aberhart. I did so because I think that we have come to the point when we must either get him to adopt the full Douglas programme or else expose him as a fraud. Our opinion here was that to get him before a Committee at which Douglas also appeared would compel him to accept Douglas-ism or else to indicate that he was in disagreement.[65]

Aberhart's efforts over the past eighteen months had been very effective in bringing his version of Social Credit to the citizens of Alberta. Now it appeared that the provincial government was taking him seriously. As Aberhart looked forward to the hearing, his main concern seemed not the importance of the occasion but whether the reimbursement for appearing at the inquiry would be adequate to compensate for the wages he would forfeit for missing several days of work at Crescent Heights.[66]

CHAPTER TWELVE

■

ABERHART VERSUS DOUGLAS

I T IS NO *surprise,*
therefore, to hear from public platforms and from
private individuals, not an exposure of the fallacies
of Social Credit, but a partial admission of all its
claims and bemoaning that it is too bad the
B.N.A. Act will not allow it to be introduced
into any one of the provinces singly.

— The B.N.A. Act and Social Credit,

by William Aberhart, 1934

The government's inquiry into Social Credit brought Aberhart and Major Douglas into personal contact. As anticipated by the U.F.A. leadership, their ideologies and personalities clashed the very first time they met. But, rather than harming Aberhart's leadership in the Alberta Social Credit movement, Douglas's visit actually strengthened Aberhart's position.

The inquiry into Social Credit was set for 19-21 March 1934, several days before Douglas was to land at Vancouver. Other "experts" called were J. Larkham Collins, Herbert Boyd (the official delegate of Kerslake's Douglas Credit League of Canada), and Professor G.A. Elliott of the Department of Economics at the University of Alberta.

Aberhart was the only witness who believed that provincial implementation of Social Credit was possible. He had nothing more than a secondhand account of a letter from Douglas (and that, practically nullified by conflicting evidence) to assure him of the support of that supreme authority. Douglas was about a week's sailing away, and it had not yet been decided whether he would even be called to give evidence. Aberhart could not tell whether Douglas would cut the ground from under his feet. He knew Douglas had to choose between supporting him and supporting the representative of the Canadian group affiliated with his own Secretariat, Herbert Boyd, who shared Kerslake's view that provincial application of Social Credit would be unconstitutional – and, therefore, impossible. But Aberhart was prepared to argue for the introduction of Social Credit into the province all the same.

Aberhart's first appearance in the Legislative chamber in Edmonton, in which much of the last act of the drama of his life was to be played, was a strange one. He had two distinct audiences: impassive and sceptical M.L.A.s, and an applauding and admiring public gallery. Many of Aberhart's followers had borrowed suits of clothes and begged rides in their neighbours' cars in order to make the three-hundred-twenty-one kilometer trip to Edmonton to hear Aberhart defend his views.

Aberhart was the first witness called to give evidence. In his opening remarks he stressed the human needs he believed Social Credit would answer:

> I am fully conscious of the responsibility that falls upon me in making an appeal for the introduction of a system of credit to solve the present depression. There are several reasons for this. In the first place it is my first appearance in this house of parliament. Many of you, it is true, have made me feel very much at home. I hope I do not get the idea of wanting to come back.
>
> Then too, the question of social credit is not very well known. I therefore am very anxious to present it in such a concise manner that there may be some interest created in it. That is all I am hoping to accomplish. To be frank with you, I feel somewhat like a young man getting married for the first time. I want to go on with it but I hardly know where it will land me. I am equally aware of the responsibility that rests upon the members of this Government in passing judgment on this matter. If the task of the juryman gives him concern when one man's life or property hangs in the balance, what must be the case when the lives, the prosperity, and the happiness of 700,000 people await your judgment.
>
> We have travelled this province from north to south, across and back, east and west, meeting people and discovering the conditions prevailing. I can assure you that these conditions are not such as to make us proud.

Let us remember that our province is potentially a land of plenty. None of our citizens should be suffering from want or privation. The granaries are full and goods are piled high in the storehouses. We have an abundance of foodstuffs that are being wasted, or wantonly destroyed. Why then should many of our people be in dire need, in suffering from worry, from privation, and from hopelessness? Many of them have no purchasing power and they cannot get work to secure it. Thousands of the youth of our land are coming out of the high schools and universities with no hope of work of any kind....

I am satisfied that any person who is going to face the public, the voters of his constituency, will have to know something about Social Credit. I shall be glad if I can help you in any way. Social Credit is the world's new road to prosperity and contentment. We shall never solve our problems until we start down this intriguing pathway.[1]

As Aberhart continued his speech he sang the praises of Major Douglas, whom he had not yet met:

The very fact that Social Credit has become a subject of world-wide interest should impress us with its vital importance. The Social Credit concept is not the product of the imagination of some hare-brained economist, seeking notoriety. It bears the marks of strength, stability and scientific accuracy. It comes to us from a genius mind. I hope that before this investigation is over, we may have with us, the gentleman himself, Major C.H. Douglas, who will speak with much more authority on the subject that I can.

He added that if the government could not see its way clear to pay the Major's expenses of $1,250, he would put up the money himself, and charge admission to meetings that he would arrange for the Major.[2]

Throughout the inquiry Aberhart maintained that Douglas's autograph on the Yellow Pamphlet proved that he had Douglas's blessing on his ideas, and he continued to argue for provincial adoption of Social Credit.[3] To illustrate his plan for Alberta, Aberhart employed charts and several illustrations. He told how, in the early twenties, he had wanted to purchase a motion-picture projector for his school. He had sold stocks to the pupils and then charged admission to cartoon films. After a year he was able to pay back the stocks worth $375 – and to pay a dividend of the same amount. A second personal illustration, at his request, was not recorded in the evidence. It probably involved his revealing how he financed the building of the Calgary Prophetic Bible Institute.[4]

Following his speech Aberhart was subjected to rigorous questioning by members of the government who had already been primed by a critique of Aberhart's Yellow Pamphlet prepared for them by Collins.[5] Aberhart fielded the questions quite well.

The next witness was Herbert Boyd from Egerton, Alberta. This attorney, the official delegate of the rival Douglas Credit League of Canada, delivered a blistering indictment of the banking system. Although he indicated that the province itself could not institute Social Credit, Boyd suggested that the

Legislature should study the system thoroughly and then recommend it to the federal government.[6]

Boyd was followed by Collins, who came to the inquiry as a private citizen. Even though Collins had been involved in having the Committee turn the tables on Aberhart, he feared that the intent of the inquiry was to discredit Social Credit entirely.[7] In his short speech, and in the question period which followed, Collins outlined how Aberhart's proposals were departures from Major Douglas's expressed beliefs and noted that the London Secretariat had repudiated Aberhart's pamphlet. In speaking of Aberhart personally, he said:

> I would like to say this with regard to Mr. Aberhart, who has interested himself in this movement for a considerable time, and to him should belong the credit for popularizing the scheme throughout Alberta. He has worked hard, and I understand always without remuneration, and if he is misled in the details, no one has questioned his sincerity.[8]

The final witness to give testimony was Professor G.A. Elliott from the University of Alberta. He was the first witness openly to challenge the basic premises of Major Douglas: he denied that there was a deficiency of purchasing power and asserted there was rather a lack of production.[9]

On 21 March 1934, all of the witnesses were recalled for comments and questioning. Almost immediately Aberhart became involved in a heated, testy exchange with Professor Elliott over the interpretation of a paragraph that Aberhart had quoted from the *Official Hand Book of Canada*.[10] Next, Aberhart argued with Collins over what Douglas had said about who should receive Social Credit dividends.[11]

Herbert Boyd tried to calm the atmosphere by complimenting Aberhart on his work:

> I have expressed to Mr. Aberhart by letter so lately as last Saturday my appreciation of the work done in educating the people of this country and my admiration of the work done, and expressed to him the hope he will continue it.[12]

During the second round of questioning, Aberhart was subjected to more pointed interrogation. Premier Brownlee asked him:

> There is something I would be curious to have you do. Having studied this whole question more than anyone in this room, probably with the exception of Mr. Collins or Mr. Boyd, at any rate more than the rest of us, supposing we ask you today to become general manager of a social credit scheme in Alberta, and to put the scheme into effect, would you mind stating to the committee just what your steps would be one by one.[13]

In his response Aberhart declared his utmost faith in Major Douglas:

> The first step would be to ask permission to engage Major Douglas to come here and organize it, and he would do the work; that is, all I would have to do is I would sit by his side, listen to him and get all the information I could, get details of the work and ask you then to give me 60 men

to meet Major Douglas and have these men instructed so they could go through the province in districts and instruct others to carry on the work.[14]

But Brownlee was not satisfied with Aberhart's reply:

> That, of course, would be a very easy way.... Are we still to conclude, in spite of all that study, all that educational work, that there is only one man in the world [who] can go into any particular place and put it into effect?[15]

To this Aberhart answered, "I think if my expenses were paid I could go to Major Douglas or someone else and get the details."

The discussion then turned to the fact that Douglas's own Secretariat, presumably speaking for Douglas, had repudiated Aberhart's plan. Aberhart hoped that the matter would be clarified when Douglas appeared in Edmonton several weeks hence. By now the Committee had decided to ask Douglas to appear before them.[16]

The final questions put to Aberhart dealt with the nature of the state that Aberhart envisioned. Premier Brownlee pointed to the authoritarian overtones: "Then, that is the same as Soviet Russia. To work out your plan then we have to put the state in a position where it is controlling the individual initiative of the man?"

Aberhart responded rather lamely: "It would not so control the position of the individual as much as the banks should do it today. The state would be a better advisor."[17] After some further questioning of the other witnesses the Committee adjourned until it could hear from Major Douglas.

As Aberhart returned to Calgary he was unhappy with the way things had gone at the inquiry; he had taken a verbal beating but still did not know what position Douglas would take at the next meeting of the inquiry. No sooner had he returned home than he received criticism from another quarter. A parent of one of his pupils complained to the Calgary *Herald* that Aberhart's going to the inquiry was a neglect of his teaching responsibilites. Aberhart should have been preparing them for their Easter exams, and when he did return after the inquiry, he was too busy with other things to give them extra instruction.[18] Aberhart, however, had gone to the inquiry with the School Board's permission.[19]

Since Major Douglas had "predicted" the Depression, its advent had brought him some prestige; and the longer it dragged on, the greater his prestige grew. By 1934 a political party espousing the principles of Social Credit was being organized in Australia. Douglas had, as noted before this, gone on a lecture tour of that country, leaving his Secretariat to handle the day-to-day affairs of international Social Credit. Presumably the first knowledge Douglas had of Bardsley's controversial letter about Aberhart's pamphlet was the copy of it he received during his Australian tour. He never repudiated Bardsley's letter, however.

The Australian tour raised extravagant hopes in Douglas. As Bardsley described the experience, "It was a royal progress."[20] From his position on public platforms all across that continent Douglas observed what seemed to be a great mass movement towards Social Credit. Sydney appeared to be a "Social Credit" city. His visit aroused great curiosity and his appearances drew large crowds. Factories were temporarily shut down so as not to interfere with radio reception of his broadcast addresses. Social Credit in Australia, under the leadership of Captain Rushworth, was by no means the non-political movement Douglas had hoped for, but since the Australian government and press were hostile to Social Credit, Douglas conceded that for the Social Crediters to run their own candidates was their only possible recourse.[21]

On his return trip to Britain, Douglas visited the Social Crediters in New Zealand and then sailed for Canada. For some months he had been planning to inspect the situation in Alberta, even if he had no invitation to address the Legislature. On 23 March 1934 he reached Vancouver, where he addressed a dinner meeting at the Hotel Vancouver under the auspices of the Kiwanis Club Open Forum.

One of the first telephone calls Douglas received in Vancouver was from J. Larkham Collins, who wanted to confirm details for public meetings that he was planning for the Major in Alberta. Earlier Collins had written Douglas seeking to have him address a mass meeting arranged by the Group of the Open Mind and the Canadian Club. The gate receipts were (after expenses) to be divided between the Canadian Club and Douglas. By this means Collins hoped Douglas's expenses would be paid and his visit to the Legislature ensured.[22] (Aberhart had had the same idea.) Douglas accepted Collins' invitation, but was later disappointed to find that his sponsors did not include serious advocates of Social Credit. Shortly after that telephone call, Douglas received a call from Aberhart, who invited him to speak over the air from the Calgary Prophetic Bible Institute. Douglas, who had no love for fundamentalism, declined the offer and left Aberhart further distressed. For some time Aberhart had hoped to have Douglas as his guest; now "the opposition" was hosting him.

Before Douglas left Vancouver, he addressed other audiences in British Columbia, including one in the Empress Hotel in Victoria. He also held informal talks with various members of the British Columbia Legislature.[23]

As Douglas's appearance in Alberta drew near Aberhart's mood grew more despondent. On 28 March 1934 he wrote to a friend in California, confiding,

> I have been assiduously pressing for the Douglas System of Social Credit, and just recently I was called upon to give evidence before our provincial government on the same. I am convinced, however, that they will pass it up for the Dominion government and this will mean its death. It makes me somewhat excited when I think of the financier holding the people of this old world so tightly in his grip, but I guess we will just have to float down the tide with the rest. I am too old a man to be able to stand the political bickering that is used in these days. I think I will send you a copy of my pamphlet on the Douglas System, just for your amusement.[24]

However, Aberhart's spirits seem to have lifted quite quickly, for he was soon on the Social Credit lecture circuit again, and on Tuesday evening, 3 April, he addressed six hundred women at the Women's Institute at Drumheller.[25]

When Major and Mrs. Douglas, and Douglas's secretary, arrived in Edmonton on 5 April 1934, they were welcomed at the station by Collins, the press, and the curious. Douglas was the man of the hour, an object of awe and speculation. Over the heads of the crowd that gathered around them the Douglases may have caught sight of a tall and massively-built man, standing uncertainly apart from the crowd, and gazing gloomily in their direction. This glimpse of the man who had been mainly responsible for their being there momentarily vanished, however, as the greetings and introductions continued.

Aberhart, who felt that he had introduced Douglas to Alberta, considered that he should have been the first to be introduced to Douglas. He was hurt by the cordiality between Collins and Douglas. Collins did finally introduce him to Douglas, but stepped aside while the two men talked. After a few minutes, however, Douglas suddenly raised his voice and said, "I think it would be much better, Mr. Aberhart, if you let me do things in my own way!"[26] He then brushed by Aberhart and walked out of the station with Collins. Such was Aberhart's first meeting with the man whom he had built up as the economic saviour of the world.

Aberhart saw a man of middle height and solid build who walked with a pronounced limp (a legacy from a shooting accident). Douglas's strong and even features, and closely-clipped grey moustache, gave him a commanding appearance accentuated by the unmistakable bearing that graces the professional soldier. Douglas was then fifty-five years old. He had none of the volatile humanness of Aberhart. Instead, he showed detachment. Since each new acquaintance could as well prove his enemy as his friend, Douglas was guardedly polite. He did not immediately identify himself with this or that faction, giving the people the lead they eagerly watched for. His refusal to become at once embroiled in the local issues gave rise to suspicions of what later became a general opinion in Alberta – that he was a theorist, withdrawn from reality.

By seven o'clock on the morning of 6 April 1934 the crowds had already gathered on the steps of the Alberta Legislative Building. They soon filled the public gallery to hear Major Douglas when he appeared before the Agricultural Committee, which consisted of the full Legislative Assembly. Douglas's testimony was also broadcast by radio. Very few people in the history of public speaking in Alberta ever had such an eager and attentive audience. Like Aberhart and the others who had been called before the Agricultural Committee, Douglas first gave an address on Social Credit theories, then answered questions from the members of the Legislature.

Douglas stated that modern technology was able to fulfil its role only by producing sufficient goods and services to enable the citizens of the world to live free from want. Since these goods and services were not sufficiently available to the consumer, Douglas diagnosed the trouble as lying in the monetary system, whose function was to transfer goods and services from producer to consumer.[27] Since much of the world's commerce was carried on by means of credit, he reasoned that the power to issue or withhold credit was the power to control the commerce of the world. This power, he believed, was in the hands of a band of bankers and international financiers who wielded it ruthlessly and arbitrarily.[28]

This theory did not seem ridiculous to Albertans who, in the Depression, could look around them and verify that in good times the banks had allowed the farmer almost unlimited credit with which to build up his farm – and that now, when credit was more essential than ever, the banks were refusing credit because the farmer was unable to repay a loan. Meanwhile, the farmer was paying more in interest than his original loan, interest that was called, bitterly, "the crop that never fails." When the farmer proved unable to pay, banks and mortgage and loan companies were appropriating the farm. There seemed, therefore, to be validity in Douglas's assertion that the banks were making fortunes out of the misfortunes of the farmer. The fact that the banks, too, lost heavily during the Depression did not impress a majority of the people. Douglas scoffed at the complaint of the banker that he too was subject to economic laws, claiming that such "laws" were artificial and of the banker's own making.

Douglas claimed that the banks did not in the first place *have* the money that they loaned out, on which loans they collected interest. It was merely what Douglas called "fountain pen money," created by the entry of a figure in a borrower's bank passbook. He stated that it was necessary for a bank to have on hand in cash only about one-tenth of the loan, and that therefore the bank was collecting interest on money that never existed. Moreover, the banks' power to withhold this credit gave them, in Douglas's view, the power of economic life or death over the public.

Douglas objected strongly to banks having power to create credit. He claimed that "credit" was a national resource that belonged to the people and should not be developed by competitive private enterprise. He proposed that the issuing and withholding of credit should become a state monopoly. Once that transfer of power was effected, it would be possible, according to Douglas, to use certain mechanisms to facilitate the exchange of goods between producer and consumer.

Unfortunately, when Douglas was closely questioned by the committee on the methods by which to remedy the situation, he showed a determined unwillingness to speak specifically – a habit that earned him a reputation for evasiveness and led to much speculation and confusion. He constantly expressed a distaste for being expected to describe a specific plan for Social Credit, insisting that there were endless numbers of mechanisms. The choice and detailed workings of a suitable mechanism would present no problem, in his opinion, to a determined man who had access to all necessary information and technical assistance.

Aberhart must have waited with considerable curiosity, if not anxiety, to hear whether Douglas would support him in his contention that Social Credit could be introduced provincially, or whether Douglas would state that provincial introduction would be unconstitutional. On this question Douglas tried not to cut the ground from under Aberhart, but admitted that even though he could put a Social Credit program in effect in Alberta or Canada in three months, it would be declared illegal.[29]

Douglas pointed out that the problem that faced them was a political or military one; the financial powers would not give up their power unless forced to.[30] He seemed to be suggesting a revolution, but commented:

> I may say that in the realms of the abstract I have not the slightest objection to revolutions or anything of that sort, but I am perfectly convinced they are absolutely futile and impracticable under the present state of affairs.[31]

As it stood, Douglas said, the B.N.A. Act would have to be changed to allow his listeners to go ahead with their program of Social Credit.[32] During the afternoon session, however, Douglas did suggest that a revolution might be a possible vehicle for Social Credit, if the existing financial system led the world into another war.[33] In one of his books he had hinted that if another war did occur, the leaders of finance should be placed in front of a firing squad,[34] presumably leaving society free to establish Social Credit economics.

Douglas's economic thought was closely tied to his political thought, although both remained vague and elusive. He had a distrust of the ability of the masses to think; they could only feel. He held to an élitist concept of government, one controlled by experts.[35] His ideas smacked of fascism. He frequently denounced fascism, but it is interesting to note that a number of his students became active fascists: Sir Oswald Mosley, leader of the British Union of Fascists; Ezra Pound, who later did radio broadcasts for Mussolini; and David Warren Ryder, who was later convicted of being an agent for Japan.[36] Professor C.B. Macpherson interpreted Douglas as being essentially fascist by 1939, with all the elements of that movement to be found in his earliest writings.[37] Douglas himself claimed only to be a "Tory."[38]

The closest that Douglas came to offering any methodology for implementing Social Credit was his suggestion that the Legislature start imposing penalties upon the banks and finance companies.[39] When the Calgary *Herald* asked Aberhart what he thought of Major Douglas's address, he dryly remarked that it was "a very satisfactory outline of the general principles."[40]

The next item on Douglas's agenda was a meeting in the Mewata Armoury in Calgary. Here Douglas was in southern Alberta, the heart of Aberhart's kingdom, and his experience at the meeting was a revelation to him of Aberhart's strength.

Several days before Douglas's appearance, there was already a brisk demand for tickets being sold by the sponsors of the meeting, the Open Mind Club and the Canadian Club. J. Larkham Collins and his associates had not invited Aberhart to the meeting and when this became known, the railway workers at the C.P.R.'s Ogden Shops announced that if Aberhart were not allowed to speak, they would prevent the meeting. Aberhart himself had very little enthusiasm about attending, but after receiving a grudging invitation, he reluctantly agreed to go.

The Armoury was filled with backless benches and chairs on which eager

Calgarians sat through the first part of the evening. The building was not designed with acoustics in mind, and the public-address system was not completely successful. Determined not to miss a phrase that fell from the lips of this man whom Aberhart had built up to almost superhuman proportions, many moved closer and stood around the platform.

Douglas's address was little more than his peculiar view of international finance, but he did elaborate a little more on how power could be returned to the people:

> you must have control of the army, and the navy and air force. That is ultimately what it boils down to or this as an alternative: you must get into such a position that it is impossible for the army and the navy and the air force to be used against you. Now that is possible. The first alternative is possible under certain conditions, but the second alternative is possible if you can communicate freely with the rest of the world.[41]

He suggested the second alternative could be achieved by electing government representatives who would work against the financial interests. If the government were controlled by enough of these men, the desired changes could be made because they would have the backing of the military. Essentially, Douglas was advocating a military *coup* against the bankers. The backing of the military was essential to his program: [We must] "strengthen the hands of those agencies which may be effective in the restoration of popular control."[42]

During Douglas's speech Aberhart was seated on the platform, probably at Douglas's suggestion. Though the meeting was sponsored and organized by Aberhart's opponents, the audience was largely made up of Aberhart's followers. They learned little new from Douglas, and it seemed to them that *he* was the disciple and *Aberhart*, the master. They longed to see Aberhart receive public recognition from Douglas. They wanted Douglas to see Aberhart in action as they knew him. Instead, Aberhart was just another seated figure in a row of dispassionate sponsors, slumped a little more heavily in his chair, perhaps, than the others.

The fact that Aberhart was not going to be asked to speak suddenly struck the audience when, after the address of thanks to Douglas, an obvious move was made to terminate the meeting. This slight to their leader, combined with the physical and nervous strain that underlay the meeting, were suddenly too much for Aberhart's followers. One of them, near the front of the hall, began to shout, "Aberhart! What about Aberhart? We want Aberhart!"[43] He was joined by others. Some of the railway workers began to rush the stage waving their chairs over their heads. At a hasty nod to the band-leader from a committee-member, the strains of "God Save the King" filled the hall, thus averting a riot.

After the meeting in the officers' mess Douglas, Aberhart, Collins, Boyd, and others became embroiled in a fierce verbal battle that lasted more than one hour. Among other things Douglas demanded that Aberhart withdraw the Yellow Pamphlet, or at least remove Douglas's name from it.[44] Both men are said to have cursed each other.[45]

Aberhart looked dejected as he came out of the officers' mess. He said to Joe Unwin, one of his supporters, "Douglas told me I am all wrong."[46] As they left the building and were going down the steps, they heard someone behind them. It was Mrs. Douglas, who was trying to heal the break. "The Major and I," she said, "would like you to come and have dinner with us at noon tomorrow." Reluctantly Aberhart agreed. What happened the next day at lunch is a matter of speculation, for both parties subsequently gave different versions of their time together.

On Tuesday, 10 April 1934, Douglas appeared again before the Legislature to answer more questions. He was asked point-blank about Aberhart's Yellow Pamphlet:

Q. Is there in existence any Douglas plan for Alberta drawn up with your authority or approval?
A. The answer to that is "no."
Q. Have you seen this pamphlet, "The Douglas System of Economics." You have probably had it drawn to your attention, and are you familiar with its contents?
A. I have seen it. I am not familiar with its contents.
Q. Do you regard it as an interpretation of the Douglas scheme?
A. I, from my own knowledge, would find it impossible to answer that question.
Q. Do you know whether the London secretariat has considered that pamphlet?
A. I believe it has.
Q. Do you know what its official opinion was?
A. Yes, I do.
Q. Did they accept this as a correct interpretation of the Douglas system?
A. No, they did not.
Q. Are you the chairman of that body?
A. Yes. I was not present in England when it was examined. It was examined while I was abroad. I have the general results of the examination. I do not know the details.
Q. They have refused to accept it as an interpretation of your scheme?
A. Yes.[47]

When asked about his autograph on Aberhart's pamphlet Douglas replied:

This pamphlet was presented to me, or was shown to me by Mr. Monger [*sic*; Munger], and he said that he felt sure that Mr. Aberhart would be very gratified if I would sign it, and I did sign it, as I write my autograph in a great many places, even in hotel registers, not turning over the pages. I have some recollection of saying something like this: that I had no doubt that it served a very admirable purpose, under the circumstances for which it was designed. It was in no sense a criticism or otherwise of the book; I have no recollection of the contents whatever. In consequence of that, this booklet was submitted to the secretariat... and the verdict of the publication committee was that it was technically unsound. That is the position.[48]

After further examination of Douglas, the Agricultural Committee adjourned for private discussions.

From Edmonton Douglas departed for Ottawa, where he addressed the House of Common's Banking Committee, as he had done once before, in 1923.[49] While in Ottawa, he received a worried letter from Collins, who wanted to know where he stood, since Douglas had not taken a strong stand against Aberhart's ideas. Aberhart had been telling his radio audience that Douglas had personally told him at their lunch date that there were only two small errors in the Yellow Pamphlet, but that he, Douglas, did not know what they were.

"How was this possible?" asked Collins. "You remarked to me when talking to you on long distance telephone from Victoria that the pamphlet is absurd and that I agreed with you when you say that Aberhart is a demagogue." Collins stated that Aberhart was also claiming that when Aberhart offered to remove Douglas's name from the pamphlet, Douglas replied that it was not necessary since they were such insignificant errors. Collins added that Aberhart and his followers seemed more convinced than ever in their aim to secure provincial adoption of Social Credit, and planned to do it with the aid of "one hundred honest men," and that they were discounting Douglas's belief that military support was necessary. Collins also remarked that if Aberhart "could be controlled, his enthusiasm might be invaluable, but he has the unhappy knack of antagonizing almost everyone with whom he comes in contact."[50]

Douglas replied to Collins, stating that he had arranged that Aberhart should submit his pamphlet to the Secretariat for revision and reissue. Douglas further commented that Collins should "plough straight ahead entirely disregarding Aberhart. He will in the end do no harm."[51]

Upon leaving Ottawa Douglas travelled to Washington, D.C., for talks with American political leaders. He left North America convinced more than ever that the current economic system would create more disaster – and from his meetings with American financiers he felt that his belief in an international banking conspiracy was very much justified.[52]

Douglas's visit to Alberta had created more controversy and conflict than had existed before his visit. Some wondered what he had in fact said.[53] One of the major results of Douglas's visit to Alberta was a further alienation of Aberhart from those who considered themselves Simon-pure Douglasites. (This had been the intent of the U.F.A. government in having the inquiry in the first place.) The dichotomy between the two factions became so marked that Aberhart's organization soon changed its name to the Alberta Social Credit League. This change of name not only signified the Central Council's emphasis on the *provincial* application of Social Credit but also subtly declared that their brand of Social Credit was different from Douglas's.

The various Social Credit factions continued their debates. Almost immediately after Douglas's testimony, Charles Palmer's New Age Club discussed the question "Was Major Douglas Right?"[54] Their continued affiliation with the Secretariat indicated that they felt that he was. J. Larkham Collins also continued his opposition to Aberhart. On 23 April 1934 he addressed the Calgary Ministerial Association, reiterating that Social Credit would work only if adopted federally. Collins claimed in a letter to Premier Brownlee that his views were well received by a number of the ministers who were opposed to Aberhart.[55]

The amount of tension created by various Alberta Social Credit factions was disconcerting to Social Crediters in Eastern Canada. Charles A. Bowman, editor of the Ottawa *Citizen* and good friend of Major Douglas, visited Alberta at Douglas's request in May of 1934, hoping to unite the groups. When asked whether the Social Credit system could be operated provincially he declared that he did not know, but stated that factional fighting had to stop.[56] Bowman met with Aberhart for lunch at the Palliser Hotel. Aberhart informed him that he had no intention of going into politics; he desired to remain a school principal and religious leader, and insisted that he would refuse to be nominated as a political candidate. He told Bowman of his efforts to convince the existing political parties to take up Social Credit.[57] Bowman's visit seems to have done little to align the various Social Credit factions. Collins paid him little heed, for on 11 May 1934 he addressed a meeting of the Economic Reconstruction Association and openly denounced Aberhart's pamphlet.[58]

Some time after the Agricultural Committee had completed its inquiry into Social Credit, it published the transcript of the hearing, along with its conclusions. The report expressed the opinion that the evidence given before it "did not offer any practical plan for adoption [of Social Credit] in Alberta under the existing constitutional condition,"[59] and cited Douglas's evidence as supporting that view. Here, in a neat package, the government thought it had a complete kit for the disposal of Aberhart's plan for provincial introduction of Social Credit and, therefore, of Aberhart's Social Credit movement. Nor were any suggestions made for steps that should be taken towards altering "the existing constitutional condition."

Feeling that there was no hope for Social Credit under the U.F.A., Aberhart soon turned his attention to the Liberals. After receiving an encouraging letter from Dr. F.W. Gershaw, federal Member of Parliament for Medicine Hat, Aberhart suggested to him that if he would take over the leadership of the Alberta Social Credit League, he was sure that Gershaw could be made premier of Alberta.[60] Aberhart also sought support from Liberal M.L.A.s,[61] but they do not appear to have been interested.

To counter the influence of the Agricultural Committee's report Aberhart and his organization issued a series of pamphlets defending their own position. One was entitled *Social Credit: History and Character*. Another, *What Would Social Credit Do For Us?* A third was *The B.N.A. Act and Social Credit*. In these pamphlets Aberhart argued that provincial application of Social Credit was indeed possible, and to be preferred to federal implementation. He also maintained that the B.N.A. Act did not preclude the province from issuing non-negotiable certificates to facilitate the use of Social Credit.[62]

These pamphlets contained humorous illustrations and cartoons drawn by Ernest G. Hansell, Aberhart's former colleague at Westbourne Baptist Church. After breaking with Aberhart, Hansell had worked as a Baptist minister in Camrose and Calgary, but marital problems and a divorce had left him without a job.[63] He went to Aberhart for help, and Aberhart, remembering that Hansell had been a newspaper cartoonist before entering the ministry, put him to work.

Aberhart and his cause were also helped by the seduction suit against Premier Brownlee that had been dragging through the courts and press since

"No more wolves at the door"
The Solution of the Present Problem
"Purchasing power in the hands of the Consumer"

Pro-Social Credit cartoon by Ernest G. Hansell, from the pamphlet What Would Social Credit Do For Us? *(1934)*.

the previous fall. In July 1934, the jury found Brownlee guilty, although the judge differed with their verdict.[64] Brownlee maintained his innocence but felt obliged to resign as premier, thus ending his political career. The leader of the Conservative Party David Duggan believed that Brownlee was the victim of a vicious frame-up by the Liberals.[65] On 10 July 1934 Richard Gavin Reid, the provincial treasurer, succeeded Brownlee as premier of Alberta.

CHAPTER THIRTEEN

■

WHERE WILL ALL THE MONEY COME FROM?

S HALL I *say then that the financiers were actually able to create money by a book keeping entry? We propose today the same for the citizens of Alberta.*

— From an article by William Aberhart, published

in the *Albertan*, 9 November 1934

One of the questions Aberhart was asked most frequently as he continued his Social Credit lectures was "Where will all the money come from to pay for the dividends?" His answers did not satisfy some, including the Calgary *Herald*, which made much of the differences between the Aberhart and the Douglas brand of Social Credit. Because of the hostile coverage that Aberhart had been receiving in the press, some of his supporters with newspaper and business experience suggested that Aberhart's organization should have its own publication. Aberhart agreed and on 20 July 1934 the first issue of the *Alberta Social Credit Chronicle* appeared. It was a weekly newspaper issued from an office a few doors from the Bible Institute. The *Chronicle* was lively, unpolished, and not afraid of carping repetition when it would drive home the necessity of having Social Credit in Alberta. News items on Social Credit group activities, mentioning individuals, were a prominent feature. Aberhart was well aware that rewards like these public pats on the back were effective in encouraging even greater efforts from his workers. Many enterprising devices for spreading the Social Credit gospel received commendation in the pages of the *Chronicle*. Some study groups had, for example, built floats that publicized Social Credit in the Calgary Stampede parade.

The circulation manager of the *Chronicle*, and also one of its reporters, was Eva Reid, who had boarded with the Aberharts some years before.[1] At first the *Chronicle* was printed by the High River *Times*, but when its circulation increased, its printing contract was picked up by the *Albertan*, another Calgary daily, where Miss Reid also worked as a reporter.

An early issue of the *Chronicle* described a Social Credit picnic on St. George's Island in the Bow River, a picnic attended by three thousand people. The crowd enjoyed a day of games and outdoor recreation in cloudless 38°C weather. A firemen's band accompanied soloists who sang Social Credit songs, often based on hymns and hymn-tunes. In his address to the people at the picnic, Aberhart reported on the speaking tour he had just made throughout Alberta. He estimated that he had travelled over twenty-five hundred miles and delivered thirty-nine addresses to approximately thirty thousand people.[2]

The itinerary on these lecture tours was intensive, efficient, and neatly organized. Two meetings a day five days a week was the rule. Aberhart arranged to have his meetings at key points in order to draw his audiences from as large a surrounding area as possible. On Tuesdays and Fridays he contrived to be fairly close to Calgary so that he could return without waste of time for his Tuesday-evening broadcasts, and on Saturday he dealt with the correspondence and other business and prepared for the Sunday services. Three stenographers were working full time on Social Credit correspondence at the Institute, much of it prompted by the radio broadcasts.

Aberhart and Manning usually travelled together, Manning serving as Aberhart's chauffeur. Occasionally Jessie Aberhart accompanied them, although she never spoke at the meetings. Sometimes the men travelled separately, when there were requests for each to speak at a different location.

They saw Depression conditions everywhere they travelled. Hopelessness was breaking the spirit of the farmers. During the growing season of that year drought had kept the farmers in the southern part of the province scanning the horizon for clouds. Long overdue, but nevertheless a welcome sight, the clouds came. But they brought not rain but hail – enormous ice pellets that broke the brittle wheat and beat it to a useless pulp. The crops around Drumheller, Calgary, and Lethbridge were preserved from the elements – only to end up feeding hordes of grasshoppers that stripped the land bare of every green thing. On 23 August 1934 a severe frost snuffed out any remaining hope of a normal crop.

The trials of the farmers in the northern part of the province in 1934 were different, but no less disastrous. Their hope was allowed to stay alive until harvest time. Then it began to rain. Day after day. The crops were drenched. Harvesting time passed. Threshing time came and went. The rain turned to a snow that covered the crops. What little grain the farmers managed to salvage was tough and damp. The price of wheat had, ironically, risen to 61 cents per bushel.

Aberhart and Manning often had difficulty in finding a building large enough to accommodate the crowds that attended their meetings. The hall in a small town might seat three hundred, but a thousand might want to listen. For that reason Aberhart and Manning often held their meetings in skating rinks; and one beautiful summer afternoon, when it became obvious that no building in the town was large enough to accomodate everyone, a local lumberman asked, "Why not come down to my lumber yard?" Aberhart always took a portable public-address system with him, and it was used that day as he stood on a high pile of fragrant seasoning wood while the crowds sat about him on other lumber piles.

At these meetings Aberhart was, as usual, asked where all the money would come from. He usually put off the question by answering, "We will not be using money, but credit." Should someone persist in his questioning and ask, "Then where will all the credit come from?" Aberhart was not at a loss for a homely illustration. He told them that the amount of credit was not important, only its circulation. He illustrated this contention with an example of how ten cents could do $15 worth of business:

> In a town there lived two Irishman, Pat and Mike. Each owned a saloon and each had a barrel of beer worth $7.50. Both set the price of beer at ten cents per glass. With the Depression business came to a dead stop. On one hot afternoon, Mike, by chance, discovered a ten cent piece in his pocket, and went across the street to Pat's saloon and purchased a glass of beer. Pat, in turn, used the same ten cent piece to buy one from Mike. They continued to patronize each other until both barrels were dry. Thus they did $15.00 worth of business with a ten cent piece.[3]

Aberhart added that they could have done the same with I.O.U.s. Unfortunately, his example did not explain how the two now-empty barrels of beer could be replenished with the dime.

The widespread support that Aberhart was receiving from the farmers, who would believe almost anything in those days of economic and agricultural despair, caused great concern to J. Larkham Collins. In August 1934 he wrote to Douglas warning him of the situation:

> I need scarcely reiterate to you my opinion of [Aberhart's] so-called plan. It is the most childish thing I have heard of, and of course would not work in his own back yard let alone the province of Alberta. The perusal of his literature forces me to the conclusion that he chiefly is interested in self-aggrandisement or as the Secretariat put it, in the development of

his own ego. May I point out to you that it would be a major error for you or your movement to become identified, or to be placed in the position of, approving of his plan.[4]

Collin's letter to Douglas was also motivated by other factors. The U.F.A.'s hopes of silencing Aberhart at the inquiry into Social Credit had not been realized. There were convinced Douglasites within U.F.A. ranks, and hoping to humour them and defeat Aberhart, the government had now decided to ask Douglas to prepare a Social Credit plan for implementation in Alberta. Collins warned Douglas about getting involved in any provincial scheme, for he felt it would fail and bring disrepute upon any eventual federal implementation.

On 28 August 1934 Norman F. Priestly, vice-president of the U.F.A., wrote Douglas on behalf of the government, asking him to prepare a Social Credit plan for the province. Douglas responded that he would do it providing that he was hired at a salary of $1,500 per annum, plus $20 per day while he was in Canada, and double first-class expenses.[5] But when Douglas heard that Robert Gardiner, president of the U.F.A., had made critical remarks about his theories, he withdrew his intention of becoming Alberta's economic consultant until the U.F.A.'s attitude was clarified.[6] Priestly replied that Gardiner could be convinced if he could be shown the validity of Douglas's thesis. At the same time Priestly informed Douglas that the government could in no way afford his terms; all that they wanted from him was a plan to consider.[7] As a result the invitation was left in suspense.

Correspondence between various Douglasites in the U.F.A. reveals that the government's courting of Douglas was intended to defeat Aberhart whose support was 75 per cent in some ridings. In a letter to W. Norman Smith, William Irvine commented:

> In my opinion there is only one hope and that is to accept the Douglas proposals officially. Then get on the air every day that Aberhart is on the air, only follow him and answer his arguments and show him up as the faker he is. This radio programme should be kept going up to the provincial election.[8]

Smith desired that Irvine should lead the campaign to discredit Aberhart before the public and Major Douglas:

> it is imperative that Doulgas should be set right. If he thinks Aberhart is going to help his cause by his demagogic humbug, he is very much mistaken. Unless a clear distinction is drawn between Aberhart and Douglas and Aberhart is definitely repudiated, the public, when the Aberhart balloon is pricked, will be in danger of having their minds closed to the whole idea of Social Credit. Having discovered that Aberhartism is quack medicine they will come to the conclusion that Social Credit is itself unworthy of notice.[9]

With opposition building up against him, Aberhart devised new methods to spread his message. One evening in October 1934, for example, he announced on the radio that Calgary would shortly be visited by a stranger from another planet.

A man from Mars, said Aberhart, was coming to Earth to study our civilization so that he might take back to his own people ideas that would enable them to live in a happier and more orderly fashion. (Aberhart had borrowed his idea from Maurice Colbourne, who had in turn used a dramatic vehicle created by George Bernard Shaw.[10]) Aberhart, who with two or three followers had begun a series of half-hour weekly broadcasts on Social Credit in addition to his Sunday broadcasts, said he had been fortunate to persuade the Man from Mars to appear on his program and report regularly on the progress of his mission. This dramatic innovation immediately captured the imagination of Albertans, and few could resist tuning in on the following Tuesday evening to find out how the trick was to be managed. They were not disappointed.

Aberhart had consulted with some of his Social Credit followers about the broadcasts, and he told them that he would hold a series of auditions for the part of the interplanetary visitor. Various disguised voices and assumed voices were assiduously practised, but the performer who best captured the required blend of celestial innocence and down-to-earth practicality was Clifford M. Willmott, a railway conductor. Willmott, already an active worker for Social Credit, combined a cultured English voice with a slow, indefinably East Indian accent and threw himself into the part with enthusiasm and a vigorous sense of theatre that delighted Aberhart.

When the newspapers were reporting that the U.F.A. had decided to postpone the provincial election until June 1935, in the hope that the issue of Social Credit would subside, Aberhart grasped the opportunity afforded him by the delay. The satirical "Man from Mars" series was on the air throughout the winter and helped to whip higher the tidal wave of Social Credit that the U.F.A. hoped was already past its crest. The series of radio skits was one of the last Canadian political broadcasts to be conducted on a "no holds barred" basis. (Later, federal legislation was passed to prohibit dramatized political broadcasts.)

The state of Aberhart's own understanding of Social Credit may be gathered from the scripts for this series, for which he had final approval. Permanent members of the cast were Aberhart, Willmott, Manning, and Charles Underhill, the Bible Institute caretaker, whose rich Northamptonshire accent, sense of comedy, and talent for animal imitations made him an asset.

The radio plays, performed before a live audience, began in the form of an inquiry into the causes of the sufferings of Albertans. There was a classroom atmosphere as Aberhart instructed other members of the cast, now and then asking questions of them and joining in discussions. Those to whom it may seem incredible that Aberhart should attempt to win the people of Alberta to a new political allegiance by means of blackboard and chalk should remember that he could teach almost anything to almost anybody, whether they were willing students or not. He had taught Presbyterians to become Methodists, Methodists to become Baptists, and Baptists to accept his own brand of Pentecostalism. An examination of his "Man from Mars" broadcasts helps us to understand the irresistible nature of his indoctrination methods.

As the "Man from Mars" wandered up and down Alberta, he came to the reluctant conclusion that, in the words of George Bernard Shaw, "this earth is the mental asylum of other planets." The transcripts of these radio plays are now lost, but in preserved extracts we find the earnest Martian speaking to a "banker":

> I am very anxious to understand. You see, my perplexity is this: I find that you are very rich in goods. In fact you have so much that you wantonly destroy your abundance. I am told that it is necessary to keep up prices. But at the same time I find that many of your people are suffering from poverty and starvation. Even little children cry for the food and clothing that your governments order destroyed. But their parents cannot buy the goods because they have no money. To get money they must work, but they cannot get work because you have invented wonderful machines to make your goods, so your people must starve in the midst of plenty. You are the manager of a bank – ah, yes! a bank – I understand that a bank is a financial institution empowered by the government to issue and control money. Therefore I ask you, sir, is there no way in which you can supply these people with money even though they cannot get work?

The following extracts from the lines spoken by the "banker" were hardly calculated to bolster the listening public's confidence in their monetary system:

> I would like to know how the people would get on without our credit. It is time the public realized that it is dependent wholly upon us for its power to live....

and again:

> I am sorry that you have been influenced by the conditions of the idle loafers who are a blight to society. It's time we had another war and got rid of them.[11]

In another installment of the series, "Professor Orthodox Anonymous," a caricature of Professor G.A. Elliott of the University of Alberta, who had given testimony at the government's inquiry into Social Credit, reflected on an impending visit from the "Man from Mars":

> Ah, well, we expect economists are getting used to interviews. The common people seem so dense these days. Always blaming their troubles onto some imaginary defect in our tried and proven economic system. They make me tired. If it wasn't for the politicians distracting their attention by throwing dust in their eyes, they'd drive us crazy.[12]

"Jerry Bluffem," leader of the "It's-Our-Turn-Next" (or Liberal) Party, gave the Martian a lesson in politics:

I am afraid that you are wasting your time worrying about the future. Remember, after we are once in power, we will have the perfect right to cancel our whole program if we so desire. I am afraid that you would never make a good politician. You do not seem to realize that the public will vote for that which they think they want whether the ultimate outcome is going to be to their advantage or not. Our policy therefore is to promise the people what they think they want, and remember once more, when it comes to an election, every vote counts....[13]

Aberhart, with vast experience in church politics, knew people. He concentrated on the majority of the voters – the unfortunate farmers who, though by now almost without hope, could nevertheless be coaxed to a grim smile by a reference to the drollness of their situation. The following is a typical passage in which Charles Underhill, in the character of "Mr. Kant B. Dunn," with a few lines of unsophisticated humour and animal imitations, brought the broadcast right into the farm kitchen. Aberhart opened the dialogue:

A: What have you in the crate?
KBD: Oh, a few chickens, a couple of turkeys, and a dandy big gobbler. Do you want to get one?
A: No, I think not.
KBD: [imitates a chicken or gobbler]
A: But look, Mr. Dunn, I'm sorry but you can't have those birds in the studio. You had better put them outside.
KBD: All right, sir. [imitates a dog yelping after being stepped on]. Get out Fido!
A: Glad you came in again, Mr. Dunn. I wanted to see you.
KBD: Well, I'll tell yer, it took 4 dozen eggs, 2 turkeys and 4 chickens to pay for my trip to town today. If this present system keeps up we'll not be able to raise enough things to get away from the farm. No, sir, I'm telling you something has to be done....[14]

Aberhart linked each family to its neighbours by pointing up the fact that they were not alone in their suffering, that "poverty in the midst of plenty" was as universal as it was illogical. Thus, he began to consolidate public opinion by uniting through their common experience all those who were suffering privation – and there were few in the province outside the bound of that circle. Having voiced the already general feeling that something must be done, and quickly, Aberhart proceeded to show that orthodox political-economic methods were inadequate to the current desperate situation. In an effort to show the various parties' proposals for dealing with the Depression, Aberhart staged a mock conference of all the parties. Even the lighter moments of the skit were carefully prepared. Consider the effect of the following opening sentence on the farmer whose children had to take turns in going to school because there was only one pair of shoes among them:

Now, fellows, go and get your dress suits on, your gold headed canes, and your plug hats. The conference is called to meet in the town of "Never Get Anywhere" at the Hotel "Have a Good Time" beautifully situated on the shore of the Lake "Tantalization." Bert, you are to be the leader of the "Hold them to it party." Dave, you are to be the representative for Revolutionville. Charles, you take the leadership of the "It's-our-turn-next party." You are the "Hon. Jerry Bluffem." Ed, you are "Mr. Fedor" from "Ization district." Now, hurry down to the convention hall and get into your places. I am going to put my hand on the switch of imagination and transfer controls to the convocation hall of the Hotel "Have a Good Time."[15]

In the same vigorous, satirical style, the debate that followed knocked down rival political arguments one by one. From the skit emerged some of Aberhart's opinions. One was that full employment was not desirable. Like Douglas, Aberhart believed that this method of providing people with purchasing power was now out of date: there was already an excessive supply of products. It would be unwise to set people to work constructing public works because they would only temporarily relieve the unemployed, and the results would raise public debt and interest charges thereon. To meet these increased debt charges, taxation would have to be stepped up, and the result would be a further reduction of purchasing power. Unemployment insurance, Aberhart explained, would not put more purchasing power in the hands of the people, either, for its cost would also have to be met with increased taxation.

By the fall of 1934 Aberhart seems to have dropped mention of Douglas's famous A + B Theorem, because he judged the pedantry of the formula a hindrance in "selling" Social Credit. Aberhart knew the farmers had an instinctive mistrust of complicated-sounding theories emanating from institutions of higher learning. He knew, too, that as principal of a Calgary highschool and possessor of a frequently-flourished B.A. degree, he was closely associated with higher education in the minds of many. Aberhart therefore emphasized instead one of the more attractive of Douglas's terms, "the Just Price," a phrase that had an honest ring and offended neither producer nor consumer (the Alberta farmer being both). Few politicians would be audacious enough to attack it openly. The A + B Theorem was nevertheless still a part of Aberhart's conception of Social Credit, though his explanations of it often conflicted and he frequently glossed over, or was vague about, crucial points.[16]

Aberhart's idea of "the just price" was expressed in the following equation:

——— Just Price ———				
A +	**B** +	**C**	=	**Selling Price**
wage cost	non-wage cost of	unearned		
of production	production	increment		
	+ legitimate	i.e. excessive		
	profit	profit		
$2 +	**$3** +	**$1**	=	**$6**

Aberhart used this formula to illustrate the cost of a pair of shoes. A manufacturer, for example, had wage costs of $2 in the manufacture of the shoes. He had other costs, too, like depreciation of machinery, insurance, freight, raw materials – and he had to make a legitimate profit. The total of those was $3. The manufacturer was fortunate to have been able to make an extra profit of $1 on the pair of shoes, and therefore he sold the shoes for $6.[17]

According to Aberhart's theory of Social Credit, a State Credit House was required. Its function would be twofold: first, to issue credit to producers and distributors at no interest; and second, to issue credit (called basic monthly dividends) to each qualifying citizen to provide them with the bare necessities of life. (Aberhart's audiences understood that this dividend would be $25 per month per adult citizen).

The State Credit House would issue the dividend by crediting the citizen's account with an amount upon which he could draw by writing cheques. When the receiver of such a cheque "cashed" it, his account at the State Credit House would be credited with the amount of the cheque, and the person who gave it to him would have his account debited by that amount. When the citizens began buying things with their Basic Dividends, the producers and distributors would be able to pay back their credit loans from the State Credit House.

As is evident by now, Albertans were not shy about asking Aberhart the question with which Douglas had so often been plagued "Where would the money come from?" Here Douglas and Aberhart said their last farewells. Douglas would not have approved of Aberhart's answer, which was: "from an unearned increment levy." That is, the government would tax away the $1.00 excessive profit shown in the above equation. Such a tax would supply funds for the monthly dividends. This, in essence, was the theory of Social Credit as Aberhart understood it, at least until August 1935.

Major Douglas's answer to the same question was quite different. On rare occasions, under unusually insistent questioning, Douglas was persuaded to give an example of how the gap between production and consumption could be bridged. The following example is taken from Douglas's evidence before the Canadian House of Common's Select Standing Committee on Banking and Commerce in 1923 and illustrates the furthest extremity to which Douglas allowed himself to be pushed on that question. Douglas suggested the case of a person buying a car for $2,000. On that person's presenting his receipt for that amount to his bank, the bank would credit his account with a specified percentage of the amount, say $500. The bank would turn the receipt over to a government department, such as the Treasury, which would credit the bank with the amount which it had credited the consumer.[18] In other words, Douglas proposed a scheme of mass subsidies at the retail level, and a government deficit. Douglas was emphatic in his denial that it would ever be necessary to recover the subsidy or rebate from the public by means of taxation. To the objection that such a constant increase in purchasing power would result in inflation, Douglas explained that if prices rose, the subsidy would become inoperative. He believed that some such flexible system of rebates, which would be based on the fluctuations of supply and demand, would be one of the many possible methods of maintaining a healthy balance between the boom-and-slump cycles that the current system appeared to follow.

By way of contrast, Aberhart believed that once stagnant credit was set in motion by the issuance of the first dividends, the velocity of monetary circulation would be increased, and prosperity would be brought about by the use of the same credit over and over again. "The poor fellow," Aberhart said of one man who asked him where all the money would come from,

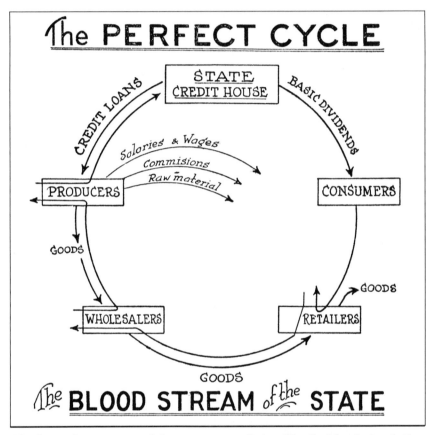

Aberhart often portrayed the economy as being like the blood-circulation system. This illustration is from his "Study Group Feature #5" (1933).

"knows nothing of the flow of credit. That is his trouble. You might as well ask where all the blood will come from to keep you on your feet for the next twenty-five years!" That was Aberhart's concept of the "Blood Stream of the State,"[19] which had been influenced by the velocity-of-circulation ideas of Silvio Gesell (1862-1930), another economic heretic who, as part of a six-day *coup* in Munich in 1919, had tried to introduce a new economic system of money that constantly depreciated. In order to keep money at par one had to affix stamps to it weekly. To avoid this tax (and it *was* a tax), people were encouraged to spend their money, thus stimulating business.[20] (Aberhart's later "funny money" was borrowed from Gesell's system.)

When Aberhart dealt with the Just Price, his definitions were not always precise. It is clear from his use of the equation for the sale of shoes that the Just Price would be equal to, or less than, the current selling price. But, when dealing with the farmers as producers, he sang a different tune. Since the price of wheat received by Alberta's farmers was considered too low by those who produced it, he gave them the impression that the Just Price could also be higher than the current selling price: "We can't wait for ten or fifteen years for a Just Price for our products and every farmer knows it."[21]

Aberhart's startling suggestion that, under Social Credit, every citizen would receive $25 worth of credit every month was the most sensational item among his collection of Social Credit proposals, and the news of the dividend became known wherever Aberhart's name was heard. The fact that it was, as he emphasized, not to be paid in cash but in "credit" detracted little from its appeal since it would presumably still purchase $25 worth of goods. To destitute Albertans the prospect of the dividend was a happy one indeed, and many observers considered it the main factor in making converts to Social Credit. Economist and humorist Stephen Leacock, for example, wrote of the Alberta farmer, "He read as far as where it said 'twenty-five dollars.' That was enough."[22]

Aberhart was pleased that the people seemed to like this idea. He assured his listeners that this was not the limit. "There is no reason," he said, "why it should stop at $25. It could be $50 or $75 in time." Though he often protected himself by the statement that the $25 was only for illustrative purposes, the $25 a month was mentioned so constantly throughout the "Man from Mars" broadcasts and elsewhere that it would have been impossible for any regular listener not to have gained the impression that Aberhart was promising him $25 a month if Social Credit should come to power.[23]

Aberhart's current concern was whether or not he should enter politics. He solved the question in his accustomed way; he left his audience confused. On 13 November 1934 he said in his "Man from Mars" broadcast:

> These broadcasts are conducted merely as an educational feature, to help the citizens of the West and more particularly of Alberta, to do a little serious thinking regarding the solution of the present unsatisfactory state of affairs in our land. In no sense of the word do we wish to make it a political broadcast.[24]

But by December he was toying with entering the political arena, although not as a "politician." He denied his political ambitions, just as he had denied religious sectarianism as he built his own religious sect:

> The Alberta Social Credit League is the organization behind this broadcast. It is against party politics and holds no party affiliation. Its aim is to introduce the System into the province of Alberta. The League therefore intends to have a candidate in every constituency, or as many as possible.[25]

At this stage Aberhart's clarion call for "One Hundred Honest Men" to become candidates to represent Social Credit in the next election was little more than a noisy threat to the U.F.A. who, Aberhart still hoped, would be shaken into activity by his persistence. But, to listeners of the "Man from Mars" series, Aberhart meant business:

> This is the first broadcast of the Alberta Social Credit League over Canadian Station C.F.C.N., Voice of the Prairies. On behalf of the cause which we represent we greet you. It is our purpose and aim to end poverty and distress in Alberta.[26]

Most people loved Aberhart for his boldness at a time when discouragement and timidity held back their leaders. When he scolded and ridiculed his own audience, referring to the public as "the simple-minded voters," they loved him as a man who was not afraid to give guidance and take responsibility when others confessed the problem too great for them. Borrowing initially from Upton Sinclair, the American novelist and social reformer, Aberhart said:

> If people wish to suffer still more under the present impossible financial system, it is still their God-given right to do so, and a vote for the old line parties will give them this privilege.
> Foolish, deluded, partisan people may still sell their birthright or claim to a living, to those who will enslave them in a bondage from which they will not be able to escape. What greater bondage could there be than to see people starve or suffer unnecessary privation in the midst of abundant plenty?
> Surely every citizen of Alberta should have enough common, ordinary horse-sense to know that there is no need to starve in a full hay paddock. Even a worm will not go hungry because the apple is too large. He invariably goes to the core of the matter and there raises his standard of living. We can if we will.[27]

Here in Aberhart was the only man in Alberta who professed to know the way out and had the courage of his convictions. The urge to get up and follow was irresistible to many. Even the members of his radio cast were overwhelmed by his personality. Aberhart had taught them how to speak in public and how to use the microphone. The result was remarked upon in a letter he read during a November 1934 broadcast when, with tongue in cheek, he admonished his cast:

> Now, you helpers, listen to me. You must speak more natural after this. Don't use my tone of voice. Spruce up. Be yourselves. Here is a radio fan who declares that I'm taking all these parts myself. He says I'm like Amos and Andy.[28]

There is little that Aberhart did not know about mass psychology. Here we hear him at work financing his broadcasts:

I am a mighty proud man tonight to have behind this broadcast one section of the Ogden Shops, who are sponsoring this broadcast. We believe that these men are hard working, clear thinking fellows. You can't put much over them. The very fact that they are standing behind Social Credit to such an extent as to finance by themselves one whole broadcast, should impress our radio audience that Social Credit is no pipe dream as some of our party politicians would have you believe....

Some members of the CPR's Ogden Shops' Social Credit study group, 1935. There were sixteen hundred such groups scattered across Alberta.

We want Ogden Shops Section #1 to be recognized by all Social Crediters as an up-to-date bunch of real live wire boosters. We want to put over thirty more weekly broadcasts. How about your district taking over one? It would please us very much to have a bunch of business men take one or two. Ten butchers or ten grocers could band together and boost Social Credit. Listen, you business men, if you could realize how Social Credit will help your business, you would get behind it in a co-operative way. You cannot expect a few of us to do all of this by ourselves. Remember then, this is the Ogden Shops Section #1 broadcast. Say, Dave, I want you to announce this every few minutes so our radio folks will not forget the splendid support of the boys at the Ogden Shops Section #1.[29]

Financially the broadcasts supported themselves. Aberhart had made no direct appeal for funds during the first "Man from Mars" broadcast, but within a week, he had received $38.20, approximately the cost of the air time. In the fourth week he got over $50, and in the ninth, approximately $140. During the week between Christmas 1934 and New Year's Day 1935 he received over $50, a remarkable sum for the post-Christmas period of that Depression-racked year.

Besides worthwhile work and long-term goals Aberhart offered his followers the temporary comfort of companionship and the exhilaration of working for a cause that already brought them echoes of happier days past and a glow of hope for the future. He acknowledged this on the broadcast of 18 December 1934, which was sponsored by the St. George's East Calgary Social Credit Group:

> One feature of their persistent endeavors is the pleasant manner in which they go about their work. They look upon Social Credit as a happy solution. It is not a bitter pill to swallow. Thus their progress each week contains a happy, humorous strain as well as a business-like discussion of the issues.
>
> Mr. Hall, one of their members, is with us tonight, and at this time he will give us a brief medley of songs.... You see what happy times this St. George's East Calgary Group have. Some who have never attended yet should go and see for themselves.[30]

Aberhart's broadcast recalled old-fashioned barn-raising socials, the atmosphere of neighbours working together and entertaining each other. His broadcast entered many a lonely farmhouse shivering in the bitter prairie wind, on an evening to which even the Christmas season seemed to bring no cheer. The families, having suffered two crop failures, now watched their cattle – their only remaining wealth – sold one by one and at a loss, because they had no feed for them, and because it was the only way they could keep a little food on the table and a few clothes on their backs until the distant spring. Through such homes rang Aberhart's voice, encouraging, scolding, telling them how to get out and help themselves, and telling them to do it with song and social gatherings.

Bible Bill was reaching out a hand to them, and not only through radio. Through winter 1934-35 many a snow-bound family saw through the frosted window a solitary visitor approaching on horseback. When the stranger reached the farmhouse and the welcome subsided, the rider produced from his saddle bag some sheets of paper on which were printed three questions:

"Have you a vote in the next provincial election?"

"Do you desire to have Social Credit introduced into Alberta?"

"Will you vote "1" for a 100% Social Credit candidate?"

[The last question referred to the preferential voting system used in Alberta, in which the voter could name his preference in order of choice.]

This was the famous Straw Vote, for which close to two hundred thousand questionaires were distributed that winter by voluntary workers. "If you do not wish Social Credit," said Aberhart, in a radio ultimatum, "say so now."[31]

In the Bible Institute Clifford Willmott was custodian of a large map of Alberta that hung in a small back room. As the Straw Votes came in he pinned flags on the map. On each flag was written the number of "yes" votes received from that particular area. On the Tuesday-night broadcasts Aberhart called on Willmott, in the character of the "Man from Mars," to read the latest results of the Straw Vote. Social Credit workers, arriving at the Institute for their evening meetings, or picking up new supplies of Social Credit pamphlets, looked in at the back room to see how their idea was spreading, and in which districts support could be expected for a Social Credit candidate in the next election.

On Christmas Day 1934 the exasperated "Man from Mars" cried, "I want to find out why it is unconstitutional to provide for the women and children of your province."[32] Drama and melodrama both rang true to the people who listened to Aberhart, for their lives were overshadowed by the threat of the creditor. Aberhart voiced their bitterness in his broadcasts:

> I wonder if the people out in Radioland are applauding as we picture the rosy scene of the good times coming. Look out your window at those broad fields upon which you have slaved for years and consider what you have to show for it. Oh, I forget, your windows are all frosted up and it is dark outside. The snow is piled high. It is bitterly cold. The cry of hungry children can be heard on every side. The distress of women and men can be seen in the midst of plenty. But we can't do anything. The people must starve. We dare not even attempt to remedy the abominable prices. A Just Price? They wouldn't allow it.[33]

By this stage Aberhart had come to the realization that a political career probably lay ahead of him. In his Christmas letter to his niece in Seaforth he wrote, "You may some day hear of me being Premier of Alberta. I am not anxious to go into politics but the people are urging me to do so."[34]

On New Year's Day 1935, Aberhart saw the new year enter a despairing world without some message of hope. Soberly he said:

> You know, I feel there is little use in wishing you a happy and prosperous New year. The words falter in their formation. It all seems a mockery as long as this outgrown, out-of-date Financial System continues. If I had the returns of our Straw Vote, we could know at once whether the year was going to be a happy and prosperous one or not.... How would it be if we postponed our New Years greetings until the first of February, after we have time to get the Straw Vote taken?... Bear in mind that this is in reality a plebiscite. It is the most important thing that we have asked you to do. Upon the result of the Ballot, the question of Social Credit will stand or fall in your neighbourhood. Do not wait for the canvassers to come to you. You go to them, mark your ballot, and have them send it in to us. If there are not sufficient ballots returned to us from any constituency, you will not have another opportunity to vote for Social Credit. We shall not have a candidate in your field. So it is now or never.[35]

On Monday evening, 14 January 1935, sixteen hundred people packed the auditorium of the Calgary Prophetic Bible Institute. Many of them were delegates to the annual U.F.A. Convention. Throughout the day, by car, bus, and train, they had poured into Calgary, all making their way to Central United Church, the largest church in the city, where the convention was being held. Because Social Credit was going to be a point of discussion at the convention, Aberhart had organized this reception for them, hoping to get another chance at convincing them of the merits of adopting Social Credit for the province.

Special speakers, special music, and drama were offered to the delegates. The *Alberta Social Credit Chronicle* reported:

> The "Man from Mars" appeared and his "perplexities" were still very uppermost in his mind as he could not understand why there were people not receiving enough food or nourishment in a land where food and clothing was being destroyed. Some people he said were driving around in big cars, well fed and prosperous looking, while others were forced to walk and did not have even the necessities of life. Mr. Aberhart informed this disciple from the far away planet that he would hear a lot about Social Credit if he could stay during the meeting and that it was the only solution that was being offered showing the way out of the present financial chaos and an answer to the present day question of "Poverty Amidst Plenty." The Mars messenger accepted the invitation and took his seat on the platform, although many ladies present cast rather suspicious eyes at the strange white bearded old gentleman from the neighbouring planet, with his bare feet and ancient garments, as he sat among them.
>
> Mr. Kant B. Dunn also managed to leave his farm for a while to make his appearance at this meeting, although he was forced to leave his turkeys and chickens together with his "Yeller" dog outside the hall, much to his disappointment. Mr. Dunn explained to the big audience how he became an advocate of Social Credit and the great amount of good it would do to all farmers in Alberta if they would only give it a trial and vote for it in the next provincial election.[36]

Noticeably absent was another member of the cast, Mr. C.C. Heifer, who usually tried to turn the discussion to the merits of socialism and whose comical presence would have been a slap in the face to many of the U.F.A. delegates who desired some form of socialism. The highlight for many that evening was Aberhart's address to the delegates.

As the Convention opened on 15 January 1935, Premier Reid pointed out in his speech some of the problems of government when revenue shrinks and expenditure grows. Security of tenure, he explained, was the object of his government, with the welfare of the people taking precedence over all. After defending his government's record he denied the wide-spread rumour that the existing split in the party would "blow the U.F.A. organization to the four corners of the wind." He emphasized that the government was willing to support anything practical and equitable, protesting that the U.F.A. had always been "the spearhead of sane reform."

During the Convention, the U.F.A. had to deal with many resolutions. Near the top of the list was Resolution 190, and as soon as the delegates of the United Farm Women (U.F.W.A.) had joined the main convention, the discussion on it began. After a preamble stating that the current financial system had failed to meet the requirements of modern civilization, Resolution 190 was worded as follows:

Resolved that a system of social credit as outlined by William Aberhart, Calgary, be put in as a plank in the U.F.A. Provincial platform to be brought before the electorate at the next provincial election.

The debate on the resolution began calmly enough. It was recalled that, on the occasion in 1934 when Aberhart had spoken before the Legislature, not one of the sixty-three members of the Legislature had gone on record as considering his plan feasible. Some delegates considered that the subject had been adequately dealt with then. Others, however, who could not ignore the gigantic shadow of Aberhart that rose before them wherever they turned their uneasy eyes, wanted a compromise that would save the U.F.A. from defeat in the coming election. Still others wanted monetary reform and believed that it could be achieved through Social Credit. The pace of the arguments quickened, and E.J. Garland, acting as chairman, was soon the busiest man in the auditorium. Immediately one speaker sat down, three others were on their feet. There were amendments, amendments to amendments, and substitute motions, and the debaters many times wandered off to other subjects, while the harrassed chairman endeavoured to keep them to the field of discussion.

The representative of one local brought a warning that was, as far as the future of the U.F.A. party was concerned, one of the most prophetic statements made throughout the whole convention. Those whom he represented wanted Social Credit, he said, and wanted it through the U.F.A.; if the U.F.A. did not give them Social Credit, they would be unable to support the U.F.A. in the provincial election. Every shade of opinion was represented as twenty speakers, one after another, voiced their opinions on Resolution 190.

At that point, Norman Priestly, vice-president of the U.F.A., remarked, with perhaps pardonable exasperation, that three hours of debate had failed to bring out what the scheme mentioned in the resolution actually was. He suggested that experts in various fields should be asked to make a survey of the situation from an unbiased, non-political standpoint, and that the convention consider their findings "with passion out and reason uppermost." That attempt to bring the convention to some agreement, however remote it might be from a decision, was followed by yet another series of motions, amendments, and a substitute motion. The meeting finally decided to invite Aberhart to appear before the Convention and explain his plan in person.

On Wednesday morning four hundred delegates and a thousand visitors crowded Central United Church to hear Aberhart speak. He had brought along his charts, one of which illustrated the "Blood Stream of the State." He hung them up on the pipes of the organ and began a ninety-minute explanation of the principles of Social Credit and how they could be applied to Alberta.

He began by saying that he wished to have this name deleted from the controversial resolution, denying credit for the idea and the benefit it might bring.[37] He called for instant action: "We cannot wait for Federal action," he said. "Let us get it going and get it going soon."[38]

Near the close of his address Aberhart indicated that he had little faith in the U.F.A.'s taking Social Credit seriously. He said that Social Credit groups would soon begin work on forming a definite platform, and plans were already in hand for holding a Social Credit convention in Calgary. He added that he was not trying to split the U.F.A., but his statements contained a threat that the matter would be fought at the ballot boxes.[39]

After an hour-long question period the session adjourned at noon, and Aberhart stepped outside. The air was clear and -33°C. Soon Aberhart labouriously eased his great form, made bulkier by heavy winter clothing, into one of the small booths in the Mandarin Cafe on Centre Street. Two men were with him, C.M. Willmott and H.D. Fawcett, a plumber. The three ordered lunch and lapsed into silence, for they were all weary. Aberhart held his head in his hands and took a cat nap. The other two had chosen this spot as one where Aberhart could relax away from the clamour of humanity in which he had spent the morning. There was little conversation during the meal, but the events of the day still stimulated their minds to a flurry of speculation.They knew that, as they sat there, discussions were beginning around countless other lunch tables all over Calgary, and that these discussions would decide finally whether they were to remain what they were – a school principal, a railroader, and a plumber – or to enter a new phase in their lives as politicians.

In the early afternoon the delegates (including the somewhat disgruntled U.F.W.A., who saw their own full schedule being gradually crowded into a shorter and shorter period of time) filed back into their seats and the U.F.A.'s fight for life continued. Aberhart joined the audience. William Irvine, M.P. for Wetaskiwin, spoke. Aberhart may have hoped that he would have the support of Irvine, who had been an early promoter of Social Credit. Irvine, however, had no such intention and instead delivered a devastating critique of Aberhart's ideas and contrasted them to Douglas's. He said that he did not believe that the province had the power necessary to put Aberhart's plan into practice until the Dominion government endorsed Social Credit. The thing to do now, he said, was to see that every U.F.A. member and every candidate was pledged to exert every effort to force its consideration at Ottawa.[40]

After Irvine spoke, other speakers followed. At four o'clock in the afternoon, with the auditorium packed to its full capacity, the chairman called a vote on Resolution 190. When the ayes were asked for hardly a hand moved. E.J. Garland, thinking that perhaps the delegates misunderstood what was before them, read the resolution again, and again called for all those in favour. Again there was hardly a response. ''I want you to make sure you know what you are doing,'' Garland said. He then put the vote to those sitting in the central section of the hall, then the left, and then the right. Still there were scarcely any votes in favour of Resolution 190. Then he called for the nays. The vote was almost solidly No.[41]

Yet, in order to satisfy those interested in monetary reform, on Thursday afternoon William Irvine rose to suggest another motion, which read as follows:

Whereas there is a growth of sentiment in the province, favourable to the introduction and establishment of social credit principles; and Whereas Major C.H. Douglas is the originator of and foremost authority upon the system of social credit; Be it therefore resolved that this convention request the provincial government to engage Major Douglas as consulting engineer in the matter of financial reform and that as such, he will be required to:

a) Advise the government to what extent his proposals are practical within the provincial jurisdiction; what helpful initiatory steps might therein be established; these proposals to be submitted to the government for their consideration and not to be regarded as obligatory of acceptance without full examination.

(b) Prepare plans for consideration with a view to the possibility of their introduction in the federal parliament.[42]

In the discussion that inevitably followed some spoke out imperturbly preferring C.C.F. principles to Social Credit ones. The Convention finally adopted Irvine's suggestion. Government members felt that their problems had been as satisfactorily dealt with as could have been expected. They took heart from the fact that the U.F.A. undoubtedly had the firm support of its party delegates in rejecting Aberhart's brand of Social Credit. By directly appealing for Douglas's aid, they could show that they were in favour of "real Social Credit" and might draw off enough of Aberhart's support to reduce him once again to a mere Bible teacher. Henry Spencer, M.P. for Battle River, felt that Douglas's appointment might make all the difference between success and failure at the polls during the summer.[43] Feeling that they had disposed of Aberhart's brand of Social Credit, the U.F.A. then turned its guns on its traditional enemies, the Liberals and Conservatives.

Aberhart's homely illustrations to answer the question of where all the money would come from had not satisfied the U.F.A. delegates. Their rejection of his Social Credit program for Douglas's was the signal for Aberhart to muster his army for the march on Edmonton. He seems to have realized that the motion to hire Douglas had not been made out of Simon-pure motives and was likely to come to naught.

Aberhart's decision to enter the political ring was made known to his friend "Hilly" Hill the day after the U.F.A. Convention rejected his program. Driving Aberhart home from school, Hill said to him, "Well, those birds have turned you down. Now is your chance to get out from under this thing." Aberhart replied, "No, Hill, I can't quit in the middle of a fight. I'll go on and organize my own party – the Social Credit Party."[44]

The call to politics had to come before his job as a highschool principal or as Dean of the Bible Institute.

CHAPTER FOURTEEN

■

ALBERTA'S MESSIAH

WE SHOULD *allow none of our fellow citizens to suffer want, and if that's what you call a dictatorship, then I'm one and I'll be glad to take the title; for I want to see men and women having a fair deal in life.*
— William Aberhart, CFCN Broadcast, 5 May 1935

Aberhart now quickly organized the Social Credit movement into a political party and prepared for the next provincial election. The much-beflagged map in the Bible Institute, which now recorded the final results of the Straw Vote, showed Aberhart's main support to be in the southern and central parts of Alberta. Of the approximately 20 per cent of the population covered by the survey it was estimated that approximately 68 per cent were in favour of Social Credit and 32 per cent against.

Many observers did not believe that Aberhart could expect to win an election against the well-established political parties. It is true that the Social Crediters were thinking in concrete terms of winning votes for the first time, but Aberhart had already prepared them for this new challenge by emphasizing that their real task was far more momentous than the winning of an election. He had painted the Social Credit movement as a crusade like the Reformation of the sixteenth century. In one of his broadcasts the dialogue between Aberhart and Manning went as follows:

> Manning: Do you remember when Latimer and Ridley were suffering martyrdom it was believed that this would dampen the enthusiasm of the whole movement? It would soon die out after this. But it didn't. Why even when they were being burned at the stake Latimer said, "Play the man Master Ridley for we shall today light a fire in England that will never be put out."
> Aberhart: But, Charles you do not mean that the Social Credit idea will never cease do you?
> Manning: Yes I do. It must be the basis of the new era of civilization.[1]

Aberhart claimed the company of the highest spiritual and temporal authorities his listeners acknowledged. An editorial in the *Alberta Social Credit Chronicle* claimed, "One of the finest and greatest exponents of Social Credit was Jesus Christ Himself. His one mission in life was to feed and clothe His people...."[2] Aberhart, recalling the comments of King George V before the 1933 World Economic Conference ("It cannot be beyond the power of man so to use the vast resources of the world as to ensure the material progress of civilization"), said on the air:

> His Majesty doesn't believe that poverty and hard work are the lot appointed by Providence for millions of people.... The King is as impatient as Alberta citizens are to see the people provided with food, clothing and shelter....[3]

With hymns and religious fervour, and confident that they had the backing of King George V and the Saviour himself, Aberhart and his followers went forth to do battle with the powers of political darkness. Aberhart's Social Credit campaign of 1935 was a political campaign *par excellence*, the like of which, say those who witnessed it, Alberta had never seen before. Poets wrote poems on Social Credit, musicians composed music to be played by the Young People's Social Credit orchestra, school children entered Aberhart's Social Credit essay competition, housewives baked pies for bake-sales and teas that drew throngs of women into the campaign and helped finance it. Most fund-raising techniques were used – except raffles, which Aberhart frowned upon. "Please remember," he said, "that I have no use for money that you are raising in that way."[4] There were mammoth picnics and mass meetings at which added attractions included such features as the personal appearance of the "Man from Mars," whose costume made him look like an Arab sheik.

The public discussions, lectures, and social gatherings of the old-fashioned political campaign were supplemented by many of the propaganda features of present-day political campaigns, except that this was in the days before professional publicity agents, speech-writers, and public-relations experts. Aberhart did without any of these specialists: he was filling all the roles himself, using the medium of radio as well as the pages of the *Alberta Social Credit Chronicle* – and made more personal appearances than one could imagine possible while he still held his position at Crescent Heights High School.

Those who attribute Aberhart's success primarily to semi-mystical qualities such as an intuitive knowledge of mob psychology or a conviction of divine mission might well consider the prosaic hard work that he applied to all his problems. He wasted nothing, sparing neither himself nor his workers. He used every suggestion that could conceivably achieve what he was striving for. With few doubts to undermine his determination he was able to apply himself – mind, body, and soul – to his task.

The expenses of this intensive campaign were incredibly small. The Honourable E.C. Manning later described the financing of the campaign thus:

> Financing the campaign was a nickels and dimes proposition. We didn't hire any workers. We had speakers going practically full time. They got their expenses only. They went out, took the collections; if there was any left they paid their gas and if there was any more they ate. Total cost was less than a lot of the orthodox political campaigns would be in one constituency – plus radio broadcasts of course.[5]

Occasionally a Social Credit speaker would be fortunate enough to encounter a Liberal or Conservative garage-owner who would do his share to undermine the U.F.A. by filling the gas tank without charge. Local Social Credit organizers of the meetings were requested to arrange publicity and sometimes to provide the speakers with supper and a night's lodging.

Clifford M. Willmott, the "Man from Mars," recalled one incident in the spring of 1935, in which someone had to be found to speak in the constituency of Ponoka, a U.F.A. stronghold represented by John E. Brownlee, the former premier. The courageous amateurs who made up Aberhart's group of speakers quailed at the thought of facing the Ponoka audience which, it was said, would "tear a Social Credit speaker to pieces." Aberhart began with the speaker on his right at the table, saying, "I want you to go to Ponoka." The date was looked up in date books and, as Aberhart asked them, the speakers one by one discovered with relief that their schedules would not allow them to take the assignment. He worked around the table until only Willmott, on his immediate left, remained. Aberhart suddenly dispensed with the ceremony of an enquiry. He turned to Willmott and gave him his instructions in two brief sentences. "Be there at two o'clock in the afternoon. Griffin will take care of you."

Mr. P. Griffin, the local dry-goods merchant and Social Credit organizer in Ponoka, arranged for Willmott to be smuggled into the hall incognito, and also had him watched over by a bodyguard of seven or eight husky farmers who had come unwashed and unfed from the fields. At two o'clock Willmott stepped onto the stage to face the "terrifying" people of Ponoka. Willmott found those people, who may hitherto have been jealously content with the U.F.A., now avidly curious about Social Credit. After the address the questions came as fast as they could be asked and answered. The hall was very warm. Willmott sipped water, he drank tea. Though usually fastidious about his appearance he divested himself one by one of his coat, waistcoat, collar, and tie. Long after six o'clock the hall was still three-quarters full.[6] Willmot's extraordinary experience was repeated many times throughout the province. Could the U.F.A. Convention delegates *really* have represented the opinion of the rank and file of the U.F.A.?

The ongoing success of Aberhart's forces was naturally of concern to the U.F.A. leaders. W. Norman Smith wrote to his friend Henry E. Spencer in Ottawa:

> Aberhart has become wild and abusive. Temporarily he has stirred up some communities to a pitch of hysteria and intolerance and created an ugly spirit. I can understand more fully now how Hitler made himself a power. Aberhart may damage us, but I don't think he can realize his ambition.
>
> It takes courage in some farm communites to stand out at the moment against him. The slightest difference of opinion is treated as an insult. Huxley district, the district southeast of Lacombe, and some others are against the action of the Convention.[7]

Aberhart's anger towards the U.F.A. was expressed loudly through his radio broadcasts. Referring to the United Farm Women of Alberta, Aberhart called them the "Undernourished Fool Women of Alberta." To defend his own position he called on more and more support from the Bible and used methods of interpretation that were hardly justifiable. Some of his comments and actions appeared paranoid. He often made biblical analogies to himself and his opponents. In commenting on his opponents he exclaimed:

> They say I won't co-operate. No Sir, I will not co-operate with the Devil. I am going to fight the Devil.... People will not be bull-dozed, buffaloed... by the people who want to graft. God will open the Red Sea.[8]

Besides comparing himself to Moses leading the children of Israel into the Promised Land, Aberhart compared himself to Daniel and even Christ.

One way that the U.F.A. tried to counter Aberhart was by transcribing his broadcasts in order to have a record of what he was saying on the radio. Copies of the transcripts were then sent to U.F.A. speakers so they could better prepare their rebuttals to Aberhart's ideas in broadcasts that followed his by several days. They made the most of his deviations from Douglas.[9]

As decided at their convention, the U.F.A. government invited Major Douglas to sign a two-year contract to act as "Economic Reconstruction Adviser" to the government, with a large retainer of $2,500 per annum, plus $2,000 for expenses on each three-week visit to Alberta.[10] Douglas accepted and planned to arrive in May to take up his duties. Douglas's behaviour stunned Aberhart's followers, to whom it seemed almost an act of treachery.

The U.F.A. government had done its best to put Aberhart in an embarrassing position and drive a wedge between the two men.

One factor that may have led Douglas to sign with the government was his personal dislike for Aberhart: Aberhart was like a bad boy in class, showing signs of becoming unmanageable and defiant, though so far publicly submissive. Douglas could not be sure that Aberhart would not bring Social Credit into disrepute with his participation in politics, his garbled adaptation of Douglas's theories, his usurpation of Douglas's position as leader, and his hasty and independent actions, thinly covered by declarations of reliance upon and indebtedness to Douglas. Douglas's conscience did not seem to trouble him when he put his name to the two-year contract.

Doulgas failed to appreciate fully the tremendous debt he owed to Aberhart, who had accomplished a widespread emotional acceptance of his ideas, something Douglas himself had never been able to do. Douglas later admitted:

> Aberhart is doing something I couldn't do. I might talk now till Christmas with the bankers and make all my points intellectually, and then they would simply say, ''Very interesting. Drop in again any time.'' Once the intellectual case is made, what is needed is husky fellows to get democracy to decide what it wants done. Aberhart is supplying the husky fellows.[11]

But though he acknowledged his debt in words, Douglas's action in accepting the U.F.A.'s offer showed his indifference to Aberhart's movement, which could not but be adversely affected by such a development.

A real personal friendship between Aberhart and Douglas would have been a difficult thing to imagine, even without the conflict of authority. A dominant personality in the religious field was a phenomenon not so common in England as on this continent. Douglas did not have a very wide knowledge of religion, and had little sympathy with fundamentalists, whose view of the Bible he summed up thus:

> The Old Testament was a record of the sayings and doings of an omnipotent if somewhat irrational Ruler, who spoke Elizabethan English and had a private staircase to Mount Sinai.[12]

Douglas did not accept the doctrines of orthodox Christianity any more than he did those of orthodox economics. Douglas's religion was his own brand of humanism, vague enough to allow men like Dr. Hewlett Johnson, the Anglican dean of Canterbury, and Aberhart himself to link his economic beliefs with their own versions of Christianity.

Douglas's first glimpse of Aberhart the year before, glowering moodily on the Edmonton station platform, probably confirmed his worst fears that he was about to meet the strange and uncongenial practitioner of some weird and obscure religion. His airforce career had not prepared the ruddy-complexioned Douglas for the austere, tobacco-less, alcohol-bereft Bible Institute atmosphere in which Aberhart thrived. No doubt the pale and intense

Aberhart, working more feverishly for Social Credit than Douglas himself, made Douglas uneasy. Aberhart's interest in Social Credit was obsessive, occupying almost all of his energy. Douglas, on the other hand, worked from 9 a.m. to 5 p.m. and, after his day's work, liked to indulge moderately in what were, in his circle, termed the pleasures of civilized living. Douglas found the U.F.A. men in Edmonton closer to his taste in these matters than Aberhart.

Another possibility that one may speculate about in trying to understand Douglas's action is that he coveted the position of "Economic Reconstruction Adviser" and the fee that accompanied the post. Affairs within the Secretariat shed light on this problem. According to Arthur Brenton, editor of *The New Age*, the Secretariat was in deep financial trouble, and any publicity or funds Douglas or his ideas received were looked upon favourably:

> To get a clear picture of the position, you must bear in mind that the Secretariat have committed themselves to such heavy expenditure (over 20 pounds per week in salaries alone) that their chief pre-occupation has become that of raising funds. Since every mention by anybody at all of the words "Douglas" or "Douglas Social Credit" or "Social Credit," whether by people like Mr. Aberhart or by any other leader or would-be leader of a movement, does serve to bring new enquirers sooner or later into membership of groups in affiliation with the Secretariat, then from this point of view you will see that fallacious as Mr. Aberhart's proposals are, his activities do advertise the existence of the Secretariat just the same as do those of sound advocates of the Theorem.[13]

The position and fee that Douglas was to receive would not only pay his salary but also provide him and his movement with publicity and a level of prestige they had never had before. The financial affairs of the Secretariat may also go some way toward explaining why Douglas had not openly repudiated Aberhart and his activites.

The U.F.A.'s hoped-for *coup* against Aberhart in their hiring of Douglas backfired. When the opposition parties learned that the government had hired Douglas without the matter having been debated in the Legislature, they were angry. They were also highly critical of the fees that Douglas was to get for his services.[14] The same feeling was held by a number of Social Crediters, who were suggesting that because Aberhart had lived in the province for twenty-five years, he was better informed than Douglas as to what extent Social Credit would work in the province.[15] The U.F.A. was further disappointed to learn that Douglas could not come for several months, thus being of little use to them in negating Aberhart's influence before the up-coming election.

Taking the suggestion of the Social Crediters, David Duggan, the leader of the Conservative Party, added fuel to the fire under the U.F.A. by introducing a motion into the Legislature that Aberhart be hired as an economic adviser, and that he prepare a Social Credit plan for their consideration. With almost all of the opposition supporting that motion, the government reluctantly was forced to negotiate again with Aberhart. Their decision to do so seems to have been motivated by the hope that if Aberhart were given enough rope, he would hang himself. Therefore the motion was passed to invite Aberhart to become an economic adviser to the government.[16]

Soon Aberhart received a disarming invitation from Premier Reid to come to Edmonton and set to work without more delay, "preparing and submitting a comprehensive Social Credit plan for the consideration of the Legislature."[17] Aberhart would have fallen into a trap if he had replied that he was incapable of formulating such a plan himself and was planning to engage Douglas, who had already been hired by Reid. Instead, before turning down the invitation, Aberhart addressed a number of letters to Reid enquiring how his work would be correlated with that which Major Douglas was expected to do, in how much detail the government wished him to draw up a plan, what use would be made of such a plan, and how much assistance he would be given.[18] The correspondence between Aberhart and Reid pattered back and forth for several weeks and was quoted at length in the Alberta press.

Another request for Aberhart to reveal his Social Credit "plan" was made by the Calgary *Herald*. The newspaper conducted an open correspondence with Aberhart, offering him one of its pages in which to set down his plan for introducing Social Credit into Alberta. Aberhart, avoiding the issue, declined the offer, saying that he would not cooperate until the *Herald* gave him fairer treatment.[19]

Demands that Aberhart reveal his "plan" for introducing Social Credit before he called upon the electorate to vote for it became more and more insistent. He had, of course, no plan, having at no time sat down with pencil and paper and worked out in detail, step by step, the methods he would use for returning the "cultural heritage" to its rightful owners, assuring a price for commodities that would be "just" to both producer and consumer, providing every man, woman, and child with the bare necessities of life and the other benefits he had promised Albertans. This was no secret, but Aberhart did not mention the fact more often than was necessary. Many confessed themselves shocked that a man should promise to give such costly presents when he did not yet know how to pay for them. Aberhart, however, was unabashed, for Douglas had faced the same question and said people voted for results, not methods. Aberhart relied on another homely illustration: one does not, he said, have to understand electricity to turn on a light switch.

Douglas's conception of representative government fitted Aberhart's case very neatly. "A mob feels," Douglas had asserted. "It does not think and consequently by whatever mechanism we represent a mob, we can only represent a desire, not a technique.... If you throw a plan to democracy, it will be torn to shreds."[20] The public should, therefore, confine itself to stating the results which it desired, not the methods by which those results could be attained. "The business of democracy," said Douglas, "is to elect representatives who will insist upon the results, and will, if necessary, pillory the actual individuals who are responsible either for the attainment of results or their non-attainment."[21]

Aberhart adopted this scheme of specialization. He himself specialized in being the politician whose duty it would be to find experts (Douglas and his assistants) and insist that they make good the election promises. Since any failure of the experts to attain the desired results would be paid for by the elected representatives' losing their jobs, the representatives would be continually putting pressure on the experts to do what was expected of them.

As the Social Credit crusade gained momentum Aberhart's position as leader of the movement was invested with, and assumed, super-politicial qualities and responsibilities. In his followers eyes he was MR. ABERHART. He was the leader, but he was also being led by his followers. That became quite evident at the first Social Credit convention held in Calgary on 4 and 5 April 1935.

In the pre-convention issue of the *Alberta Social Credit Chronicle*, its editor Charles K. Underwood intoned:

> There is one important thing you happen to be blessed with, YOU POSSESS A LEADER WHO IS ONE MAN IN A MILLION, a man of foresight, a man of intelligence and a man with GOD GIVEN GUIDANCE....
>
> There is one great thing that your worthy leader relies on, the same thing that men, like Gladstone, Salisbury, Gordon, Kitchener, Cromwell, Nelson, Laurier, Lincoln and other noted statesmen and soldiers of history relied on, that one thing is PRAYER. In this scientific age this may seem superficial, but in spite of the advances of science that same faith in the Almighty, after all is said and done, He is the only real guide in this great question, He and He alone is the mainstay of the whole business, and the very minute God Almighty stays away from Social Credit then you may just as well throw away your aspirations and intentions for this cause into the discard, you may just as well go home and forget it. Pray for that great guidance from Him; if your leader Mr. Aberhart can do it, with courage, hope and success, surely you as delegates can do likewise.[22]

The first Social Credit convention was designed for delegates south of Red Deer. A parallel convention for delegates from the northern part of the province was planned later. The southern convention was a carefree affair, during which the Bible Institute was filled with the pandemonium of two thousand delegates and visitors. The crusading spirit was still there. They were fighting against great odds and were trying to bring a new era of happiness to their fellow-Albertans, but this was no cause for excessive solemnity. "O God Our Help in Ages Past" still opened their sessions and the Institute auditorium echoed again to the familiar tune of "Who is He in Yonder Stall?" but this time the words were different:

Who is he in yonder hall
Calling to Albertans all?
Aberhart 'tis he with glory
Sending forth a wond'rous story....

The meetings progressed to more boisterous tunes. "John Brown's Body" now contained the line "We'll keep the 'Man' in Manning and the 'Heart' in Aberhart...." This prostitution of hymns for political purposes was not unlike that in contemporary Germany, where Hitler, like Aberhart, was receiving adoration from various religious groups. There was, for example, the nazified hymn:

Silent night! Holy night!
All is calm, all is bright
Only the Chancellor steadfast in fight
Watches o'er Germany by day and by night
Always caring for us.

Silent night! Holy night!
All is calm, all is bright
Adolf Hitler is Germany's wealth
Brings us greatness, favour and wealth
Oh give us Germans all power![23]

One of the main points discussed and decided upon at the southern convention was a very unusual method of nominating candidates. Seven delegates from each constituency would together nominate three or four candidates for their constituency. Aberhart and an advisory committee appointed by him would then select the best candidate from among those nominated. The resolution proposing this system was immediately conceded by the convention after Aberhart told them, in a statement reminiscent of many a deacons' board meeting of the past, "If you are not going to let me have any say in the choice of my supporters, you will not have me as your leader."[24] The passing of that resolution was openly opposed by only two of the delegates. Archie F. Key, a newspaper editor from Drumheller, who had been leading the Social Credit group there, complained to the Convention that that resolution would establish Aberhart as "another Mussolini" by giving him such dictatorial powers.[25] Another voice of warning came from Mrs. N. Campbell, an elderly woman and one of the seven delegates from Pincher Creek who spoke against the autocratic selection of candidates. She received no response other than a brief period of silence following her remarks.[26]

Another resolution passed at the convention was that Aberhart should not cooperate with the U.F.A. government. Aberhart himself had already decided that the government's asking him for a Social Credit plan was a political trick, so the resolution merely gave him a reason to turn down the invitation.[27]

The delegates also decided that in the upcoming election Aberhart should not run as a candidate, but should rather devote his entire activities to the overall campaign. Should they win enough seats to have a majority in the Legislature, Aberhart would be made premier. According to Clifford Willmott, that decision was made because it was felt that if Aberhart ran in any particular constituency, the opposition would go to any length to defeat him, thus damaging the prestige of Aberhart and his movement.[28]

The convention closed on Friday evening with Aberhart being the main speaker. He levelled broadsides at his opponents, mainly ex-premier Brownlee and the Calgary *Herald*. Waving a recent editorial from the latter, he quoted:

The mixing of religion and politics is never agreeable to the thoughtful observer and it cannot be doubted that the leader of this movement has used and is using a tabernacle built in the name of religion to promote what is rapidly becoming a political party.

Responding to it, he said:

That surely is a polite way of saying it. "We are very religious down here at the *Herald*. We do not believe in mixing our religion with politics...."
You know I have always believed that a religion that amounts to anything should be practised in every span of life.... The day is past when religion should be put on the shelf and taken down on Sundays.[29]

Interspersed throughout the Sunday-afternoon broadcasts were readings of names of Social Credit supporters, dates and locations of Social Credit rallies, announcements for the Radio Sunday School, and the reading of letters for and against Social Credit. As Aberhart read opposing letters he posed as a persecuted martyr without political ambition. When he attacked his opponents and the Calgary *Herald* his audience cheered him wildly and booed the opposition. The atmosphere was more like a vaudeville show than a religious service. On at least one occasion Aberhart became so involved in Social Credit matters that he did not have time to start his sermon.[30]

His sermons were as confusing as the order of his broadcasts, and were mixed with prophecy and Social Credit. Sometimes he implied that Social Credit was a fulfilment of prophecy. As he read biblical passages dealing with wickedness he launched attacks on the old-line politicians, there being no doubt in his listeners' minds as to whom he meant: ex-premier Brownlee and O.L. Mcpherson. He called them "fornicators, grafters, and reprobates concerning the faith."[31]

When Aberhart used such tactics, the U.F.A. and other opposition groups struck back in their own radio broadcasts. Some of their leaders were ministers of the United Church of Canada and able speakers. In a series of broadcasts over CFAC given by Harry Humble, a railway worker, former Calgary alderman, and sometime evangelist with the United Church of Canada, Albertans were warned:

If you do not desire to hear what I have further to say about the so-called social credit plan for Alberta then turn your radio dial, but I urge you, if you are a church member or if you are interested in the Christian religion to hear me out in this matter. I appeal to all those who are jealous for religion and the freedom which has been associated with it, to protest that an attempt is being made to use God as a rubber stamp for the political ideas of one man.... The inference has gone abroad that a person must be a social crediter to be a Christian, and furthermore, not just a social crediter, but an Aberhartite. Last Sunday, over a Calgary radio station, a service was broadcast wherein the so-called social credit plan for Alberta was discussed. A member of the Prophetic Bible Institute offered prayer in these words, "We thank Thee, O Lord, for Thy truth, which has gone out on Social Credit this afternoon." In these words an attempt is made to use God as a rubber stamp for the ideas of the sponsor of the so-called Social Credit plan for Alberta.[32]

In another broadcast Norman Priestly, a former clergyman, said:

> No other party in this election contest has used a church pulpit and cheap broadcasting time, cheap because it is supposed to be for religious purposes, to broadcast news and make announcements of political meetings, giving instructions to speakers and candidates, etc. Nor has any other political party in this election enveloped its political doctrines with the singing of hymns and the praying of prayers and the building up of a Sunday School and a Back to the Bible movement. Nor has any of those contesting this election, excepting the leader of the new political party, imported a foreign evangelist to talk about the love of God for humanity in one sentence and then in the next cast aspersions on their political opponents suggesting that they were evil smelling, like nigger babies (so said the evangelist) and getting a laugh from an audience supposed to be assembled for religious worship.... What other political party in Canadian history ever descended to such base tactics?[33]

The following excepts from Aberhart's broadcasts illustrate what his opponents were objecting to:

> The principles of the old-line politicians and their henchmen are like those of the man who betrayed the Christ. Gold was his god and millions have suffered because of it. The money changers upheld his right and crucified the Christ and they have been crucifying everyone since who follows in the steps of the Saviour....[34]
>
> Are conditions not similar today to those when the Master took a whip of small cords and drove the money changers out of the temple? Do not the common people need leaders and shepherds today, the same as in the days when the Christ had compassion on them and fed the 5000 with five loaves and two small fishes? The Easter message is a message of hope. There is deliverance. There is salvation. God can and will work even a miracle to bring his people into the place of joy and prosperity. Is that not a message for all believers in Social Credit.[35]

In another homily, Aberhart used Christ's parable of the nobleman and the ten pounds to illustrate the "flow of credit":

> Then he called his followers and gave them their Unearned Increment in the form of one dividend. You will find it in Luke 19:16. The result was that Number 1 started his pound on the flow of credit and made 11 pounds. The second man did the same and came out with six. The third man said it was a fool idea. It couldn't be done. There could be no flow of credit, so he rolled his pound in a napkin and blocked the whole works. In other words, the result was that three pounds produced eighteen pounds, or i.e., a velocity of circulation of six.[36]

Aberhart's mixing of religion and politics should not be seen as merely manipulative; it was the expression of his theology, which was undergoing yet another metamorphosis. Aberhart's shift in theological emphasis continued to draw criticism from some fundamentalist quarters. Early in April 1935 J. Fergus Kirk, the President of Prairie Bible Institute, who had participated with Aberhart in evangelistic crusades in the early twenties, published a mimeographed letter in which he claimed that Aberhart had abandoned his dispensational theology and was now preaching materialism and communism.[37] Aberhart responded on the radio with a bitter attack on Kirk and Prairie Bible Institute, not only attacking their theology concerning the atonement and salvation, but also comparing them to the priest and Levite in the Parable of the Good Samaritan.[38] That attack on Prairie Bible Institute lost Aberhart the support of some fundamentalists; but, at the same time, Prairie Bible Institute was said to have lost two-thirds of its financial support for not backing Aberhart.[39]

Aberhart claimed that he had not changed his dispensational theology one iota,[40] but his preaching had changed so much that it was approaching a vague universalism. In one of his sermons he stated:

> A new Christianity, a new type, a true type, is appearing. The old prejudiced denominationalism is giving place to the era of Christian brotherhood. Let the critics howl; they can never stop it. We shall combine and co-operate so that we may become our brothers' keepers.[41]

In another sermon, after reading a letter from a Roman Catholic who praised his work and suggested that he was following in the footsteps of the Pope and Father Coughlin (a Hamilton-born radio priest centered in Detroit, who championed economic reform and later anti-Semitism and fascism), Aberhart commented:

> I was rather glad to read that. You know I think it's touching on the right chord. The chord that must be struck today. That chord consists of many varied notes but harmonizing together in one thing – the love of fellow man. It's helping to blot out the bias and blind prejudice that has separated us for so long. Why cannot we not see that after all we are all sojourners here below. We might as well make it more pleasant for one another.[42]

That was quite a departure from the strong separatist stance that Aberhart had taken before taking up the cause of Social Credit. He was now associating with people who represented the opposite end of the theological spectrum, including Theosophists, Mormons, and United Church of Canada ministers. Aberhart's shift was inevitable as he sought to broaden the base of his movement.

Within the mythology of Alberta history, there has been an assumption that much of Aberhart's political support came from the fundamentalist sects. This idea, which formed the basis of W.E. Mann's study *Sect, Cult and Church in Alberta*,[43] needs re-evaluation. It appears that support for Social Credit varied within denominations. While some United Church of Canada ministers ran as Social Credit candidates, other ministers of that church strongly opposed Aberhart. A similar situation existed among the sects. We have already seen that some of the leaders of Prairie Bible Institute took a stong stand against Aberhart's mixture of religion and politics, but Roger Kirk, who was the brother of J. Fergus Kirk, was an avid Social Crediter.[44] Many of the "closed" Plymouth Brethren opposed Social Credit, but some of the "open" Brethren supported it.[45] Just before the election, a Mormon apostle came from Salt Lake City and warned the Stake Conference at Lethbridge that they should not be carried away by radicalism[46]; yet at least four Mormons were elected as Social Credit members of the Legislature, including Nathan Tanner, who was a bishop of that sect. The leaders of the Seventh-Day Adventist college at Lacombe feared that if Aberhart's party won the election, there would be a religious dictatorship; but there were some Seventh-Day Adventists who supported Social Credit.[47] Even within Aberhart's own church there were those who were opposed to his involvement in politics – which was one of the reasons why Dr. Imrie had broken with Aberhart. All in all, it appears that support for Social Credit crossed denominational lines and church members responded individually to Social Credit.

Two recent studies that examined the history of the Social Credit Party in Alberta from 1935 until the late 1960s may shed some light on the religious affiliation of Aberhart's supporters. Both studies suggest that most of the support for Social Credit came not from the members of religious sects as suggested by Mann, but rather from members of established churches. H.L. Malliah's study of the legislators of Alberta has revealed that the average Social Credit M.L.A. was a member of the United Church of Canada.[48] Owen Anderson's analysis of the membership of the Social Credit Party has indicated that almost 30 per cent of party membership belonged to either the Anglican or United Church, while only about 11 per cent were members of fundamentalist sects[49]:

> The general impression of the party as being composed primarily of fundamentalist Protestants is not the case. But it can be said that these groups are over-represented compared to their incidence in the general population.[50]

Because Aberhart had shifted the emphasis of his preaching away from his extreme sectarian theology (which he continued to teach within the confines of the Bible Institute Baptist Church), he was now preaching a quasi-social gospel that attracted a great variety of people.

In spite of such support, Aberhart's critics did not stop and Aberhart's feud with the press escalated after the southern Social Credit convention. So many letters were being received by the Calgary *Herald* on the subject of Social Credit that the paper threw open several of its pages to readers' correspondence – which shows that the controversy that always boiled about Aberhart had by this time spread throughout the whole province and beyond. The Calgary *Herald*'s criticism of Aberhart's use of religion for political purposes brought a retort from one reader who said that "Social Credit is merely Christianity in practice." The letter continued:

> Just as God chose Moses to lead the children of Israel out of bondage, we firmly believe God has also ordained Mr. Aberhart a second Moses, who will lead the people of Alberta into a better and higher standard of life and into their rightful heritage....[51]

Another defender of Aberhart saw him in messianic terms:

Jesus Christ abides in Mr. Aberhart. He walks every moment by his side. When Christ came it was to save the sinners.The self-righteous rejected Him and crucified Him. They jeered and sneered and your Paper is doing the same to the one whom Christ has chosen to lead us out of this depression....[52]

The Calgary *Herald* also had its defenders:

Mr. Aberhart is a pretty good hand at slinging the Bull but there is no sense in letting him Bull-doze the people of Alberta and get away without even a protest from us.... Let us have some more Editorials dealing with the Aberhart plan of Social Credit. Give us both sides of the case as much as you can, as it is only through reading and studying that we can form a worth while opinion on any issue.[53]

Yet another critic of Aberhart wrote:

We read in the Bible that in the last days false prophets will appear on earth and it looks as if we have one appearing right in the city of Calgary. He is parading under the cloak of religious teachings to cover up his political campaigning from the pulpit during his Sunday deliberations and in these deliberations he abuses anyone who does not belong to his party by obnoxious remarks far from being expected to come from a pulpit when in the next sentence he was asking the public to be born again.[54]

The manner in which Aberhart planned to choose the Social Credit candidates for the coming election again came under criticism. In his Sunday-afternoon broadcast on 7 April 1935, Harry Humble, who represented the Labour Party, commented:

First, let me say, Major Douglas is a democrat, and Mr. Aberhart is a dictator. Two weeks ago I charged that the Aberhart movement savored of Fascism. It is now a matter of record that Mr. Aberhart has dictated the terms on which he would undertake the leadership of the new political party and no dictator of the modern world has been more exacting in his demands. Those of you who have been reading the daily press, but did not understand the nature of this organization, were no doubt shocked when you read that the mailed fist of dictatorship was to control the affairs of the party even to the point of naming the candidates for the various constituencies in the Province of Alberta. No doubt the sponsor of this movement is well read-up on Mussolini and his methods.

The leader of this new so-called social credit party of Alberta has been quite outspoken regarding the old political parties and their wire-pulling tactics, but no political party leader in Canada has attempted to pull the strings to the extent that every member of the party sitting in the parliament would be the personal choice of the leader and a mere rubber stamp man.... Surely no one is going to be fooled by the crude attempt to cover up this procedure by what is to be called "an advisory council" of three members, because even the advisors are to be chosen by the dictator himself. There is not an atom of democracy left in the whole proceedings and Canada has now one who is making a definite bid for dictatorial powers.[55]

When the Communist *Daily Worker* of 2 March 1935 had called Aberhart a fascist, the *Alberta Social Credit Chronicle* responded in anger[56]; when Harry Humble said the same, the *Chronicle* accepted his comments thus:

"Major Douglas is a democrat and Mr. Aberhart is a dictator" says Harry Humble. Quite a nice compliment Mr. Humble. A democrat so stated by the dictionary is one who is out solely for the people; a dictator is one who is invested with authority and capable of leading people. Really a wonderful combination to lead Alberta out of their present chaotic mess.[57]

Archie Key, president of the Drumheller Social Credit Group, was less fortunate in his opposition to Aberhart's domination of the selection of the candidates. On 11 April 1935 the Drumheller Social Credit constituency meeting demanded his appearance. Feelings were running so high that he refused to go, fearing he would be beaten up. He was henceforth expelled from the party.[58]

Although Aberhart was waging a campaign without parallel in Albertan history, it should not be thought that the other parties were napping. The other parties fought hard, and if Aberhart had the economic crisis of the land in his favour when he propounded Social Credit, the other parties had an enormous supply of ammunition and they used it. Social Credit, that large, vague, many-headed thing, was an easy target.

One pot-shot that surely could not miss was a remark by the opposition broadcaster Harry Humble, that *he* held no mortgage on the radio station over which he broadcast. He swiftly followed that insinuation with the accusation that Aberhart forced CFCN to carry his broadcasts by means of a mortgage by which he virtually owned the radio station and had the owner in his power.[59] This was one of the few accusations that embarrassed Aberhart. He chatted to his radio audience about the matter, not denying that there was a mortgage, but misleading them by implying that the sum quoted was owed by, and not to, the Institute. "We are not trying to cover up anything," he explained. "It is all above board. We have a bonded indebtedness on the Institute of $5000 bearing interest at 8% payable half yearly." It was, he said, due in 1937. In the tone of one struggling Albertan to another, he ran through other major expenses of the Institute:

You see, at any rate, just taking the Radio Sunday School and taking the broadcasts and taking this $5000 that we have to pay and the interest on that, we'll have to have by 1937 easily $18,000. Now if any of you know how we are going to get it and if you think we are going to have an easy time to get $18,000 in times such as this, you'll know we have not any money to flash around.... It's rather hard, you know, to find them throwing stuff at you, when you almost have to stay awake nights to wonder how you're going to make everything go and meet the bills when they come. However, it's alright as long as you understand that I'm not getting anything out of it anyway. It's straight above board as far as I am concerned.[60]

What Aberhart said was a half-truth. The mortgage on the Bible Institute was due in 1937,[61] but the facts that he was trying to conceal were as follows. The Calgary Prophetic Bible Institute had made its first loan to the Voice of the Prairies Ltd. in September 1928. The amount loaned was $600 and no interest was charged. The loan had been repaid in the form of air time. That arrangement seems to have been almost solely to the advantage of the radio station, which was glad enough to have a guaranteed sale of air time, paid in advance. The mortgage to which Harry Humble referred was arranged when CFCN again got into financial difficulties during the Depression. It is said that at that time, Aberhart could have bought the station for $200. Instead, in 1934 the Institute loaned the Voice of the Prairies Ltd. $8,000 at an interest rate of 8 per cent per annum.[62] (The mortgage was to have been paid in full by 1936, but Aberhart granted extensions that enabled the radio station to defer discharge of the loan until 1939.) The mortgage no doubt safeguarded Aberhart's broadcasts during those years, when they were particularly controversial and when the greatest pressure would have been put on the radio station to discontinue carrying them.

Harry Humble's closing comments cut to the core:

> In the light of these facts, which you can verify for yourselves, what confidence can you have in the Aberhart political program which talks about reduction of mortgages by means of distribution of basic dividends and then in the same breath about lower interest rates?[63]

Most of Aberhart's supporters did not wish, however, to verify the facts for themselves. Aberhart's reassurances were sufficient for them.

Within weeks of the first Social Credit convention held in Calgary a similar convention was held in Edmonton. Aberhart's most pressing campaign problem was the northern part of Alberta, where the Straw Vote had shown his support to be weakest. This area of the province was not easily accessible to him since he was still a full-time employee of the Calgary School Board and CFCN, his main communications channel with the public, was not received clearly north of Edmonton.

During the Easter holidays of 1935 Aberhart travelled to Edmonton, where the northern Alberta Social Credit convention was being held in McDougall United Church. Much of the preparation for that convention was the work of Earle Ansley. Aberhart had met Ansley when he had stayed with Ansley's parents in Killam in the course of his lecturing tour in the summer of 1933. After hearing Aberhart speak, Ansley, who had been a highschool teacher himself, began lecturing on Social Credit, and during the next eighteen months, he became well-known in central Alberta. In January 1935 Ansley had received a telegram from Aberhart asking him to abandon his current lecture tour to build up the campaign. He did so, speaking throughout the capital and arranging meetings for two other speakers, Joe Unwin, a salesman, and Edith Rogers. A series of weekly Social Credit broadcasts were also put out over CFRN, Edmonton.

Aberhart spent the whole Easter vacation at the convention. To a crowd of about seven thousand he declared that he had been called the "Pied Piper from Hamelin'' and added that he liked that characterization ''because the Pied Piper drove the rats out of the capital city.''[64] He reiterated his earlier statements that he was quite ready to assist Major Douglas in every way to promote Social Credit when the latter took up his position with the government.[65]

The coverage that the Calgary *Herald* had given to the northern convention angered Aberhart. During his Sunday-afternoon broadcast on 28 April 1935, he announced that his supporters should boycott newspapers that were unfavourable to Social Credit:

> I don't think you will miss it if you don't have it. I think you can get the news in another way. Some of the citizens of this province cannot distinguish falsity from truth. I'm cancelling my subscription tomorrow. What about yours?[66]

The following day the Calgary *Herald* editorialized:

> Surely, it is very surprising to find the leader of a Christian movement and the head of a political party inviting his followers to injure an established industry which employs a large number of citizens. These employees of the *Herald* have contributed largely in the past and still do to the payment of Mr. Aberhart's salary as principal of Crescent Heights High School.
> Is everyone opposed to the political opinions and plans of Mr. Aberhart to be boycotted? He has invoked a most dangerous precedent and has given the people of this province a foretaste of the Hitlerism which will prevail if he ever secures control of the provincial administration.[67]

Many of Aberhart's followers obeyed him, and soon sales of the Calgary *Herald* dropped considerably. Archie Key's newspaper at Drumheller was so affected by the boycott that it was forced out of business.[68] The boycotts of newspapers next spread to other businesses. Social Crediters were encouraged to buy only from Social Crediters. Advertisements in the *Alberta Social Credit Chronicle* frequently emphasized ''the Just Price.''

Reaction to the boycott was varied. The following indignant remonstration came from a reader at Drumheller:

> In the *Herald* plant are employees who are union men to their finger-tips, men who are respected citizens of Calgary for long years past, men whose future happiness and welfare are dependent upon the work they perform for the *Herald* and the wages they receive from there and yet Mr. Aberhart would boycott these men onto the breadline, just because the *Herald* justly and fairly criticizes his theory....[69]

Another reader, J.J. Zubick, a veteran newspaperman of whom we will shortly hear more, claimed that the Calgary *Herald* was to some extent responsible for its own situation because it had been too fair in its treatment of Aberhart. Had the Calgary *Herald* taken a firmer stand against Aberhart he would not now have his present power: ''If the press will take its gloves off and put some real punch into its wallops this province can still be saved from the mess into which he would plunge it."[70]

Aberhart's opponents attacked him on three fronts, claiming that his program would not work, that his mixture of religion and politics was unwarranted, and that he would be a fascist dictator. In his broadcasts he attempted to convey the impression that he was not seeking office. Even after the southern Alberta Social Credit convention passed a resolution that he would be their premier if Social Credit won the election, he commented, "That Mr. Duggan, or Mr. Reid, or Mr. Howson be your next choice for premier is satisfactory to me. I have no desire or inclination to seek any office of that kind."[71] In May he protested:

> I'm not seeking office. No sir, I am not. I have a work here in the Institute that is dearer to my heart than the Premiership of Alberta, or even of Canada or the Presidency of the United States. Cannot the people of this Province give a citizen of twenty-five years standing the credit of being honest in his altruistic endeavors. I'm getting up in years. I'm not ambitious. The spirit of Christ, the greatest man that ever lived, has gripped my life.... We should allow none of our fellow citizens to suffer want, and if that's what you call a dictatorship, then I'm one [*sic*] and I'll be glad to take the title, for I want to see men and women having a fair deal in life.[72]

As the opposition fired away at him, Aberhart claimed their attacks did not hurt him since he had a "rhinoceros hide."[73] But, the more he mentioned it, the more his opponents felt he was protesting too much. Aberhart had acquired a taste for battle and began tilting at accusations that he had prophesied, in the course of his Bible teaching, that wheat would be $4 per bushel in 1932 and that the world was coming to an end in 1934. His great-grandfather, he protested wryly, had not been hanged for sheep-stealing in Arizona. With suppressed emotion he complained:

> Anyway, could I be held responsible for what my great-grandfather did? I have been a resident of the City of Calgary for a quarter of century, twenty-five years. People here have known me. I have taught their children faithfully during all this time. Surely I have served my time and should be given a clean sheet, don't you think so after all these years?[74]

Aberhart's opponents must surely have sometimes felt as though they might well employ their time in *discouraging* criticisms of him, for he was fast becoming not merely a crusader, but a martyr.

He was also facing criticism from his old adversary, the Calgary School Board. Now that a political distraction had been added to a religious one, Aberhart was less popular with them than ever. Annoyance had already been expressed at School Board meetings over his request for the four days' leave of absence granted him in May for speaking engagements in distant cities; but the School Board ruled that if he wished to have any more time away from school, he would have to ask for leave for the remainder of the term.[75] He managed to conduct the campaign without missing a single day in June. His position was made vulnerable by the personal animosity felt for him by his employers, and he decided not to give them any more tangible cause for complaint.

Aberhart had said earlier that he could transform the province with "one hundred honest men." From those men the Social Credit candidates would be chosen. At the constituency nominating conventions, which began in May,

IS THIS FASCISM?

IN ITALY MUSSOLINI AND HIS HENCHMEN SELECT THE CANDIDATES WHOSE NAMES GO BEFORE THE ITALIAN ELECTORATE.

IN CALGARY MR ABERHART AND HIS HENCHMAN SELECTED THREE CANDIDATES WHOSE NAMES WERE NOT ON THE LIST APPROVED BY THE SOCIAL CREDIT CONVENTION.

OUR FIGHT IS POLITICAL DEMOCRACY VERSUS FASCISM.

Anti-Aberhart cartoon linking him with fascism, from J.R. Love's pamphlet A Cross Examination of Aberhart's Plan of Social Credit *(1935).*

not less than three and not more than four prospective candidates were chosen by ballot. Aberhart, with a few of his headquarters' staff, formed an advisory committee and toured the province. Apart from Aberhart the personnel of the Advisory Committee changed from one occasion to another, but Ernest Manning was usually a member. The Committee interviewed in each constituency the seven delegates who had attended the main conventions, hearing from them the "claims and merits" of the three or four prospective candidates. After that, the prospective candidates themselves appeared before the Advisory Committee for interviews, on the basis of which the Committee made the final decision as to who should be the Social Credit candidate for each constituency.

The prospective candidates had been asked several questions to test their knowledge of Social Credit theories, but the main thing Aberhart wished to determine was their degree of attachment to any other political parties, since the Social Credit party had been in existence only a matter of months. Aberhart tried to prevent the incorporation of divided loyalties into the foundations of his party. In his radio broadcast of 9 April 1935, in answer to an open letter printed in the Edmonton *Journal*, which alleged that the nomination method was dictatorial, he had said: "There is an epidemic of old-line politicians who are seeking office under our banner and it is essential that they be not allowed to destroy our cause."[76] Needless to say inquiries were also made to ensure that the candidates were men of good character. Scandals like those that had precipitated the decline of the U.F.A. would not lower the tone of *his* crusade, if Aberhart had any say in the matter.

Although the Advisory Committee began its series of interviews before the provincial election was called, none of its decisions was made known until after July 23, and all nominees were expected to campaign actively during that time. "Four candidates," said Aberhart, shrewdly, "should be able to cover much more ground than one. Why not let four do it?"[77]

While Aberhart was on the march with his Advisory Committee in search of his "One Hundred Honest Men," Douglas was crossing the North American continent on his way to Edmonton in May of 1935. His presence now aroused considerably more public interest than had his previous visits. Reporters boarded his train in every province and his words appeared in newspapers in many parts of the world. The Alberta government was the first in the world that appeared to be taking Douglas seriously.

Douglas's name was becoming well known in Britain now, as the number of those in his movement increased and famous names became associated with his. The most colourful of British churchmen, the Very Reverend Hewlett Johnson, dean of Canterbury, was now director of revenue for Douglas's Social Credit Secretariat. As was the case with many other Social Crediters, the Dean's use of Douglas's ideas was one rung in a ladder to other political ideologies. Johnson later became an apologist for communism.[78] The Earl of Tankerville and the Marquis of Tavistock were other impressive names on Douglas's roll of active supporters. Tavistock claimed to have tried to interest Hitler in making Social Credit the basis of Nazi economics, and during the Second World War he would be a Nazi sympathizer.[79] Ezra Pound, the poet who later joined Mussolini's Fascist Party, declared "Gibbon's *History of Rome* [*sic*] is a meaningless jumble till a man has read Douglas."[80]

Social Credit was the subject of discussion everywhere in 1935. The Labour Party of Britain, after examining Douglas's evidence before the Macmillan Committee in 1930, had concluded that the "Douglas Scheme is not only an intellectual nightmare, but an administrative monstrosity."[81]

These were the days when Hitler's fascist Black Shirts and Brown Shirts were marching in Europe. Douglas, too, was not without his marching, uniformed Social Crediters. They were known as the "Green Shirts." The uniform of this organization consisted of a green shirt and a beret bearing a piece of Douglas tartan. They participated in regular drilling, and their activities included "Study, Propaganda, and Demonstration." The organizer of this troop of young men was John Hargrave, who had organized his own semi-occult movement devoted to "outdoor life" after he had left a leadership position in the Boy Scouts. Hargrave called his group the "Kindred of the Kibbo Kift" and its manual was borrowed by the Nazi youth movement. When Hargrave was converted to Social Credit he added this ideology to his movement. Alberta would soon hear more of him.

Once in Edmonton, Douglas was cordially entertained, and he enjoyed a round of golf with the cabinet ministers. Aberhart was hurt that Douglas was conferring with those who were desperately trying to prevent Social Credit from being instituted in the province. "How do you account for the fact," Manning had asked of Aberhart on the 9 April 1935 broadcast, "that he accepted the present government's proposal?" "I do not know," was the restrained reply. "Time will tell."[82]

If there was any doubt in Aberhart's mind that Douglas would be willing to cooperate with him if he won the election, it must have caused him some anxious moments. He never expressed any such doubts in public, but the strain under which their acquaintance laboured, and Douglas's facile acceptance of the U.F.A. government's invitation can hardly have bolstered Aberhart's confidence in the future of his alliance with the Social Credit founder. Should Douglas refuse to return and institute a system of Social Credit, Aberhart would indeed be in a serious predicament.

When Douglas was asked by a reporter how he regarded Aberhart's promise of a $25 dividend to each adult, he was less than enthusiastic: "This is technically possible," but it would result in "much political trench warfare."[83] On 22 May 1935 Aberhart went to see Douglas in Edmonton, and it appears that Douglas made a promise to return to Alberta to assist him, should he come to power.[84] Still no "plan" was made public, and no one knew specifically how the Aberhart-Douglas team would set about introducing Social Credit if Aberhart got into power. Douglas doubtless had some ideas, but he had already said:

> Nothing can be more fatal to a successful issue than the premature publication of cut and dried arrangements which are likely to be out of date before their adoption can be secured.[85]

On 23 May 1935 Douglas submitted his report to the government of Alberta, a report that was entirely predictable. Since the appearance of Douglas at the inquiry a little over a year before, Aberhart's movement had gained in impetus and size, and it looked now very much as though Aberhart might become the leader of the world's first Social Credit government, no matter what Douglas might say about the matter. He could hardly have been expected to close the door on the commencement of the first experiment in his own theories. Douglas recognized that neither he nor his movement stood to lose, and might gain much by repeating those of Aberhart's arguments that appealed to him as reasonable. In his 1935 report, therefore, Douglas changed his view on the constitutional question. He emphasized current doubts as to the ability of the B.N.A. Act to prevent the provincial introduction of Social Credit.[86]

Douglas suggested three steps towards the eventual introduction of Social Credit. The government would, first, need a systematic news-circulation system that would be unchallengeable. Second, a special credit institution would have to be organized. Third, the government would need systematically to accumulate federal currency, stocks, and bonds – which could be used for the purpose of "foreign exchange," that is, for interprovincial trade.[87]

In a covering letter to Premier Reid sent along with his report, Douglas added that it might be necessary to form a coalition government (presumably with Aberhart) if Social Credit were to be realized. He also stressed that the government's public-relations department would require the power to discourage, "by suitable methods, loose accusations of defective administration" that might be levelled against the government.[88] Here the authoritarian implications of Douglas's ideas showed through.

Douglas's report was disappointing to those members of the government who had hoped that he would attack Aberhart's ideas. Therefore, J.F. Lymburn, the attorney-general, submitted to Douglas a transcipt of one of Aberhart's radio broadcasts, asking him to criticize it. Douglas's comments, which were included by the government in his published report, implied that Aberhart should not have been giving elaborate details to the general public. Douglas also noted that Aberhart's concept of "the Just Price" differed from his and that he did not see how Aberhart's program for increasing purchasing power would work.[89]

Unsatisfied even with that, the U.F.A. decided that Douglas was no longer any use to them. Soon they released to the public findings on Social Credit by the 1935 Agricultural Committee, which had heard testimony from Dean Weir of the Faculty of Law and Professor G.A. Elliott of the Department of Economics, both of the University of Alberta. Their evidence suggested that Social Credit, whether it be Aberhartite or Douglasite, was constitutionally and economically impossible.[90]

To answer the government's latest publication, Aberhart issued in June 1935 a successor to the Yellow Pamphlet that had come under fire from Douglas's Secretariat. The new booklet was called the *Social Credit Manual* and became known as the "Blue Manual," also because of its cover. Its appeal was wider than the urban working class and addressed issues of particular concern to farmers.[91] Many read it eagerly, hoping that they would find in it a detailed account of how Aberhart would put Social Credit into being if he came to power; but they were disappointed. The booklet contained yet another summary of the evils of the current monetary system, and abbreviated descriptions of some of the features of Social Credit that Aberhart thought most desirable for Alberta. The rest of the booklet consisted of sixty questions and answers on Social Credit.

The Blue Manual modified to some extend the radical proposals for which

Aberhart had been criticized by the Secretariat. In it, Aberhart stated that there would be no confiscation of bonds or bank deposits, and he allowed for the operation of banks. He claimed that his program would recognize individual enterprise and individual ownership, but would also prevent exploitation of the consumer.[92] The nature of the State was better defined. Dividends would be given for loyalty to the State; if a person refused to work, or refused to join the Social Credit movement, he would not receive dividends.[93] If he abused his privileges under the new economic system, the Credit House inspector could withdraw his dividends and put him on an "Indian List." The latter expression was not defined, but Aberhart may have had in mind the reservations or concentration camps that Bellamy had described for non-sympathizers.[94]

Aberhart planned to place restrictions on income: "No one should be allowed to have an income that is greater than he himself and his loved ones could possibly enjoy, to the privation of his fellow-citizens."[95] To prevent a mass immigration into the province, dividends would only be given to bona fide citizens, that is, those Canadian citizens who had resided in the province for at least one year.[96] Should a person not want to remain in the province, there might be restrictions upon anyone carrying out of the province more than he and his loved ones could use for the rest of their lifetime.[97]

In spite of the authoritarian overtones in those proposals, Aberhart disassociated his plan from socialism, nationalization, confiscation, communism, fascism, and nazism. He protested that Social Credit would make the individual supreme, and the State, he claimed, would bend all its efforts to protect the individual's rights.[98]

In regard to the dividends that each citizen was expecting, he was even more specific than in his Yellow Pamphlet:

> Basic dividends should be $25 a month for every bona fide citizen, male or female, twenty-one years or more. Children of bona fide citizens, sixteen years old will receive $5 a month. Those seventeen and eighteen years will receive $10 a month. Those nineteen, $15 and those twenty, $20 a month. [He added:] These figures are merely suggested for illustrative purposes.[99]

Emphasizing that the dividends would be issued in credit, he repeated, "There will be no new money issued."[100] In answer to the question "How long will it take to introduce Social Credit into the Province of Alberta?" he wrote:

> That is a difficult question to answer with precision. Much information will need to be gathered. Expert investigations will have to be made. I would judge that 15 or 18 months might be required.[101]

The Blue Manual did not embody a complete Social Credit plan. Aberhart was relying on Douglas to come and do the job for him. Aberhart's getting away with such vague promises was undoubtedly made easier by the desperate problems of unemployment and the federal government's callous attitude towards those in need. In June 1935 the problems of unemployment and the conditions in relief camps came to a head. In the hope that Parliament would listen to them, hundreds of young men left the relief camps in B.C. and boarded the roofs of box-cars and headed for Ottawa. Their ranks swelled as the trains rolled eastward. It was a peaceful and well-organized journey until they reached Regina.

Fearing that the Trekkers were planning a communist overthrow of the government, Prime Minister Bennett ordered the R.C.M.P. to stop them at Regina. While the Trekkers were listening to speeches given by their leaders, the R.C.M.P. and local police charged the group. In the mêlée that followed, one city police detective was killed and hundreds of Trekkers, policemen, and onlookers were injured.[102]

Commenting on the Regina Riot, the *Alberta Social Credit Chronicle* charged the government with being "capricious, arbitrary, and dictatorial, showing neither tact, intelligence, nor respect for the rights of citizens." It further implied that if the Trekkers had communists among their ranks, it was the government's own fault:

> herding jobless citizens into isolated camps, putting them under something like military discipline, and paying them 20 cents a day for occasional jobs is a first class method of making converts to the Communist party.[103]

As a result of that confrontation, the Trekkers were halted at Regina and they returned to the work camps and homes, promising themselves that they would see R.B. ("Rotten Bastard") Bennett defeated in the next federal election.

On 16 July the provincial election date of August 22 was announced. Almost immediately Aberhart announced the names of the candidates that he and his Advisory Committee had selected. The criteria that he had used to make the final selection of candidates were puzzling. In an interview, Dr. Victor Wright, who had served on the committee, claimed that he had given the candidates marks for intelligence, personal appearance, and general knowledge, but that Aberhart seemed to have his own marking scheme, which he did not share with his advisors.[104]

Although it was expected that Aberhart would select his Social Credit candidates primarily from among his religious supporters, Ernest Manning was the only one so picked. Manning, the slim, ascetic-featured young man who was secretary of the Bible Institute, had shared Aberhart's experiences of the past three years and now found himself involved in Aberhart's politics. As in Bible studies, Manning had been an apt and eager student of Social Credit. Now he was Aberhart's right-hand man in the political campaign, dealing with correspondence and many other details that would normally fall to a campaign manager. Manning was in great demand as a speaker, being by now a "radio personality" and accepted as an authority on Social Credit, one who was closer than anyone else to the leader of the movement. He was naturally shy and retiring, but the excitement and urgency of the times had converted him into the sort of man described by a member of his audience when Manning spoke in a small country town. Manning had been delayed, and it was already a few minutes past the time scheduled for the opening of his address, when the door of the crowded hall opened and in hurried Manning. He strode down the hall, up the steps onto the stage, and began talking to the audience about Social Credit as he was removing his overcoat.

Ernest Manning, Edith Gostick (an early Social Credit student of Aberhart's), and four other candidates were selected to run in the multi-member constituency of Calgary. Three of these candidates had never been nominated by the Calgary constituency convention but had been selected by Aberhart himself. Immediately there were cries that Aberhart had used fascist methods. One writer to the Calgary *Herald* commented on the selection of O.G. Devenish, a veteran oil man:

> Some distrust has been evident in the ranks by the entry of big oil interests in the person of O.G. Devenish, into an organization primarily to promote the welfare of the common people.

The same writer complained of the number of competent workers for Social Credit who had been shelved as candidates, J.R. Boon, for example:

> The rejection of J.R. Boon, one of the earliest pioneers and a promi-nent speaker of the movement came as a surprise to many. Associated with Mr. Aberhart for a number of years in church work, Mr. Boon has long been a familiar figure to the numbers attending the Bible Institute with whom his personality has made him extremely popular. His expert knowledge of the deeper problems of agriculture and his efficient work in this line for years past would have made him an asset in a slate in which only twelve practical farmers have been chosen. Possibly, however, his propensity to stand by his convictions at any cost would not have made him a very docile member of the legislature.[105]

Once the election date had been announced, the Social Credit campaign moved into high gear. Not only was it a campaign, it was a crusade. At one of his meetings Aberhart is reported to have prayed, "Oh Lord, grant us a foretaste of Thy millennial reign."[106] In another of his broadcasts he com-mented:

> Ladies and gentlemen, let us be at once assured that the God of Heaven is behind the great crusade that we see manifesting itself in our province. We trust that there will sweep over this province and over this western land such a wave of reverence and adoration for the God of heaven that has never previously been known. I am persuaded myself that it is only by the grace and power of God that our people shall be delivered from the awful conditions that threaten us. This is a time when all Christian people, of whatever creed or church should join hands in friendship and com-radeship to help one another to help himself.[107]

Throughout the campaign Aberhart talked of Social Credit being "applied practical Christianity"[108] and said it would produce charity and brotherhood; but the movement appeared to produce the opposite results. It was reported that in some churches the Social Crediters sat on one side of the church while supporters of other parties sat on the other. It was also reported that if the supporters of other parties had a car breakdown, Social Crediters would not stop to help them.[109] Feelings ran very high. Some of Aberhart's supporters believed that opposition groups were trying to keep them in poverty. Opposition candidates claimed that when they held their political rallies, their meetings were sometimes broken up by Social Crediters – who banged fenceposts on the walls of the buildings, or stopped their cars outside the halls and blew their car horns until the speakers were forced to quit. They also claimed that Social Crediters slashed their car tires and put sand and sugar in their gas tanks.[110]

Aberhart did little to discourage the actions of his supporters. When O.L. Mcpherson, the minister of Public Works who had been involved in the spectacular divorce suit, attempted to question Aberhart at a political rally, Aberhart appealed to his supporters and said, "Are you going to let this man cross-examine me?" The crowd responded by shouting down Mcpherson's questions.[111]

Aberhart's radio broadcasts at this time had an estimated audience of over 300,000 people on Sunday afternoons. Aberhart had a larger audience than Jack Benny, whose comedy program followed *The Back-to-the-Bible Hour*. Aberhart played heavily on western alienation by denouncing the so-called "Fifty Big Shots" of central Canada, and the "high mucky-mucks."

As election day drew nearer, Aberhart's call to prayer went out from the transmitter of CFCN. He instructed people how to pray and what to pray for, and he rejected the suggestion that the standard prayer for the Social Credit movement should be "If Social Credit is good for us, please give it to us." It was, he said, "too wavering."[112] He turned down a suggestion by one of his followers that they could conduct an all-day prayer meeting. "When you start to pray all day," he told them bluntly, "some of you only pray ten minutes and that is the finish of you." He suggested instead that they pray for a short time every evening, at home or in the Institute. The series of prayers was not to interfere with, but to be an integral part of, the Social Credit campaign. "Some of you have a Social Credit meeting on one night of the week," he reminded them. "All right, you will have to attend that. The others don't have it. Come down here." He would look on the response, he said, as an indication of whether the campaign was going to be successful:

> I believe I could tell better by the praying people in this province than we could by the folks that are shouting too much for Social Credit. Let us pray and shout both. I don't want you to stop shouting but I do want every last man of you to join in a Bible study and a little prayer meeting.[113]

The other parties, especially the U.F.A., continued their oppposition to Aberhart's mixture of religion and politics. They attacked him in their broadcasts and public meetings, and in pamphlets containing cartoons satirizing his proposals.

One Sunday evening, while Aberhart was preaching in the Bible Institute, someone in the audience caught his eye. A young man, sitting a few rows from the front, was studying him intently. Aberhart had the uneasy feeling, however, that his words were passing this man by. On the man's knee was propped a sketchpad, his busy pencil recording Aberhart's features and gestures; he was distracting the attention of those sitting nearby. This twenty-three-year-old artist, motivated at the time by no feeling of malice toward

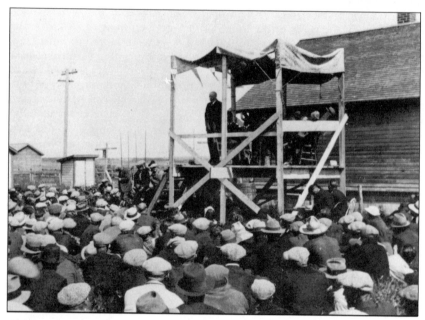

Aberhart campaigning in 1935.

Aberhart, but merely endeavouring to earn a living by his pencil, was to become a deadly but dispassionate enemy of Aberhart, giving him the devastating new experience of having his most earnest words greeted by the derisive laughter of a nation. He was Stewart Cameron, whose father J. McKinley Cameron, a prominent Calgary barrister, was said to have suggested themes for his son's anti-Aberhart cartoons.

Aberhart's features – his bald head with a slight fringe of hair on the sides, his thick lips and fleshy jowls, his pince-nez glasses, and his expansive waistline – made him a cartoonist's delight. Of all the attempts to capture Aberhart on paper, Stewart Cameron's caricatures were the most skillful. Soon his cartoons were featured in *The United Farmer* and the Calgary *Herald*.

During the campaign Aberhart worked like a man who meant to win an election. He spared no one, least of all himself, and he spoke at as many as four meetings in one evening. Yet somehow all the work seemed no more than the habit of years. Those closest to Aberhart say that he could hardly believe at this stage that it was possible for him to win the election; it was even hard for him to get used to the idea that he was actually in the game of politics. He seldom stopped to consider the strange and swift sequence of events that had catapulted him at the age of fifty-seven into a position in a field that had never before held any special interest for him. To Aberhart, it was like a hobby run wild.

The 1935 Alberta election was governed by the preferential voting system, whereby the election was decided by taking into consideration the total of first-, second-, and third-choice votes a candidate received. As early as December 1934 Aberhart had begun to persuade the voters that they could vote for Social Credit without withdrawing their suppport from whatever party they usually voted for.[114] His argument was based, first of all, on the

One of Stewart Cameron's earliest anti-Social Credit cartoons, from the United Farmer *(9 August 1935, p. 16).*

dubious claim that Social Credit was not a political party, but a people's movement, and secondly, on the fact that under the preferential voting system used in Alberta, the voter would be able to give his first vote to Social Credit and his second to the party for which he usually voted. The latter part of Aberhart's argument was not easily refuted: a vast number of voters were confused by the statistical complexities of their voting system.

Having brushed up his own knowledge of the workings of the preferential voting system, Aberhart, through the pages of the *Alberta Social Credit Chronicle*, gave the general public a course of instruction in the subject, illustrated by charts and sample completed ballots.[115] This helpful information was followed, nearer to the election, by the mailing of printed cards to the electorate at large, demonstrating exactly how the ballot should be marked in each district. In the multi-member constituencies of Calgary and Edmonton, these cards were marked in such a way as to make the best possible use of the second-choice, third-choice, and subsequent votes. Ads telling

CALGARY
BOARD OF TRADE
TAKES STAND ON
SOCIAL CREDIT

It having been represented to the Calgary Board of Trade that people were looking to it for some statement regarding Social Credit, the Council of the Board, after very prolonged and careful consideration of the arguments for and against the proposals, has decided to submit the following as its considered conclusions on the subject:—

1.   The proposals must necessarily involve crushing taxation entirely beyond the capacity of the people of Alberta to pay.

2.   Any attempt to fix just prices can only result in incredible confusion and paralysis of business to the detriment of every producer and consumer.

3.   The suggestion that dividends can be paid out of cultural heritage and undeveloped natural resources is impracticable and impossible.

4.   The Social Credit monetary proposals will lead to a condition similar to that which occurred in Germany, involving the Province, the farmer, the wage earner, etc., in financial disaster.

5.   The Social Credit proposals will isolate Alberta and render it impossible for either the farmer or the business man to buy or sell to advantage.

6.   Finally, such an experiment as is outlined by the Social Credit proposals will lead to chaos, and entail great suffering, from which the Province would not recover for many years.

Inserted By The

ECONOMIC SAFETY LEAGUE

Hon. Dr. W. Egbert
President

CALGARY

Jesse Gouge
Secretary

Many businessmen feared the effects of Aberhart's proposed changes to the economy. This anti-Social Credit ad was placed in the Calgary Herald *(8 August 1935, p. 3).*

people how to vote were also carried on "telephone time."[116] Near the end of the campaign Aberhart gave a public demonstration in ballot-marking at the Labour Temple.

Though Social Credit proposals were the main issue of the campaign, other planks in the Social Credit platform had a certain interest: the elimination of borrowing from outside the province; legislation for the relief of debtors and mortgage defaulters; and the refinancing of municipal and provincial debts at lower rates of interest. Greater standardization among the various provincial educational systems was called for, and vocational training was promoted.

This Social Credit platform was designed to appeal to a wide range of people, much wider than those interested in Social Credit economics. The "Socreds" proposed to assist agriculture by securing new export markets, lower freight rates, revising the system of grading produce, maintaining rural roads, and raising the quality of livestock in Alberta. Irrigation, eradication of weeds, assistance for drought areas, and amendments to homestead laws were proposed. The improvement of legal facilities, the organization of a provincial police force, and revision of taxation methods were also mentioned. The following statement in the Social Credit platform also appeared almost word-for-word in the U.F.A. platform: "We are favourable to the ultimate introduction of State Medicine into Alberta."

The low state of U.F.A. prestige, and the suspicion felt by most Social Crediters that almost everyone in the government was a scoundrel, was indicated by the pronouncement "Every Department of the Government needs to be reorganized and to be put on a business basis to eliminate the present enormous waste of taxpayer's money."

The final plank of the 1935 Social Credit platform was intended to dispel any lingering misgivings in the voters' minds about Social Credit:

> The Social Credit Government when in power will pass legislation to the effect that candidates submit to the voters right of recall if they fail to carry out the proposals made prior to the election.[117]

This promise would be regretted by Aberhart in due time.

The U.F.A. platform included evidence of its connection with the C.C.F. when it advocated the creation of a National Wheat Board and the extension of provincial ownership into utilities and monopolistic natural-resource industries. Yet another political creed crept into the U.F.A. platform in the form of a weak Social Credit plank, designed to satisfy those within the party who wanted some form of Social Credit without frightening those who were opposed to Social Credit. This plank called for the nationalization of the Bank of Canada, the public ownership of the monetary system, and short-term and immediate credit.

Despite the comprehensive nature of their platforms, the issue between the U.F.A. and Social Credit in the campaign was clearly Social Credit itself – its feasibility and desirability, or otherwise. Aberhart himself best summed up the attitude of his party when, in his election-day speech, he said that whereas the Liberal Party had made twenty-six promises, the Social Credit

Party had made only one – to attempt to provide all citizens with the bare necessities of life.

Other groups in Alberta besides the formal political parties found Aberhart's promises ludicrous. The Economic Safety League was formed by businessmen who feared economic chaos for the province if Aberhart came to power. One member of that organization, the Calgary Board of Trade, warned that Aberhart's program would result in crushing taxation, business paralysis, financial disaster, provincial isolation, and "great suffering from which the Province would not recover for many years."[118]

In the final days of the campaign it became obvious that the U.F.A. was fighting a losing battle. One U.F.A. leader related what he termed a "typical experience" at a political meeting at Wetaskiwin, a place that was afflicted by hail in 1935. He finished his address, and the meeting was thrown open for questions. A young farmer rose and told the crowd of the low prices he was currently receiving for his wheat and his cattle. "I sell a steer," he concluded, "for hardly enough to pay the freight. Now, would you tell me what I have got to lose in trying Social Credit whether I believe in it or not?" That unanswerable question was cheered by the farmer audience.[119]

On the night of 14 August, eight days before the election, Norman Priestly, vice-president of the U.F.A., was scheduled to speak at Ponoka. As he stood in the school yard, waiting for the audience to arrive, he and some of his supporters talked about the upcoming election. The spring of 1935 had been late and cold, but it had come and there had been plenty of rain at the right time; the crops were still green and they looked good. The U.F.A. speakers glanced at the sky. It looked as if frost was in the air. "If it freezes tonight," said Priestly, "we can count on a Social Credit win." That night, three quarters of the crops of Alberta were damaged by a cruel unseasonable frost.[120]

As the campaign approached its climax, Aberhart continued to deny he was seeking power. In his broadcast of 11 August 1935, he had remarked:

> You know a man is not [sic] without honour in his own province. I fear I could never command the utmost confidence of our people. Major Douglas on account of his wide experience and in coming from a distance might gain it. I am strongly in favour of Major Douglas introducing his system. He is the originator and I am a disciple. Please get it out of your head that I want to be a dictator. If you want me to answer it in another way I would say this – I shall be very glad indeed to refuse any government position of honour or authority if that will help you think I would not be a dictator. I am not going to be a dictator.[121]

However, in his private conversations with friends, Aberhart was very convinced that he would assume power. On 20 August 1935, while working at Crescent Heights High School preparing for the fall term, he was asked by Lettie Hill, still the school librarian, what he felt his party's chances were in the election. Aberhart replied, "Oh, the election is all over, it is in the bag, so to speak." He estimated that they would obtain between fifty-five and sixty seats: "It's a fact alright. You see, I've got the greatest political organization that this province or country has ever seen."[122] After telling her that he would accept the premiership if his party got more that fifty seats, he suggested that she should move to Edmonton to become the provincial librarian and his research assistant. Subsequent entries in "Hilly" Hill's diary indicate that this was a genuine offer.

Many thought Aberhart's election victory a foregone conclusion, and a potential catastrophe for the province.

In a last-minute attempt to warn the public against Aberhart, the Calgary *Herald* published the Stewart Cameron cartoon depicting a car containing the people of Alberta. It approaches a concealed railway crossing. A train labelled "Common Sense," unseen by the people in the car, is also approaching the intersection, at high speed. Aberhart, leaning out of the "Social Credit signal tower," beckons the car on, saying, "All's clear. Don't stop, look, or listen."[123]

The same evening, Calgary Social Credit candidates and Aberhart addressed a mass meeting in the Victoria Arena. Apart from his short holiday in Vancouver, Aberhart had not spared himself. Those who attended this meeting recall him on one knee at the edge of the platform, with perspiration rolling down his forehead, shaking hands with the dozens of people who pressed forward. After the meeting he went to the CFCN studios, where with other Social Credit speakers, he gave a final broadcast until 11 p.m.

In that final pre-election broadcast, Aberhart lambasted the other parties:

Never in the history of elections in this Province has the public been inflicted with such a campaign of falsifications, lies, threats, and what not.

The few men in financial power are determined to maintain it at all cost...
I am sure that the intelligent voting part of the public are well aware that
it is not a safe proposition for them to support candidates who have connection with this diabolical, slanderous, vicious style of propaganda work.
If they will lavishly spend money for the purpose of getting their candidates
into power you may rest assured that they have their own selfish interest
at heart. The more cultured, dignified, honest-to-goodness voters in our
land, I am sure, will recognize that if these men will stoop to such tactics
in order to get into parliament, what may they expect after they have been
put there. If they fail to recognize it, it is a poor time to complain after
the election when graft and greed and injustice with little regard for the
people's welfare is found in the circles of government.[124]

One of the "falsifications and lies" to which Aberhart referred was a news
story that had appeared in the Calgary *Herald* that day, reporting Aberhart
was a defendant in a lawsuit involving his Blue Manual. When he had prepared
the booklet in May of 1935, he had made James Rogers, an unemployed man,
his advertising and publicity agent. Rogers was to secure advertising to be
placed within the booklet; the ads would pay for the publishing costs. To
assist Rogers's task, Aberhart had written him a letter of introduction. Rogers,
in turn, had hired others to obtain the advertising and had not paid them
their commissions. These salesmen were now suing both Aberhart and Rogers
for non-payment.[125]

The *Alberta Social Credit Chronicle* reported that Aberhart was annoyed
at the press report. He denied having anything to do with the financing
of the Blue Manual and claimed the booklet and the letter of introduction
were Rogers's ideas; he had supplied only the questions and answers.[126]
Months later he was still paying Rogers's bills.[127] If anything, the incident
revealed Aberhart to be a poor judge of character, with questionable
business sense. The scandal did not, however, have any impact on the
election.

The position of importance that Aberhart had given Social Credit in the
minds of Albertans is perhaps best illustrated by the following experience
– recalled by one who sat in her family circle beside the radio listening to
election returns on Thursday, 22 August 1935. Mussolini was threatening to
seize Ethiopia at the time, and the radio announcer said, "Today the eyes
of the world are on Alberta and Ethiopia." "Why?" enquired a member of
the family. "Have they got Social Credit, too?"

Voter attendance at the polls was unprecedented. Throughout the
crowds, Social Credit workers tried to influence voters by handing them
sample ballots indicating how people should vote, just as they had done
at the advance polls.[128] Here and there were cries that this was a violation
of the Election Act, but little seems to have been done about it. In some
ethnic areas, a frequent question was asked: "Vich vun twenty-five dollar
man?"[129]

The returns, as they were coming in and being counted, revealed a political
landslide such as Alberta had never seen before. Out of 63 seats in the legislature,
Social Credit secured 56, the Liberals 5, and the Conservatives 2. Not a single

U.F.A. candidate was elected, and many of them lost their deposits. In contrast to this, the standing of the parties on 22 July 1935 had been: U.F.A. 36, Liberals 13, Conservatives 6, Independents 4, and Labour 4. Social Credit had received 163,700 votes – 54 percent of the popular vote.

Many stories have been told to illustrate how Conservatives, Liberals, and U.F.A. supporters had voted for Social Credit, many making last-minute decisions to do so. In one country district the members of a certain U.F.A. family were said to have gone to the polling station with no other ostensible intention than that of voting for their U.F.A. candidate. When the votes were counted, however, not a single U.F.A. vote had been polled in that station, an embarrassing fact for that particular family – each of whom, had there been even one U.F.A. vote cast, might have claimed it as his own.

That evening at the victory celebration at the Calgary Prophetic Bible Institute, Aberhart was almost too excited to use the speech he had prepared that afternoon. His speech was broadcast over CFCN. Perhaps for the first time, he permitted himself to realize the enormous responsibilities he had undertaken:

> Anything I might say now, must be said with great consideration for when we're fighting a fight to get into power everything we say must be carefully said just as everything we do must be carefully done. I feel this myself more especially tonight in the face of victory than I have ever done before.

To those who feared the Social Credit victory, he addressed the following words:

> Those of you who have investments or money or savings, Social Credit will not confiscate them. Social Credit will work for the welfare of the people collectively, not only for a few. Great care will be taken in carrying through this new Social Credit Order. You may rest assured that nothing rash will be done. We want your confidence because we want to serve you. We would ask you to bear in mind these words: we hope that Alberta will lead the world. The eyes of the world are on Alberta.

In conclusion he commented:

> I want personally to give thanks to the Almighty God in Heaven for His guidance and direction in this whole matter. I assure you that it is our intention to submit our deliberations to His Divine guidance and wisdom. Since He seems to be calling us to a place of leadership we trust that our people will put their trust in Him and not fail. Follow your Government with your prayers. Remember our theme song: "O God Our Help in Ages Past." Fear not, thank you, ladies and gentlemen.[130]

In six months, Aberhart had wrestled control of Alberta from the orthodox political parties.

The Social Credit victory can be attributed to many factors. Aberhart's organization and propaganda were much more effective than those of his opponents; he had a radio station at his disposal. The U.F.A. government's chances of being re-elected had been destroyed by sexual scandals, disunity and alienation within the party, and lack of charismatic personality in Premier Reid. Aberhart's promises of economic reform had won the support of most farmers and the urban working classes.[131] The $25 carrot he had dangled in front of the voters had also helped him gain votes. As an economic Moses, he had taken his party through the Red Sea of the election; he was to find, however, that the Promised Land was a long way off.

CHAPTER FIFTEEN

■

"VICTORIOUS! WHEN COULD YOU COME?"

O N AUGUST *15, 1935,*
Mr. Aberhart said: "You don't have to know all
about Social Credit before you vote for it. You
don't have to understand electricity to make use
of it, for you know that experts have put the system
in and all you have to do about Social Credit
is to cast your ballot for it, and we'll
get experts to put the system in."
— William Aberhart as quoted in the
Calgary Herald, 30 January 1937

The Social Credit victory in Alberta generated international interest. In London, John Hargrave and his Green Shirts, with their flags flying, trumpets blasting, and drums beating, marched around the Bank of England announcing that Aberhart's victory marked the doom of the existing financial powers.[1] Among Social Crediters in Alberta excitement was high. They were ready for Aberhart to lead them in an exodus out of the Depression. The task ahead of him was great enough to challenge even Aberhart – the administration of an impoverished province with a government not one member of which had ever sat in the Legislature before, but which promised economic recovery for the province, and food, shelter, and clothing to every citizen.

Canadian Liberal leader William Lyon Mackenzie King, upon hearing of the Alberta election results, believed that Aberhart's victory announced the coming defeat of the federal Conservative Party and his own return to the prime ministership. He noted: "It is a weird business – a fortunate thing it is for Canada as a whole, that this fanatical flame has thus far been kept within the bounds of a single province."[2]

International press reaction to the Social Credit victory was mixed. The Philadelphia *Record* remarked:

> The Alberta experiment ought to settle finally whether the Social Credit theory is economic hogwash, or something smarter and more genuine than most people suspect.

The Boston *Herald* was highly critical: "Alberta goes crazy," it headlined. A similar view was voiced by the Chicago *Daily Tribune*: "Greetings to the Canadians. Who's loony now?"

Within Canada most newspaper editorials were just as critical. The St. Catherines *Standard* claimed, "The whole thing is a chimera, a nightmare that passeth all understanding,"[3] while the Montreal *Star* commented:

> They have voted for an untried man and a policy whose workings he ostentatiously refused to explain before polling day. He was reported as saying that it was not necessary for the electorate to understand electricity and yet they turned it on. Thus they could turn on his social credit scheme, and he would guarantee that the light would come.
>
> So they took his word and turned it on. They are in frame of mind to try anything once. It is a dangerous frame of mind, but it is a mental condition that our public men may well heed.[4]

The Toronto-based *Pentecostal Testimony* wished Aberhart well, but added, "Personally, we question whether the movement, however commendable, can ever attain its ends. We are rather inclined to believe conditions now extant are indicative of the end times... and we feel that only the Millennium can bring about a reign of justice and equity."[5]

The Ottawa *Citizen*, edited by Charles A. Bowman, Major Douglas's friend, was the only major Canadian newspaper to welcome the victory:

> The Social Credit victory in Alberta is one of the most momentous decisions ever made by the people of a self-supporting State in recent times.

It may sound the death-knell of an archaic financial system which demonstrably fails to fit the facts of modern production, and it will come as a stupefying shock to those in other parts who dismissed William Aberhart as a sort of comic character suitable for the barbs of their misinformed derision.[6]

Some Alberta newspapers analyzed the vote as the result of economic and psychological deprivation. The Hanna *Herald* noted the psychological forces at work:

It is easy for a person in favorable circumstances to be logical in mind and philosophical in temperament. But strip a person of his belongings, take his job away from him and expose him to the cruel vicissitudes under which the poor have to live and there is no telling how his mentality will operate.[7]

The Edmonton-based *Alberta Labour News* remarked:

Indeed, it was a radical vote. It was a vote that was seeking to find expression in the proposals that appeared to offer the most striking challenge to the present social order. The Labour vote went Social Credit. Much of the U.F.A. vote went Social Credit. It went that way because the people were seeking to find a more immediately effective means of voicing protest against things as they are.[8]

Its editor Elmer E. Roper, who had been a member of Aberhart's Bible class at Grace Presbyterian Church many years before, expressed the hope that the new Aberhart government would become more left-wing and would soon find itself allied with the C.C.F.

The Calgary *Herald* also saw the Social Credit victory as a mass revolt against the Depression.[9] The Calgary *Albertan*, which had been more sympathetic to Aberhart's movement and had printed the *Alberta Social Credit Chronicle*, wished the new government well, but added that it would rather have had Social Credit "tried in Major Douglas's native Scotland, or Ethiopia or anywhere but Alberta."[10]

It was not surprising that the *Alberta Social Credit Chronicle* was overjoyed with the election results. One of its staff writers saw eschatological significance in what was happening: "The world is just about to pass into the seventh period, a period of reajustment, reconstruction, and harmony, the period which is frequently referred to as the Millennium."[11] Another of its correspondents pictured Aberhart in messianic terms. She described how she had seen a mother present her children to Aberhart at a picnic that summer:

When the mother at last reached the goal, she presented these two Sunday scholars to our Leader, and, oh the joy, to witness that great man welcome so tenderly and joyfully these youngsters. It made one's thoughts revert to One Who many years ago did likewise here on earth.[12]

The *Alberta Social Credit Chronicle* poured out eulogies upon Aberhart and his wife, whose lifestyle had little in common with Aberhart's average Alberta family clad in gunny sacks and eating gopher stew. A reporter for the *Chronicle* wrote:

> Did you ever enter a typical Western Canadian home, where comfort, homeliness and cleanliness greet you as you enter the door? You climb a long winding stone staircase, through grass terraces intermixed with flowers in profusion, and you are met by a gracious and sweet faced, grey haired lady in her early fifties, although looking much younger, and as she takes your hand, a warm smile of welcome lightens her face, the first thought that comes into your mind is one word – "Mother." This is what comes to mind as you meet Mrs. William Aberhart, wife of the leader of the victorious Social Credit party.
>
> Mrs. Aberhart's home in Elbow Park although luxuriously furnished, is one in which you immediately find rest and comfort, and as you sink into one of the big comfy easy chairs you at once feel the warm welcome that is extended to you.[13]

Jessie Aberhart appeared to be happy with her husband's political success. However, when Aberhart's aged mother Louisa, whom he had not seen for some years, was interviewed by the *Huron Expositor*, she claimed that she was not at all enthusiastic about her son's entrance into politics and wished that he had stayed with his preaching. She added that she had not bothered to stay up to hear the election results.[14]

In spite of this small sour note, the Social Credit victory brought many honours to Aberhart. Babies were named after him, and telegrams and letters flowed in from around the world. As he read these congratulations over his radio broadcasts, Aberhart appeared as happy as a child at a birthday party. Major Douglas had cabled him: "There will be others, but only one first."[15] Dr. Hewlett Johnson, dean of Canterbury, also cabled his regards: "Magnificent. Congratulations. Given best Social Credit skill to produce watertight scheme and pressing it forward courageously, Alberta will kindle a worldwide torch."[16]

Other letters came from Aberhart's past schoolmates, and from students he had taught over the years, as well as from almost anyone interested in Social Credit.

On 24 August 1935 Aberhart sent the following cable to Major Douglas in London: "Victorious: when could you come – Aberhart."[17] Two days later, he received the following reply: "If necessary could sail middle September. Suggest calling me telephone ten morning Edmonton time – Douglas."[18]

Every evening for the following week, Douglas stayed by his telephone, expecting to receive a call from Aberhart. No call came. It would be interesting to know what matter Douglas wished to discuss with Aberhart by telephone rather than commit to paper. Perhaps Aberhart also speculated on what it might be, and may have guessed that Douglas wished to discuss the financial arrangements of his proposed visit to Alberta. Douglas's two-year contract with the Alberta government stipulated the sum to be paid Douglas for only one stay of three weeks in each year. He had already visited Alberta once in 1935, and if he were to make a second visit, the fee would have to be negotiated. On the very day Aberhart was supposed to telephone Douglas, Aberhart received a telephone call from Premier Reid that must have been a shocking revelation to him of the financial position of the province and may have caused him to decide, as he afterwards explained to Douglas, that there was absolutely no use trying to bring Douglas to Alberta in September or October without even enough money or financial credit to pay his expenses.[19]

Premier Reid requested that Aberhart come to Edmonton as soon as possible to take over the government, since the financial situation of the province was growing desperate. At the news of the Social Credit victory, said Reid, a wave of apprehension among the holders of Alberta savings certificates had caused them to cash their bonds at a higher rate than normal. There had already been a run on the banks as many people had transferred their deposits to banks in other provinces.[20] The Alberta Treasury could not stand even a slight increase in withdrawals, and Reid proposed to suspend payments temporarily. Aberhart agreed with this step. The U.F.A. government was in a distressing situation because, having been defeated, it was unable to borrow money, yet a large loan was an absolute and urgent necessity in order to carry on even the immediate routine business of the province.[21] Aberhart said he would go to Edmonton on the following day, immediately after the close of the first Social Credit caucus.

On Wednesday 28 August 1935 the first caucus of Social Credit M.L.A.s was held in the Calgary Prophetic Bible Institute. Aberhart entered the familiar building that had been the summit of his ambitions eight years before, to hear himself unanimously chosen leader of the parliamentary group, and therefore, in effect, premier. Aberhart did not as yet hold a seat in the Legislature, for he had not run in the election. The caucus therefore passed resolutions allowing him to choose any seat he wished from those that his party had won.[22] Aberhart was also given the authority to force any Social Credit M.L.A. to vacate his seat should he wish to fill it with someone else. Further, he was given complete authority in the choosing of his cabinet. Two other matters were dealt with in that first caucus meeting. It was decided to run Social Credit candidates in the coming federal election, and decisions had to be made regarding help from Major Douglas.

Immediately after the caucus, Dr. Victor Wright, who had assisted in the campaign and served on Aberhart's advisory committee, drove Aberhart, Manning, and John W. Hugill up to Edmonton. On Thursday Aberhart set about investigating the exact financial position of the Treasury and arranged that the swearing-in of his government would take place on 3 September 1935.

When Aberhart returned to Calgary late Friday night, he announced his selections for cabinet ministers. Long before the election he had, of course, singled out possible candidates. In only one known case did the election results make it necessary for him to revise his choice. The prospective minister of Lands and Mines O.G. Devenish had been defeated in the election, having been viewed with suspicion by the working class because he represented big oil interests. Upon Dr. Wright's suggestion, Aberhart then appointed a Liberal, Charles C. Ross, a former district supervisor for petroleum and mines with the Dominion government, to the ministry of Lands and Mines.[23] A seat would have to be vacated for him.

None of the other choices for cabinet positions was much surprised when he was contacted by Aberhart: each already had a fair idea that he was to be included. Aberhart had already discussed the list of ministers with John Hugill, K.C., a successful candidate. Hugill, formerly a law partner of R.B. Bennett and legal advisor to the C.P.R., was one of the few members of Calgary's élite who openly supported Social Credit. He was consul for Sweden and vice-consul for the Netherlands, held the rank of major with the 24th

Aberhart and his cabinet ministers, 1935. None of them had ever sat in the Legislature before. Aberhart flanked by John Hugill and Ernest C. Manning.

Infantry Brigade, was captain of the Calgary Polo Club, and held many other offices in civic, social, and recreational clubs.[24] When he and Aberhart discussed who would be attorney-general, Aberhart replied knowingly, "You know who that is."[25]

For provincial treasurer and minister of Municipal Affairs, Aberhart chose Charles Cockroft, an accountant and a general merchant from Gadsby, who had also been mayor of that town and otherwise prominent in civic affairs. William N. Chant, the new minister of Agriculture, was a farmer from Camrose. William A. Fallow, mayor of Vermillion and agent for the Canadian National Railways, became minister of Public Works, Railways and Telephones. Dr. W.W. Cross of Hanna was chosen as minister of Health.[26]

Ernest C. Manning, who had headed the polls in Calgary, became the new provincial secretary. At twenty-six, he was the youngest cabinet minister in the British Empire, and so deficient in that breadth of experience usually considered essential to a cabinet minister, that even the *Alberta Social Credit Chronicle* could say of him only that he had "shown his ability along secretarial lines." "His honesty and integrity," added the editorial reassuringly, "can be vouchsafed."[27] The only remaining portfolio, Education, was taken by Aberhart himself.

As a novice premier Aberhart had made a fairly good choice in selecting his cabinet; they were men with practical experience related to their portfolios and, as we will soon see, they were not simply "yes men."

Continuity with the previous government was maintained when Aberhart chose as his personal secretary Fred Stone, who had previously been the personal secretary of the outgoing premier R.G. Reid. Stone had been one of Aberhart's students at Crescent Heights High School and had gone on to study economics and political science at McGill University. During the school year 1932-33 he had written a master's thesis on unemployment relief in western Canada. Aberhart came to depend upon Stone as a speech-writer, adviser, and confidant.[28]

For the next few days Aberhart found himself occupied with housekeeping duties; he had to clear up unfinished business in his other endeavours. On 31 August 1935 he wrote to the Calgary School Board requesting an indefinite leave of absence from Crescent Heights High School. His request was granted.[29]

The other big interest in Aberhart's life, the Calgary Prophetic Bible Institute, had to be managed during his absence. To that responsibility he appointed Cyril Hutchinson, who had been his student off and on since the early twenties. For the preceeding few years Hutchinson had been a clerk with the city of Calgary's relief department and had been a supply preacher for Aberhart. The pastoral duties of the Bible Institute Baptist Church were to be continued by the Reverend M.L. Burget, who had been hired in 1934. Aberhart, however, still remained the central figure in the various organizations sheltered within the Bible Institute; he continued to be the president of the Calgary Prophetic Bible Institute Church, dean of the Calgary Prophetic Bible Institute, and apostle of the Bible Institute Baptist Church. To maintain this control, he and Ernest Manning would travel to Calgary on alternate Sundays and conduct the necessary services and business.

On 3 September 1935 the public crowded into the galleries of the Legislative Chamber to watch the ceremony as Aberhart and his cabinet were sworn into office. That was one of the least important things on Aberhart's mind at the time. His investigations had revealed that before 31 March 1936 he would be faced with bond maturities of $5,200,000, interest charges of about $2,800,000, relief payments, and maturing bank loans, bringing the government's total obligations to $14,915,000. The financial position of the Treasury had not yet been ascertained exactly, but Aberhart recognized that a loan from the federal government was essential and urgently needed. He telephoned Prime Minister R.B. Bennett in Ottawa, who assured Aberhart that he would do anything he reasonably could to help; and it was arranged that Aberhart would, if necessary, travel to Ottawa to discuss the matter.

There was not even enough money to pay civil servants' salaries that would come due on 15 October 1935, and the obtaining of the loan from

The Alberta Legislature Building.

Ottawa exceeded in urgency the visit of Major Douglas to Alberta and the introduction of his long-term Social Credit plan. Aberhart asked Douglas for his written instructions, however. On the day after his government was sworn in, Aberhart acknowledged three cables he had received from Douglas on various subjects:

> Cables gratefully received. Before taking further action executive council wishes full information by letter or preliminary directions.[30]

Douglas, nearly 10,000 kilometers away in Fig Tree Court, set about composing a letter in reply to Aberhart's cabled request. Douglas was vaguely aware of the immediate crisis in Alberta, but he did not know that Aberhart was asking for a loan of $18 million from the federal government.[31] In his letter Douglas suggested that the Alberta government should persuade one of the chartered banks to credit its account with the sum of, possibly, $5 million. The bank should agree not to call in the loan and the government should pay only the bank interest of one-and-a-half percent, as well as some bookkeeping charges, both of which, Douglas considered, should cover the cost of the bank's services. The government would be able to draw upon that account only by cheque, and all cheques had to be deposited in the bank that made the loan. That would, said Douglas, "prevent any variation in the bank's cash ratio and would not subject them to any financial difficulty whatever."

Douglas suggested an alternative measure to be used if that was unacceptable to the banks (as it surely would have been). The government should obtain securities held by private Alberta citizens by exchanging them for short-term Alberta bonds, and use the securities as collateral for obtaining a loan from a bank under ordinary commercial arrangements.

"The general outlines of a permanent plan," said Douglas, "are well under way but it seems expedient not to commit them to paper at the present moment, in case the information should come into the wrong hands." Douglas was not, then, attempting to give complete blueprints for introducing Social Credit into Alberta, but only to deal with the immediate crisis in the province. Aberhart had, however, already done this by approaching Bennett for a loan.

To aid Aberhart's movement, Douglas was also sending the Dean of Canterbury to Canada on a speaking tour, and he suggested that Aberhart use the Dean's influence to good advantage in gaining the support of the well-to-do and conservative sections of the population.[32]

Before he dispatched the letter Douglas read in The *Times* about Aberhart's intended visit to Ottawa. "I quite agree with this policy," Douglas wrote in a note which he enclosed with the letter, "if on reasonable terms."[33]

On 6 September 1935 Dr. Wright drove Aberhart and John Hugill to the C.P.R. station in Calgary, where several hundred people waited to watch the premier and the attorney-general leave for Ottawa to negotiate the loan. This was not Aberhart's first trip back to his native province, but it contrasted oddly with his journey west twenty-five years before. Now he was the centre of interest on the transcontinental train, discreetly pointed out at dinner and curiously studied in the observation car. Some of the bolder passengers sought his acquaintance and offered him well-meaning advice on how to solve the problems of government in Alberta, and others regaled him with their opinions on the consitutionality of Social Credit and the feasibility of the theory.

Aberhart's train was looked for all across the country – at Medicine Hat by an entire Social Credit nominating convention, which had interrupted its preparations for the federal campaign and adjourned to the station to cheer him. At Winnipeg, Social Credit organizers for Manitoba boarded the train to confer with him, and Allan Bond, a family friend of Hugill's, was introduced to him. Bond worked for the National Trust Company, and he and Aberhart discussed the advisability of employing auditors to check the financial position of Alberta. Bond mentioned that he had a high regard for Robert J. Magor, a Montreal economist who had straightened out the finances of Newfoundland, and offered to write Magor on Aberhart's behalf. This seemingly blameless conversation was to result in dark suspicions about Hugill and much controversy among Social Crediters.

Aberhart went directly to Ottawa, where he met with R.B. Bennett and his cabinet. There are no descriptions of his negotiations with the federal government, but he was successful in securing only a $2,250,000 loan.[34] That was a far cry from the $18 million previously mentioned, but Bennett had pointed out that he could authorize a loan to cover only the time remaining before the federal election.

Even though the Social Credit League was fielding candidates in the upcoming federal election, Aberhart had expressed the wish before leaving

Attorney-General John Hugill and Aberhart with Prime Minister R.B. Bennett in Ottawa, 1935. They went seeking $18 million from the federal government to stabilize Alberta's economy before they tried to implement Social Credit.

for Ottawa that R.B. Bennett should not be opposed by a Social Credit candidate in his home riding of Calgary West. Within the Social Credit League there was considerable debate over this issue, but it was decided to follow Aberhart's wish in the matter.[35] To some it seemed that Aberhart was using this as a lever to obtain Bennett's good will.

On Aberhart's assuming office Bennett had written him a very warm letter,[36] but when it came to Social Credit, Bennett was not as enthusiastic. He had appointed, early in 1935, a commission including his brother-in-law W.D. Herridge, the Southam brothers, and Charles A. Bowman to investigate the possibility of distributing dividends to all Canadians, although nothing came of the inquiry.[37] Bennett pointed out that the loan to Alberta had nothing to do with Social Credit; it was only to keep the province going.[38] When asked about Aberhart, he remarked, "Mr. Aberhart is a friend of mine. He is a great teacher, but he has not yet proved himself a great statesman."[39]

One of Bennett's suggestions to Aberhart was that a loan council be formed to administer Alberta's debt. When Major Douglas heard of this he immediately wrote Aberhart claiming that it was a trick designed to bring the Alberta government under the influence of Montagu Norman, governor of the Bank of England, who had already talked to Bennett about Alberta's situation. To Douglas, Montagu Norman was one of the arch-conspirators within his anti-Semitic mythology.[40]

With only part of the necessary $18 million being provided by the federal government, Aberhart turned to other sources for help. During his conversations with Charles Bowman of the Ottawa *Citizen*, Aberhart had asked him to accompany him to England, where they would seek the aid of Major Douglas in finding money for the Alberta government from British banks. Bowman cabled Douglas, who advised against this action.[41]

Aberhart then suggested that Bowman go with him and Hugill to interview Henry Ford, who had bypassed the banks in the financing of his projects. Without an appointment, they set out for Detroit via Kingston and Toronto. They visited Queen's University at Kingston, from which Aberhart had earned his extramural degree. On the train to Toronto Aberhart met Sir Joseph Flavelle, president of the Canadian Imperial Bank of Commerce, and the simultaneous alighting in Toronto of the two men, the financier and the anti-financier, was eagerly recorded by the waiting reporters whose stories, when published in London, gave Douglas more than a moment of uneasiness.

The following day Aberhart had a number of conferences with Toronto bankers, but little came from the talks. He then spoke before a luncheon meeting of the Canadian Club. Generally he made a good impression, but he discovered that in these new social surroundings, his attorney-general was more at home than himself, and that perhaps emphasized the differences apparent between the two men from the beginning.

John Hugill was the type of man whom Aberhart was never able to understand fully or appreciate. Hugill was of slight build, had extremely elegant tastes, and a keen appreciation of the refinements of "civilized" living. His education in England at the City of London School, and later in Canada at Dalhousie Law School and the University of King's College, Nova Scotia, had imparted to him considerable polish, which Aberhart's set of values did not allow him to appreciate. Aberhart looked with distaste on the sensuous delights of fine wines and expensive cigars, and neither shared nor understood Hugill's acute pleasure in riding a pedigreed polo pony. Hugill disguised his own ability and application to his work with a fashionable flippancy that left Aberhart puzzled. "I never know when to take you seriously," he once said to Hugill in exasperation.

In a similar state of incomprehension Aberhart listened to Hugill at lunch in a Windsor Hotel, remarking favourably on the Ontario government's allowing liquor to be served with meals in hotels. "Do you mind," Hugill asked their host, the manager of the Ford plant in Windsor, "if I have a bottle of the burgundy which is served here?'' Upon the wine being brought, Aberhart remarked in a semi-serious manner to their host, "I hope you don't mind my Attorney-General. He has peculiar habits."[42]

From Windsor, Aberhart and the others travelled to Detroit to interview Henry Ford but, having not made an appointment, discovered that Ford was away at his summer home. Aberhart then had a meeting with Herbert Bruce Brougham who, since 1919, had been Major Douglas's official representative

Aberhart conferring with Father Coughlin in Detroit.

in the United States. A journalist by trade with experience on the New York *Times* and the Philadelphia *Public Ledger*, Brougham was currently preparing an article on the Social Credit movement in Alberta for the *Atlantic Monthly*. He had contacted Aberhart while he was in Ottawa and arranged to meet him when he came to Detroit. He had also arranged a meeting between Aberhart and Father Charles Coughlin, another controversial figure.[43]

Coughlin was a Canadian-born Roman Catholic priest who had gathered an enthusiastic following in the United States and Canada through his radio attacks on capitalists and bankers, among others. Aberhart had often expressed his admiration for the priest; Coughlin was in turn interested in Social Credit, and now eagerly took advantage of the opportunity to meet Aberhart. The meeting, which lasted for an hour, was held privately, even Hugill being excluded, and no word of what was said was apparently ever made public by either man. However, Aberhart said of Coughlin, "He has a keen intellect and is absolutely fearless. He has a correct appraisal of world conditions."[44]

After the meeting with Coughlin, Brougham drove Aberhart and Hugill north to Seaforth, Ontario, where Aberhart planned to visit his mother and brothers. On the way Brougham discussed his involvement in the drafting of the American Social Credit Bill (H.R. 9216) that T. Alan Goldsborough, congressman for Maryland, had introduced into the House of Representatives on 22 August 1935, the day of the Social Credit triumph in Alberta. From his conversations with Aberhart and Hugill, Brougham departed with the impression that they had invited him to come to Edmonton to draft a Social Credit plan for the Alberta government.[45]

On the afternoon of Saturday, 14 September 1935, the mayor of Seaforth and his council stood about in the Town Hall waiting for the return of William Aberhart. The little town had not radically changed since he had last lived there almost forty years before. There was a flutter of mild excitement in the air as Aberhart arrived. This was the third time that Huron County had had a native son become a provincial premier: W.M. Martin and James G. Gardiner, both premiers of Saskatchewan, shared this honour with Aberhart.

However, there had been no wild rejoicing in Seaforth when Aberhart's movement had swept the polls in Alberta. "I don't know," exclaimed his mother, "why he went and got into politics. No, I certainly do not approve of it." "However," she conceded, "he is old enough to know what he wants." Neither his mother nor his eldest brother Charles claimed to understand Social Credit theories any better than their neighbours. They had, they said, not seen Bill lately. His brother Louis, however, now the owner of a chopping mill, did not need to understand Social Credit in order to have faith in his brother. "I was sure he would win," exclaimed Louis. "And this is only the beginning. He will show the way to the rest of the Dominion, and you will see the United States swing that way, too."

The other inhabitants of Seaforth, reading accounts of Aberhart's election promises in hostile or indifferent newspapers, shook their heads sceptically. However, they delved back into their memories and recalled that Bill Aberhart had been an honest, hardworking lad from an honest, hardworking family – and were forced to come to the conclusion that, as his brother Charles said, "If he says these things can be done I know he feels they can be done."[46]

During Aberhart's visit to Seaforth he had a brief, nostalgic hour of glory – the civic reception, the reunion with his mother, his brothers, nephews, and nieces. He greeted old friends and recalled his boyhood days, but spoke as often of the task ahead of him in Alberta and of the people he was trying to help. On Sunday evening, Aberhart mounted the pulpit of First Presbyterian Church in Seaforth, where he had attended as a youth, and told the congregation of conditions in Alberta and how he had become distressed when his school graduates could not find jobs. He asked for their support and said, "If you allow us to fail, remember hungry hearts and wild-eyed men and women may turn to violence. We are fighting to save the people from revolution."[47] He tried to reassure conservative Easterners that although the conditions in Alberta had almost turned him into a communist, revolution could be avoided through Social Credit economics.[48]

From Seaforth Aberhart returned to Toronto for more talks with bank officials. Nothing definite was decided, but Aberhart claimed that he had found a friendly spirit prevailing, and that they had asked him to submit his plans in detail to them before any loans to Alberta could be considered. On his way back to Alberta he stopped at Winnipeg and Saskatoon, in both cities addressing luncheon meetings of the Canadian Club.

On his return to Edmonton Aberhart found stacks of mail that had accumulated in his absence. He took his job seriously and, at first, tried to answer all of his mail personally. Many letters contained questions on theological matters, requests for advice or financial aid, or congratulations.

Three letters that Aberhart opened eagerly were from Major Douglas. In them Aberhart hoped to find a complete plan for the introduction of Social Credit. Finding only Douglas's two alternative measures for dealing with the shortage of money that now was not as pressing, he was disappointed. He wrote Douglas dismissing his first suggestion of obtaining a loan as "a matter of detail that will be taken up later when we are prepared to start the system,"[49] and saying that the exchanging of privately-owned stocks for Alberta bonds "would alarm our citizens to a very grave degree, and would give the opponents a splendid opportunity to attack viciously the whole method of procedure."[50]

The securing of Douglas's written plan for Social Credit was now becoming important in Aberhart's mind, and he appealed at some length for Douglas to send him a complete plan:

> I am looking forward to receiving the general details of a permanent plan which you are preparing. I feel satisfied that you need not hesitate to let us have this in definite form at your earliest moment. I am sure the government will be careful not to let the information fall into the wrong hands.
> The question of your remuneration in the matter of your second visit to the province in any one year is important. As you are aware, our treasury has been greatly depleted. We would, therefore, like to hear from you regarding this.[51]

Aberhart also assured Douglas that he had been treated fairly by R.B. Bennett and the bankers he had visited. He claimed that he was not going to run ahead of Douglas's advice.[52]

In the meantime, without guidance from Douglas, Aberhart set about directing the affairs of the province with the aid of his cabinet. As we have already seen, Aberhart had difficulty accepting Hugill's values; but Hugill had even more difficulty accepting Aberhart's. He was shocked at Aberhart's dependence on the occult, having learned for example that Aberhart had chosen a cabinet of seven advisors because seven was the "perfect" number.[53] Numerology was one of the ideas Aberhart had picked up in his flirtation with British-Israelism. Then, for the benefit of the cabinet Aberhart explained the numerological significance of their names, and some sought license plates with their "number."[54]

On 24 September 1935 Aberhart announced that the government was going to sell "prosperity bonds" to offset the $150 million provincial debt, saying he believed that in ten years the province would be debt-free. He also added that those bonds had nothing to do with the introduction of Social Credit; they were only intended to balance the budget.[55] A public-works program was also announced, to improve the main highways and enlarge the mental hospitals.[56]

In order to clear the way for his own administration, Aberhart began cutting other expenditures and staff. A number of department heads in the civil service were asked for their resignations,[57] a measure undoubtedly to get rid of those people who might not be sympathetic to Social Credit. Forced retirements were imposed on all civil servants past retirement age.[58] These moves were in direct contradiction to Aberhart's speech the night before the election:

> I told all the official civil servants that they have nothing to fear whatever from the Social Credit government. We are not a political party. We have no great number of henchmen that must be [given] positions.[59]

Aberhart made his friend Dr. Victor Wright chairman of the Workman's Compensation Board. To the position of King's Printer he appointed his Jewish friend Abe Shnitka.

While all of this was taking place there were repeated questions as to when Social Credit would become a reality. Douglas's immediate arrival in Edmonton was looked upon as the most urgent step to be taken if Social Credit was to have an opportunity of being tried in Alberta. Neither of the two people who alone could arrange this, however, were showing any great anxiety to hasten the visit.

Douglas had already postponed his visit when he had said in his letter of 5 September 1935, "On the face of it it seems desirable that any visit I might make to Alberta would be more useful after the Federal Election."[60] It is understandable that the federal election, which was to be held on 15 October, would assume greater importance for Douglas than for Aberhart, who was preoccupied with provincial problems.

Douglas had already taken one big step to influence what he considered the promising federal election, when he persuaded the Dean of Canterbury to make a speaking tour of Canada before it. He had told Aberhart that the tour "will turn election if suitably supported."[61] He had also emphasized in his letter of 5 September 1935 the "immense importance of getting the largest possible favorable 'bloc' of members at Ottawa."[62]

Dr. Hewlett Johnson landed at New York on 15 September and then commenced a speaking tour of Canada on behalf of the Social Credit movement. Though the Dean described his mission as "educational," it was in fact a crusader's march across the country with enormous propaganda value. His route intersected, and his meetings coincided with, those of politicians of all parties who crossed Canada in preparation for the federal election.

The Dean's appearances in Alberta were made under the auspices of the New Age Club (still the official representatives of Douglas's organization). Aberhart complained to Douglas that his own Social Credit organization had not been allowed to act as host to Dr. Johnson, but he did not comment publically on the matter.[63] For the huge crowds who attended the meetings in Calgary and Edmonton the Dean's presence gave the impression that the Social Credit victory had been a great triumph of Christianity over politics.

The presence of the Dean in Aberhart's pulpit of the Calgary Prophetic Bible Institute left some of Aberhart's religious followers with the impression that the Dean was a fundamentalist. One member of the congregation went up to the Dean after the meeting and said to him, "Dean, I used to attend the Church of England, but I left because it was too 'cold.'" He replied to her, "Well, my dear, you had better go back and warm it up."[64]

Dr. Johnson was closely followed in Alberta by William Lyon Mackenzie King, leader of the federal Liberal Party who, in Calgary on 30 September 1935, made his "hands off Alberta" speech, which was afterward notorious in the province. In seeking the support of Albertans, Mr. King said he would "give Alberta every chance to work out what she is seeking to do."[65] Mackenzie King's visit to Alberta also involved an interview with Aberhart. In his diary King commented on Aberhart's cabinet: "I was appalled at the immature look of those around or rather on both sides of the table, all with paper and pencil in hand."[66]

As the federal election approached, Social Crediters were campaigning for sixteen of the seventeen seats in Alberta. On Aberhart's instructions they had not opposed R.B. Bennett in Calgary West. Aberhart took almost no part in the organization of the federal campaign, as his time and energies were fully occupied in the problems of the provincial government. The Alberta Social Credit League, however, was very much involved. Letters were sent on 1 October 1935 to those firms that had done business with the Alberta government and asked them for donations to its federal campaign. When some businessmen objected, they received another letter that threatened boycott if they did not reconsider.[67]

The major problem facing Aberhart was putting the province on a firm financial basis. On the suggestion that he had received from Allan Bond in Winnipeg, John Hugill began negotiations with Robert J. Magor, the Montreal financier and president of the National Steel Car Corporation of Hamilton, to come to Alberta and advise the government on financial affairs.[68]

Another matter of concern was the pressing demand from the people of the province for their promised dividends. Aberhart responded that the dividends would not be supplied until Social Credit was put into force, and he had still seventeen months to do that.[69]

The third matter urgent for Aberhart was the finding of seats for himself and C.C. Ross, whom he had appointed minister of Lands and Mines. Aberhart chose to run for the seat for the Okotoks-High River constituency that had been vacated for him by the Reverend William Morrison, a minister of the United Church of Canada. Aberhart claimed that he chose this riding so he could be M.L.A. for the Prince of Wales, whose ranch was located there.[70] The seat of Athabaska was vacated by Clarence Tade so that C.C. Ross could run in the by-election.

On 15 October 1935 the Conservative government at Ottawa paid for its inability to banish the Depression, and a Liberal government under Mackenzie King was elected. King, a practicing spiritualist, was so elated at his victory that he hugged and kissed the busts of his deceased parents, and went from room to room in his house praying to their pictures that adorned the walls.[71] The West had no monopoly on the bizarre.

For the first time in history seventeen Social Credit members sat in the House of Commons in Ottawa, the third largest of the ten parliamentary groups, though not large enough to wield much political power. Many of those Social Crediters were Douglasites. The leader of the federal Social Credit members was John H. Blackmore, a Mormon. The Social Credit candidates had taken all of the Alberta seats but two (one of those two being that of R.B. Bennett, who was re-elected in Calgary West). Aberhart's former colleague from Westbourne Baptist Church, the Reverend Ernest G. Hansell, was one of the successful federal Socred candidates. In Saskatchewan, two out of the twenty-one Social Crediters were elected. The results in Manitoba and British Columbia were disappointing: not one of the Social Credit candidates was elected.

The limited success of the Social Credit party in the federal election was very disappointing to Major Douglas. It now became clear that he had to work in close cooperation with Aberhart if he wished to assist with the work of Social Credit in Alberta. Aberhart had reassured him in every letter that he desired his help, but his letters were not as frequent as Douglas's. Douglas felt that he did not have sufficient authoritative information to sum up the situation accurately, though what he did know did not please him. He was expecting the Dean of Canterbury back shortly and would receive from him a complete account of the Alberta situation, from which he could form a well-founded opinion of Aberhart's actions. That was in his mind when Douglas sat down to write another letter to Aberhart.

This cold but courteous letter is interesting, for it contained Douglas's response to Aberhart's request for "general details of a permanent plan." Douglas replied that these details could be found in his *First Interim Report*, which he had already given to the U.F.A. that year. He added another proposal, that Aberhart should make an arrangement with a bank to obtain "sums of financial credit as may be required from time to time" under the terms suggested in his letter of 5 September 1935. Failing that, similar arrangements should be made with an organization that the government itself might set up. He commented upon the only step towards Social Credit that the government had been making:

> I regard the survey of production, resources, etc., to which you refer, as being quite secondary to action of the character I have outlined, and consider the existing details quite sufficient for the purpose of inaugurating a sound Social Credit system.

As to a visit to Alberta that fall, he remarked:

> I should much prefer not to make a second visit in the early future since the sum agreed upon does not, in fact, nearly compensate me for the direct and indirect cost of a visit to Alberta.[72]

Douglas was apparently trying to obtain more than the $2,000 paid to him for his previous visit to Alberta that year.

Aberhart was not happy with Douglas's reply; Douglas was being as vague as ever on the question of how Social Credit would be established. Aberhart discussed the matter with his friend "Hilly" Hill. They agreed that one of

The Macdonald Hotel, the Aberharts' home in Edmonton.

Douglas's recommendations from the *First Interim Report*, that the government have at its disposal a newspaper and radio station, was a good idea. The weekly and unprofessional *Alberta Social Credit Chronicle* was not adequate for their needs, and contrary to his critics' beliefs, Aberhart did not control CFCN. Hill suggested that the Social Credit League purchase the *Albertan*, which had been somewhat favourable to the Social Credit movement. He believed the newspaper could be obtained if Social Crediters purchased its stock, the sale of which could be handled by the firm of O.C. Arnott and Company by whom Hill was now employed.[73]

The matter of Alberta's financial situation was still very much on Aberhart's mind, and Major Douglas had been of little help. Therefore negotiations with Robert J. Magor were completed, and he arrived during the latter part of October to assist Aberhart. Magor's employment, the government explained, was not part of the Social Credit plan itself. "He has been retained," said Ernest Manning, "for the purpose of building a solid foundation on which the super-structure of Social Credit can be erected."[74] His task was to clear up the results of alleged maladministration by the previous U.F.A. government, and he was to be paid $600 per month plus expenses for his services. He would spent only a limited amount of time in Alberta; most of his work would be done in his Montreal office.[75]

When Aberhart had assumed the office of premier he found it necessary to rent out his pleasant white bungalow, with the terraced garden, in Calgary, and move to Edmonton. Not wanting to purchase a house in Edmonton that they might be forced to sell if the Social Credit experiment did not work, and feeling that they did not want to rent a house, Aberhart and his wife moved into a two-room suite in the Macdonald Hotel in Edmonton. There, for a while, they formed a part of a strange little colony. Next to the Aberharts were Dr. and Mrs. Victor Wright. (Wright was now head of the Workman's Compensation Board.) Next door to the Wrights was Attorney-General John Hugill, and a few doors away lived Ernest Manning.

This little community was subject of considerable speculation in the hotel. It might reasonably be expected that a glittering social circle might in time revolve around the little colony on the third floor, but the Social Crediters lived up to their reputation for godly austerity. No wild merry-making or lavish tipping enlivened the Macdonald on Aberhart's arrival, and the only lamp burning late in the Aberhart suite was on Aberhart's desk. There he worked, between the tall windows that looked down to the North Saskatchewan River. Jessie had made the suite familiar with things brought from their Calgary home.

When in Calgary the Aberharts stayed at the Palliser Hotel. Their living in such fancy hotels brought a certain amount of criticism from some of the electorate, who felt that the Premier should set an example of thrift. Aberhart replied that because he paid for his accommodation out of his own pocket, it was his own business where he lived.[76]

Nonetheless, the destitute state of the province and Aberhart's own somewhat austere tastes did govern their lifestyle. Jessie Aberhart's entertaining seldom went beyond an occasional tea party for the ladies of her acquaintance. She was, however, a person of much dignity, charm, and refinement, and performed her quiet office as wife of the premier with much graciousness – and perhaps with more ease and pleasure than she had while being the wife of a fundamentalist religious leader.

Every morning Aberhart and Dr. Wright breakfasted in the hotel cafeteria. Out-of-town visitors and Edmontonians alike would be on hand in unusually large numbers to watch them peform the humble task of carrying their trays to a vacant table, and to marvel at the heartiness of Aberhart's and Wright's appetite, as if the two men were a new breed of polar bear being fed at the zoo.[77] From that peaceful domestic spectacle the onlookers turned once again

Aberhart and his closest advisors: John Hugill, Ernest C. Manning, and Dr. Victor Wright.

to their morning newspapers and read of the predicted revolutionary activities of the new government.

The third-floor colony at the Macdonald Hotel soon dwindled. Hugill moved away to a house as soon as his wife was able to join him in Edmonton, and the Wrights moved to a suite on the first floor. The Aberharts remained in the two rooms of Suite 301 that now became their permanent home.

On 20 October 1935 Aberhart announced over his Sunday-afternoon religious broadcast that Major Douglas would be leaving England on 1 November and would arrive in Edmonton two weeks later to confer with the Alberta government.[78] Aberhart's announcement seemed to have had no basis in fact, for no correspondence exists between him and Douglas over the details of any such visit. That the visit might have been arranged by telephone is a possibility; however, Douglas's statement that he had never received any specific invitation from Aberhart casts doubt upon it. What is most likely is that Aberhart made the announcement in order to calm the clamour about when Douglas was coming. He may have been taking a gamble that Douglas would come.

Such, however, was not to be. Douglas's own correspondence with Aberhart over the past two months, and the account of the Alberta situation he had received from the Dean of Canterbury, brought him to the conclusion that he could never work successfully with Aberhart. On 29 October he had written a searing letter. In it he said that he believed Magor's employment by the Alberta government had been engineered by a group of Montreal bankers. In Aberhart's chance meeting in Winnipeg with Allan Bond, who recommended Magor to him, Douglas saw the sinister designs of the "money power" at work. He saw Hugill as an agent of the bankers to work on Aberhart's inexperience and susceptibility to flattery. Douglas looked upon Magor with the deepest suspicion. Magor, he said, had been active in the introduction of a financial policy in Newfoundland (then still a British dependency) "which has been murderous to the population of Newfoundland though satisfactory to the Bank of England." (The fact that Aberhart hired practically the first man who was recommended to him was indeed a sign of his inexperience, though not necessarily of any preconceived plan on the part of the bankers.)

In the rest of the letter Douglas vented his anger, for the first time revealing that he had been keenly disappointed in Aberhart's behaviour since the election, and listing his grievances at length. Aberhart had not kept Douglas sufficiently informed of what was happening in Alberta and omitted to telephone him. Douglas had gathered from Aberhart's three letters of 24 September that "he preferred to work in co-operation with the banks." He pointed out that this was directly opposite to the policy advocated in his *First Interim Report*. He discounted the effects of U.F.A. maladministration (which Aberhart had said was the reason for his employment of Magor), indicating that he felt that Aberhart's policies would damage the general cause of Social Credit and suggesting that his own contract with the Alberta government be "terminated by mutual consent."[79] Should Aberhart's behaviour change in the next six months, however, Douglas was willing to renegotiate with him at that time.

Even before Aberhart received this letter, the public was aware that there was some kind of rift between him and Douglas. On 1 November newspapers reported that Douglas was angry about Magor's hiring, and that the earliest Douglas might come to Alberta would be in the following spring. When Aberhart was questioned by reporters about the situation, he denied any rift with Douglas, but admitted that there had been no official decision as to when Douglas would come to Alberta.[80]

Not knowing the full state of affairs between Aberhart and Douglas, Social Crediters still looked forward to the full operation of Social Credit. Spurred on by the successes of their provincial and federal candidates, they now sought to have Social Credit governments at the local level. Calgary's civic election provided them with their first opportunity. Among the full slate of candidates who vied for civic office in Calgary were Charles R. Pearce and Fred Battisto, both members of the executive of the Calgary Prophetic Bible Institute. They ran for the positions of school board trustee and alderman, respectively. Their bids for office, however, were not successful; but five other Social Crediters filled three aldermanic and two school board seats.[81]

While the Calgary civic election campaign was on, by-elections were also being held in the constituencies of Okotoks-High River and Athabaska.

Because no other parties contested the elections, Aberhart and C.C. Ross, the minister of Lands and Mines, won the seats by acclamation.[82]

In mid-November Aberhart again found it necessary to approach Ottawa for a two-million-dollar loan in order to carry on normal government business,

Aberhart, still the sportsman at heart, kicking off a football game in Calgary, 1935.

but Mackenzie King's Liberal government responded with only one million.[83] Again Aberhart reiterated that the loan had nothing to do with Social Credit; it was only to clean up bad debts incurred by previous administrations. People were becoming anxious about Aberhart's own administration; so far every major step he had taken "had nothing to do with Social Credit." There was an increasing cry of "Where are the dividends?" and one writer to Aberhart threatened that if the first dividends were not paid by Christmas, Aberhart would suffer the consequences. Aberhart replied that it would take eighteen months before Social Credit dividends could be distributed.[84]

Some citizens were not satisfied with that reply. Mr. A.S. Shandro of Edmonton took advantage of the controversy and formed the Social Credit Dividend Association of Alberta, promising to help citizens register for the proposed dividends and to interview Aberhart on their behalf. Membership in the organization cost one dollar.[85] Aberhart considered this organization a racket and notified all postmasters to remove its posters from all post offices.[86]

Aberhart was soon faced with another crisis. At the beginning of October H.B. Brougham, whom he had met in Detroit and with whom he had travelled to Seaforth, had arrived in Edmonton and had taken up residence in the Macdonald Hotel.[87] On 21 November a copy of an economic plan that Brougham had drafted allegedly disappeared from his room while he was at breakfast.[88] When he released that story to the press, Aberhart immediately denied that he or Hugill had hired Brougham as an economic adviser. He denied that Brougham had arranged the interview with Father Coughlin.[89] Brougham responded by calling Aberhart a liar. In a letter to Aberhart he complained:

> You have brutally and unequivocally challenged my truthfullness. Why you should wish to discredit me with the people of Alberta, and why you should treat a stranger within your gates, whom you invited as a guest, with such distinquished discourtesy I shall leave, for the time, with your conscience.[90]

The documentation that Brougham supplied to Aberhart indicates that he did, in fact, arrange the interview with Coughlin, but correspondence between Brougham and Charles A. Bowman suggests that Brougham was a self-appointed economic adviser.[91]

Brougham's plan for Alberta involved the establishment of a large cooperative association that would provide dividends of $10 per month and discounts of 25 per cent. Aberhart declared this plan worthless because it duplicated existing cooperative organizations.[92] Since Brougham claimed to be Major Douglas's official representative in the United States, the press took particular interest in this dispute. When Douglas was contacted by reporters, he stated that Brougham had ceased to be his representative in 1932 and that Brougham's work in Alberta was in no way sanctioned by him.[93]

Aberhart's reaction to Brougham seems to have been governed by several factors. He apparently felt that Brougham was a spy for Major Douglas and had been filling Douglas's ears with untruths about Robert Magor. In Aberhart's letter to Douglas on 27 November, he claimed that Brougham (although unnamed) was unhappy because Magor had been hired in preference to an American whom Brougham was trying to promote.[94] Also, Aberhart was becoming increasingly testy because of his own problems with Douglas. In the same letter to Douglas, Aberhart emphasized, "Nothing can be gained by your assuming the position of dictation rather than advice." Further, Aberhart was embarrassed by the necessity of having to shake off this unwanted assistant, who found the press eager to air his complaints against him.

Aberhart still felt he needed advice from Douglas. In his letter of 27 November, he tried to placate Douglas while at the same time holding him to his contract with the Alberta government. He explained to Douglas the immense problems that had immediately faced him on coming to power and reproached him for believing what he read in the newsapers (which Douglas had himself said were the propaganda organs of the financiers). Surely Douglas could give him some more detailed and practical instructions than he had hitherto done. Aberhart pointed out the hopelessness of expecting the banks to make loans *without* interest when they would not even make them *with* interest.

Aberhart remonstrated with Douglas, "It's your duty, surely, under contract, at least to complete your agreement. So we therefore ask you to communicate at your earliest convenience your detailed advice regarding our steps of procedure. Be more specific."

To please Douglas, Aberhart revived discussion of his proposed visit to Alberta: "Would it be better for you to come early in January or would your visit be more effective if it occurred immediately after the session of parliament?"

During the next ten days Aberhart was also harrassed by preparations for his attendance at the Dominion-Provincial Conference that Mackenzie King had called to take place in Ottawa early in December. On 1 December 1935 Aberhart said over the air from the Bible Institute that he was going to attend the conference in order to ask for assistance to put Alberta on a sound financial basis. "I am not talking of Social Credit," he said, "or twenty-five dollars a month... We shall send for Major Douglas to discuss the whole matter in detail in all good time."[95]

On 5 December Douglas cabled Aberhart: "No letter received. Will you announce resignation or shall I?"[96] With all the build-up Aberhart had given Douglas, the announcement of his resignation was the last thing Aberhart needed at this time. Quickly a cable was sent to Douglas, presumably by Ernest Manning, acting on Aberhart's instructions: "Letter mailed week ago. Have patience. One year not up till March – Premier Aberhart."[97]

While this exchange of cables was taking place, Aberhart was in Montreal consulting with Robert Magor about his negotiations with the federal government. He and Magor had worked out a plan to save the province money by decreasing the interest on Alberta bonds and by asking the federal government to reduce the interest it was charging the province for its past debts. The total provincial debt of Alberta amounted to about $160 million. The debts of Calgary and Edmonton brought the figure to approximately $200 million. The interest on these debts was taking about half the province's income. To improve the province's financial picture further Aberhart and Magor planned to ask the federal government to assume responsibility for relief payments, the operation of the mental hospitals, and the collection of income tax.[98]

Aberhart assured Eastern reporters that these negotiations had nothing to do with Social Credit. He denied he had promised a $25 dividend to each adult each month. "The $25 bonus was a figure of speech," he claimed. "The important thing," he asserted, "is that every individual should be guaranteed food, clothing and shelter."[99]

In his dealings with the Eastern press Aberhart became very angry. He denied over and over reports that even the *Alberta Social Credit Chronicle* had carried. While preaching in Ottawa's St. James United Church he lambasted the Canadian Press for carrying a story that said twenty-five additional R.C.M.P. officers had been assigned to Alberta to protect him because he had received threatening letters. "I have never had any threatening letters. Not one. Why should they threaten me? I have not done anything."[100] The Canadian Press's general manager quickly responded and implied that Aberhart was a liar. The press had never said that the Mounties had been sent to Alberta to protect Aberhart. The following day Aberhart claimed that he had been misquoted.[101]

The Winnipeg *Free Press* was another target for Aberhart's anger. He claimed that it had misrepresented him by depicting him as a tall, slender man with red hair. Archie Dale, the cartoonist for the *Free Press*, took advantage of the situation. In his cartoon of 11 December he hinted that Aberhart was attacking straw men in order to take the pressure off himself for not providing the dividends.

While in Ottawa Aberhart had lengthy talks with Mackenzie King. He told King that he did not know much about politics and hoped that he could call upon King for advice at any time. King recorded in his diary that Madame Taschereau, wife of the premier of Quebec, had told him she felt that Aberhart was a Liberal at heart and could be groomed to be King's successor.[102]

When Aberhart returned to Edmonton, he found another angry letter from Major Douglas. Douglas was implacable; he threatened to break his contract with the Alberta government on the grounds that Aberhart had committed a breach of contract by the "consultation of various authorities without reference to me, and the appointment of a technical advisor reporting to your Government without consultation with me."[103]

Aberhart tried appeasement again with the following cable: "Council decided to request you to come to Alberta no later than January 6th if possible. Parliament meets February 6th. We are now prepared to receive your full counsel."[104]

Douglas then suggested that he would meet Aberhart in Ottawa at the end of January, but he would not come to Alberta until their differences had been settled. Aberhart replied in another cable: "Impossible to meet Ottawa end January. Legislature meeting February sixth causes rush. We expect you to fulfil contractual obligations. You have no responsibilities apart from government. We do not understand your attitude."[105]

Douglas then asked to see Magor's contract, reports, and any proposed action. He claimed that if his assistance seemed practicable, he would sail fourteen days after receiving such information.[106] Aberhart replied that there was no written contract with Magor and that he had made no recommendations regarding Social Credit. He added that if Douglas could not come immediately, he should postpone his visit until after the Legislature met.[107]

On 31 December 1935 Douglas sent Aberhart another letter claiming that Aberhart did not understand what Social Credit was. He reiterated that he needed to see all of the recommendations that Magor had made if he were going to be of any assistance, and that he would require a month's time from the moment the material was sent to him to the day he set out.[108]

Aberhart was in difficulty; he felt he needed Douglas and yet he found Douglas very difficult to deal with. He wrote to Charles Bowman and asked his help:

> The more I confer with Major Douglas, the more impossible he seems in so far as his attitude is concerned. How can we possibly use him when he takes this high hat position? On two occasions at least I have asked him to give us definite advice that he would give to any government. Then on the 20th of December, as you know, I invited him to come to Alberta at our expense to review the whole situation. His reply was that he would go to Montreal; that before he came further he had to review the whole

position in which we were. It would seem to me that he thinks that the steps we are taking are placing the province beyond the reach of the application of social credit principles. The whole position is ridiculous. It is the first time that I have heard a suggestion from him that a province could be so far down that he could not help them. I want to assure him that we have improved the condition in Alberta by getting free as far as possible of the power that may be exercised by finance. I am persuaded that it will take a little time to introduce social credit, and there must be no checkmating on the part of finance while this aim is being done. Can you give me further advice as to what may be done to get this man off his high horse and bring him down to a place where we can talk to him.[109]

Douglas had insisted that anything Aberhart might have done in the province for the introduction of Social Credit had been automatically prejudiced by the employment of an orthodox economist. Aberhart disagreed with this and remonstrated that all he had done was to make "immediate arrangements to look after the civil service and necessary conduct of the affairs of government." He asserted his right to use his own discretion:

> You will pardon me, I am sure, when I say that I personally do not intend to sink my right as premier to express my opinion upon your advice or that of any other person in the employ of the government. I am responsible to the people, and I of course shall be called to account for any mistakes that are made.[110]

Thus was brought into the open the irreconcilable differences between Douglas's and Aberhart's conceptions of their own and each others' functions. This was the point they had arrived at by the time of the opening of the first session of the Alberta Legislature on 6 February 1936. Gone was the hope of a constructive partnership between the two men. While Albertans waited, thinking them in close consultation, the two men in fact sat in separate rooms, Douglas considering his future, and Aberhart juggling the day-to-day problems of the premiership.

Douglas could see the only opportunity for trying out his Social Credit theories that had ever occurred quickly slipping away. Success in Alberta would have meant the vindication of his ideas. He wondered if, even now, it might not be too late to guide Aberhart away from actions that might discredit Social Credit. Aberhart himself could feel a million pairs of eyes on him – hopeful, trustful. He had promised the people of Alberta prosperity. Perhaps he could see the mood-change – and the mob, as had been prophesied for him, swarming up the Legislative Building steps, demanding its dividends.

On 6 February 1936 Aberhart and Douglas sat down to write each other in a calmer mood, neither motivated by friendly personal feelings but rather, as Douglas put it, "actuated solely by a desire to forward the cause...." Douglas cautioned Aberhart against the proposal that had been made in Alberta's brief to the Dominion-Provincial Conference, to place the collection of income tax in the hands of the federal government.[111] Aberhart, in his letter, asked for "any suggestions" Douglas might have for dealing with the next crisis that faced the Alberta government: the maturity on 1 April 1936 of $3,200,000-worth of Alberta bonds.[112]

The expectations created by the campaign still drove the Social Credit M.L.A.s, and their eagerness to press ahead with the introduction of Social Credit was no doubt responsible for Aberhart's note to Douglas on 20 February 1936. It informed Douglas bleakly that he was expected in Edmonton in early March. Douglas had already seen rumours in the press of this request, and a letter in reply was already on its way to Aberhart. Douglas spelled out several options; he renewed his request that Aberhart come to London to confer with him, and failing that, he set out conditions under which he would come to Alberta. He insisted that his contract with the Alberta government be considered terminated before he left England, and that he would be free to state publically his opinion on all matters and to advise at his own discretion anyone in Alberta who wished to effect financial reform. He also insisted that the government should undertake to put into practice certain of the recommendations he had already made. The letter indicated that if his conditions were refused, he would wash his hands of the entire business.[113]

After sending this letter, Douglas received Aberhart's urgent one of 6 February asking for advice concerning the maturity of the government bonds. In answer to this request Douglas suggested an ingenious scheme that was, however, no more practical than his previous suggestions for procuring interest-free loans. A gesture should be made, he advised, to persuade the federal government to take over the loan, renewing it on a two-and-one-half-per-cent basis – the provision of the interest to be the only obligation on Alberta. If the federal government refused, the bond-holders should be offered an alternative of renewing the bonds on existing terms or exchanging them for credit of the value of 115 per cent of the value of the bond. This credit would be made available to the former bond-holders and could be used by them for buying any product on sale in Alberta.[114]

Aberhart's dependence upon him gave Douglas an advantage that Douglas used to the utmost in order to try to force the premier to accept his directions. Aberhart and Douglas had always represented the practical and the theoretical, respectively. A compromise had been the only basis of hope for cooperation between them, but as the time for action had approached, they had instead moved further away from each other. Now they had withdrawn so far that there was no hope of reconciliation. Aberhart had realized immediately upon his taking office that Douglas's theories of "rule by expert" and the subsidiary role of the politician were completely impracticable, and that if he blindly obeyed Douglas's every instruction, he would be betraying the trust the people had reposed in him. He was, however, completely reliant upon Douglas for a "Social Credit Plan." Feeling the pressure of his own party, Aberhart cabled Douglas on 12 March trying to persuade him to come to Alberta and promising "full co-operation" when he came.[115] In his response Douglas properly reminded Aberhart that his contract with the Alberta government did not require him to provide a Social Credit plan but merely to advise and give directions upon all questions and problems of organizing in relation to the present financial and economic conditions of the said Province of Alberta and to advise and/or give directions upon any matters desired by the government related thereto.[116]

Douglas did not draw attention to the fact that neither did the contract require the Alberta government to take all of his advice when he chose to give it. This unreasonable requirement was what Douglas was, in fact, demanding, relying on Aberhart's helplessness.

Recognizing the unthinkable situation in which Aberhart would be without him, Douglas must have felt fairly confident that Aberhart would capitulate and accept his terms, however harsh. Then suddenly he changed his mind and decided to send a colleague rather than go to Alberta himself and have to deal directly with Aberhart.[117] Over the next eight days a cabled dialogue, discussing terms, dates, and contracts, argued the matter to a standstill, and ended with a letter from Douglas, dated 24 March 1936, breaking off negotiations with the suggestion that Aberhart could obtain his Social Credit advice locally:

I am confident that it is desirable that you should obtain the co-operation of Mr. Spenser [sic], the late M.P. for Battle River, Mr. Herbert C. Boyd, M.A., of Edgerton, and Mr. Larkham Collins, F.C.A., of Calgary.[118]

These three men whom Douglas now suggested Aberhart consult for expert advice on the introduction of Social Credit into Alberta had already declared their opinion that the B.N.A. Act made the introduction of Social Credit into a single province unconstitutional. Douglas's suggestion was surely a slap in the face, for Douglas knew that Aberhart and Collins were long-standing enemies. Since Douglas had suggested no alternative to this unacceptable course, "diplomatic relations" between him and Aberhart ended at once.

Aberhart was now on his own. He did not have a Social Credit plan, and it seemed that Douglas did not have one, either. Douglas appeared to be either a confidence-man or a meglomaniac seeking power only for himself. He had no love for democracy and, before the Macmillan Committee in 1930, he had said "if I were Dictator...."[119] The closest Douglas ever came to giving a concrete suggestion of how Social Credit would be put into force was his letter to Larkham Collins and his speech at the Mewata Armories in 1934, when he said control of the armed forces would be required.[120] Aberhart would not accept such a suggestion, for a military *coup* was foreign to his makeup. So he would have to try other advisers and methods to introduce economic prosperity into the province.

CHAPTER SIXTEEN

"I AM GLAD THERE WILL BE NO NEWSPAPERS IN HEAVEN"

T HE PRESS *is becoming a nuisance. The people of the world are beginning to realize that they will have to own and control their own press. We don't want to go into the publishing business but we won't be afraid to go into it. If some of these days I tell you that Social Crediters are going to have a daily paper I hope you'll support it.*

— William Aberhart quoted in the *Alberta Social Credit Chronicle*, 10 January 1936

While Aberhart was having his troubles with Major Douglas, he was waging a battle that eventually resulted in legislation censuring the press. Aberhart had been having his fights with the press, particularly the Calgary *Herald*, during the election campaign, and he had tangled with them since. Nonetheless, Aberhart was gratified by the attention they paid him; and during his first days in office, he had been open-hearted and free with the many out-of-town reporters who solicited interviews. It seemed, however, that Aberhart was unable to convince them of the feasibility of Social Credit. The articles that appeared on his desk weeks later were critiques of his ideas, containing penetrating analyses of why his proposals would not work. Other articles were written tongue-in-cheek, and some contributed to the general hilarity of their subject with elaborate descriptions of Aberhart's personal idiosyncrasies and appearance.

When Aberhart said of those who managed the nation's finances, "They haven't got a soul at all!.... The Lord Jesus Christ was crucified by the money changers...," he was under the impression that he was attacking, not reasonable people with clear consciences, but personifications of evil. He was always surprised to find that they attacked him personally in similar terms. It was not easy for his opponents to accuse him of immorality or greed, so they discredited him with the one weapon to which he was most vulnerable – laughter.

Early in January 1936, a copy of *Maclean's Magazine* crossed Aberhart's desk. In that issue was an article by H. Napier Moore, entitled "What of Social Credit? Impartial Notes on the Progress of Alberta's New Prophet."[1] Moore had given a brief history of Aberhart's pre-political activities, and recalled the rumours that he had made a bundle of money out of his Bible Institute and radio evangelism. Moore commented that he believed Aberhart was sincere when he first began with Social Credit, but that now he had reservations about him. He listed the incidents when Aberhart had denied making statements, such as that about receiving a threatening letter (a letter that Moore himself had heard Aberhart read over the air). Moore reported that in all of his travels around Alberta, and in his talks with government inspectors, he could not find one case of people subsisting on gophers, as Aberhart had claimed some did. Moore said some people were so convinced that they were going to get the $25 dividends that they had reserved berths on transatlantic cruises.

In his radio broadcast of 5 January 1936, Aberhart was noticeably angry. He lashed out at the press, calling reporters "nuisances" and stated that he was "glad there will be no newspapers in heaven."[2] He hinted that the press would have to be controlled and suggested that a daily Social Credit newspaper was needed. Aberhart was obviously hurt by Moore's article; he said he was glad he had "a rhinoceros hide and was now developing Abyssinian [presumably thick-soled] feet." Because Moore had made a number of factual errors in his article, Aberhart was able to deny or dismiss most of Moore's comments. Moore had incorrectly stated that Aberhart was the publisher of the *Alberta Social Credit Chronicle*, and in reference to the mortgage that the Bible Institute held on CFCN, Moore claimed that CFCN was owned by the Bible Institute. A picture in the article incorrectly indicated that CFCN was housed in the Institute building.

In a further article, Moore stated that people were becoming restless for their dividends. Why were the dividends being held up until the budget could be balanced if money was only "the stroke of a fountain pen" as Aberhart had claimed? Why could not the non-negotiable certificates handle the problem of Alberta's debt? Moore said that Aberhart believed that all of these problems would be solved because he felt the Divine Hand was guiding him.[3]

The treatment Aberhart received from Moore was nothing compared to what was to come. Walter Davenport, an American writer whom Aberhart had received graciously, and whose questions he had treated with gravity and patience, described Aberhart in *Collier's Magazine* in brilliant and sadistic prose, in an article entitled "Milk and Honey, Ltd.":

> He was sitting at his desk at a completely relaxed loll. When Mr. Aberhart sits down there is no nonsense about it. He gives himself with whole-hearted entirety to the chair and the rest is up to the chair. He is large, heavy and slumberous.... He has a vast colorless face. His pallor seems to extend far below the surface. He has some white hair on the sides of his bomb of a head but the whole is so pale and pigmentless that you don't notice it. As he spoke to us his tired, neutral, close set eyes closed tightly as though he'd like to shut out the world – and in particular the sight of those who couldn't believe. But most of all you remember his mouth – a narrow, left slanted mouth with soft, extra-heavy, bloodless lips which don't quite meet and through which he breathes wetly. Huge, waxen, hairless, weary; you wondered whether he'd bleed if stabbed.[4]

Aberhart could not understand what led to such abuse. He could not even recognize the events of the past few months in Davenport's jazzy description:

> he announced that... his version of Major Douglas's theme would pay monthly dividends. And that brought them to their feet. They could understand dividends and leave such matters as "increment of association" to the bugle-heads. All they wanted to know was how much, how often and how soon.[5]

The months had gone by, and the dividend had not been paid, and the world, less patient than Alberta, was laughing:

> He implored the national government at Ottawa for current expenses of government, for official salaries including his own, for electric current to light his desk as he pondered at night, for laborers to shovel the snow from the parliament building steps, for the wages of the policemen who would protect him from the mob that wanted its money....[6]

The dividend, the visiting reporter strongly suspected, was a myth, Aberhart a fraud, and Social Credit a hoax.

It was impossible for Aberhart to understand this scepticism.[7] The world did not appreciate what he was trying to do for it. He still believed he could not fail, if only he had the strength to outlast his adversaries. Publicly, therefore, he never wavered. But in his personal contact with strangers could be seen the deep scars on his feelings. Interviews with him soon became difficult to obtain and the jovial manner was glazing over with an icy reserve. He tried to sum up his new acquaintances – no easy matter for him, in spite of his quick and accurate assessment of the collective mind. He employed more frequently a means of discouraging impertinence that he had used during his teaching days. In silence he would scrutinize the one under suspicion. The cool blue eyes in their pallid setting would be steadily trained on their subject – penetrating, impersonal as the lens of a camera – as though trying to discover some weakness in the victim. Thirty seconds under that glacial gaze was an unnerving ordeal.

Throughout his experience in office, aggravated by continual attacks from the press, hurt and mystified, Aberhart kept his confidence and his belief that his cause was still intact. Publicly he brushed aside the personal attacks, continually exhorting Albertans to patience, assuring them that U.F.A. mismanagement had left untold problems that he had to deal with before he could begin to implement Social Credit. When he was ready he would invite Douglas over; nothing else delayed the Major. The eighteen months he had declared necessary to institute Social Credit had hardly begun, and nothing could be achieved without the loyalty, cooperation, and patience of the people.

In order to provide himself with a news outlet that would present and support the government's actions, Aberhart set about with "Hilly" Hill to purchase the Calgary *Morning Albertan*. The newspaper had had a poor financial history, and had been subsidized by the Calgary *Herald* in order to keep it out of the afternoon market.

On 15 January 1936 George Bell, publisher of the *Albertan*, announced that the newspaper had been purchased and was now the official organ of the Alberta Social Credit League.[8] The *Alberta Social Credit Chronicle* was to be merged with it.[9] Besides the newspaper, the Alberta Social Credit League also obtained radio station CJCJ, which was owned by the *Albertan*. The newspaper company would soon be offering preferred and common stock to the public, a first in Canadian journalistic history.

Aberhart, in his initial public statements, expressed great surprise at hearing that the *Albertan* had been purchased, but he was party to the purchase from the beginning.[10] Actually, a company he had formed with his friends had only an option to purchase the newspaper. Sales of stock were necessary to complete the purchase. Publicly, Aberhart denied any control over the newspaper, but privately he exercised control through one of his lieutenants, Charles R. Pearce, secretary-treasurer of the Calgary Prophetic Bible Institute, whom he made vice-president of the company that operated the *Albertan*.[11]

Soon Aberhart was promoting the sale of *Albertan* shares over his Sunday afternoon radio broadcasts, which now emanated from both Calgary and Edmonton. The Edmonton press was highly critical that Aberhart was using religious services to promote stock sales.[12]

The acquiring of a daily newspaper and a radio station were part of the recommendations of Douglas's *First Interim Report*. Not only was their acquisition important for government propaganda dissemination, but at that time Aberhart hoped that their purchase would prove to Douglas that he was following his advice. Aberhart made much of that point in a letter to the Dean of Canterbury during the time he was trying to get Douglas to come to Alberta.[13]

While Aberhart was fighting with the press, he received continued criticism from the U.F.A. At its convention in January 1936 ex-premier Reid defended his past government's actions, and demanded that Aberhart stop his allegations of mismanagement on the part of the U.F.A. or give proof of the same. Reid contended that there was no financial mess inherited from the U.F.A.; that had they been asked to carry on, there would have been no difficulties. These difficulties arose from Aberhart's own radical policies, which created a rush on bond redemptions and caused the withdrawl of normal lines of credit. He emphasized that the perilous financial state of the province had been disclosed many times, had the Social Crediters cared to listen.[14]

The U.F.A.-C.C.F. attack on Aberhart was carried on by William Irvine through a series of open letters to Aberhart published in the *People's Weekly*. Those letters began on 25 January 1936 and continued for ten weeks. Irvine informed Aberhart that the treatment he had received from the press had been very fair, considering the promises he had made. He noted that Aberhart seemed now to favour the "Big Shots" by appealing to bankers and financiers for help. He rubbed it in that Aberhart had had to borrow, for a *third* time, two million dollars from the federal government in order to meet the payments for bonds that matured in January. Where was Aberhart's "fountain pen"?[15] In another letter, Irvine wondered why Aberhart would seek aid from financiers when he himself admitted there was no soundness in the current financial system. Ex-preacher Irvine illustrated his question with a homely example:

> Let me put this matter to you frankly in language in which you will not fail to understand my point of view, however much you may then disagree. You are a preacher of the gospel. You are greatly interested in saving souls. Would you advise a sinner to patch up his soul and try to get it on a sound basis before he becomes converted? Or would you advise a drunkard to take another shot of Scotch to put him on a sound basis before you invite him to repent? I do not think you would dream of giving advice to anyone as unsound as that. You would demand an immediate abandonment of the sin by the sinner and urge his acceptance of the new way of life at once as the only way to achieve a sound basis for his life.
>
> Why, then, do you give such ridiculous advice in respect to a new financial system? The principle is the same. The present financial system is either sound or unsound, it is either right or wrong. If it is a wrong system, as I believe it is and as you have often declared it to be, then why should you want to monkey with it at all? You were elected to give us a new system. Now you say you cannot begin the new system until you have got us a sound basis by further use of an unsound and wrong system. You surely do not expect to fill the baskets of your promises with grapes and figs from the thorns and thistles of the "Big Shots'" system. That is wrong thinking, sir.[16]

The amount of criticism Aberhart was receiving was much on his mind as he prepared for the first session of the Legislature. He referred to it in an address he gave in Calgary on 17 January 1936, but what was intended to gain him more support, backfired. In referring to the hard time he was having, he commented:

> It brought to my mind the story of the young lady in the maternity ward who was in agony; she asked the nurse if there was a young man in a brown suit and brown fedora outside in the corridor. The nurse said, "Yes, I saw one out there when I came in."
>
> "Well," said the girl, "tell him that if this is anything like married life, the engagement is off!"[17]

Although Aberhart won much laughter with his joke, he was later beseiged by complaints that he had told such a "lewd" joke during a religious broadcast, and attempts were made to have him taken off the air.

The soon-to-mature Alberta bonds were one of the most pressing problems that faced Aberhart when his government assembled in the Legislative Chamber in Edmonton on 6 February 1936. Foremost in the minds of the M.L.A.s, however, was the mission for which they had been sent to Edmonton, the introduction of Social Credit. Uppermost in the minds of the public was the question of how the M.L.A.s would act. Did M.L.A. stand, as Stewart Cameron implied, for "men like Aberhart"? Had Aberhart chosen pliant candidates to act as rubber stamps for his legislation? Would they press for the dividends? To Aberhart's chagrin, they would.

After the opening of the Legislature, a party was held at Government House. Because of Aberhart's stand on alcohol, wine was not served with the dinner; but after dinner, in order to oblige those so inclined, the lieutenant-governor placed several bottles of liquor in his study. Others played bridge and billiards. Aberhart and Mrs. Edith Gostick, an M.L.A. for Calgary, did not want to join in, so a checkers board was found for them.[18]

Aberhart did not speak in the Legislature during the first session (indeed his maiden speech was not made until 1939). He saw no need to voice his opinions in the Legislative Chamber. Anything he wished to communicate to the people he gave to them directly over the air, and he could communicate with Social Credit members in caucus. His own followers already knew his views, and it was a foregone conclusion that the opposition would not agree with them. Aberhart seemed to be afraid of having to defend his position in the Legislature; he was not a man who would accept open challenges to his authority. The caucus therefore gained unprecedented importance; it was said that the Social Crediters met four nights a week during that first session. Cabinet meetings were often held in Aberhart's suite at the Macdonald Hotel. Jessie Aberhart is reported to have attended those meetings, busily knitting beside her husband. Whenever he lost his temper, she would reprove him: "Now, now, William!"[19]

Even though the opposition in the Legislature was small, they found enough support among unhappy Social Credit M.L.A.s to pass a motion by David M. Duggan, Conservative leader, that all the correspondence between Aberhart and Douglas be tabled in the Legislature. The disintegrating relationship between Douglas and Aberhart was now revealed, and W.R. Howson,

Liberal leader, made a motion that Douglas be brought before the Legislature for questioning, along with Robert Magor, regarding Alberta and the federal loan council. The motion was defeated.[20]

During the adjournment of the Legislature the final break with Douglas occurred. Douglas claimed he would not come because Aberhart had not been following his advice, and wanted the world to know that Aberhart's version of Social Credit was not his.[21] For the remainder of the nine-week session the untiring legislators worked out their energy in passing no less than one hundred and eight acts, and amendments to acts. Included in them were many positive social and labour acts that provided for minimum wages,[22] tradesmen's qualifications,[23] and free treatment for tuberculosis patients.[24] Some of those acts no doubt came from the civil service, but none were specifically "Social Credit"; they could have been passed by any progressive government.

Aberhart's much-discussed campaign promise to provide for the recall of members of the Legislature became law on 3 April 1936. The Act provided that a petition containing the signatures of 66.66 per cent of the total number of voters registered at the previous election in his constituency would be sufficient to unseat an M.L.A.[25]

Credit must be given to Aberhart as minister of Education for legislation passed during that session that even the most ungenerous observer must admit accomplished great and necessary reforms in the Alberta school system, though at the time they met with bitter opposition from the school boards and members of the teaching profession. It was Aberhart who gave Alberta teachers professional status by making it compulsory for them to belong to the Alberta Teachers' Association – that organization that he himself had refused to rejoin and the presidency of which he had declined in 1927. Now he forced into the hands of the teachers a means of safeguarding their common interests.[26] The consolidation of the rural school districts, a long-overdue piece of reorganization, was indignantly condemned by the Alberta School Trustee's Association convention, but even protest delegations were unable to dissuade Aberhart from pressing this measure which both saved money and extended educational opportunities for rural children.[27] Aberhart's own fights with school trustees, since his days in Brantford, had much to do with that legislation.[28]

Much of the other legislation was piloted through the house by Ernest Manning. Into his hands had been placed the modifications to the Trades and Industry Act passed by the previous U.F.A. government. An order-in-council clause of that Act allowed for the setting up of minimum prices, but Manning planned to set maximum prices. Aberhart had claimed that such price-fixing was, in effect, the establishment of the Just Price system.[29] These measures were not welcomed by the Calgary Board of Trade[30] but, at the first session of the Legislature, were put into force,[31] along with legislation requiring the licensing of all trades, businesses, and occupations. Failure to register would result in fines and/or imprisonment of up to three months.[32] This Act had ominous overtones, for it could and sometimes did deny business licenses to those who were opposed to Social Credit or were considered undesirables, particularly Orientals.[33] It also had ironic similarities to what Aberhart and Manning feared the Antichrist would set up in the near future: unless one had the "mark of the Beast," one could not buy nor sell. The Antichrist and the coming Tribulation were still an important part of their theology and radio broadcasts.[34]

Another Act extended the powers of the Liquor Control Board, thus providing an added source of revenue.[35] Aberhart received considerable criticism from religious people regarding this action. He read in his radio broadcast a letter from a person in Saskatchewan who complained that he should not be conducting a Bible class while his government was making money selling booze. Aberhart replied that if he could have his own way, he would bring in total prohibition; but it would not likely work, given the way people were thinking; they would likely smuggle it in from Saskatchewan.[36]

More criticism was received with regard to Bill 5, which provided enabling powers for the establishment of Social Credit. Lieutenant-Governor W.L. Walsh warned Aberhart that he might not pass this Bill because some of the undefined measures could be unconstitutional.[37] The undefined nature of the Bill was deliberate. Ernest Manning defended the Bill thus: "Don't you think it would be foolish for the government to make all the details of its procedure public so that our enemies would have further means of attacking us?"[38] When the Bill came up for third reading it had a difficult passage. G.H. Van Allen, a Liberal member for Edmonton, claimed: "The proposal to proceed by order-in-council will be regretted; if it is done by order-in-council, it will be 100 per cent dictatorial legislation."[39] Opposition to the Bill reached even into the Social Credit party; S.A.G. Barnes, the Socred member for Edmonton, voted against it. The Bill was passed, however, and received royal assent.[40]

The nightmare that disturbed what little sleep Aberhart had during the session was the bond maturation, about which he had written to Douglas on the day the session began. Douglas's suggestion, that the public be asked to accept 115-per-cent credit for their bonds, or that the federal government be asked to accept responsibility for the bonds, requiring only that Alberta pay the interest,[41] was considered too radical by Aberhart.

In Douglas's eyes, Aberhart was altogether too open to suggestion from the federal government; in the opinion of the federal government, however, Aberhart was a stumbling block to federal-provincial cooperation in schemes to relieve the Depression. Where the federal government appeared to be attempting to reduce existing provincial autonomy, Aberhart held fast to the privileges of his province. He refused to accept the loan council set up by the federal government. The loan council, dominated by the federal government, would assist the hard-pressed provincial governments so long as the latter submitted to the council's restrictions on borrowing and budgeting. "It seemed to us," Aberhart had explained to Douglas, "that the Dominion Government was attempting to deprive us of our autonomous rights with respect to borrowing."[42] When, of course, Aberhart attempted to finance the bond maturity for April with a federal loan and was told that it must be dealt with through the loan council, he would not comply with that requirement.

The federal government refused to grant a loan on any other terms, and as a result Alberta defaulted on its bond payments on 1 April 1936.[43] The default did nothing to help Alberta's financial reputation or the confidence of her people.

Some of the other Acts passed during the first session were not met by enthusiasm from the public; increased taxes were placed on fuel oil, income tax was raised, and a 2-per-cent retail sales tax was levied.[44] Those actions were no doubt taken to increase the revenue of the province because it could not get federal money on its own terms. Fred Kennedy, the Calgary *Herald* reporter assigned to cover Aberhart, whom Aberhart had known for some time and with whom he had a loose friendship, taunted Aberhart that this was a "dividend in reverse."[45]

PSALM 1936
The Social Credit leader is my shepherd,
I am in want;
He leadeth me beside the still factories,
He disturbeth my soul.
He leadeth me in the paths of distraction
for the party's sake.
Yea, though I walk through the valley of the
shadow of Depression,
I anticipate no recovery, for he is with me.
He prepareth a reduction in my salary
in the presence of my enemies.
He anointeth my small income with taxes;
my expenses runneth over.
Surely unemployment and poverty shall follow
me all the days of my life,
And I shall dwell in the mortgage house forever and ever.[46]

On 7 April 1936 the first session of the Alberta Legislature under Aberhart came to an end. After catching up on his correspondence Aberhart took part in the wedding of his friend and assistant Ernest Manning, who on April 14 married Muriel Preston, who had served as Aberhart's pianist since she was a young teenager. Aberhart gave away the bride, and after a reception in the Palliser Hotel, the Mannings and Aberharts departed for Vancouver, still the Aberharts' favorite holiday spot, where both their married daughters were still living.[47]

Aberhart was very tired after the long hours and bitter controversy that he had experienced during the first sitting of the House. He had also drawn fire from the major religious denominations. Since moving to Edmonton he had begun a Prophetic Conference there that met in a theatre. Plans were being made for establishing a permanent headquarters for his religious work in Edmonton.[48] His services were being held on Sunday afternoons and were broadcast live. Their political content caused the synod of the Anglican Diocese of Calgary to pass the following resolution:

Therefore be it resolved that this Synod deplores the use of Sunday for political propaganda by means of public meetings and radio broadcasts and respectfully but strongly urges those engaged in public life to do everything in their power to prevent it.[49]

Several months later the Alberta Conference of the United Church of Canada passed a similar resolution.[50]

Aberhart found rest playing with his grandchildren in Vancouver. His affection for them can be noted in a letter he sent to his son-in-law a few months before:

> There is only one little piece of advice that I would attempt to offer you, and that is this – Do not attempt to make the success of your business the one greatest purpose of your life. I mean by that that you should see that you and your loved ones are living with medium happiness and comfort at the same time when you are pressing hard in your business career. You have a little girl coming up now that needs your most careful attention and influence, and you must not allow your business to deprive her of her happy moments with her father in the evenings. I do not offer this advice to you because I feel you have been neglectful in any way. I can quite understand that success in any year is apt to urge one on to greater efforts the next year, and he ["her father"] is apt to forget some of the things for which we are living in his attempt even to increase the profits of the previous year's business.
>
> I am so pleased to know that you are getting along that you will pardon me, I am sure, for this advice. It bespeaks to you, of course, that I am getting old whenever I offer you or anyone else advice. I suppose that is the privilege of an old man, and I trust you will understand me in this regard.[51]

One suspects that Aberhart may have had regrets of his own for the little time he had spent with his own children during the years they were growing up.

Now that Aberhart and Douglas had ceased their correspondence Aberhart had to find a way of bringing in Social Credit without Douglas's aid. Therefore, Aberhart set up a committee of M.L.A.s to devise a method of increasing purchasing power in Alberta, which should if possible be based on Social Credit principles, but which should in any case be constitutional. This committee, operating under the Social Credit Measures Act,[52] created Aberhart's "funny money" scheme.

On 23 April 1936, before Aberhart returned from Vancouver, the government announced that it would issue "scrip." As we saw during his campaign, Aberhart was susceptible to the argument that the Depression was largely due to the slowing down in the velocity of the circulation of money. The scrip system, designed to remedy this aspect of the Depression, was based on the theories of Silvio Gesell, who had taken part in an ill-fated *coup* in Bavaria in 1919.[53] Like Douglas, Gesell was not a professional economist, but he held strong views on economics and evolved his own theories concerning it. Gesell reasoned that the owner of money held an unfair advantage over the owner of goods because money did not depreciate and could be exchanged for any kind of goods the purchaser might choose. When the interest rate fell, the money-owner would decide not to invest his money. That decision aided and perpetuated Depression conditions. Gesell's aim, therefore, was to make money perishable.

The Alberta government adapted Gesell's method of persuading the public to keep money in circulation. The "scrip" documents were called "Prosperity Certificates." On the backs of the certificates, which resembled dollar bills, were spaces for the attachment of one-cent stamps, one of which had to be added each week, thus making it desirable to dispose of the certificates before the stamps came due. The $1.04 in legal tender, which the government would collect in payment for the stamps on each certificate at the end of two years, was intended to be used to redeem the certificates and to pay for the expenses of the scheme.

Scrip schemes had been tried with varying degrees of success at some municipal levels in Austria, the U.S.A., and elsewhere in Canada. The town of Raymond, Alberta, in fact had used a scrip system when the town could not obtain bank loans to pay school-teachers' salaries; but it was not depreciating currency, and the Raymond system would not have worked if the town had not had a sugar factory providing it with a healthy tax base.[54] It remained to be seen, however, whether Aberhart's scrip system could transport money about Alberta faster than it had moved hitherto. No one, not even Aberhart, claimed to be quite sure. The first issue of the scrip was to be, he said, "experimental."

Before launching this radical experiment Aberhart informed Robert Magor that his services were no longer required.[55] He had been trying to defend Magor's employment to the Douglasites both in Alberta and abroad, but their suspicions of him did not abate.[56] Aberhart may have even come to question Magor's motives. Magor was not very disappointed to be released, but he did advise Aberhart to continue to aim at balancing his budget.[57]

With Magor gone, Aberhart engaged another economic "expert," E.S. Woodward, of New Westminster, B.C., the national executive secretary of the Free Economy League of Canada, a society promoting Gesell's theories. For many years Woodward had been an alderman in Victoria, a leader of the Anti-Vaccination League and a member of Clem Davies' religious cult, the Victoria City Temple.[58] Shortly after the Social Credit victory, Woodward had offered Aberhart his services, as had a lot of other people with unusual backgrounds and ideas.[59] During Aberhart's holiday at the Coast he engaged Woodward to help him with the scrip program.[60] Woodward hoped that his job would become permanent,[61] but Aberhart hesitated to commit himself; he replied that he had had some rather unhappy experiences with economic "experts."[62]

Aberhart and his cabinet ministers travelled about the province, explaining the plan and imploring merchants, school boards, and town councils to accept scrip. Scepticism was freely expressed by the press and many citizens. Scrip, everyone agreed, bore no relationship whatsoever to Social Credit, and although attempts were made to reassure those who feared the revolutionary nature of Social Credit, they soon realized that scrip was also revolutionary. The press detected in this sudden espousal of a theory as wild as Douglas's (though otherwise totally unlike it, and denounced by Douglas) a hint of panic in the Aberhart administration.

Indeed, there was panic. Because of the government's defaulting on its bonds, there were fears that the Bond Holders' Protective Association would take the government to court. Aberhart, in his conversations with "Hilly" Hill, felt that they could block such legal actions, but Hill disagreed and said that Aberhart had no power over the courts in Alberta.[63]

As the press made the most of the opposition that Aberhart was receiving for defaulting on the bonds and introducing scrip, Aberhart continued his threats to license the newspapers. The Calgary *Herald* began fighting Aberhart with humour by hiring Stewart Cameron, whose cartoons in various newspapers and the Conservative Party pamphlet *The Amos and Andy of Social Credit* had been very popular. Since January 1936 Cameron had been working for Walt Disney Studios on *Snow White and the Seven Dwarfs*, but he was unhappy there. He returned to Calgary when he saw that the political situation in Alberta required his talents, and approached the Calgary *Herald* for a job.[64]

That was the first time in its history that the *Herald* had employed a staff cartoonist. Aberhart must have been unique as a politician of merely provincial stature to have an artist of such a caliber work full-time cartooning him. For the next four years the important news covered by Alberta papers was taking place within view of their own city desks. Newspapers from all over the world were sending reporters to take up residence in Edmonton to cover the local situation, and Cameron's cartoons were reproduced in many parts of the world. A more delightful situation for a cartoonist would be hard to imagine. Aberhart's features lent themselves to caricature, his unguarded words and unorthodox activities, to ridicule; and Cameron was an able draughtsman who used the opportunity to the full. Throughout the series of cartoons that came from Cameron's pen, Aberhart was depicted as bullying, egotistical, unreasonable, and stupid.

Cameron's return to Calgary coincided with Aberhart's promotion of the scrip scheme. In one cartoon Cameron showed Aberhart teetering on the end of a high-diving board, in the garb of an old-time circus diving girl. Below stood a barrel of water labelled "Scrip Scheme," and the crowd bit its fingernails and wondered, "Will she do it?"

Aberhart had been claiming that the "worst enemies of the [scrip] plan were not those who opposed it, but those who wanted the government to go too fast with it." "Don't rush me," he said; then in July, with considerable fanfare, he took the plunge. Some 500,000 Alberta Prosperity Certificates, in one-dollar denominations, were printed by Abe Shnitka, the King's Printer.

Even before the Prosperity Certificates were off the press a hitch developed in Aberhart's program. A heated argument developed between E.S. Woodward and the cabinet. Certain cabinet members wanted scrip to be given out in the form of dividends; Woodward objected, stating that that would bankrupt the Treasury. He also objected to the government's statement that scrip could not be used for the payment of fines and taxes, or for the purchase of liquor. He felt that the public would not have confidence in the scheme if the government would not accept its own currency,[65] but Aberhart wanted the system to stimulate the business community. Scrip flowing into the Treasury would not accomplish this. Aberhart's conception of the scrip system obviously differed from Woodward's. Conflict ensued; Woodward tried to dictate to Aberhart and was fired.[66] Thus exited Aberhart's fourth economic "expert."

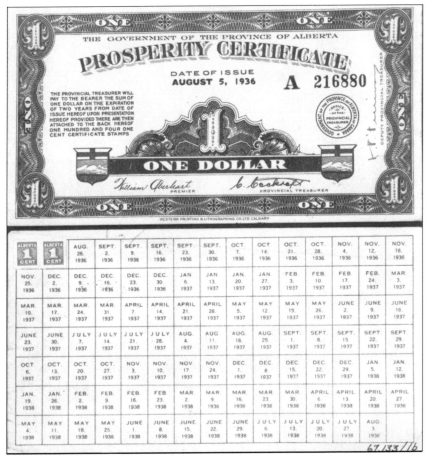

A specimen of Aberhart's celebrated "funny money." In order to keep the money valid, people had to affix stamps to the back each week.

Such was the state of affairs when the Prosperity Certificates finally appeared on 5 August 1936. Workmen engaged in government-relief road-building projects were the first to receive it.[67] Long overdue accounts at corner stores were paid in scrip, and some small merchants welcomed it;

but when they attempted to cash it in the banks, it was not accepted. Then the merchants tried to pay their wholesale suppliers, often located outside the province, only to find that outside Alberta the scrip was worthless and

This Form to be retained by Citizen.

TRADE AND INDUSTRY DEPARTMENT

ALBERTA CITIZENS' REGISTRATION COVENANT

I, _____hereby covenant, promise and agree as follows:—

    (1) To co-operate most heartily with the Alberta Government, and with my fellow citizens of the Province of Alberta in providing food, clothing and shelter for every one of us.

    (2) To work whenever possible, and to accept my remuneration in Alberta Credit as far as I can reasonably do so. In the event of receiving the whole or the greater part of my income in Canadian Currency, I shall exchange as much of it as is convenient for Alberta Credit.

    (3) To make no claim nor demand, at any time, for payment in Canadian Currency, of Alberta Credit held by me.

    (4) To tender no Alberta Credit in payment of Provincial taxes, licenses, royalties, fines, etc., until such time as the Alberta Government shall be able to accept all or part on the taxes, etc.

In return for my agreement, I understand that the Alberta Government covenants and agrees as follows:—

    (1) To establish, as early as possible, and maintain a just rate of wages with reasonable hours of labour.

    (2) To grant interest-free loans in Alberta Credit on such terms and security as shall be mutually agreed upon, not exceeding 2% for administration charges, for the building of a home or the establishment of the Registered Citizen in his own enterprise if conducive to the economic requirements of the Province.

    (3) To give monthly dividends to all registered Alberta Citizens, and to increase the same as the total production of the Province will allow.

    (4) To redeem when possible, Alberta Credit with Canadian Currency for the purpose of allowing the member to take up residence outside the Province or for other essential requirements.

With full understanding of these several declarations, I gladly enter into covenant with the Alberta Government and with my fellow citizens.

In witness whereof I affix my signature in the presence of

Witness: Signed:

R. C. MacMillan   *H. B. Luck*

58.84

Specimen of a registration covenant, 1936. In order to receive the proposed Social Credit dividends, Albertans had to sign such documents. The dividends never materialized, however.

wholesalers refused to take it. Branches of the big department stores refused it for the same reason.

Business leaders in Alberta were extremely worried and sent letters to Mackenzie King asking him to intervene,[68] but because the scrip system was regarded as a purely internal matter, Ottawa did not make any public comment on it. To persuade wholesalers to accept scrip the government then decided to allow merchants and wholesalers to redeem it for Canadian currency to facilitate out-of-province payments. The public was even allowed to use it to pay sales tax; but their confidence in the program was not helped when even cabinet ministers hesitated to accept it as part of their salaries.[69] As Aberhart pressed on with his scrip system, orthodox Douglasites complained that scrip had nothing to do with Social Credit.[70] S.A.G. Barnes, one of the M.L.A.s from Edmonton, shared these views and, for his opposition, was expelled from the caucus and the Alberta Social Credit League.[71] Soon federal Social Credit members also became involved in the issue. Percy J. Rowe, M.P. for Athabaska, advised the residents of Alberta to throw Aberhart out of office if he did not fulfill his campaign promises.[72] Another group of Alberta M.L.A.s got in touch with Major Douglas, who replied that he would come to help them if Aberhart was removed from office.[73] In response to that criticism Aberhart sought to alleviate the public's demands by promising to commence a registration program for the dividends immediately. An earlier program started by Manning in September 1935 had ceased after Aberhart found Alberta had no money. Where he was going to get the money this time was not divulged, but he may have had in mind giving dividends in the form of scrip, one of the issues he had debated with Woodward.

On 31 August the registration program was explained in the *Albertan*. More than just registering for dividends, citizens were required to sign a covenant "to co-operate most heartily" with the Alberta government. A second requirement was that citizens exchange their Canadian currency for "Alberta Credit." "Alberta Credit" was not explained. Did it mean scrip, dividends, or government bonds? Other requirements were that citizens were to make no claim upon the government that they be paid in Canadian currency for their "Alberta Credit," nor were they to use "Alberta Credit" in the payment of taxes, licenses, or fines until the government changed its policy. Along with the registration covenant, citizens had to complete other forms disclosing all of their assets, liabilities, sources of income, and other personal information. Special registration forms were designed for farmers and merchants; farmers had to sell 50 per cent of their produce in exchange for "Alberta Credit."[74] Fine print on the forms indicated that in order to retain the right to obtain dividends, citizens would require the permission of the local manager of the State Credit House if they desired to leave the province for more than one month.[75]

The authoritarian, even totalitarian overtones of this program brought immediate cries of "fascism" from many of Alberta's leading citizens.[76] A "League of Freedom" was formed by F. Surry, an Edmonton bookstore-owner, to fight the proposed registration program, after he had been told by an M.L.A. that if he refused to sign, he could lose his business license.[77]

On 10 August 1936, five days following the introduction of the controversial scrip system, citizens of Alberta rushed to sign the registration and covenant forms for the proposed dividends. Many did so fearing government

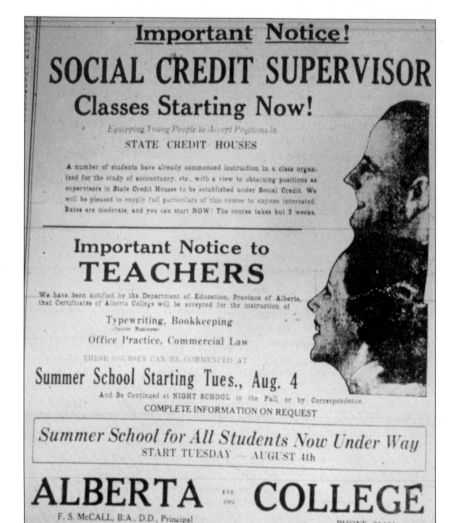

Aberhart's proposed State Credit Houses, which would replace banks, created widespread anticipation of new jobs, fanned by advertisements like this one in the Edmonton Journal, *1 August 1936.*

retaliation if they refused or simply failed to do so. Aberhart's friend W.P. Harvey urged his wife to return at once from a vacation in Detroit in order to register.[78] He was doing only the same as many others who confidently expected to receive the dividends immediately. Others hesitated to register, however, fearing they would be fired by their employers.[79]

Another feature of the registration program was the creation of State Credit Houses that would process all financial transactions within the province. Ernest Manning described the program as a giant bookkeeping system. Special non-negotiable certificates were being prepared to serve as credit instruments.[80]

After discussing the registration program with Aberhart, "Hilly" Hill recorded in his diary that they had a bitter argument. He noted that Aberhart was "becoming more autocratic every day – a second Hitler" who could not brook opposition.[81] Hill recorded that opposition to Aberhart's program reached into the cabinet. He had learned from Charles Ross, the minister of Lands and Mines, that Fallow, Maynard (minister without portfolio in charge of the scrip program), Cross, and several others were meeting secretly to oust Aberhart, but when presented with that information, Aberhart claimed not to believe it.[82]

A year after his victory at the polls Aberhart was in an unenviable position. The fulfillment of his election promises seemed further away than ever, and the despised scrip system was sluggishly completing its uninspired journey. Nevertheless, on 22 August 1936 and on the following day, mammoth anniversary celebrations were held.

On Saturday afternoon a giant picnic was held at St. George's Island Park. "Hilly" Hill, who attended the event, described the scene thus:

> There must have been at least 10,000 people there, but what a moth-eaten crowd. They looked to be almost the average age of 45 and hopeless, without a pot to piss in or a window to throw it out of. What a god awful band. God, I feel sorry for Abie if they ever turn on him. They stood and watched him eat his picnic lunch like crows or like as if they were watching God. He would reach for a piece of bread and they would follow him with all eyes, as much as to say, "there now he is eating bread." Then, "there, now he is drinking coffee." Then, "there, now he eats cake." Oh, the poor deluded fools. The worst thing there was that terrible awful band. I never heard such awful sounds from band instruments before in my life. I left very depressed.[83]

The following day a giant thanksgiving service was held in Victoria Park, and again over ten thousand people attended. Aberhart addressed them in a voice resonant with conviction and confidence. He had great news to tell them of achievement in the registering of citizens for the dividend. He had, of course, no idea when he was going to be able to pay the dividend; nevertheless he reported great progress in the work. He gave some impressive figures to the crowd; 30,475 people, he said, had registered by that time, and registrations "were pouring in continually."[84]

It was as if Aberhart had a tiger by the tail and dared not let go. With a determined smile on his face he assured the crowd that dividends were on their way. He declared, "In spite of the fact that I told you that it would be 18 months after we were in power that the first dividend would be paid, we are making a systematic effort to pay it at an earlier date." No hint of uncertainty was there as the voice of authority rang out in the old familiar way. He autographed programs, he joked about his baldness, he grew angry

Aberhart and his supporters at Social Credit Anniversary Picnic, 22 August 1936.

with financiers. "Unto thy brother thou shalt not lend upon usury," he cried. "The interest racket must cease!... What do you want interest for anyway if you have your food, clothing and shelter provided for you?"[85] The crowd roared. He had given them neither food, clothing, nor shelter, but they applauded; he still believed he could give them prosperity, and therefore they believed it. As usual he levelled broadsides at the press. He claimed that the Calgary *Herald*'s circulation had dropped 50 per cent because of the boycotts, and hinted that a "constitutional whip" would soon be employed to rescue the people from the financiers and the press.

True to Aberhart's promise at the anniversary celebrations, the second session of the Legislature, which commenced the following week, saw the enactment of several pieces of legislation that put more teeth in the fight with the banks and financiers.

Act I legalized the registration program, the establishment of the State Credit Houses, and the creation of non-negotiable certificates that acted as cheques. The Act also provided for broad orders-in-council to provide for further developments. To aid the expansion of agriculture, manufacturing, industry, or the building of private homes, loans at 2-per-cent interest were offered to those who had signed registration covenants.[86] The money for such projects was probably going to come from the sale of Prosperity Certificates.

Act II cancelled interest payments on all debts contracted before July 1932 and established a Debt Adjustment Board to rule on repayments and property seizures. Lieutenant-Governor Walsh cautioned Aberhart that the Act might be unconstitutional because creditors had rights, just as debtors did. Walsh warned that he might withhold royal assent,[87] but eventually he allowed the bill to pass into law.[88]

Act III was of a similar nature. The Debt Adjustment Board was given authority to stop legal actions against residential homes and farms, and referees employed by the Board would assist debtors to program their repayments. Decisions of the Debt Adjustment Board were final and could not be appealed through the courts.[89]

Act IV legalized the earlier issuance of Prosperity Certificates that was being challenged in the courts.[90] Another Act legalized the government's reduction by 50 per cent the interest payable on their bonds and savings certificates.[91] Finally, Act XVI amended the Judiciary Act so that members of the Executive Council were immune from legal action or prosecution because of any of their legislation. No doubt this piece of legislation was aimed at protecting the Council from irate bond-holders and other dissidents. The amendment was made retroactive to 1 September 1935.[92]

These acts, needless to say, did not inspire confidence among members of the business community. "Hilly" Hill warned Aberhart that government bonds were not selling well and that the State Credit Houses were apt to be a failure.[93] Rumours abounded that bank deposits and securities were being transferred out of the province by scared businessmen. Aberhart blamed the panic on financiers.[94]

The public's confidence in Aberhart's schemes was probably best expressed in the amount of support they had given to buying shares in the *Albertan*. As early as April 1936 Nathan Tanner, the Speaker of the House and Mormon bishop, who had been put in charge of the sales of *Albertan* shares, informed Aberhart that the public did not have much money to spend on the scheme. He warned that if sufficient stock was not sold to complete the purchase of the newspaper, they would lose the confidence of the public. Aberhart had encouraged him to stick with the project and emphasized its importance to the cause,[95] but as the summer progressed, stock sales declined. "Hilly" Hill, who was deeply involved in the sale of stock, found that he and the others had to promise government patronage in exchange for stock purchases.[96] Aberhart discovered, to his disappointment, that the only ones who were really interested in buying the stock were the liquor interests,[97] and even with his promotions of the stock sales in his radio broadcasts, the venture did not prosper. Within a short time the option to purchase the newspaper had to be dropped, and Aberhart had to think of other ways of obtaining "fair" news coverage.

As Aberhart's plans failed one after another, he objected to the press coverage he was receiving, accusing the media of distortion and lying. The press in turn claimed that Aberhart could not stand the truth.

Week after week Aberhart lectured the press, banks, mortgage companies, businessmen, and churches for not cooperating; he blamed them for his failures and denied his own responsibility. He continued to assert that Social

Aberhart had formed a company to buy and control the Calgary Albertan, *but the project failed. Stewart Cameron captured Aberhart's dilemma in the Calgary* Herald, *8 October 1936.*

Credit was "an economic system from God himself."[98] His threats against the press were becoming more definite; he was considering legislation to license newspapers so they could not "print lies to cause a disturbance among peace-loving contented people."[99] At about that time, "Hilly" Hill showed up at the newsroom of CFCN with a message from the government stating that the station "must stop reporting news of an adverse character against the government, *or else.*" The news editor of CFCN refused to be muzzled and reported the incident in the next news broadcast.[100]

The public was far from being as contented as Aberhart implied. Unemployment was rising, and all Aberhart seemed to be doing was making speeches. The dividends were nowhere in sight. Without federal government aid Alberta was forced to default on its bonds maturing on 1 November 1936, the second time that year.

With pressure being exerted upon them from all quarters, Aberhart and his cabinet burned much midnight oil trying to develop a plan for the introduction of Social Credit. The stress under which they were operating soon manifested itself in breakdowns in their health. Aberhart, who had appeared to have an inexhaustable supply of energy to this point, became ill himself. When his son-in-law suggested that he had been working too hard, Aberhart brushed aside his advice with the comment "If overwork is the only cause of sickness, I know some fellows that never will be sick."[101] While denying the reality of his own situation, he was indeed worried about Ernest Manning who had recently suffered a complete physical collapse. Aberhart confided to Fred Kennedy that Manning had "sacrificed himself for the cause."[102] For the next few months Manning was out of action while recuperating from tuberculosis. During Manning's absence Aberhart had the Reverend E.G. Hansell, his former colleague at Westbourne Bapitist Church (who was now the Social Credit M.P. for Vulcan), Cyril Hutchinson, and Norman B. James, M.L.A., assist him in his religious services.[103]

The same stresses that contributed to Manning's illness also affected Charles Ross, minister of Lands and Mines, who found that his health was shattered from constant cabinet meetings that lasted late into the night, by the dissensions and the battles. By the end of the year Ross submitted his resignation and left the party.[104]

By Christmas 1936 the scrip system had ground to a standstill. Little damage had been done to the province; the province had even claimed a profit of $32,300.[105] The only harm of the "Aberhart money," "baloney dollars," "wooden money," "funny money" or "monkey money," as it was variously called, was to Aberhart and his government. The episode provided excellent opportunities for Archie Dale of the Winnipeg *Free Press*, Stewart Cameron of the Calgary *Herald*, and the press at large to poke derisive fingers at Aberhart.

As the year came to a close, the eighteen-month period that Aberhart had predicted would be necessary to implement the dividend program was also running out. The public and many of the M.L.A.s were like racehorses chafing at the bit, wanting to get on with the race for economic recovery, and Aberhart was accused of hesitating at the starting line. During the past two years he had felt that he had been mistreated by the press; the treatment forthcoming from within his own caucus far exceeded anything he had yet received.

THE ALBERTAN'S PRAYER
Our father who art in Edmonton
Aberhart be thy name
Thy will be done in Canada
As it is in Alberta
Give us this day our dividends
And forgive us our impatience,
As we forgive those that elected you.
Lead us not into the hands of the "big shots,"
For thine is the kingdom, the power and the glory,
Until the next elections come around.[106]

CHAPTER SEVENTEEN

■

THE REBELLION

T HE *Douglasites*
criticize me for not going ahead quicker.
They have no idea of the constitutional
difficulties we have to face.

— William Aberhart quoted in the
Calgary Herald, 25 August 1936

Aberhart and his cabinet had been searching frantically for a constitutional way of implementing Social Credit but met continual disappointment. Dr. W.W. Cross, minister of Health, described their activities and their dilemma:

We have considered the advice of economists. We have considered plans submitted to us from all parts of the world by hundreds – but when they say "give us experts" there is no man in the world that has had any experience in introducing Social Credit.[1]

Although Major Douglas had no more practical experience than Aberhart in instituting Social Credit, many of the restless Douglasites in Aberhart's caucus, stimulated by the scrip fiasco, felt sure that Douglas or someone from his organization would be able to bring it off. Their hopes were raised by the appearance of an unexpected visitor.

In December 1936 an interesting traveller from England came to Edmonton on his own initiative, eager to be consulted by Aberhart and his caucus.

John Hargrave, leader of the "Green Shirts" in England, came over to assist Aberhart during the winter of 1936-37. Though he did not stay long, he managed to generate a backbenchers' revolt in Aberhart's caucus.

He was John Hargrave, mentioned before as leader of the Green Shirts. The Green Shirts were now known as the Social Credit Party of Great Britain and Northern Ireland, for they had unsuccessfully run candidates in Britain's general election of November 1935. Hargrave's personality and political activities had alienated Douglas, who described Hargrave as a man "with a strong power complex." Hargrave no doubt hoped to make a name for himself in Alberta, and had come to advise Aberhart after one of his Green Shirt officers had reconnoitered the situation in Alberta.[2]

Having heard so much about Hargrave, Aberhart invited him up to his suite in the Macdonald Hotel on the evening of 17 December 1936 for a meeting that lasted until 2:30 the next morning. In his description of this interview Hargrave gave a valuable clue to Aberhart's thinking at the time:

> Premier Aberhart's outstanding difficulty, during the whole of this discussion, was summed up in the question he reiterated a number of times, "If I issue a dividend, how do I get it back?"[3]

Where, in other words, would all the money come from? This was the question that, according to a Conservative writer during the election campaign, was "always the cause of riotous mirth for the believer in Social Credit."[4] Aberhart, however, had by this time analysed the joke and found it wanting in humour. The question was serious, and he did not know the answer.

At a meeting with the cabinet the following day, Hargrave was told of the doubts about the constitutionality of Social Credit. Hugill said that in his opinion the B.N.A. Act would prevent the introduction of Social Credit in one province alone, to which Hargrave made the crushing rejoinder "Surely the electorate ought to be told."[5] Aberhart explained quickly that the government members were doing their best to find a way through the constitutional difficulties.

Hargrave later claimed that Aberhart asked him to draft a Social Credit plan for Alberta. He set up a committee of four government members to which, after two days of investigating the temper of the M.L.A.s, he submitted a brief draft of a plan. Under the plan Alberta's exports would have to pay for her imports and extraprovincial debts, and "transfer tickets for goods and/or services" would be issued by the Alberta government for use within the province. Hargrave admitted the unconstitutionality of his plan, but like the revolutionary he essentially was, he believed that the province could successfully defy Ottawa, which would not dare to enforce the law. This was the very argument that Aberhart had used before the election but which, afterwards, had been overshadowed by his indebtedness to the federal government.

What Hargrave did not tell the committee, which was meeting while Aberhart was at the Coast for his Christmas holiday, was that his draft recommendations, known as the "eleven-point program," were designed so that if his ideas were not promptly adopted by the Aberhart government, they would form a rallying point for dissatisfied M.L.A.s who, Hargrave had observed, were increasing in numbers, but were unorganized.[6]

On the evening of 29 December 1936 Hargrave received a telephone call from Joe Unwin, Socred M.L.A. for Edson and also party whip, asking him to explain his eleven-point program to a group of seventeen M.L.A.s who were at that moment gathered in the Legislative Building. Hargrave took advantage of the offer. That was the first of several actions that precipitated some of the most sensational events of the next two years – without doubt, the most turbulent years in the history of the Alberta Legislature.

The day after Hargrave's address to the seventeen M.L.A.s the eleven-point program monopolized the headlines in Alberta: "New Social Credit

Financial Order Now Looms,'' said the Edmonton *Bulletin*; "Drastic Laws
are Forecast at Social Credit Meet,'' announced the Edmonton *Journal* ;
"Legislation Planned in February Session,'' said the *Albertan*, and so on.

After the Hargrave story broke, Aberhart was besieged by reporters in
Vancouver. To Aberhart at this time his period in office seemed to consist
of what he called "simply one awful thing after another.'' He felt that he
had been unfairly used by Hargrave and the M.L.A.s who had spoken in support of Hargrave's recommendations in his absence and without his sanc-
tion. Aberhart lost no time disassociating himself from Hargrave's plan. "I
have no such intention of drastic legislation,'' he said in his broadcast from
the Institute on 3 January 1937.

On his return to Edmonton, Aberhart attempted to tame the tempestuous
energy of Hargrave. Aberhart joined the committee and discussed the eleven-
point program. After studying the plan, he declared that neither he nor the
cabinet could recommend it.[7]

Meanwhile, other M.L.A.s were arriving in Edmonton to prepare for the
legislative session, which was to begin on 25 February. A three-day caucus
starting on 12 January called upon Hargrave to explain his program. His
account of the meeting indicates that there was a deep division in the party,
between the moderate faction of whom Hugill was an outstanding member
and an impatient though leaderless group of rank-and-file M.L.A.s. Hugill's
unenviable isolation was vividly depicted by Hargrave. No one else in the
provincial government was in a position to see so clearly the illegality of
Douglas's or Hargrave's Social Credit schemes as Hugill was. Hugill's
outspokenness embarrassed the government, and his cabinet colleagues failed
to support him publicly or defend him when the backbenchers ridiculed him,
as happened at that caucus meeting. "You realise, Mr. Hargrave,'' said Hugill,
"that this scheme you are putting forward would not be legal?'' "I am not
interested,'' replied Hargrave, "in legal arguments.'' According to Hargrave,
his own rejoinder was hailed by applause. Hugill's next question was "What
would you do if your legislation was disallowed and your parliament
dissolved?'' Hargrave replied:

> There is only one way in which such a government could be
> "dissolved,'' and that is by sending in troops to throw it out, physically,
> neck and crop, down the steps of this parliament house. Does the Attorney-
> General suggest that any authority anywhere in Ottawa or elsewhere would,
> in those circumstances, march troops into Alberta?[8]

We can sympathize with Hugill's giving up the attempt to deal single-
handedly with a collective state of mind in which the above outburst by
Hargrave was greeted by cries of "Never!'' "The Attorney-General,'' related
Hargrave, "smiled rather wanly, and appeared to relapse into a state of
unheeding contemplation.'' An M.L.A. discouraged Hugill from rejoining the
discussion by taunting him with reminders of his own election campaign
speeches. Derisive laughter echoed through the room.

It seemed that Hargrave had been successful in making his program a
focal point for the dissatisfied M.L.A.s. There was little moderation in

Hargrave's makeup and, in the current situation, which he thought needed stirring up, he became more and more troublesome to Aberhart, sharply criticizing the government in press interviews, denouncing Aberhart's concepts of the capital levy and scrip as irrelevant to Social Credit, and flourishing his own program like a red flag.

Aberhart was now seriously worried by the adverse publicity that the government was receiving at the hands of Hargrave and attempted to persuade him to cooperate in regaining prestige for the government. Aberhart's method of persuasion with Hargrave was a little more heavy-handed than any he had used so far. He presented Hargrave with letters recanting his criticism and pressed him to sign them.

Recognizing that he had worn out his welcome, Hargrave decided to "deliver a shock" that might act as the signal for a revolt.[9] Without a word

The expert was called in

On August 15, 1935, Mr. Aberhart said: "You don't have to know all about Social Credit before you vote for it. You don't have to understand electricity to make use of it, for you know that experts have put the system in and all you have to do is to push the button and you get light. So all you have to do about Social Credit is to cast your ballot for it, and we'll get experts to put the system in."

Hargrave very quickly and publicly washed his hands of Aberhart. Stewart Cameron cartoon, Calgary Herald, *30 January 1937.*

or a sign, Hargrave left his hotel on the morning of Monday, 25 January, and deposited with the press a lengthy statement, generally derogatory about the government. He claimed he was leaving because he "found it impossible to co-operate with a government which I consider a mere vacillating machine which operates in starts, stops and reversals." He described the government as "groping its way like a man stumbling along on a pitchblack night."[10] He then stepped quickly on the eastbound train for Ottawa, where he intended to go to stir up the federal Socreds. The news of his departure was comforting to Aberhart who, no doubt with some relief, deposited in his desk drawer the eleven-point program that, though he did not notice it, had begun, very faintly, to tick.

Trouble was never far from Aberhart. In the course of a January 1937 caucus meeting the newspapers were, as usual, brought in and placed before Aberhart as soon as they were issued. On the front page of the Calgary *Herald* appeared the words "Cockroft and Chant to be fired from the Cabinet." Without a word Aberhart tossed the paper across the table in front of Cockroft who, though resignation had been in his mind for some time, had made no statement to the press. In failing health, Cockroft was also unhappy because his advice had not been heeded by Aberhart. He objected to Aberhart's plans to invest the Sinking Fund in questionable projects, and he also had had disagreements with Aberhart, as did Chant, over the question of government patronage.[11] Cockroft resigned on 29 January 1937. Chant did not resign at the same time, but rumours of his and also of Hugill's possible resignation made the Alberta government seem increasingly unstable.

Three days after the opening of the Legislature, Aberhart admitted to the people of Alberta, during his broadcast from the Bible Institute, that he had been unable, in the eighteen months he had asked for, to pay the monthly dividends he had promised them. Aberhart said he had no intention of resigning unless the people desired a change in leadership or party. What he now asked for were the people's instructions. He asked the constituency association presidents to call zone meetings of all registered Social Crediters and have them express their decision on this matter by resolution.[12]

Aberhart explained to them that "opposition and blocking tactics" had been more determined than he had anticipated. Some of the blockages to which he referred were recent court decisions that had declared his Debt Legislation Act and Provincial Securities Interest Act *ultra vires*. He also declared that Manning's illness had slowed up the implementation of Social Credit. To that comment the Calgary *Herald* retorted that if the success of Social Credit depended on Manning's health, no wonder he was ill.[13]

Yet Aberhart was not anxious to rush his followers. He noted that because the roads in the rural areas were in bad condition during the spring, the zone meetings should be delayed until early June, by which time they would know of the legislation the government proposed to pass during the current session.

The Calgary *Herald* reacted angrily to Aberhart's suggestion that only registered Social Crediters would determine his future. Registered citizens amounted to only about 10 per cent of the population; an issue like this, said the *Herald*, demanded a general election. The editorial compared Aberhart's suggestion to "a similar early referendum conducted by Herr Hitler who rode to a dictatorship on the shoulders of a small minority of the German people."[14] From then on, the Calgary *Herald* and Stewart Cameron's cartoons portrayed Aberhart in fascist terms and images.

Aberhart had as usual gone straight to the people, not relying on their elected representatives to deliver their demands to him. He was aware that had he put his question to the M.L.A.s at this point, it would be revealed that he had lost the confidence of a number of them. How many he was not sure.

It is estimated that in the first two weeks of this particular session, the Social Crediters spent eighteen hours in session and more than twice as many in caucus. In caucus Aberhart was confiding and apologetic about the delay in implementing party promises to the constituencies. When there were murmurs of dissatisfaction, he reproached those who complained and appealed to them to have faith in the government. He tried with all his eloquence to keep the party united and felt that he was succeeding tolerably well.

What Aberhart did not know was that a growing number of members were, upon leaving the caucus, going secretly to the Corona Hotel, where they met and discussed their dissatisfactions. According to Fred Kennedy, who kept in close touch with the dissidents, the first active malcontents were Earl Ansley (Leduc), A.V. Bourcier (Lac Ste. Anne), W.E. Cain (Brooks), A.L. Blue (Ribstone), and Joe Unwin (Edson). They were soon joined by eight or ten others. For a year and a half now, these M.L.A.s had had to face their electors and explain why Alberta did not yet have Social Credit. They had answered as best they could the questions of when and how the government was going to pay them dividends, why Major Douglas had not come, and why prosperity still eluded them.

Time had not improved either the living conditions or the temper of the farmers. There was restlessness and dissatisfaction in the constituencies, but from the accounts of those who witnessed the protest movement among the members, it seems that the greatest indignation was felt by the members themselves. They were disappointed that the broad road they had marched along so hopefully seemed now to be petering out in barren country. Hargrave's program had been dropped, and there was no plan afoot that might move them closer to Social Credit. Conducting the government of the province along orthodox lines kept the cabinet ministers busy, but no such satisfaction awaited backbenchers in the humiliating job of boosting the reputation of a government whose courage and sincerity they themselves had come to doubt. They prepared, therefore, to take matters into their own hands.

Aberhart was probably aware that his personal influence over some of the M.L.A.s was not strong. Earl Ansley adhered strictly to Douglas's conception of Social Credit. He was deeply disappointed in the collapse of relations between Aberhart and Douglas, and was inclined to place the blame on Aberhart. He also despised the scrip system, even though he had sat on the committee that had produced the idea.[15] He was supported by A.V. Bourcier, another Douglasite, whose mercurial temperament now flared to revolutionary intensity. The problem of finding a leader did occupy the rebels for a time, but by 4 March 1937 they had chosen H.K. Brown, a dental surgeon who represented Pembina, to lead them.

All the Social Credit M.L.A.s were approached by the insurgents at one time or another, and their views were sounded out. Many were adamantly loyal to Aberhart; but some were torn between the two and had to be reasoned with and persuaded to throw their vote to the rebels when the time came. One or two remained borderline cases, and kept the rebels in agonizing

Aberhart made secret plans to go to the coronation of King George VI. When his machinations were exposed, and objections were made that Alberta could not afford the expense, Aberhart denied he had ever planned to go. Stewart Cameron cartoon, Calgary Herald, *6 March 1937.*

suspense as the number of their declared supporters in the caucus crept up towards the halfway mark.

On March 12 came the explosion. Solon E. Low, the new provincial treasurer, a Mormon representing Warner, brought down the budget. It contained no provision for Social Credit and was at once labelled by the rebels a "banker's budget." Aberhart was immediately confronted by a party insurgency. A.L. Blue, the Socred member for Ribstone, shocked the assembly by supporting the criticism of David Duggan, the Conservative leader. Blue also objected to Aberhart's plans for attending the coronation in London, because the province could not afford the expense.[16]

The coronation of King George VI and Queen Elizabeth, which was planned for May 1937, spread a little royal splendor and pagentry as far afield as Depression-ridden Alberta. Aberhart, as first minister of the province, had been invited to witness the crowning of the monarch and was anxious to attend. The cabinet had agreed, and he had booked a tentative passage to England on the *Duchess of Atholl*, hoping that Charles Bowman would travel with him and his wife.[17] Upon hearing of Aberhart's plans, Major Douglas offered to host him in London during his visit and told Aberhart that he would publish this invitation if it would help.[18] Douglas's change of attitude towards Aberhart seems difficult to understand, but Douglas's own difficulties with his Secretariat may explain his behaviour. Many of Douglas's followers in England were very unhappy with his lack of leadership, and his hesitancy to cooperate with the world's first Social Credit government.[19] Hargrave was seriously challenging Douglas's leadership, and since Aberhart had refused to take direction from Hargrave, Douglas may have felt that Aberhart still might be of some use to him. A member of Douglas' Secretariat was even planning a speaking tour for Aberhart.[20]

After the adjournment of the day's sitting in which Blue had attacked Aberhart's plans for the Coronation trip, there was much bustling in the corridors of the Legislative Building. There was a special, hurried cabinet meeting, followed by a special caucus. Blue, it was rumoured, was to be called to explain himself. By the time the caucus assembled, Aberhart had neatly collected his wits. Blue was gathered to the bosom of the government and praised as a worthy Social Crediter who had spoken his mind without fear or favour; he was a brave man and the government was proud of him. The incendiaries were momentarily nonplussed to find that Aberhart had slipped out a side door of the burning building and was working with them, shoulder to shoulder, ostensibly heaping fuel on the blaze.

Aberhart was not above using "dirty tricks" to help his position; while the insurgency was taking place, he was busy trying to build up public support for himself. With the aid of a supporter who worked for a life insurance company, Aberhart appears to have ghosted an editorial that was sent to a number of rural newspapers, comparing Aberhart to the showman P.T. Barnum. It quoted Aberhart as saying that average people had the mentality of thirteen-year-olds and that they were "suckers." The purpose of planting this editorial was to give Aberhart "proof" of the slanders of a hostile press and the control over the press exercised by financiers and life insurance companies, because they printed such editorials.[21] He appears to have rewarded his helper with a government job.

In spite of the criticisms he had received about the coronation trip, Aberhart still planned to go, and arranged for interviews along the way.[22] He was scheduled to sail on 28 April.

After Aberhart had disarmed Blue, the insurgents badly needed time to gather their thoughts, reassemble their ranks, and plan their next moves. On

17 March the new lieutenant-governor, S.H. Primrose, a former Royal North West Mounted Police officer and Edmonton police magistrate, died suddenly. According to custom the Legislature adjourned until a replacement was appointed by Ottawa. That gave the insurgents five days in which to reorganize their campaign.

Tension was in the air. The public gallery held only 240 people, so to be assured of a seat on the day that the session reopened, people took their places throughout the morning and sat patiently until the session began at three o'clock, meanwhile eating lunches they had brought with them in paper bags. On that afternoon of 22 March, A.V. Bourcier was the first to speak. He denounced the government at length. That was the first stage of a long siege the insurgents had planned, to delay indefinitely the vote on the controversial budget. Other Socred M.L.A.s followed Bourcier in a three-day attack.

Aberhart sat hunched in his chair, silent, glancing now and then at the clock, and aimlessly doodling on a piece of paper. Edith Rogers, one of Aberhart's earliest and most active supporters, now took up the cudgels and belaboured the government. W.E. Cain and Earl Ansley followed. The rising of each new speaker came as a blow to Aberhart, who had not realized to what extent he had lost the loyalty of the M.L.A.s. The newspapers gloated that these were the people whom Aberhart himself had hand-picked. On 24 March Dr. Harry Brown moved an adjournment of the Legislature. The motion was carried, over Aberhart's objection, by twenty-seven votes to twenty-five. The triumphant rebels regarded this as a vote of non-confidence in the government.

Because of a mere procedural point Aberhart refused to consider the vote a vote of non-confidence and gave notice that he would move closure of the budget debate on 29 March and put an end to the nonsense. This was the first time in the history of Canadian politics that a premier had threatened closure on his own party.

On 27 March the insurgents announced that they now numbered thirty. Dr. Brown took the cabinet to task for not having brought Douglas over to help put in Social Credit. Brown revealed that some time before, Aberhart had said he would "play second fiddle to no man."[23]

Aberhart, realizing that he would be risking his government by putting the budget to a vote,[24] announced in his Easter Sunday broadcast that he would withdraw his closure motion and ask for a temporary money vote instead. The next day, hundreds of people were waiting to get into the public gallery before the session opened. Demonstrators carrying a six-foot-long stovepipe made up to look like a fountain pen, with which Aberhart had once said he would create credit for their dividends, demanded to see Aberhart, but he was not available. The crowd far exceeded the capacity of the public gallery and loud-speakers had to be set up in the rotunda so that they could listen:[25]

When the session opened Aberhart tried to get the unanimous consent of the Legislature to allow him to withdraw his closure motion, but it was refused; the motion was put to a vote and defeated. The insurgents were confident that they could also defeat the government's interim supply motion, without which Aberhart had only two alternatives: to accede to whatever the insurgents might demand, or to resign.

For four hours that night in caucus Aberhart bargained with the insurgents. A compromise was reached whereby, if the insurgents supported the interim supply bill, the cabinet would introduce an amendment to the Social Credit Measures Act to provide for the establishment of a five-to-seven-man board that would appoint a commission of "experts" who would implement Social Credit in the province.

The insurgents then allowed the interim supply bill to pass, but when Aberhart introduced the bill to amend the Social Credit Measures Act, the insurgents claimed that it was not as *they* had drafted it and would not vote for it. There was much talk among the rebels of demanding the resignation of Aberhart and his cabinet. On 31 March a delegation confronted Aberhart with this demand, saying the rebels were prepared to take over the government within twenty-four hours. With the understanding Aberhart would submit his resignation if they allowed the third reading of the supply bill to pass,

In an attempt to quell a rebellion by impatient back-benchers Aberhart raised their salaries. Stewart Cameron cartoon, Calgary Herald, 3 April 1937.

the insurgents passed it. Then, when Aberhart did not resign and denied that there had been any such deal,[26] they felt they had been tricked.

Aberhart made it known that the only way they would defeat him was if a general election were called and the people decided to throw him out.

The insurgents did not want an election, feeling that they could not compete with Aberhart's radio broadcasts. He tried to sidetrack their plans by having Solon Low introduce a motion raising the sessional indemnity of the M.L.A.s raised by $200. The insurgents turned down the bribe.[27]

Because of the intense opposition Aberhart had been receiving to his proposed trip to the Coronation, he finally abandoned his plans to go. Politically, with a major revolt underway, he could not afford it. From the pulpit of the Bible Institute, and in his correspondence, he denied that he had ever definitely stated he was going to the Coronation,[28] but his own correspondence establishing appointments in England shows that he lied.

On 8 April 1937 Solon Low introduced a new, comprehensive bill – the Alberta Social Credit Act. Here at last was what the insurgents had been seeking even more than Aberhart's resignation. The new bill provided for the creation of "Alberta Credit" and the establishment of credit houses for its distribution and transfer, and for the payment of subsidies to producers and distributors. The controversial registration covenants were also cancelled. The Act also set up a Social Credit Board of non-cabinet members of the Legislature empowered to appoint a commission of from three to five experts to administer Alberta "credit" and advise the Board on Social Credit legislation.[29]

Other legislation passed during the session was intended to modify previous acts declared invalid by the courts. Act IX amended and strengthened the Debt Adjustment Act, making its decisions final and beyond the jurisdiction of any court, with a *caveat* attached, however, containing a contradictory clause stating that the Act could be cancelled if the federal government enacted similar legislation, or if the Act was declared *ultra vires*.[30] In Act XI court actions against the province for not redeeming its debentures were prohibited, unless special permission was granted.[31] Acts XII and XIII reinstituted the reduction of interest payable on provincial securities, which had recently been declared *ultra vires*.[32] The government's failure to redeem its bonds was further legalized.[33]

The Social Credit Board, which had just been established, was composed of four moderate insurgents and one loyalist, Floyd Baker.[34] The cabinet denied all responsibility for the Alberta Social Credit Act, and the insurgents were already disagreeing among themselves about its details. By disassociating themselves from the Act, cabinet members hoped to be able to absolve themselves from all responsibility if the Board failed. Aberhart and his cabinet, therefore, were in a position, strange in a cabinet system of government, of being ruled in the matter of economic policy by a board of private members that would be under the influence of Social Credit "experts," somewhat in the manner that Douglas had in mind when he advocated voting for results, not methods. The duty of the Social Credit board was to find "experts" who would in turn find "methods."

Aberhart, nervously awaiting developments, was at least able to reflect that he was still in office. The insurgency had been a great blow to him. That so many of his followers had overpowered him shook his confidence as nothing else had before in his life. He had always maintained command; his whole career was based on his quality of leadership, and this demonstration of weakness in his influence over those who followed him seemed to undermine the whole basis of his life. He grew uncommunicative and suspicious; he looked uncertainly at those about him – even at those who were not in the government – not knowing whom he could trust. He broke a long silence at the breakfast table one morning by asking Dr. Victor Wright suddenly, "Are you mixed up in this insurrection?"[35] To find out how much support he did have, Aberhart and a loyalist member prepared a petition calling for his resignation and for that of his cabinet,[36] but suspicious of its origin, the insurgents refused to sign it.[37]

The crowded press room in Edmonton was filled with tension over what would happen next. Teletypes had to be installed, and finding space for the many correspondents who crowded into the press room was a major problem. It held, at one point, more correspondents than there were in the press room in Ottawa. They had begun to arrive from all parts of the world during the 1936 session. The Alberta press gallery, instead of its usual six or eight men, now held thirty. The New York *Times* had its correspondent on hand. The telephones rang continuously. London, New York, and Boston wanted to know if the insurgency was bringing Social Credit nearer. Alberta was still news and continued to be so for another eighteen months.

The first task of the Social Credit Board was to find "experts" who could put in the system. Everyone expected Douglas to be brought over to Alberta. The Calgary *Herald* editorialized that if Douglas did come to Alberta, "it will be the first time he has accepted any administrative responsibility throughout his long and profitable crusade on behalf of his own special theories." The *Herald* agreed with the Winnipeg *Free Press* that even if Douglas had been come over to help Aberhart, "Alberta would still be in the mess it now is."[38] If Douglas would not come, other "experts" would have to be found. Stewart Cameron's cartoon in the 17 April issue of the Calgary *Herald* was very sceptical of the success the Social Credit Board might have finding these "experts."

For many months now, the insurgents had been in correspondence with Major Douglas. Immediately after the Social Credit Board was established, its chairman G.L. MacLachlan cabled Douglas:

> Board appointed by Legislature with full authority independent of political influence to establish Social Credit. Unanimously request your services as expert with free hand to direct operations and choose colleagues. Need you immediately. Cable reply collect, stating earliest possible date you can come.[39]

Douglas, however, still hesitant about cooperating while Aberhart still held the premiership, refused to come, but suggested instead that a representative from the Social Credit Board should come to London to discuss the direction that the Board should take and the possibilities of his coming to Alberta later.[40] In his correspondence with his own supporters, Aberhart indicated that he was hoping Douglas would come over to direct the establishment of Social Credit, but one wonders how sincere he was at this point.[41]

On 29 April 1937 MacLachlan left Edmonton for Ottawa on the first leg of his journey to interview Douglas. Arriving in London on 9 May he was met by Bardsley, secretary of the Secretariat. Douglas was at his fishing lodge, where MacLachlan visited with him and made arrangements for two of Douglas's representatives to come to Alberta to assess the situation. Should they submit a favourable report to Douglas, he would then come to Alberta to direct the operations of the Social Credit Board. A sum of two thousand dollars was immediately wired for the travelling expenses of Douglas's technicians.[42]

While MacLachlan was away, Aberhart's feud with the insurgents continued. He insisted that he would "stick to his guns" and not give up his office unless he was kicked out. The more he made comments about his "rhinoceros hide" the less it appeared that he had one. The latest crisis had been sparked by his firing of W.N. Chant, minister of Agriculture, who was known as a Douglasite.[43] Chant's role in the insurgency was unclear, but Aberhart may have suspected that he had been leaking cabinet information to the rebels. Aberhart had asked for his resignation, but Chant refused to give it without a good reason for doing so. Aberhart accused him of being inefficient and lacking in aggressiveness[44]; Chant claimed he was dismissed because he had refused to abide with Aberhart's method of patronage.[45] The truth seems to be a combination of both accusations: Chant's ineffectiveness as minister of Agriculture and his fight with Aberhart over patronage.[46]

One man decided that the conventional newspapers had not done enough to expose Aberhart's régime and therefore founded his own, one devoted exclusively to attacking Aberhart, his government, and the Social Credit Board. J.J. Zubick of Calgary had long been an opponent of Aberhart's Social Credit views and feared their results. Born in Siberia he had moved as a child to Canada and, during the First World War, had served with the Canadian armed forces. For a number of years he had been a school teacher and newspaper editor in Saskatchewan. He was a Conservative in politics and a dedicated Lutheran.

Zubick's paper *The Rebel* exposed and attacked Aberhart with satire, lampoon, and ridicule. He called Aberhart every name in the book, short of profanity. In his first issue Zubick let loose:

> Aberhart has been treated as though he were an honest, honourable man trying to introduce Social Credit; whereas the truth is that Aberhart is a dishonest, dishonourable, lying, blaspheming charlatan, who insinuated himself into power by deception and misrepresentation, and is morally unfit to hold the office of premier... You gained power by using the highest and noblest thing in life – religion – to appeal to the lowest – to greed, selfishness, cupidity. By using this fiendish combination, you set loose an uncontrollable flood of passion. You set neighbour against neighbour, friend against friend, brother against brother, man against wife. And then you crucified a suffering people upon the cross of your vanity and ambition.[47]

In another issue Zubick claimed:

> No, Aberhart is not insane. He is just a person of low mentality and perverted moral perceptions who has gotten himself into a "jam" through

the exercise of an ego inflated beyond his intellectual capacity, and who, lacking courage to face the facts, is forced through circumstances of his own creation, to resort to the only course left to any coward – pretense and deception. And the only way to bring a pervert of this type to his senses is to "treat him rough," to force him into a position where he must either fight honourably or quit – and then he will give in, like the yellow quitter he undoubtedly is at heart.[48]

Aberhart's misuse of religion for political purposes was especially serious in Zubick's mind:

> Mr. Aberhart may not be a seducer of innocent girls, such as a former premier is alleged to have been. No, but unblushingly and brazenly he openly prostitutes the Word of God for political purposes.[49]

Zubick sent copies of his paper to Aberhart, addressing them to "The Wolf in Sheep's Clothing" at the "Calgary Pathetic Bible Substitute."

Zubick continued *The Rebel* for almost three years; his criticisms of Aberhart far surpassed anything that Aberhart had ever experienced from the Calgary *Herald*, the other newspapers, or American magazines. The intensity of Zubick's attack no doubt increased Aberhart's hatred for the press and contributed to the forthcoming legislation to control it.

As MacLachlan and the first of Douglas's technicians made their way back to Alberta, Douglas's latest book came off the press. *The Alberta Experiment: An Interim Survey* outlined Douglas's impressions of what Aberhart's government had achieved so far, and he published all the correspondence between them up until March 1936. He concluded that with a little redirection, the Alberta government would be able to establish a Social Credit system.[50]

MacLachlan and George Frederick Powell, who had been employed as a salesman with a major tire firm, arrived in Edmonton on 10 June 1937. One of Powell's first duties was to prepare a pledge of unity. Nearly all of the Social Credit M.L.A.s and the members of the cabinet signed the pledge binding them "to uphold the Social Credit Board and its technicians." The second technician from Major Douglas arrived in Edmonton several weeks later. L.D. Byrne, who had left an insurance business in Southhampton, had been sent by Douglas because of his vast knowledge of Social Credit, and he was expected to accomplish the bulk of the work, while Powell managed the public relations.[51]

As the Social Credit technicians commenced their work, there were increasing rumours in the press of forthcoming regimentation because of the fascist direction the government appeared to taking. Stewart Cameron's cartoons reflected this concern.

The insurgency was virtually dead after Byrne and Powell began to supervise the Social Credit Board. The backbenchers felt that now Social Credit would be realized. Secret meetings were held behind closed doors while radical legislation was being planned. Occasionally rumours filtered out: one of which was that bond-holders would have to register in order to receive a settlement on the defaulted bonds. The opposition saw this as another sinister move on the part of the government.

As 3 August 1937, the date for the opening of the special session of the Legislature, approached, people competed to gather from the rumours that

After Major Douglas's lieutenants Powell and Byrne began to direct the affairs of the Aberhart government, Stewart Cameron depicted Aberhart in fascist poses. The Social Credit salute was an outstretched hand, saying "Give me my dividends!" Stewart Cameron cartoon, Calgary Herald, *26 June 1937.*

filled the air something of the nature of the new Social Credit legislation being drawn up. Byrne claimed that his offices had been broken into and his desk rifled.[52] There was speculation among businessmen and bankers about how the new legislation would affect them, and politicians in Ottawa watched carefully, with a copy of the B.N.A. Act ready for immediate consultation.

CHAPTER EIGHTEEN

■

ABERHART VERSUS THE CONSTITUTION

I BELIEVE *we have*

in this province the greatest example of true

democracy that the world has ever seen," the premier

said. "By this I mean a government elected

by the people and for the purpose of

carrying out the will of the people."

— William Aberhart quoted in the

Calgary Herald, 18 August 1937

Under the direction of Powell and Byrne, Aberhart's government passed radical legislation concerning the press, the banks, and civil rights that brought it into serious conflict with the federal government. The special legislative session of 3-6 August 1937 was short and to the point. The first three of a proposed series of revolutionary bills devised by the Social Credit technicians were pushed through the House.

The Credit of Alberta Regulations Bill required every bank and every bank employee to obtain a license from the provincial government. Upon being licensed each bank would have a local directorate appointed by the Social Credit Board to supervise all of its activities, thus giving the Social Credit Board complete control over their credit policies.[1] The Bank Employees Civil Rights Bill prohibited any unlicensed bank or bank employee from having any access to the courts.[2] The Judicature Act Amendment Bill prohibited any court action over the constitutionality of any enactment of the Alberta Legislature.[3]

Immediately the Opposition labelled these Bills "Hitler legislation." Stewart Cameron's next cartoon depicted Aberhart setting fire to the "Temple [Reichstag] of Civil Rights."[4] Soon the Lethbridge Board of Trade sent a telegram to the lieutenant-governor asking him to withhold assent because the bills were in violation of the B.N.A. Act.[5]

On August 6 the business of the session was complete except for the obtaining of royal assent to the bills. John

After Aberhart's government introduced legislation restricting banks and civil liberties, Cameron depicted Aberhart burning the "Reichstag," the Temple of Civil Rights. Stewart Cameron cartoon Calgary Herald, 7 August 1937.

Campbell Bowen, the new lieutenant-governor and a former Baptist minister, requested that Aberhart and John Hugill come to his office. Knowing their opposite views on the legislation, the M.L.A.s watched curiously as the oddly-matched pair left the Legislative chamber for their interview. The press gallery was full of speculation about whether Bowen would refuse royal assent to the Social Credit legislation and employ his powers of reserving them for consideration of the governor-general.

In the office of the lieutenant-governor a strange little drama ensued. Brief though it was, the episode, as described by Hugill, raised the age-old question of the duties, privileges, and behaviour of a vice-regal personage in relation to a provincial government. In the more leisurely days of Lieutenant-Governor Walsh, Hugill and his legislative counsel would be sent for when the lieutenant-governor wished to discuss the legal aspects of any legislation, and the three men would speak freely over a cup of tea. However, on this occasion, when the lieutenant-governor asked Hugill for his opinion of the bills, Aberhart was waiting for him to approve, glowering ominously over the conversation. Hugill was embarrassed by the presence of Aberhart, but unintimidated he said that in his opinion the bills were unconstitutional. Aberhart could see the Social Credit legislation stumbling at the first hurdle and, without waiting for Hugill to advise the lieutenant-governor to withhold his assent, Aberhart insisted that Bowen sign the bills. He would, he said, take the responsibility himself. The lieutenant-governor signed, and in this bizarre manner the controversial bills became law.[6]

As Aberhart and Hugill walked back to the Legislative Chamber, where the assembly still waited to prorogue, Aberhart said, "You know what this means, don't you?" The Legislature prorogued at five o'clock, and shortly afterwards Hugill came into Aberhart's office and tendered his resignation.[7]

Even though Aberhart had kept Hugill in the dark about some of the Social Credit legislation, Hugill could have refused to advise the lieutenant-governor but, in advising him, Hugill obeyed the letter of the Alberta law that set out his duties. In deciding what advice to give, Hugill had to choose between his duty as a cabinet minister and his duty as a legal adviser. He decided that since the question related solely to the law, he must allow his oath as a barrister and his position as a King's Counsel to take precedence over all others, even if it meant his own political destruction. It also seemed a fortuitous time for Hugill to leave, because as one who had never accepted the Social Credit ideology, he had been becoming very uncomfortable in cabinet.

Eleven days after the controversial bills were made law, the federal government disallowed all three.[8] Aberhart was informed of the disallowance while he was addressing a Social Credit picnic near Edmonton. He was handed a note and stopped to read its contents. When he told the audience of the disallowance, someone shouted from the crowd, "Give me a gun!" Aberhart quickly tried to calm the crowd: "No! No! None of that! This is not bloodshed!" He asked his supporters to send letters and telegrams to Mackenzie King. He said that Alberta would not leave the Dominion, but the threat was there, for soon afterwards he read telegrams from Australian Socreds who were advising secession for Alberta.[9]

The revival of the power of disallowance, which was considered by Aberhart to be obsolete since the Statute of Westminster gave more autonomy to the provinces, put an effective stop to the advance of Social Credit. It was a dramatic demonstration of the hostility of the federal government to Social Credit political and economic theory.[10]

As some of Aberhart's critics had predicted, his legislation backfired. This development, however, was not unwelcome to Douglas, Byrne, and Powell, who certainly knew that the legislation would inevitably be tested in the courts even if they had not thought it would be disallowed by the federal government. After the *ultra vires* decisions on the 1936 Reduction and Settlement of Debt Act and the Provincial Securities Interest Act, they could not have expected that legislation interfering so radically with the banks and preventing future testing in the courts of Alberta would be allowed to come into force without protest.

Immediately after the disallowance Douglas wired Powell and Byrne: "Magnificent. Getting busy. Give Mounties notice. Organize provincial police. Ultimate success now certain. Congratulate Aberhart."[11]

Douglas's desire to rid the province of the R.C.M.P. was the first stage in his plan for the Social Credit *coup*. Plans were already underway for the creation of a provincial police force, candidates for which were expected to be 100 per cent for Social Credit.[12] J.J. Zubick, editor of *The Rebel*, feared it would be another Gestapo.[13]

After his initial visit, Byrne decided to stay in Alberta as a special adviser to the Social Credit Board. He was offered a contract with a $2,750 retainer and a salary of $6,000 per annum, plus expenses.[14]

Byrne and Powell persuaded Aberhart that only by making a martyr of himself would he stand any chance of gathering the support of public opinion against the federal government. The practice of moderation that Aberhart had followed on the advice of Hugill and other moderate members in his cabinet (all of them now gone) seemed to have brought him nothing but revolt and political near-lynching. Aberhart therefore entered with a will into the new order of the day, throwing moderation to the winds. The Social Credit Board had now put into his hands a Social Credit weapon, and he was no longer regarded as a mere disturber of the peace, but as a full-fledged radical against whom the federal government itself had moved with a show of strength.

It seems strange to think that Douglas's technicians and the Social Credit Board drew up their legislation believing that it would be prevented from coming into effect. However, that was the case: far milder legislation had met a similar fate, and Powell afterwards admitted, "The disallowed Acts had been drawn up mainly to show the people of Alberta who were their *real* enemies, and in that respect they succeeded admirably."[15]

The strategy was beginning, however, and the Social Credit Board pressed on, drafting new legislation in secret, and organizing propaganda. Powell and Byrne held daily classes in the Legislative Building teaching the principles of Social Credit to the Socred M.L.A.s. They wished, no doubt, to expunge from their minds any loose and inaccurate ideas they may have acquired from Aberhart's "unsound" interpretations. Instead, they now absorbed Douglas's "true" concept of Social Credit and the international plots of its "real enemies."

Shortly after the disallowance the federal government announced the formation of a royal commission on federal-provincial relations. Both Douglas and Aberhart interpreted this royal commission as an attempt by "international finance" to meddle in Alberta's affairs. Therefore the Alberta government refused to cooperate in the discussions.[16]

On 30 August the Social Credit party celebrated its second anniversary at St. George's Island. A march past Aberhart's reviewing stand was planned, but called off, possibly because of a Stewart Cameron cartoon that appeared two days before. Cameron had depicted Social Crediters as fascists with a characteristic salute, a hand stretched out asking for dividends.[17]

Fears about what Aberhart and his government would next do to erode civil liberties were so intense that a coalition of all opposition political parties was formed to fight the government. That group, the People's League, attracted huge crowds to its meetings, which were held all over the province. An estimated ten thousand people attended one such meeting at the Victoria Pavilion in Calgary on 8 September 1937. A motorcade of more than one hundred cars came from Aberhart's own riding. When the building could not contain the audience, loud-speakers were installed outside to facilitate the overflow crowd. That meeting, chaired by Mayor Andy Davison, called for the immediate resignation of Aberhart and called on the C.B.C. to prohibit Aberhart's Sunday-afternoon broadcasts because of their political content.[18]

Hugill's last act as attorney-general was his attendance at the Canadian Bar Association meeting in Toronto. After returning to Edmonton, he described Alberta as fast developing into a "tyrannical dictatorship" whose leader would exceed the actions of Hitler and Mussolini if not soon stopped.[19] Aberhart retaliated by having Hugill's expense account cancelled, forcing him to pay the bills from his recent trip. Hugill responded by calling Aberhart a "teutonic dictator," a meglomaniac and the most sadistic man he had ever met.[20] He then crossed the floor of the Legislature and henceforth sat as an independent with Hansen, Ross, Cockroft, and Chant.

The defection of Hugill was welcomed by the press and the legal community. At the same time, however, they expressed the feeling that Hugill's "repentance" came a little late; if he had allowed his integrity to rule earlier, the province would not be in its present peril.[21]

As part of his penance for his past "sins" Hugill joined the People's League. Later, he prepared a critical exposé of Aberhart and his government. When Aberhart heard that Ryerson Press was going to publish Hugill's manuscript, he warned them that if they did so, he would cancel Ryerson's contract to supply school textbooks in Alberta. Hugill's manuscript was never published.[22]

Following Hugill's forced resignation, Aberhart assumed the role of attorney-general, adding it to the premiership and the Education portfolio he already held. Hugill felt that Aberhart's taking that office was highly irregular, for Aberhart neither held the title of King's Counsel nor was he even a member of the bar.[23] His only preparation for this office was a brief correspondence law course he had taken some ten years before from an American school. Because of Aberhart's ignorance of the law, the lieutenant-governor requested that he submit all proposed legislation to an independent solicitor for review. Aberhart refused.[24]

The ideology of Aberhart's Social Credit movement in Alberta was still markedly left-wing in 1937. Earlier in the year W.R. Herbert, head of the Calgary Constituency Association of the Alberta Social Credit League, described its ideology as half-way between communism and fascism.[25] During the summer of 1937 Powell and Byrne held a secret meeting with the leaders of the Communist Party and after that Communist speakers were featured at Social Credit rallies.[26] The Communists, who were at that time in their "common front" stage, were trying to infiltrate other radical parties. In their literature the Communists claimed that they were not Social Crediters; but there were enough common elements in their aims to unite for the defeat of the Conservative-dominated People's League and the federal Liberal Party.[27] Aberhart, who had been receiving opposition from so many quarters, acknowledged the help of the Communists in distributing and obtaining signatures on the Alberta Blue Pledges, which replaced the Registration Covenants.[28]

Public opinion varied in interpreting Aberhart's government. Calgary's mayor Andy Davison claimed that, since the insurgency, Social Credit had ceased to be democratic.[29] William Irvine declared that Aberhart was a fascist dictator who used socialist terminology without being committed to socialist principles.[30] The head of the Canadian Fascist League Dr. R.M. Johnstone also claimed that Aberhart was a fascist, but "through certain religious quirks he hasn't got around to realizing it."[31] The *Financial Post* depicted Aberhart as a communist.[32]

Although Aberhart's critics disgreed on where his government ranked in the political spectrum, there was agreement that it was verging on totalitarianism. According to at least one definition of fascism, the Alberta Social Credit government at that time could be classified as left-wing fascism.[33] The government was fascist because of its charismatic leadership and its emphasis on state control of the economy, regimentation, no distinction between government and party, rule by order-in-council, restrictions on a free press, boycotts of non-sympathizers, and repression of civil liberties. At the same time there was anti-capitalist rhetoric and some positive social legislation in education, health care, relief, and labour relations.

As Douglas's emissaries guided the direction of the Alberta government, another backlash developed. For the past few years the press had severely criticized Aberhart for not being an orthodox Douglasite; now that the actions of the technicians from Douglas could be observed, the press turned its guns on Douglas, who was viewed as an evil genius working behind the scenes. Aberhart was only a pawn in his hands. In various quarters it was felt that Douglas had no interest in establishing Social Credit at all, but only in stirring up controversy that would publicize his theories and sell his books, which were reported to earn him $75,000 per year in royalties.[34]

Opposition to the Social Credit government was steadily increasing. Almost all of the newspapers in the province were demanding a general election. They felt that in order to defeat Aberhart a united front composed of all opposition factions was required.[35] Aberhart continued his battle with the press. The following extracts from one of his broadcasts in September, 1937 illustrates how he harangued his audience and gained their approval for his subsequent legislation against the press:

I can see that in spite of all that one can say in protest, the newspapers who are the mouthpiece of the financiers persist in publishing falsities that are entirely unfair and untrue! They determine to confuse all who they can beguile into reading their spurious articles and they want to give Alberta a black eye in the sight of the world. We've had letters from South Africa, Australia and New Zealand and they tell us that what is put in their papers about Alberta would make you sick. Not a bit of it true, copied from this paper, and copied from that paper, our own papers.... Now ladies and gentlemen if this is done in the name of the liberty of the press we must question such liberty! [Applause]. I fear that I am going to be forced to come to the conclusion that the caliber of the men who are managing these papers is so low as to be unsafe to claim liberty at all. They shouldn't be at large! [Applause].... This again I say to you is the statement of a disordered, distorted, mad brain. The only purpose seems to be to place the Premier of this province in a bad light in the eyes of the people of this province as well as in the eyes of the world. Why else would they tell such a confounded falsity from beginning to end?... I feel certain that the citizens of Alberta will soon come to the judgment that something should be done to curb the mad-dog operations of certain of the financial newspapers! [Applause].... We license doctors, we license lawyers, and school teachers and businessmen and auto drivers and hotel keepers for the protection of the public. Why shouldn't the newspapers be licensed also? [Applause] and licensed for the protection of the public – just the same thing – be required to live up to a certain standard of truth and honesty in their publications? I wonder if such an action would meet with the approval of the citizens of this province? [Applause]. Alright! This is a matter that will receive my immediate attention when I return from the Coast after a little holiday! [Applause]. I hope they are listening in so they'll know what is coming. [Applause]. I hope they don't start to holler like the bond-holders: "you never gave us notice." [Applause]. They know it now! [Applause]. I want to show them that if we can handle their bosses, the financiers, we can handle the henchmen! [Applause].[36]

As Aberhart promised, the fall session of the Legislature saw radical legislation directed against the press. The Accurate News and Information Act required that every Alberta newspaper publish any statements furnished by the chairman of the Social Credit Board "which has for its object the correction or amplification of any statement relating to any policy or activity of the Government of the Province." The bill further directed that newspapers could be ordered to reveal in writing all sources of their information and the names and addresses of such sources, and the names and addresses of the writers of any editorial, article, or news item appearing in their papers. Failure to abide by this ruling would result in the prohibition of the publication of the said newspaper, the prohibition of the publication of anything written by an offending writer, and the prohibition of the publication of any information emanating from any offending person or source. Fines up to one thousand dollars per day would be levelled against those who failed to comply.[37]

Additional legislation was directed at the other "enemy," the banks. The Bank Taxation Act planned to levy taxes of one-half per cent per annum on all paid-up capital of the banks and one per cent per annum on their reserve funds and undivided profits.[38] The Credit of Alberta Regulation Act, which had recently been disallowed, was rewritten to drop all reference to the banks and substitute the words "credit institutions." All such credit institutions were to come under the direction of the Social Credit Board.[39]

When Aberhart refused to submit these bills to the Supreme Court of Canada to determine their legality, Lieutenant-Governor Bowen refused to grant them royal assent and reserved them for the consideration of the governor-general.[40] That was the first time in the history of Alberta that the lieutenant-governor had exercised such powers.

Other legislation that was of a controversial nature, but which did receive royal assent, further extended the registration and licensing of all trades and businesses and persons associated with such occupations.[41] The Calgary *Herald* objected to the arbitrary powers this Act granted to the provincial secretary Ernest Manning, a young man with no business experience. His decisions were subject to no appeal.[42]

Another piece of legislation passed during the third session of the Legislature in 1937 was the repeal of the Recall Act, the first of its kind ever passed in the British Empire, and the first piece of legislation Aberhart's government passed. The constituents of Okotoks-High River had begun a petition demanding the recall of Aberhart. By the fall of 1937 they had the necessary 66.66 per cent of the voters supporting the recall petition. In order to save Aberhart's seat, the government revoked the Recall Act retroactively to the date of its passage.[43] Aberhart justified that action by claiming that many of the oil companies in his riding had intimidated workers into signing the recall petition.[44]

Just before the Recall Act was rescinded, speculation was that had Aberhart been successfully recalled, the caucus would have made Douglas's envoy George Powell premier in Aberhart's place. Liberal house leader J.J. Bowlen claimed that this would not really have been much worse since, for all practical purposes, the province was *already* being administered from Fig Tree Court.[45]

The repeal of the Recall Act by the Alberta government, along with the press "gag" law and the taxation of the banks, were seen by the opposition as more evidence of a growing fascist dictatorship. The Press Act also alienated the *Albertan*, which now sided with Aberhart's opposition.[46]

During the third legislative session of 1937 yet another storm broke. David Duggan, the Conservative leader, mentioned in the House that he had seen a pamphlet that labelled him and other prominent Edmontonians by name as "bankers' toadies." The back of the pamphlet read:

> My child, you should NEVER say hard or unkind things about Bankers' Toadies. God made Bankers' Toadies, just as He made snakes, slugs, snails and other creepy-crawly, treacherous and poisonous things. Never therefore, abuse them – just exterminate them!

After a number of complaints were lodged, Edmonton police raided the headquarters of the Alberta Social Credit League and seized 7,000 copies of the pamphlet. Joe Unwin, the party whip, and George F. Powell, Major

Douglas's technician, were arrested for preparing and distributing the pamphlets. They were charged with defamatory libel and counselling to murder.[47] As attorney-general, Aberhart attempted to stop the prosecution of Unwin and Powell by withdrawing the Crown prosecutor from the case. The trial judge then appointed a public prosecutor and set the trial for November.

During his trial before judge and jury, Joe Unwin described how he had offered to prepare a series of pamphlets for the publicity department of the Social Credit Board. The cost of printing those pamphlets was paid for by order-in-council, and they were circulated under the fictitious name of the "United Democrats," having as its address Unwin's home. Powell had supplied Unwin with the text of a cartoon from the Gladstone era of British politics and added the words "Bankers' Toadies." Unwin had sent Powell's copy to the printers and was surprised to find the final product with the names of prominent Edmontonians printed on the back of the pamphlet. Unwin claimed that he had tried to suppress the pamphlet and put the blame on Powell. After hearing much contradictory testimony the jury found Unwin guilty of defamatory libel, and Justice W.G. Ives of the Supreme Court of Alberta sentenced him to three months with hard labour in Fort Saskatchewan Penitentiary.[48]

Powell's trial commenced immediately after Unwin's. Powell elected to be tried by judge alone. His testimony was contradicted on many points by Unwin, who was again put on the witness stand. Powell denied having given Unwin the list of names for the reverse side of the pamphlet and accused him of lying. The judge, however, finding Powell to be a difficult and dodgy witness, accepted Unwin's testimony and regarded him as a "glorified messenger boy." Testimony by Unwin's secretary linked Powell with the inclusion of names on the pamphlet. Mr. Justice Ives then sentenced Powell to six months with hard labour in the same penitentiary as Unwin, along with a recommendation that Powell be deported from Canada following his enforced accommodation.[49]

Major Douglas was angered by the jailing of his personal representative and commenced a series of letters to Mackenzie King. There was some talk about Douglas coming over to Alberta to lead the fight against the opposition, but his letters reveal that he had fears that he, too, might be jailed.[50]

Unwin and Powell appealed their sentences, but lost. Aberhart found himself in a conflict-of-interest situation; as attorney-general he had to uphold the law, but he frequently discussed and criticized their sentences during his radio broadcasts and encouraged his supporters to write to Mackenzie King asking for clemency for the two men.[51] Aberhart attempted to evade the seriousness of the charges against Unwin and Powell by claiming that the pamphlet was only a harmless piece of political humour.[52] Even the defence attorneys had not attempted this defence.

The federal government replied to letters asking for clemency for Unwin and Powell by stating that "such a drastic and immediate exercise of clemency would be construed throughout Canada as a direct interference by the federal executive with the free and proper functioning of our courts." Mackenzie King added that "in the opinion of the government, attacks upon the judiciary

Many thought Aberhart was not in control of his own government. Most of the legislation inspired by Major Douglas was disallowed by the federal government. Stewart Cameron cartoon, Calgary Herald, *16 October 1937.*

[by Aberhart] can hardly be expected to be conducive to an exercise of clemency."[53] Unwin and Powell were regarded as martyrs by Social Crediters, many of whom loaded themselves into cars every night and formed a caravan

Major Douglas and his two "experts" Powell and Byrne, forcing a seemingly reluctant Aberhart to "rob" the banks of Alberta. Stewart Cameron cartoon (Calgary Herald*).*

that travelled out to the penitentiary to show their support for their jailed colleagues.

Before half of their sentences were completed Unwin and Powell were released from prison. Political expediency had a lot to do with it. On 21 March 1938 a federal by-election was being held in East Edmonton. Hoping to win some support, the federal government announced the release of Unwin on the day of the election. Upon receiving the news of his impending release, the Socred M.L.A.s broke into jubilation and performed a snake-dance in the Legislature. The Liberals' hopes of winning support, however, failed. Social Credit candidate Orvis Kennedy won the election, and that night a huge victory rally was held in honour of Kennedy and Unwin. Joining them on the platform was Jan Lakeman, leader of the Communist Party in Edmonton, who had helped with the Social Credit campaign. Lakeman was thanked by Kennedy for his support, and Lakeman in turn thanked the voters "for giving an overwhelming defeat to the forces of reaction in the dominion." Leslie Morris, secretary of the Canadian Communist Party and correspondent for *Pravda,* who had also helped in the campaign, took part in the victory celebrations.[54]

Powell was not released until the end of April 1938.[55] As he departed for England, the Alberta goverment passed an order-in-council granting Powell $4,000 for his trouble.[56]

In the meantime, other legal battles had been raging. Aberhart had reluctantly submitted the three bills that had been reserved by the lieutenant-governor to the Supreme Court for a ruling on their constitutionality. As the Supreme Court of Canada considered the legislation, R.B. Bennett, former prime minister and M.P. for Calgary West, waded into the fray by claiming that Alberta was being discriminated against because some of Ontario's legislation had not been disallowed. Social Credit and C.C.F. Members of Parliament copied Bennett's argument.[57] On 4 March 1938 the Supreme Court ruled that all three bills were unconstitutional and that the federal government had the right to disallow provincial enactments and upheld the right of the lieutenant-governor to reserve his assent to provincial legislation.[58] Members of the Alberta government and the Social Credit Board were unhappy with

Aberhart often went to visit his daughters in Vancouver. Cameron felt Aberhart had a much easier life than the average Alberta farmer under the Social Credit government. Stewart Cameron cartoon, Calgary Herald, *22 April 1938.*

the Supreme Court's ruling, claiming among other things, their inability to tax the banks now denied them two million dollars of expected revenue,[59] even though the legislation probably had been designed to create a negative reaction from Ottawa.

In another act of posturing, the Alberta government took another swipe at the press. Don Brown, a reporter for the Edmonton *Journal*, was arrested on orders from the government for allegedly misquoting a backbencher and thereby misrepresenting the business of the Legislature. A trial was staged after Brown was hauled into the Legislature, convicted of the charge, and sentenced to jail; but two hours before he was to enter jail the sentence was dropped.[60] Thus ended the Alberta government's attempts at legislating the press. For their efforts at opposing the Alberta government the Edmonton *Journal*, the Calgary *Herald*, the *Albertan*, the Edmonton *Bulletin*, the Lethbridge *Herald*, the Medicine Hat *News* and ninety other weekly newspapers in Alberta were awarded the 1938 Pulitzer Prize.[61]

The spring of 1938 saw Aberhart's government taking retaliatory measures against the lieutenant-governor for his refusal to give assent to the controversial Social Credit legislation the previous fall. During the new session of the Legislature, it was announced that Government House, the official residence of the lieutenant-governor, would be closed immediately and that the government would no longer provide the lieutenant-governor with an official car and a secretarial staff. However, an office would be retained for him in the Legislative Building, and should he need transportation or secretarial services, he would have to call upon the motor pool and the secretarial pool. In letters to Aberhart, Mackenzie King claimed that such actions showed disloyalty to the Crown. However, Aberhart insisted on the new arrangements.[62]

The office of lieutenant-governor had been a hotly contested issue in the history of Alberta politics, especially during the Depression. On more than one occasion, the previous U.F.A. government had talked of closing Government House as an austerity measure.[63] When Lieutenant-Governor Bowen had refused to give assent to Social Credit legislation, some Social Crediters had written to Aberhart demanding not only the closing of Government House but also the abolition of the position of lieutenant-governor.[64] Aberhart, however, refused to act that drastically.[65]

As the conflict continued between Aberhart and the federal government, more legislation was passed by the Alberta government to strengthen its cause and raise its revenues. The Alberta Social Credit Act was replaced by the Alberta Social Credit Realization Act which broadened the powers of the Social Credit Board.[66] To make up for the disallowance of the Bank Taxation Act, a 50-per-cent increase in taxes was levied against the banks.[67] To break the power of the banks over the people the government encouraged the establishment of Credit Unions.[68] Mortgage holders were also affected; a 2-per-cent tax was imposed on unpaid principle amounts of first, second, and third mortgages on land.[69] Any bank, mortgage, or finance company planning to foreclose on a private home had to post a $2,000 bond payable to the owner of the home if the foreclosure was completed.[70] Legislation affecting farmers was a mixed blessing; the Alberta Hail Insurance Act was created,[71] but farmers were hurt by a 7-per-cent tax imposed on all agricultural produce.[72]

His Favorite Actors

Aberhart's fight with the federal government generated more cartoons that depicted Aberhart's fascist leanings. Stewart Cameron cartoon, Calgary Herald, 19 March 1938.

The extra revenue was badly needed by the Alberta government, which was near bankruptcy. Succession duties were raised by 20 per cent.[73] By June 1938 the province had been again forced to default on its payment of over $3.25 million worth of bonds.[74] Then the federal government disallowed or declared *ultra vires* the following pieces of recent legislation dealing with taxes and debts that would have raised the province's revenues. On 15 June the Securities Tax Act, which placed a 2-per-cent tax upon the owners of mortgages, and the Home Owners' Security Act were disallowed by the federal government, which declared that those Acts were coercive, oppressive and repudiatory, violating contractual obligations.[75] The federal government's action had resulted from widespread petitions raised by banks, finance companies, and boards of trade from across Canada and the United States.

Aberhart's inability to solve the financial problems of Alberta had a profound effect upon the fortunes of the Social Credit movement in Saskatchewan, and in June 1938, a provincial election was held in that province. Aberhart and a group of volunteers launched a speaking tour in Saskatchewan in support of the forty-one Social Credit candidates he had selected there, with the hope that a Social Credit government would be elected. As huge crowds turned out to hear Aberhart, who for many was a voice they had often heard on the radio, some press correspondents and Aberhart's supporters predicted another landslide victory for Social Credit. However, the Saskatchewan Socreds only received 16 per cent of the popular vote, and only two Social Credit candidates were elected.[76] It appeared that the people had come to see Aberhart more out of curiosity than out of political conviction.

For Aberhart the Liberal victory in Saskatchewan was a great blow, after all the hard work he had put into the campaign. But, as Fred Kennedy pointed out, had the Alberta Social Credit government been able to fulfil its own promises, Social Credit might also have won in Saskatchewan. However, with its many failures at home, it was not surprising that another province turned it down.[77]

The political fortunes of Aberhart's government were declining. Toward the end of June 1938 a caucus meeting was held in Edmonton to plan coming strategy for the Social Credit government. Several backbenchers who suggested that a general election be called were shouted down. Following that caucus meeting Aberhart made a tour of his own riding of Okotoks-High River. There he found that dissatisfaction with his government was rampant. On more than one occasion fist-fights erupted during his meetings.[78]

The opposition that Aberhart was experiencing was very taxing on his health. He found himself exhausted and headed to Vancouver to spend another holiday with his daughters and grandchildren. This holiday rejuvenated Aberhart somewhat, and upon returning from the Coast, he took retaliatory measures against another "enemy" by firing Magistrate A.H. Gibson, who had committed Unwin and Powell to stand trial the previous year.[79]

The battle between Alberta's Legislature and its courts continued. On 24 September the Alberta Court of Appeal ruled that the 7-per-cent tax on all agricultural products was *ultra vires*.[80] It appeared that most of Alberta's legislation was doomed to failure.

In an attempt to regain public support, the Social Credit caucus in June 1938 had commissioned L.D. Byrne to create another Social Credit plan; part of that plan was the resurrection of the program to establish State Credit Houses throughout the province to replace the banks, which had indicated that they would withdraw their services entirely from the province unless recent legislation was withdrawn or disallowed. Some of the banks in rural centres had already closed their doors.[81] The new credit institutions were to be called Treasury Branches and were legalized during the fall sitting of the Legislature.[82] When Provincial Treasurer Solon Low approached Lieutenant-Governor Bowen for approval to use unlimited funds to establish the Treasury Branches, the government was turned down and allowed only

$200,000 for the purpose. That became another incident in the long-lasting battle between Aberhart and Bowen.

The Treasury Branch program had some unusual features, in that non-negotiable transfer vouchers were issued to deposit-holders instead of cheques. These vouchers could be deposited only by the person receiving them. On each one was a place for the merchant to record the total amount of Alberta-made goods purchased. At the beginning of each month the Treasury Branch would credit to each deposit-holder a bonus of 3-per-cent of the value of Alberta-made products he or she had purchased during the previous month. The intention was to promote Alberta's own products. The program carried the slogan "What Alberta makes Makes Alberta."[83] As in the earlier experimentation with Prosperity Certificates, merchants were hesitant to accept Treasury Branch vouchers. They were easier to redeem, but were still worthless for extraprovincial transactions. By 1945 this aspect of the Treasury Branch program was phased out.[84]

Another feature of the Treasury Branch system was that all civil servants would have to deposit their pay cheques in the Treasury Branches to avoid a 2-per-cent penalty. This was seen as another demonstration of the dictatorial nature of the Alberta government, and because of widespread opposition, the order was suspended. By 1939 there were 315 Treasury Branch facilities operating in the province. They did provide an alternate banking system for some people who did not have easy access to chartered banks, but the business community was suspicious of the Treasury Branches because most of Aberhart's other economic ventures had been disasters. It took quite some time for them to become accepted, and they never seriously challenged the existence of the banks.

A piece of legislation far more important to the prosperity of the province than Treasury Branch legislation was passed during the fall session of 1938; it concerned regulation of the oil and gas industry. For many years the oil companies in Turner Valley had been burning off excess gas, and the amount burned was so extensive that the reddened sky from the flares could be seen as far away as Calgary. The Alberta government declared that this practice was a waste of energy and had to stop.[85] Although that legislation was unpopular with the oil companies, the conservation of oil and gas reserves was a practical and positive action on the part of the government. The establishment of the Oil and Gas Conservation Board would eventually do far more to improve the economy of Alberta than Social Credit legislation could ever do. However, economic recovery was still a long way off.

During the first three-and-one-half years in office Aberhart had never spoken publicly in the Legislature. His maiden speech came in February 1939, after members of the opposition had commented that the Speech from the Throne had contained so little Social Credit rhetoric that they wondered whether Social Credit had finally been abandoned. Aberhart replied that the government had not abandoned Social Credit and defended his government's record, noting the establishment of the Treasury Branches, the promotion of Credit Unions, the enlargement of the school districts, the progress of the government towards State Medicine, the extensive road-building program, and oil and gas conservation measures. Noting that his speaking in the House was not his usual policy, Aberhart stated that he felt that such speeches were a waste of time because the opposition would not accept anything he said,

Aberhart did not deliver a single speech in the Legislature until 1939. As always, he feared open debate, and he depended on this radio broadcasts to communicate with the public. Stewart Cameron cartoon, Calgary Herald, *20 February 1939.*

anyway. The important people, the public, he could reach by radio.[86] During the Legislative Session that followed the debate on the Speech from the Throne, only one piece of legislation appeared to have any relation to Social Credit. The government established a Provincial Marketing Board

Aberhart and his wife greeting King George VI and Queen Elizabeth during their tour of North America in 1939.

to control and regulate the transportation, packing, distribution, and marketing of all natural products within the province.[87] Aberhart made Charles R. Pearce, secretary-treasurer of the Calgary Prophetic Bible Institute, head of the Board. Several other pieces of legislation made minor amendments to debt legislation that had been declared *ultra vires*. The rest of the Acts were of such a nature that they could have been passed by any other provincial government. As the opposition members had noted, Social Credit was quickly disappearing from the government's agenda.

During the rest of the spring of 1939, Aberhart was busy preparing for the visit of King George VI and Queen Elizabeth. As one who had a predilection for all things British, he looked forward to the event with great anticipation. However, in some quarters there were complaints that Aberhart should not be allowed to meet their majesties because of all the un-British things he and his government had done: the closing of Government House, the official guest house in which their majesties would have stayed; the talk of firing the R.C.M.P.; restrictions on the press and civil liberties; and the breaking of covenants in defaulting on the bonds.[88]

Mackenzie King, Jessie Aberhart, King George, Aberhart and Queen Elizabeth at the head table during a banquet for the royal visitors, 1939.

The royal visit again brought to the fore Aberhart's fight with the lieutenant-governor, and what transpired was a comic opera. Aberhart had planned to have his granddaughter Kaye MacNutt present flowers to the queen, but after much protest, a girl from an orphanage was given the honour. On more than one occasion Aberhart found himself uninvited to and locked out of functions Lieutenant-Governor Bowen had planned for the royal couple. Mackenzie King, who accompanied the royal entourage, noted in his diary that he had been kept busy keeping the king and queen ignorant of the hostilities between Aberhart and Bowen.[89]

In spite of those difficulties Aberhart was happy with the royal visit. He had been proud to present his daughters to the royal couple. In his conversations with the king he had even asked him about the British-Israelite belief that the British royal family were direct descendents of King David. The king replied that it was an interesting theory.[90]

During the fall of 1939, election speculations were in the air. Even before the royal visit, Aberhart had commented on his radio broadcast that he was willing to resign if the people wanted it that way. "I have done my best, and

I am prepared to be cast aside like an old shoe.''[91] When he further announced that he would be visiting all the Social Credit constituencies, the opposition groups suspected that an election was near. As Aberhart and Manning travelled the province during the next two months their actions gave substance to election speculations.

Part of Aberhart's propaganda was the distribution of a booklet entitled *The Records Tell the Story*. This booklet listed the failures of previous Alberta governments and the accomplishments of the Social Credit government. It

Aberhart attempted to defend his government so far, in a tendentious booklet The Records Tell The Story. *Cameron felt it needed even more data. Stewart Cameron, Calgary* Herald, *5 August 1939.*

was filled with statistics, even to the last gopher tail collected by the government.[92] The document, however, seemed to convince only those already converted and came in for severe criticism from the opposition groups. Although there was no election in 1939 and Aberhart's talk was merely a smoke screen, the refutation of *The Records Tell the Story* became a major item in the opposition's fight in the 1940 election campaign.

Opposition groups claimed that Alberta's economy was worse off in 1939 than it had been when Aberhart had become premier. Actually, the economy had started to improve despite Aberhart's efforts. But, in truth, his critics noted that very little distinctive Social Credit legislation was in force; most of what had be passed had been declared *ultra vires* or was disallowed by the federal government. Aberhart had tried many maverick schemes. His refusal to abide by the dictates of the federal loan council had caused the unnecessary repeated defaulting on Alberta bonds. Unemployment was still rife and provincial relief camps for the single unemployed continued long after the federal government abolished its camps in 1936.[93] The opposition sneered that the only ones who seemed to benefit financially from the Social Credit movement were Aberhart, the M.L.A.s, and the economic "experts" sent over from England.[94]

CHAPTER NINETEEN

■

THE WAR YEARS

L ET THEM *go ahead*
and print their malicious, revolting cartoons,
in their financially servile muck-raking press.
It will get them no farther than it did in 1935
because the people know that kind of
scare-mongers for what they are.

— William Aberhart as quoted in the *Calgary Herald*

during his election campaign, 1 March 1940

Because of his interest in biblical prophecy, Aberhart had a deep concern about what was happening on the international scene, viewing with alarm the activities of Hitler and his expansionist plans.[1] When Hitler threatened to seize the Sudetenland ringing western Czechoslovakia, Aberhart was also critical of Britain, France, and Russia for promising to come to the aid of the Czechs. Aberhart felt that such promises could draw Europe into another military conflict. During his Sunday broadcast of 25 September 1938, he attacked all parties concerned:

> The German people are being fired by that particular type of mad patriotism that drives them to fight if any member of their race in any country does not get even more than most ordinary citizens ever have. And the British, French and Russian people are being stirred up by that other equally foolish concept of contractual obligation which demands its fulfillment no matter what the conditions are.

He compared the Allies' promises to Czechoslovakia to the promise that King Herod had made to Salome: no matter what the contract was, it had to be fulfilled, and John the Baptist lost his head.[2]

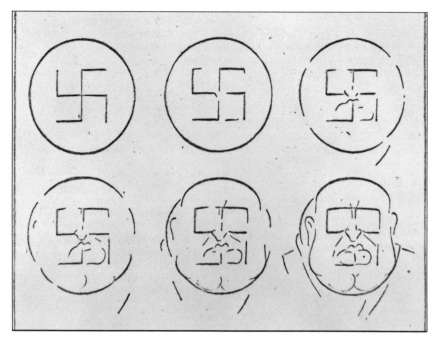

'Oh–You–Nazi Man'

Cameron ingeniously found a swastika hidden in Aberhart's face. Stewart Cameron cartoon, Calgary Herald, *28 September 1938.*

As a result of this statement Aberhart was seen as disloyal to Britain and was branded as a Nazi or at least a German sympathizer.[3] The cartoonist Stewart Cameron took advantage of the situation and discovered a swastika hidden in Aberhart's face.[4] Being a Nazi or a German sympathizer was the farthest thing from Aberhart's mind, and in spite of his German descent, Aberhart had very little regard for things German. In his eschatological scheme Germany was always the villain. He believed that the Germans descended from the ancient city of Gomorrah.[5] One wonders how much Aberhart's relationship with his German father had influenced that interpretation, for he almost always identified with his English mother and spoke of "we British."[6]

After Hitler seized the Sudetenland, the British government sought to settle a number of German-Czech refugees in Canada. In February 1939 officials of the Canadian National Railways and the Canadian Colonization Association met with Aberhart and his cabinet with the hope of settling some of those families in Alberta. The railway was prepared to sponsor these families for a period of two years, and asked only that the Alberta government grant refugees unused land in the northern part of the province. While some of the cabinet were enthusiastic, Aberhart was against the idea. He stated that instead of Britain asking Alberta to give aid to foreigners, Britain should be giving aid to Alberta. When it was pointed out that these German-Czech families were industrious and would quickly add to the economy of the province, Aberhart disagreed. He claimed that settlers of German origin in Alberta had no particularly favourable record with respect to relief, and when they did go on relief, they were more demanding than settlers of English-speaking origin. Another of Aberhart's statements shocked the delegation: he remarked that if after two years the refugees ended up in a state of semi-starvation in Alberta, "it would have been better if they had been lined up and shot at the time of the crisis [in Sudentenland]."[7]

When Canada declared war on Germany on 10 September 1939 Aberhart quickly pledged his support to the Allied war effort. Albertan civil servants who joined the armed forces were promised that their jobs would be waiting for them when they returned.[8] Hitler's suppression of Christianity in Germany caused Aberhart to see the war as a battle between Christianity and paganism.[9] He saw Hitler as a "demon-possessed" man, although he did not identify him as the Antichrist as some fundamentalists were doing.[10]

Aberhart had little sympathy with those who refused to get behind the war effort because of religious principles. When the Hutterites, the anabaptist group known for their communal farms and pacifism, refused to enlist or purchase war bonds, various patriotic and veterans groups demanded that the Alberta government prohibit further land sales to them.[11] Aberhart's government did pass laws to prevent further land purchases or leasing of land by Hutterites for the duration of the war. The Alberta Statutes classed them as enemy aliens.[12] When another conscientious objector, a member of the Jehovah's Witnesses, wrote to Aberhart asking if her children could be excused from saluting the flag at school, his answer to her insisted on strict obedience of the law:

> I assure you that there is no real argument that can be offered for us not to declare our loyalty to the British ideals at a time such as this. Of course you will be held responsible no doubt for the action of your children. The local School Board has the right to demand obedience on the part of the children in such exercises and would of course suspend a child

whose parents refuse him an opportunity of carrying out his duties in school.

If the military authorities decide to intern the parents the children would of necessity be taken care of and be sent to school under the authority of those who would look after them. The whole situation is too unhappy to be worth any objection being taken in such a simple matter.[13]

Although Aberhart had been quite prepared to see others' freedoms restricted by the war, he soon found himself in a situation that he described as persecution by federal authorities of his religious and political activities. Because of war-security measures the C.B.C. ruled that Aberhart's religious broadcasts could no longer have political content, personal greetings, or special requests. All political broadcasts had to be made from a studio, and CFCN was warned that if Aberhart did not comply, it would lose its radio license.[14] As war-censorship regulations were increased, Aberhart was forced to do most of his religious broadcasting from the studio of CFCN, and the members of the audience at the Calgary Prophetic Bible Institute had to listen to him via a radio installed on the platform.[15] Aberhart complained publicly that these regulations were an infringement on his freedom because Mackenzie King could broadcast live without such restrictions.[16]

The limits that the federal government had imposed on Aberhart's legislation and activities convinced him that Social Credit needed a stronger position in Ottawa than the seventeen seats that had been won in 1935. In 1939 Aberhart aligned himself with a new movement called New Democracy, founded and headed by W.D. Herridge, a former Canadian ambassador to Washington and brother-in-law of R.B. Bennett.[17] Herridge had been impressed with Roosevelt's New Deal legislation and had tried to have an analogous approach adopted by the Conservative Party. After being turned down, he decided to gather various reform groups together to work for economic reform. Aberhart gradually warmed to Herridge after some Eastern Social Credit supporters such as Charles Bowman and H.A. Southam began identifying with Herridge's program. Aberhart had hopes that Herridge would lead the federal Social Credit movement and went so far as to publicly call him "our leader."[18] But, when Herridge was reluctant to declare himself completely for Social Credit, Aberhart's enthusiasm began to wane.

During the fall of 1939 a rift developed between Aberhart and Herridge over the war situation. Herridge proposed that the federal government institute conscription. Aberhart, on the other hand, demanded that before there be any conscription of manpower, there should be a conscription of wealth by "placing an embargo on capital and capital assets as at the date of declaration of war" and "requiring that financial institutions and corporations reveal all undisclosed resources as at the declaration of war, and that these be forthwith conscripted by the Dominion Government."[19] Aberhart's emphasis on financial conscription before manpower conscription placed him much closer to J.S. Woodsworth than to Herridge, whose emphasis on manpower conscription also alienated the Quebec Socreds, who thereafter refused to be associated with New Democracy.

Almost all the federal Socred members of Parliament adopted Herridge's attitude and listed themselves as New Democracy M.P.s. When Aberhart learned that some of them had dropped the name Social Credit because of party failures in Alberta, he was less than happy. He still maintained that Social Credit could stand on its own merits and was critical of New Democracy's ties with the Conservative Party, which he claimed had "been devoid of a new idea for years."[20]

Aberhart and W.D. Herridge, leader of the New Democracy party, 1939. Aberhart's hopes that this party could be a national vehicle for Social Credit "doctrine" were soon disappointed.

In October 1939 O.B. Elliott, the Social Credit M.P. for Kindersley, Saskatchewan, resigned his seat so that Herridge could contest it in the by-election that would follow.²¹ Aberhart stated his lack of enthusiasm for the idea, claiming that it was not wise for a leader of a party to enter Parliament by means of a by-election, "especially for one session only."²² (Had he forgotten that this was the way he himself had entered the Alberta Legislature?) Herridge, however, never had an opportunity to try for the seat because Mackenzie King refused to call a by-election. Some felt that this was a deliberate move to keep Herridge out of Parliament.

Aberhart's first term in office was up in 1940, and he had to call an election sometime during that year. This matter formed the major part of the agenda at the annual Social Credit convention held in Calgary in January 1940. Elaborate preparations were made for both the provincial election and the federal election that also had to be called during that year. Aberhart decided he would call the provincial election as soon as the federal one was announced. By doing so, he could take advantage of the strife between the major parties. Over the past months Liberals and Conservatives had combined forces in opposing his government. However, during the federal election they would be at each other's throats and their hostility would spill over into the provincial campaign, thus destroying united opposition to Social Credit.

Among resolutions at the Social Credit convention were calls for a new Recall Act that would exempt the premier and cabinet from recall until they had first been dismissed or expelled from the cabinet, demands that Social Crediters be given first chance in obtaining government jobs, and demands that the government encourage birth control for the purpose of eugenics.²³ Another resolution called for the attorney-general's department to investigate the Social Credit League's dealings with the *Albertan*, and the paper's subsequent economic losses and departure from Social Credit ideology.²⁴ On Aberhart's prompting, in his radio broadcasts, many people had invested their entire savings in *Albertan* stock so the paper would be owned by Social Crediters. When the agreement for sale fell through because of inadequate stock sales, those who had invested lost their money and asked Aberhart for help. He could do nothing for them²⁵ and treated these economic failures cavalierly. When confronted, he is reported to have said, "What if these charges are true? Mistakes under the direction of God are not mistakes but stepping-stones to success."²⁶ It was almost like a wolf being asked to investigate the disappearance of sheep. The final matter dealt with at the convention was the method of selecting candidates for the coming election. Amidst charges of "dictation" Aberhart insisted that they follow the same procedure as in 1935, when he and his advisory board had had the final say in the choice of candidates.²⁷

With a provincial election in the wind, opposition groups mounted a fierce attack on the government as soon as the Legislature opened in February 1940. Lieutenant-Governor Bowen's objection to having the Speech from the Throne broadcast on the radio was an indication of the mood that was to prevail during the legislative session. On the first day of the session, four Social Credit members announced that they were crossing the floor and desired to be known henceforth as Independent Progressives. They included Charles Cockroft (former provincial treasurer), S. Barnes (who had been expelled from the caucus in 1936), and A.L. Blue and A.E. MacLellan (both former insurgents).[28] Barnes attacked Aberhart's method of ruling by caucus

When Aberhart promoted the purchase of the Albertan, *many of his supporters invested their life savings. When the scheme failed, Aberhart was unresponsive to their complaints. Stewart Cameron cartoon,* Calgary Herald, *20 January 1940.*

and demanded that this "pure brand of modern dictatorship" be abolished and "open government be implemented."[29]

During the throne speech debate David Duggan, the Conservative leader, revealed that in 1938 the Alberta government had made a deal with Jack James Sousa of Los Angeles to negotiate the refunding of Alberta's debt of $150 million. Sousa represented an American syndicate connected with the New York firm of Kuhn, Loeb and Co. Ironically, this firm, according to Major Douglas, was one of the leaders in the so-called Jewish financial conspiracy.[30] Sousa was an unknown underwriter, and his only credentials were two form-letters written by Calgary's mayor and chief of police. According to his contract with the government, Sousa was to travel across North America and buy up Alberta bonds below par. Those bonds would be turned over to the Alberta government, which would then issue a new series of bonds for $150 million that would mature forty-five years later. The scheme failed, however, because the interest offered on new bonds was much lower than could be received elsewhere. The venture had also cost the government a considerable amount of money in the form of Sousa's travelling expenses.[31] As the opposition berated the government for its clumsy handling of the refunding problem, Aberhart and his cabinet at first tried to deny Duggan's charges. However, the evidence that Duggan produced, including a copy of Sousa's contract, made the government squirm.

Another matter that Duggan raised was the use of government funds for Social Credit publicity. On several occasions, speeches by Aberhart and his cabinet members had been printed at government expense.[32] An investigation into other improprieties was demanded by Liberal leader E.L. Gray, who charged that graft was operating in the department of Agriculture. The investigation by the public accounts committee was cut short by the government's proroguing the Legislature so that an election could be called for 21 March 1940.[33]

Now that the election had been set, Aberhart campaigned on the record of his government and emphasizing the labour and debt legislation they had enacted. He downplayed his failure to provide the promised dividends:

> I can stand all the abuse heaped upon me when men whose farms I have saved by my debt legislation grip my hands in thanks.... Never mind the dividends, let them go. After getting 95 percent, are you going to pluck me on that?[34]

Nevertheless, Socred candidates claimed that dividends could be issued, and Aberhart himself suggested that if Social Credit economics were implemented each family would have a hundred more dollars in purchasing power.[35]

Part of the Socred publicity program was another distribution of their booklet *The Records Tell the Story*, filled with statistics claiming Social Credit successes and the economic failures of previous administrations. Because those booklets were printed and distributed at government expense the opposition complained that the government was using tax money for propaganda purposes.[36] The Socreds justified their actions by claiming that the party could not obtain adequate news coverage any other way.

The opposition groups responded with their own booklets. The Unity Council of Alberta issued *The Truth About the Records*, which claimed that the Socreds had distorted statistics to support their case. The thrust of this pamphlet was that the past governments had put the province into debt, but it was justifiable debt, caused by the building of schools, hospitals, court houses, highways, the University of Alberta, and other government and public buildings. The pamphlet had humorous touches: "The Records boast 1,313,098 gophers died in Alberta in 1937 under a Social Credit government. Even the Gophers can't stand it."[37] Sprinkled throughout the booklet were extracts from the speeches of the insurgents in 1937 when they accused Aberhart of being a Hitlerian dictator.[38]

A similar pamphlet entitled *The Trail of a Truth Twister: An Answer to "The Records Tell the Story"* was written by William Irvine for the C.C.F. campaign. Irvine made much of Aberhart's promises and his failure to fulfil them, emphasizing the expense to the province.[39]

The Calgary *Herald* had, as part of its program of opposition to Aberhart, panels in which his promises and failures were prominently featured.[40] Another feature was a two-part article by Charles Cockroft, former provincial treasurer, which provided a stinging critique of Aberhart's mistakes and an assertion of the economic impossibility of Social Credit.[41]

Opposition groups dared Aberhart to run again in the constituency of Okotoks-High River, where recall proceedings had been brought against him. Feelings against Aberhart still ran high because the recall deposit had been retained by the government, even after it had rescinded the Recall Act.[42] Instead, Aberhart decided to run in the relatively safe multi-seat constituency of Calgary. The top vote-getter for Calgary in 1935, Ernest Manning, was moved to contest the other multi-seat constituency of Edmonton.

Aberhart found the 1940 campaign harder than the one in 1935. In a letter to his brother Charles he remarked that he was having to watch his health and get adequate rest.[43] Restrictions placed upon his broadcasts made campaigning more difficult, because he could not use his effective political dramas on the radio. However, he still used them before live audiences, who laughed at the ideas of ex-professor Muddlepuddle, late professor of Misconomics at the University of Foozelem, and the Rt. Honourable Aloysius Marblehead, Prime Minister of England, and they sided with the likes of Bill Simple and John Wyse.[44]

As Aberhart campaigned he lashed out at his enemies. His experiences during the past five years had not dampened his vitriol:

> It will take more than all the money the big-shots can pour into this election or the most ridiculous cartoons some moron can conceive, it will take more than the most unscrupulous lying, whispering campaigns the minds of depraved reprobates can devise to wheedle the votes out of these mothers, wives and daughters who know these things. Yes, this is your friend Aberhart. I am determined to bring home to the money powers, whose stool-pigeoning lawyers are listening and making dictaphone records of what I say; this is Aberhart telling the enemies of the people a few cold truths.[45]

In the midst of the campaign the Privy Council in London ruled that the Alberta government's reduction in its interest paid on bonds was *ultra vires*. In spite of this ruling Provincial Treasurer Solon Low announced that interest rates would continue at half-rate. It was also learned that the government had not set aside any funds to cover the back-interest payments in the event that the Privy Council ruled against it. The amount of back-interest payments amounted to $11 million.[46]

As election day approached the Calgary *Herald* was confident that

Aberhart and his party would lose the election. Stewart Cameron predicted that Aberhart would retire to a mansion he was said to own in Vancouver. Aberhart denied that he had built a house there,[47] but he had in fact bought the mortgage on his son-in-law's elegant home when the latter was about to lose it. Aberhart allowed him to amortize his debt on an easier basis.[48]

As in the 1935 campaign Aberhart was better organized than his opponents and had a platform that contained many positive planks dealing with agriculture and health.[49] The main opposition parties, which had temporarily united under the label of Independents, had only one plank in their platform: "get rid of Aberhart."[50]

Aberhart and his party won the election, but the results showed how much Aberhart had lost the public's support. The Social Credit Party secured only 36 seats, a drop of 20, and obtained only 43 per cent of the popular vote, a drop of 11 per cent. In the multi-seat riding of Calgary, Aberhart came second to the Independent candidate, Andy Davison.[51] Another Independent candidate, J. Broomfield, won Aberhart's previous constituency. Solon Low, the provincial treasurer, was the only member of the cabinet to lose his seat but, in order to keep him in the cabinet, another member vacated his seat. In spite of the drop in support, Aberhart still maintained that his party's win in the election indicated they continued to have divine favour.[52]

The results of the federal election slated a week after the Alberta provincial election were even more disappointing to the Socreds and devastated the Social Credit-New Democracy union. The Socreds running on the New Democracy label lost their two seats in Saskatchewan as well as five other seats across Canada. They now had only ten representatives in Parliament (all from Alberta), rather than the seventeen they had had in 1935. The Liberals under Mackenzie King once again formed the government.

The election results also aggravated the incompatibility between Aberhart and Herridge. Herridge, who ran in the riding of Kindersley, Saskatchewan, was one of those who failed to win a seat. His loss convinced many Socreds that he was not the leader for their federal movement. Relations between Aberhart and Herridge quickly deteriorated. Aberhart chided Herridge for his inactivity: "The people of Canada, I fear, will demand from you greater evidence of sincerity than merely a few speeches intermittently given without consideration of purpose or objective."[53] Besides the incompatibility in their ideologies, one suspects deep tensions between their personalities. Aberhart's letters to Herridge were written in strong paternalistic tones and suggest that he really did not want Herridge as leader of the New Democracy movement. The federal Social Credit members continued to use the name New Democracy for some time, but soon they repudiated Herridge's leadership as Aberhart had done. John H. Blackmore again became the leader of the federal Socreds.[54]

Within a short time after being returned to office the Alberta government again ran into conflict with the federal government. One of the Socred promises during the provincial election had been the creation of a provincial bank that could offer services beyond the powers of the Treasury Branches. In this regard Provincial Treasurer Solon Low sought a bank charter from the House of Common's Banking and Commerce Committee. During questioning by members of the committee Low was grilled on the economic failures of past Social Credit schemes. Regarding the dividends, Low claimed they were never promised and then, almost in the next breath, stated that they were possible and would be eventually instituted.[55] When asked about the Alberta government's reduction of the interest payable on its bonds, Low remarked that it had been done on the advice of Robert Magor. In a letter to the chairman of the committee Magor denied he had recommended such an action. On the contrary, he had advised the Alberta government to co-operate with the federal loan council in order to refund its debt.[56] The committee also received a telegram from Jack J. Sousa who desired to appear before the committee because he believed that Low had misrepresented his involvement with the refunding scheme.[57] Other letters were received from various chambers of commerce in Alberta requesting that no charter be given. These submissions further weakened the credibility of the Alberta government and the charter was never granted. It was felt that the Alberta government's past record in economics was no guarantee that the deposits of an Alberta bank would be secure.

Aberhart's next controversy with the federal government involved the Rowell-Sirois Royal Commission on Dominion-Provincial Relations. The Commission had been created in 1937 to re-examine "the economic and financial basis of Confederation and of the distribution of legislative powers in light of the economic and social developments of the last seventy years." An important aspect of the investigation was to find a more equitable system of taxation. Aberhart had refused to cooperate with the commission and prevented civil servants from giving evidence.

When the report of the commission was released in 1940 Aberhart and members of his party condemned it as advocating centralization of power in the hands of the central government.[58] Douglasites viewed it as part of an international financial plot against provincial autonomy. Aberhart's critics responded by saying that it was strange for Aberhart to object to centralization:

> Just how long since has our premier come to the conclusion that centralization of power is undemocratic? Every Act passed by his government since 1935 has tended to centralize all provincial power at Edmonton. Does the present School Act give more power to the local trustees? How about all the various licensing Acts, and all those disallowed by the federal government and those found ultra vires by the Privy Council, each and every one of which aimed to centralize power at Edmonton? It looks very much like a case of whose ox is gored.[59]

The report of the Rowell-Sirois Commission proposed that the federal government take over all provincial debt and assume full responsibility for all unemployment relief. In exchange the provinces would have to give up their rights to collect income taxes, corporate taxes, and succession duties.[60] A federal-provincial conference was called for January 1941 to negotiate the acceptance of the recommendations of the Commission. Along with Aberhart, Ontario's premier Mitch Hepburn declared his lack of sympathy with the report. Duff Pattullo, premier of British Columbia, also voiced his criticisms of the recommendations.[61]

The conference, which began on 14 January 1941, started on a bad note; Aberhart's train was late arriving in Ottawa, and it was decided that the conference should not begin until he had arrived. In opening the conference Mackenzie King tried to be conciliatory and attempted to alleviate fears that the recommendations of the Commission were attempting to rewrite the

When premiers Aberhart of Alberta, Hepburn of Ontario, and Patullo of British Columbia refused to agree to the recommendations of the Rowell-Sirois report on Dominion-Provincial relations in 1941, Cameron accused them of helping the German war effort. Stewart Cameron cartoon, Calgary Herald, 18 January 1941.

Constitution or rebuild the structure of Confederation, or to centralize power in Ottawa. However, he emphasized that a certain measure of adjustment of taxation was necessary in order to finance the war effort.[62]

The conference ground to a halt the day after it started, as the opposition of Hepburn, Pattullo, and Aberhart made further discussions pointless. Hepburn declared that Ontario had to come before the Dominion,[63] Pattullo claimed that the proposed financial changes would not finance the war for thirty days.[64] Aberhart was the least antagonistic of the three, and had it not been for Hepburn and Pattullo, Mackenzie King and some members of the press felt Aberhart might have agreed to continue the discussions.[65] Aberhart's main argument was that the recommendations of the Commission be set aside until after the war, when they could be discussed at leisure; disunity over the Rowell-Sirois report was detracting from the unity necessary to complete the war. (His line of argument was possibly a bluff, because he had opposed the Commission even before the war.[66]) Aberhart suggested that the federal government try "Social Credit economics" as the best way to finance the war.[67] In his diary Mackenzie King described Aberhart's address as "amusing, plausible," and "pretty much all humbug."[68]

The actions of the three dissenting premiers received severe criticism across the country, for they were seen as traitors to Canadian unity and the Allied war effort. It was claimed that they had acted without the mandate of their citizens and against the wishes of many members of their governments.[69]

Within a month of his returning to Alberta, Aberhart and his government met for the first session of the Legislature since the 1940 provincial election. Of the original fifty-six Social Credit members in the House only twenty-eight remained. A very strong and united opposition promised a lively session. In the Speech from the Throne the government promised to enter into the life insurance field, create more debt legislation, and introduce new petroleum and natural gas regulations to stimulate more exploration. Missing were any mention of dividends and the usual Social Credit rhetoric.[70]

The opposition groups responded by flaying the government for losing valuable grants by rejecting the Rowell-Sirois recommendations, and Aberhart was criticized for his foolish performance at the conference. Since it appeared that he had set his mind beforehand against the Commission's recommendations, he could have saved the province a great deal of expense by simply mailing his negative response rather than personally delivering it with the aid of several cabinet ministers. The Treasury Branches were also attacked as a needless expense and just another financial blind alley, costing the province $1,000 per day.[71]

With new legislation passed and the session over, Aberhart looked forward to the convocation of the University of Alberta to be held on 19 May 1941. The university had been created by the government of Alberta shortly after the province was formed, and the provincial government still had considerable control over the university's affairs. Aberhart had been asked to give the convocation address, and a committee of the university senate had decided to bestow upon him the degree of Doctor of Laws, on account of his past work in education. The granting of an honorary degree to the premier upon the commencement of his second term of office had become something of a tradition; there were also rumours that Aberhart was to be the next president of the university.[72] In honour of Aberhart a number of his friends had purchased an academic gown for him. While he was visiting his daughters and grandchildren in Vancouver, he wrote a speech that was filled with humour, much of it home-spun. Characteristically, he joked about his baldness: "I am not particularly concerned about the extra letters. I shall have added to my name B.A. L.L.D. I have been b-a-l-d for many years, even without the Degree."[73]

In high spirits Aberhart returned to Edmonton looking forward to the honour that awaited him. Jessie Aberhart remained at the Coast with her daughters. On 12 May 1941 the university senate met to ratify the recommendations for honourary degrees. This was usually a formality, but in an unexpected move, a majority of the senate overruled the committee's recommendation and voted that Aberhart should not be the recipient of an honourary degree. A second vote produced the same result. Those who had voted against the motion felt first that Aberhart had not made any contribution to the cultural or academic life of the province to justify such a degree being granted. Second, they felt that the granting of such an honour would be an endorsement of Aberhart's Social Credit theories and all that went along with them – the broken promises, no dividends, no Just Price, and no interest-free loans.[74] Aberhart was at home at the Macdonald Hotel when Dr. G. Fred McNally, his deputy minister of Education, came bearing the sad news. Aberhart was deeply hurt and without his family, who heard the news through the newspapers and wished that they could have been with him.

Under the circumstances Aberhart decided that he would not address the convocation. Letters of sympathy for Aberhart poured in from across the province. The Alberta Teachers' Association passed resolutions condemning the action of the university.[75] Even the Edmonton *Bulletin*, long an opponent of Aberhart, described the affair as "one of the most despicable tricks, one of the most tactless fiascoes and one of the most undignified procedures ever to occur in the Dominion of Canada."[76] For his part, Aberhart suggested that a purge of political influences at the university was needed.[77] During the 1942 session of the Legislature he got his revenge on the university senate by cutting it in half and limiting its functions.[78]

Aberhart's claim that political interference had kept him from an honourary doctorate was true, but in a different manner than he claimed. For the past months he and his party had been interfering with the administration of the university and had created a lot of enemies. In October 1940 Aberhart had suddenly dismissed Chief Justice Harvey, the chairman of the university's board of governors.[79] The dismissal of other members soon followed. Then, within a short time Aberhart's government loaned the university $30,000 to expand its radio broadcasting station. Aberhart had appointed a new committee, which included three Social Credit stalwarts, to supervise the new facility. Opposition groups interpreted this as a move to use the university and its radio station as a propaganda device.[80]

As Aberhart had been fighting real and imagined enemies he adopted more and more of the paranoid views of Major Douglas and his cohorts. His acceptance of Douglas's conspiratorial theories often led to the suggestion that he was anti-Semitic. Aberhart added to that misunderstanding by employing anti-Semitic jargon used by Douglas.

However, Aberhart disassociated himself from anti-Semitism and pronounced the controversial *Protocols of the Elders of Zion* a forgery.[81] His own eschatology, which had been influenced by the pro-Zionist apocalyptic novels of Sydney Watson, placed great emphasis on the return of the Jews to Palestine and the future theocratic rule of a resurrected King David during the Millennium. However, Aberhart's eschatology and the British-Israelite concepts he increasingly used contained latent anti-Semitism of which he seems to have been unaware.[82]

For the most part, the Jewish community in Alberta and western Canada saw Aberhart as a friend. The Jewish press frequently solicited his greetings to the Jewish people at the time of their celebrations, and Aberhart freely gave them.[83]

As Major Douglas's anti-Semitism became more rabid, Aberhart received increased criticism from Jewish supporters and the press. In September 1938 the Edmonton *Journal* had remarked on one of Douglas's diatribes that described the Jews as parasites who choked the original cultures of host countries through the "black magic of finance, salesmanship and advertising." Douglas claimed that the "Bank of England rules the country and the Jews rule the Bank of England." The Edmonton *Journal* noted that Douglas's impressions were not realistic and that his thinking had much in common with Hitler's.[84] Aberhart reacted angrily to this editorial in the *Journal*, and claimed that it had distorted Douglas's words. He heaped abuse on the press for suggesting such a connection, stating that "the Social Credit movement as we understand it, not only is opposed to anti-Semitism, but condemns it in the strongest possible terms." However, his interpretation of what Douglas had said could be regarded as anti-Semitic. Aberhart claimed that two groups of money barons controlled the finances of the world: the Jewish group and the Anglo-Saxon group (which was equally sinister). He suggested that the Jewish group of financiers in Germany had been responsible for the persecution of Jews in Germany and had themselves remained untouched and were prospering economically.[85] The Edmonton *Journal* responded that it was useless for Aberhart to deny Douglas's anti-Semitism, and that Aberhart's comment that the Jewish financiers were sacrificing their own people was out of keeping with the facts. The Edmonton *Journal* regarded Aberhart's comments as just another example of his wild accusations.[86] Undoubtedly his comments reflected the anti-Semitic Social Credit literature that he had been reading.

Douglas's paranoia reached absurd heights during the war. Allegedly, Douglas had written to Hitler before the war, praising him for persecuting the Jews.[87] There was also hope within the British Social Credit movement that the Nazis would be establishing Social Credit economics in the Third Reich.[88] When the latter did not happen Douglas started to believe that Hitler was part of the Jewish conspiracy, being, as Douglas claimed, the grandson of an illegitimate daughter of Baron von Rothschild of Vienna.[89] Douglas declared that there was no real destruction of Jews happening in Europe; Hitler had only started a sham persecution in order that his Jewish-Nazi agents disguised as refugees could infiltrate the rest of the world and bring to it further economic and cultural ruin.[90] Douglas hinted that Jewish financial leaders in Britain should be executed.[91] Most of Douglas's paranoid anti-Semitic ideas were propagated in Alberta by his emissary L.D. Byrne, who was directing the Social Credit Board and who seems to have written some of Aberhart's speeches.[92]

Aberhart came under criticism from many quarters because of the anti-Semitic views appearing in Social Credit speeches and publications. Many Jewish supporters of his government demanded that he break all links with Douglas and purge his party of anti-Semitic elements. Aberhart replied that he did not have the dictatorial powers that people were ascribing to him, but he said he was doing everything he could "to put the brakes on this foolish spirit of anti-Semitism."[93] As Aberhart became aware of the real plight of the Jews in Europe, he saw it as his duty to defend them. His publication, *The Prophetic Voice*, newly revived, repeatedly denounced anti-Semitism and noted that any nation that harmed the Jews would be cursed by God.[94]

Convinced that there was a federal plot against the province of Alberta Aberhart organized a national convention on monetary reform that was held at the Marlborough Hotel in Winnipeg at the end of October 1941. He had hopes that a new federal party could be formed to field candidates in the next federal election. Aberhart led a twenty-man contingent from Alberta that joined sixty other delegates, most of whom came from the West. Neither New Brunswick nor Quebec were represented, and only one or two delegates came from Ontario. Noticeably absent was W.D. Herridge, who had founded the New Democracy movement. Rumours suggested that the new party would only have success if Aberhart agreed to lead it, even as other rumours suggested that his health had been deteriorating and that he had been advised to take it easy.[95]

When Aberhart spoke to the convention, those who had expected oratorical fireworks from him were disappointed. He spoke in a very low voice, which sometimes was almost inaudible, and told a few anecdotes about his childhood. Fred Kennedy, the political reporter for the Calgary *Herald*, noted that Aberhart's old fire had gone; he appeared to be a tired old man.[96]

The convention adopted a ten-point program of monetary reform aimed at post-war reconstruction. It stressed a commitment to British ideals and Christian principles.[97] In spite of such objectives the convention quickly barred the press from their meetings, and Aberhart himself resumed his war with the media.[98]

From what is known of the convention before the battle with the press erupted, it appeared that Social Credit had been cast aside for monetary reform in general. This was only a ruse. A booklet that Aberhart had written for the convention, and which was on sale there, contained the usual Social Credit rhetoric. Other speakers mouthed catch-phrases such as "What is physically possible is financial possible," "Money Power is the synagogue of Satan," and "Dethrone the Antichrist, the power of International Finance."

Aberhart had adopted Douglas's opposition to the "Union Now" movement, which sought to establish a federal union of democratic countries to oppose fascism. "Union Now" was seen as part of the international plot to control the world. In September 1941 Aberhart had adopted Douglas's position and criticized the "Union Now" movement by saying he was "opposed to the centralization of financial power under the control of Wall Street, New York."[99] He went on to say that it was "plainly an attempt to impose a world dictatorship, a super-world-state, that would involve a tyranny worse than anything mankind has ever known."[100] He suggested that under such a system, with an international police force and army, "we would have brutal regimentation, concentration camps, the gestapo, and all the evils of totalitarian dictatorship."[101] Independent members of the Legislature taunted Aberhart that his own deeds – his interference with civil rights, the courts, and the Mounties – were leading in this very direction.[102]

Aberhart's opposition to the "Union Now" movement seems to have been influenced also by his eschatological fantasies about the future world kingdom of the Antichrist (see chapter IV). He may have hoped that monetary-reform movements could slow down the alignment of nations he believed would join with the Antichrist. We do know that there were eschatological ideas discussed at the convention, even though they may not have been exactly what Aberhart had taught. Dr. W.W. Cross, Alberta's minister of Health, warned that "Satan and all his imps [would] oppose them in their fight for monetary reform, but if they stayed together and co-operated fully, victory would be theirs."[103]

It was not surprising that Aberhart was elected leader of the new organization after all the work he had put into the convention. At the convention he was eulogized as "the greatest organizer the world has ever seen," and as responsible "for the greatest educational system in the whole of Canada." A.J. Hooke, M.L.A. for Rocky Mountain House and former insurgent, declared that they would almost give up their lives for Aberhart. The audience broke into "For He's a Jolly Good Fellow."[104]

Soon after the convention Aberhart, and Ernest G. Hansell made elaborate plans for organizing the Democratic Monetary Reform Organization (D.M.R.O.) into a political force that would be ready for the next federal election.[105] Aberhart realized that any movement wishing to capture the federal political scene had to have a strong representation in Quebec. To prepare for the Quebec campaign Aberhart started studying French with the aid of a recorder. Taking Quebec was going to be a difficult task; he had not only linguistic gaps to bridge, but also religious ones. Cardinal Villeneuve had denounced Social Credit as charlatanism and stated that priests were to have nothing to do with it.[106]

In his own province Aberhart began a massive organizational campaign for the D.M.R.O. At the annual convention of the Alberta Social Credit League it was officially linked to the D.M.R.O.[107] A Democratic Victory League was formed to raise funds for the publication of campaign literature. The movement also had a spiritual arm, the Fisherman's Club, operating under the auspices of the Calgary Prophetic Bible Institute.[108] The movement was portrayed as a Christian crusade for the preservation of democracy and civilization.

Aberhart's religious zeal, however, soon produced difficulties within the D.M.R.O. As the war progressed Aberhart's increased acceptance of British-Israel theories had come to dominate many of his pronouncements. Such ideas had been treated occasionally in Aberhart's earlier preaching, but after the royal visit in 1939 Aberhart gave these theories more credence. He was particularly interested in the claim that Joseph of Arimathaea had visited Glastonbury, England. In his own way Aberhart "researched" this tale and apparently accepted it as a fact.[109]

Following the royal visit Aberhart had begun an active correspondence with members of the British-Israel movement and publically acknowledged use of their material in his radio broadcasts.[110] At the same time, however, he still rejected their date-setting for the return of Christ, based on measurements in the Great Pyramid.[111] After the Second World War had broken out, Aberhart preached and published a series of sermons on the scriptural significance of the British coat of arms.[112] Through a questionable mixture of heraldry and prophetic interpretation he maintained that Britain and the United States would win the war.[113]

Aberhart's strong pro-British views were rejected by Paul Prince, the French-Canadian leader of the D.M.R.O. in Manitoba. He claimed that Aberhart's views were just as racist as Hitler's, only with a different race being venerated.[114] This internal conflict of ideas was one of the many problems that contributed to the downfall of the Democratic Monetary Reform Organization. Before long that name was dropped, and the Social Credit banner was again unfurled. Name-changes by the federal group, first to New Democracy and then to D.M.R.O., had not been successful.

During the latter part of 1942, Aberhart launched his last campaign for post-war reconstruction. That was the theme of his last three booklets and a conference held in Edmonton that December. He maintained that a new social order had to be created if Canada were going to be a worthwhile place to live in following the war. He feared that the regimentation and economic restrictions imposed by the war would be continued, and that the soldiers' sacrifices would be worthless if drastic steps were not taken.

While most groups had plans for post-war reconstruction, Aberhart's were particularly molded by his distorted world view. He came to believe that not only did the international bankers control money, the press, and governments but they also masterminded wars to make a profit.[115] Aberhart's thinking seemed to be more and more dominated by the delusions of Douglas, Byrne, and the Social Credit Board.

The publications of the Social Credit Board maintained that the "international conspiracy" had to be stopped if the post-war period was going to be any better than what had preceded it. For an answer to the problem the Social Credit Board returned to the old message of Social Credit, but was just as silent as Aberhart had been in 1935 as to the mechanics of its implementation. Again, the Social Credit Board advised that the problem should be left to the "experts," an elusive group that they had failed to find during the past eight years.[116] A Post-War Reconstruction Committee was created by the government to hire technicians to obtain information and to formulate plans for economic reconstruction. That group, with duties much like the Social Credit Board, was given a budget of one million dollars.[117]

When Aberhart considered post-war reconstruction plans of other groups – the Beveridge Plan, the Marsh Plan, "Union Now," Roosevelt's National Resources Planning Board, the League for Social Reconstruction's *Social Planning for Canada* – he saw them only as evidence of a gigantic international conspiracy. He lumped these groups with the Nazis, Fascists, and Communists.[118]

The Privy Council's ruling in February 1943 that Alberta's Debt Adjustment Act was beyond provincial jurisdiction[119] was seen by Aberhart as more evidence of that conspiracy:

> For the past seven years we have witnessed a continuous parade to the courts by the money-lending corporations to challenge the validity of one act after another. And with a consistency which has increased the disillusionment of people, the moneylending concerns have always obtained a favourable decision against the Crown representing the people.
>
> This onslaught has been in the nature of a legal war being waged by the money-lending corporations against the people generally and the farmers in particular, for the dual purpose of territorial gains by divesting them of their property, and of placing them in utter subjection to the dictates of these financial over-lords. Their objective is to acquire a land monopoly to strengthen the stranglehold of financial power.
>
> When this country was plunged into war beside Great Britain to fight for our very existence, at least these money-lending corporations could have assisted the war effort by declaring an armistice. Instead they not only carried on this private war against the people, but they intensified their attack. I hope the full significance of that will not be overlooked by Canadians.
>
> Finally, the High Command of the moneylenders unleashed a blitzkrieg. They succeeded in breaking through what they considered to be the main defence which stood between them and the people by having the Debt Adjustment Act declared *ultra vires* and by having the Moratorium tied up in the courts. No doubt they feel that now all they have to do is march in and take possession.[120]

Early in 1943 Aberhart commenced coast-to-coast broadcasts on the theme of post-war reconstruction.[121] He was also looking for help in the federal campaign from Mitch Hepburn, former Liberal premier of Ontario, who had recently been dumped by his party because of his opposition to the Rowell-Sirois Commission.[122] In reality Aberhart had no economic plan, knew of none which would work, and was only grasping at straws; he had little sense of direction now. He attributed his failures to federal or international conspiracies.

CHAPTER TWENTY

■

THE PREACHING PREMIER

I T SHOULD *be clear to every student of the Bible that the British Commonwealth, the United States, and their allies are truly God's battle axe at this time. His covenant for us is to be found in Isa. 54:17. It reads like this: "No weapon that is formed against thee shall prosper, and every tongue that shall rise against thee in judgement, thou shall condemn."*

— William Aberhart from his booklet called *Post-War Reconstruction: First Series*, 1942

During Aberhart's years in political office his religious organizations experienced considerable controversy and stress. Changes had gradually taken place in his theological emphases and in his radio preaching. Some of these changes were related to the broadening effect political life had upon him. At the same time, however, he retained a strong sectarian stance within his own religious organizations, and the resulting tensions caused repeated controversies and schisms.

Within a few months after Aberhart had assumed office in 1935 difficulties had arisen at the Bible Institute Baptist Church in Calgary. Quite a few people had joined the church "on the coat tails" of Social Credit, and the Reverend M.L. Burget did not have a forceful enough personality to control the various factions that tried to exert their own leadership in the church during Aberhart's absence.[1] All important church business had to have Aberhart's approval because of his continuing position as apostle, and a steady stream of letters went back and forth between church officers in Calgary and Aberhart in Edmonton.[2] This "remote control" was difficult for Burget, who found himself out of sympathy with certain of Aberhart's doctrines and the political nature of Aberhart's sermons. As their relationship deteriorated Aberhart appears to have stopped contributing personally to the minister's salary account – a by-now-familiar ploy. In the fall of 1936 Burget threatened to quit unless his promised salary was paid.[3] Like the Reverend Andrew Imrie before him, Burget found that these stresses were taking their toll on his health. He found it almost impossible to work in his office at the Bible Institute because of the noisy Social Credit meetings being held in the building and the constant interruptions by people coming into his office to seek political information. A year later Burget's physical and mental health were broken and he resigned. He left the ministry, and later took a much quieter position with the Colorado Fish and Game Department.[4]

Burget was succeeded by E.L.J. Hughes, whose background remains a mystery.[5] He was extremely disliked by the congregation for his tactlessness and coarse manners. He earned the epithet "uncut diamond" because he seemed allergic to soap and water and often entered the pulpit wearing a shirt and tie stained with soup.[6] When the congregation demanded that Hughes be replaced, Aberhart at first refused to do so. However, after the protests continued, Hughes was dismissed in the fall of 1938.[7]

In their search for another pastor the congregation advertised widely, and eventually the Reverend Ralph C. Crouse of Denver was hired. Crouse's ministry lasted approximately four months, and he left after a crisis that was as intense as the one Aberhart had experienced with the insurgents in his caucus. It began when Crouse objected to the political content of Aberhart's Sunday-afternoon broadcasts.[8] Crouse also felt muzzled when he was preaching because Aberhart's lieutenants were always criticizing his sermons.[9] Further, he objected to Aberhart's control over the church and refused to recognize him as the apostle of that church.[10] When Crouse had attempted to establish a foreign-missions program in the church, Aberhart's lieutenants thwarted it. The sectarian identity that Aberhart had imposed on the church was another source of conflict. Crouse had not been allowed to exchange pulpits with other ministers in the city or to have any fellowship with other Christian groups. Apparently Aberhart alone was free to associate with leaders of other denominations. Crouse therefore submitted his resignation.

After a week went by without his having heard whether his resignation was accepted, and not having received his salary, Crouse took his story to the Calgary *Herald*, which was only too delighted to publish anything against Aberhart. For the next few weeks the Calgary *Herald* reviewed the history of Aberhart's religious activities in Calgary. It described the dictatorial ways in which Aberhart controlled the affairs of the Bible Institute Baptist Church through a board that he had appointed and which was beyond the reach of the congregation; how the ownership of the Institute building had come under the exclusive control of about six persons; how that board had refused to publish a financial statement and had loaned $8,000 to CFCN at 8 per cent while Aberhart was attacking the banks and "money barons" for doing the same thing; how the Bible Institute Baptist Church was only a tenant of the Institute building and could be evicted even though members of the congregation had paid for the Institute through their contributions; and how the Bible Institute Baptist Church could not afford to pay the excessive rent the Institute board demanded.[11] Many of the issues that Crouse raised were the same that had caused Westbourne to break with Aberhart ten years before.

Crouse was very popular with the congregation, and when these revelations were broadcast, a large percentage of the congregation took his side. During the church meetings that ensued shouting matches developed. The fight was so intense that pages were later removed from the minute book.[12] Many of those who sided with Crouse also objected to the political content of Aberhart's preaching. When Crouse's supporters demanded a congregational meeting at which Aberhart and Crouse could be questioned, Aberhart and his board refused to allow it. As a result Crouse and many of the leading members of the congregation withdrew and held meetings elsewhere.

Some of those who sided with Crouse were Aberhart's oldest supporters. Mrs. Perkins, who had attended Aberhart's meetings since 1916, demanded that he resign as apostle of the church.[13] Another stalwart member who left was Mrs. W.P. Harvey. She told the dissidents that every minister who had left the church had left broken-hearted.[14] She knew the feeling: her husband had experienced the same thing. W.P. Harvey had actively supported Aberhart's political program and had hoped to secure a government position when Aberhart's party was elected. Aberhart and Harvey had been very close and usually phoned each other every day. After Aberhart entered office this practice stopped. One day Harvey asked Aberhart why he did not phone him when he came to Calgary. Aberhart is reported to have said, "I am the Premier of Alberta now. I am too busy to talk to you. Besides it costs ten cents to phone from the Palliser Hotel."[15] Harvey quit the board of the Bible Institute, resigned as deacon of the church, and worshipped elsewhere.[16] Thus Aberhart lost his oldest and closest friend. Several years later Aberhart expressed regret at their friendship having been broken, but he seems to have done nothing to restore it.[17] Such was the fate of one of the many who had put their trust in Aberhart. He inspired and demanded intense loyalty of his followers. However, when they no longer served his ends in achieving power, he cast them aside. Another man who experienced Aberhart's quest for power described it as "satanic."[18]

The Crouse incident was short-lived, but the fact that Crouse was able to depart with so many of the congregation indicated that Aberhart's charisma was wearing thin even in his own church. Aberhart and his lieutenants went through the motions of answering Crouse's charges by knocking over straw men (such as Crouse's lack of Canadian citizenship), but evaded the real issues by deception.[19]

Crouse attempted to establish another church for the dissidents, but within a short time he returned to the United States. Some of those who supported Crouse returned to the Bible Institute Baptist Church, but only after having to beg to be reinstated.[20] For the majority of those who had left with Crouse this was their last dealing with Aberhart.

The pulpit at the Bible Institute Baptist Church was then filled by a graduate of the Bible Institute, Arthur D. Cornell. Soon he was joined by two of his fellow-students, William J. Laing and Ed Phillips.[21] By having his own graduates fill the pulpit, Aberhart was able to bring peace to the church for a time at least, but within ten years the same issues erupted again into a schism that closed the doors of the Calgary Prophetic Bible Institute.[22]

Aberhart's failure to fulfil his election promises had been one of the reasons why so many of his religious supporters had lost their faith in him. The matter of dividends was still very much in their minds. Note the tone of the following letter:

> Just a few lines to let you know I'm all through work now as there isn't anymore work around here. I didn't get much work this fall as there wasn't much around here to do. My rheumatism has been bad. I'd like to know when the dividend is coming through because I need it now for food. Please answer right back and let me know when you think its coming through. I sure could use it now. There's no such a thing as getting any work around here. I'll be expecting word from you right away. I have a shack to stay in for the winter.[23]

Or the tone of this one:

> We have been waiting for the dividend because our mother has promised us a lot of things when we got it but it never came. She promised my big brother a pair of rubber boots and my younger sister and brother each a pair of rubber boots and a party table and chairs and me a pair of rubber boots. But the dividend never came so we never got it. We have been waiting for over a year.[24]

The revolt against Aberhart that had taken place at the Bible Institute Baptist Church was not an isolated incident; it was indicative of widespread dissatisfaction among his pre-Social Credit supporters. Among the members of his vast radio audience there was unhappiness with the content of his broadcasts. Those who desired biblical homilies were tired of listening to Aberhart's defence of his actions, his unsolicited denials, and his attacks on his opponents. He had lied, from his pulpit and over the radio, about never having said he was going to the Coronation. In 1938 he lied again from the pulpit when he bought a custom-built Buick limousine equipped with an intercom to the chauffeur's compartment and a radio-telephone. He protested that he had not bought a new car. But when a car-dealer wrote to Aberhart, stating the facts of the purchase and noting that the car was being stored in a government garage, Aberhart casuistically claimed he had told the truth; he had not paid for the car yet, so he had in fact not bought it. After Aberhart began using the car, he threatened to have any press photographer who attempted to photograph it arrested.[25] Henceforth, the limousine became a regular item in Stewart Cameron's cartoons.

For some of the public Aberhart's broadcasts had become a desecration of the sabbath.[26] Others turned their radios off as soon as he began to talk about Social Credit.[27] Some dispensationalists continued to write him, telling him that he had no business being involved "in the affairs of the world."[28] Aberhart was usually very brisk with his religious critics, replying to them with biblical quotations such as "rebuke not an elder," or "judge not that ye be not judged." He maintained that God had put him in his present position and that his actions should not be questioned.[29]

Sometimes Aberhart defended his actions by employing his own brand of ultra-dispensationalism. He argued that many of the biblical passages his critics had directed against him did not apply to the present dispensation. For example, some had argued Aberhart's "something for nothing" program was contrary to the verse in Genesis that states "man shall eat by the sweat of his face." Aberhart explained that verse away by claiming that the sweat was caused by the chewing action of the face muscles, not from actual work.[30] Another verse hurled against him was St. Paul's comment that if a man did not work, he should not be allowed to eat. Aberhart claimed that modern technology had made such a belief obsolete and that it did not apply to the present dispensation.[31]

Aberhart's public preaching after he had entered the political realm had become quite ecumenical and reached a wide spectrum of the religious community. However, it should not be assumed that the same ecumenical spirit pervaded the Bible Institute or the Bible Institute Baptist Church. The staff of these institutions retained Aberhart's pre-Social Credit theology, which was other-worldly, eschatologically oriented, separatist, and possessing a peculiar doctrine of the Holy Spirit. Thus, there were considerable differences between Aberhart's behaviours in his various spheres of activity. Those local and radio supporters whom he had indoctrinated before his involvement in politics could not identify with the quasi-social gospel that had become the main emphasis of his public preaching. At the same time, however, Aberhart's ecumenism was his own.

By 1938 Aberhart finally admitted that the focus of his preaching had changed. To supporters in Saskatchewan, who had complained of the decreasing biblical content in his broadcasts, Aberhart wrote:

You know, dear friends, the older I get, the more I am becoming more convinced that it is not more Bible teaching that people need, it is the application of what they have. Probably it is this deep conviction that is altering somewhat the emphasis that I put in my sermons. I wonder if I am wrong. I do not wish to go down a blind alley and get nowhere, but I see so many church people who have no interest in anything that might tend to uplift their fellowmen.[32]

When students from the Bible Institute, who were still preaching Aberhart's pre-Social Credit sectarianism, attempted to minister in various churches, problems usually arose. At the time of the Crouse controversy Aberhart had his hands full because of a row started by one of the students, Dave Stewart, who advertised himself as an "outstanding Canadian Fundamentalist." He had been conducting evangelistic meetings in some Lutheran churches in the Camrose area. Quite a controversy arose due to his methods and doctrines. Letters of protest were sent from Lutheran church leaders to Aberhart, asking him to correct the situation. Aberhart, however, advised Stewart to carry on in spite of criticism.[33]

Aberhart's refusal to correct Stewart later blew up in his face when Stewart was ministering in a church in Innisfail that was associated with the Bible Institute Baptist Church. Dave Stewart disagreed with a number of Aberhart's doctrines and left with some people of like mind. Stewart knew that the pro-Aberhart congregation did not own the building in which they had been meeting, and he asked the owners, the Baptist Union of Western Canada, to rent it to *his* group. The Baptist Union, which still had no love for Aberhart, agreed to do so. The pro-Aberhart group was ordered to vacate the building.[34] When Aberhart's supporters sought his help, he instructed them not to turn the keys of the building over to the Baptist Union.[35] Some of Aberhart's lieutenants from the Bible Institute even went to Innisfail to prevent the seizure of the building.[36] When diplomacy failed the Baptist Union secured a court order evicting Aberhart's group. Aberhart soon became involved in yet another conflict-of-interest situation. As attorney-general he had to uphold the law, yet he was busy supplying his supporters with advice on how to fight the case.[37] Finally, the Baptist Union padlocked the building, whereupon Aberhart's lieutenants from Calgary cut the lock off.[38] A similar situation happened at Red Deer, where a congregation affiliated with the Bible Institute, pastored by Ed Phillips, one of Aberhart's former Bible students, broke with Aberhart, and joined the Baptist Union.

Aberhart's relationship with the fundamentalistic Regular Baptists was not much better. In 1937 the Reverend T.T. Shields, with whom Aberhart had worked in the mid-twenties, wrote a stinging critique of Aberhart's theology and political activities.[39] The following year Shields wrote:

> The simple fact that anyone advocating such absurd economic principles as Mr. Aberhart, could become Premier anywhere, or leader of any party outside of an insane asylum, is symptomatic of the perilous political possibilities of the times.[40]

On the whole, Aberhart's political activities and the shift that had taken place in his theology had alienated him from many of his former fundamentalist associates. He found much of his political support from ministers of the mainline denominations,[41] even though their denominations had denounced him for mixing religion and politics. In March of 1941 Aberhart had the lieutenant-governor proclaim a provincial Day of Prayer to petition God for an Allied victory. Protestant, Catholic, and Jewish congregations held special prayer services in compliance with Aberhart's call to prayer.[42]

When vacationing in Vancouver Aberhart worshipped at St. Andrews-Wesley United Church. He maintained friendships with several ministers of the United Church of Canada: the Reverend G. Harrison Villett, the Reverend Herb Ashford, and the Reverend George W. Kerby.[43] Their social-gospel emphasis had a lot of similarities to Aberhart's new emphasis. In 1942 he preached a sermon in which he labelled those who refused to improve their society by political involvement as "being worse than infidels." The ideas expressed in this sermon were diametrically opposite to views he had published in 1926.[44] At times Aberhart seemed to suggest that the Kingdom of God would be achieved when Social Credit was completely implemented.[45]

Political life had certainly broadened Aberhart's theological horizons, but the broadening process was not yet complete. He still retained many elements of his pre-Social Credit theology, with its sectarianism and apocalypticism. Until the end of his life his sermons and letters contained the themes of the Rapture, Tribulation, and the Antichrist.

Aberhart found, to his disappointment, that political life had its costs. During the war the C.B.C.'s broadcasting restrictions affected his radio audience and the audience at the Bible Institute. People complained that his studio broadcasts cramped his style as they had known it, and people at the Bible Institute were not happy listening to a radio when they liked to see Aberhart in person.[46] Aberhart was left with few alternatives: either he had to give up the radio broadcasts and appear at the Bible Institute in person, or he had to confine himself to the radio broadcast and have Cyril Hutchinson and Bill Laing conduct the actual meetings.[47]

Aberhart decided to continue his broadcasts. In order to retain the intimate contact with his audience that had been destroyed by the C.B.C.'s refusal to allow him to broadcast dedications, greetings, sponsorships, acknowledgements, or requests for political support, he resurrected *The Prophetic Voice* in July 1942.[48] Charles R. Pearce, the superintendent of the Radio Sunday School, was made editor of the magazine. It contained reprints of Aberhart's earlier lectures and sermons, the material the C.B.C. prohibited, and material reprinted from other religious publications.

Limitations on his broadcasts was one of the prices that Aberhart had to pay for being a politician. Another limitation was imposed on his vigorous opposition to the theory of evolution being taught in public schools. As minister of Education, Aberhart wanted to include the creationist position in all science courses that dealt with evolution. He prepared a manuscript on the subject and had various friends criticize it for him.[49] He hoped that the government would approve the pamphlet and underwrite its costs.

Aberhart's deputy minister of Education Dr. Fred McNally, a Baptist, suggested that it would not be politically expedient for Aberhart to pursue this project; it would raise more controversy and it would be a conflict of interest for a minister of Education to take sides on an issue by propagating his own theories.[50] Reluctantly Aberhart accepted McNally's opinion and decided that he would have his pamphlet published apart from the government.[51]

The 1943 session of the Legislature was the most strenuous Aberhart experienced since the insurgency in 1937. Political bantering across the floor of the House became very personal and involved open attacks on his religious beliefs by some of those whom he had taught in school and Sunday school. Aberhart and his government were accused of having wasted time and money by passing legislation they knew would be overruled, and then having had the affrontery to appeal court decisions concerning it. Elmer Roper, leader of the C.C.F., charged that the purpose of most of the Social Credit legislation had been largely political – to illustrate the so-called financial conspiracy that existed in the deluded minds of Douglas, his cronies, and Aberhart. Roper also accused Aberhart's government of starving widows and orphans by not raising the widow's allowance. Roper, who many years before had attended Aberhart's Bible class at Grace Presbyterian Church, continued his attack by quoting Scripture: "Woe unto you, scribes and Pharisees, hypocrites, for ye devour widows' houses and for a pretence, make long prayers."[52]

Aberhart received another personal attack from James C. Mahaffy, leader of the Independents, who remarked that he hoped Aberhart was "taking a refresher course in elementary constitutional law along with his French lessons." That remark seems to have hurt Aberhart deeply, for Mahaffy had been one of his students at Crescent Heights High School. He had tutored Mahaffy for the debating society. As he glowered at Mahaffy, he replied more in sorrow than in anger: "Some young men are like tacks. They can go no further than their heads will let them."[53]

During the session Aberhart's eschatological views were openly attacked in the press:

> Mr. A's mind does not, it seems, operate in this matter-of-fact world at all. He lives in an Alice in Wonderland realm, peopled by wild beasts and imaginary monsters. To him, Great Britain is not merely centre of the world's greatest and most enlightened Empire; it is The Lion which was forecast by someone many centuries ago. To him, Russia is not merely the home of a great people, suddenly modernized and inspired with patriotic fervor, and therefore a nation which exerts a tremendous influence in world affairs; it is The Bear which was similarly foretold. To him, international finance is not the intricate, and perhaps faulty, result of our complex modern relationship, it is the sinister creation of malevolent Machiavelli bent on making Mr. A and you and me their slaves through the promotion of world wars.[54]

During the years of Aberhart's premiership the opposition he had received, and his own failures at implementing economic reform, began wearing thin the confidence that he had had after he won the election in 1935. He had been convinced that God had placed him in office and that God was guiding him. As difficulties presented themselves he began to search for evidence of divine guidance from other sources. In the past Aberhart had condemned occult practices,[55] even though his own star studies and belief in numerology were occultish, and during his years in office, he picked up palmistry and taught it as "psychology."[56] His increasing interest in British-Israelism and his acceptance of Douglas's conspiracy theories also reflected his search for certainty. In 1940 he thanked an acquaintance for sending him a horoscope,[57] and later he appears to have commissioned one himself. This horoscope, now in his private papers, warned him to beware of his advisers and to watch the condition of his liver.[58] Both warnings were "prophetic."

The aging premier, c. 1941.

The deterioration of Aberhart's mind corresponded to the deterioration of his physical health. In 1941 people had become aware that his health was failing. He seemed to have lost his spark. During the summer of 1942 he visited his aged mother in Ontario; she had broken her hip in a fall.[59] Members of Aberhart's family noticed that his own health had deteriorated, and meals had to be specially prepared for him.[60]

Aberhart's pace during his final years had remained much the same as it always had – a life of relentless activity. He did enjoy chess, but even that was competitive. Sometime his granddaughter Kaye MacNutt was able to persuade him to take her to a movie and what little leisure reading he did was in detective fiction.[61] For the most part, Aberhart could not or would not relax. When his friend Charles R. Pearce offered to take him to the Calgary Stampede, he declined, stating that he did not have the time and "would not be at all interested."[62] When another friend suggested holding a spiritual retreat, he replied that a retreat would not "be of any value to any movement at the present time. What is needed is activity – bold, aggressive, and courageous activity."[63]

During the legislative session of 1943 it became more apparent that Aberhart was ill, but neither he nor those around him took it very seriously. He found that he had difficulty shaving in the morning and was frequently bothered by motion sickness.[64] Mention of his illness began appearing more and more in his correspondence. He complained of weakness and had to cancel obligations.[65] After a medical examination he was ordered to take a rest. He decided to go to visit his daughters on the West Coast. He expected to be away only two or three weeks and then planned to travel to Ontario to visit his mother and brothers and carry on the federal campaign.[66] Upon leaving the Legislature for the last time he is reported to have said to Alf Hooke, one of the M.L.A.s, "Alf, I did not know that a man could feel as weak as I do and still walk around."[67]

On 18 April, William and Jessie Aberhart left Edmonton. On their way to Vancouver he was very ill on the train. When he arrived at the home of his daughter Khona, she, being a registered nurse, realized he was a very sick man. Under duress he entered hospital for a check-up. As one who had avoided hospitals all his life he found the experience very trying. The smells nauseated him as usual. After a week Aberhart could stand the hospital no longer and returned to Khona's home. The situation there was quite hectic. Khona's youngest daughter had chicken pox. Jessie Aberhart also took sick and had to be nursed. Khona's other daughter Pat was sent over to Ola's home; but it was soon learned that Ola's children had another childhood disease, so Pat came home and had to be isolated. It was altogether a trying time for everyone.[68]

Aberhart seems to have realized that he would have to cut his pace; he talked of retiring. He said to Jessie, "When I retire, mother, I'm going to spend all my time writing all my sermons."[69]

On 17 May, Aberhart had another check-up. He was immediately rehospitalized and the public was told that he had a serious liver ailment.[70] Privately he was told he had an enlargement of the liver, more commonly known today as cirrhosis.

Cirrhosis is normally associated with alcoholism, but it can also be caused by other factors: overwork, lack of sleep, and inordinate stress. For years Aberhart had been working himself to death. So far as we know he had remained an abstainer from alcohol; the only reason he would allow for occasional drinking would be medicinal purposes,[71] but he himself seems to have resisted even that.

During Aberhart's second stay in hospital he became quite upset when a nurse gave him a needle without telling him what it was for. He was not used to this kind of treatment, for he had always been in control of most situations. From then on, his daughter Khona took over his nursing care in the hospital.

Back in Alberta acting premier Ernest Manning denied rumours that

Aberhart was seriously ill and about to retire: "There are no grounds whatever for assuming that Mr. Aberhart will no longer be able to lead his government."[72] Speculation was rife on who might replace Aberhart. Ernest Manning and Solon Low were seen as the chief contenders.[73] Manning again denied that there were any plans for replacing Aberhart.[74]

Aberhart was told by his doctor that in order to live he would have to have weekly intravenous treatments. He replied that that would be too much to bear; he was too squeamish. Refusing any further treatment he resigned himself to death.[75] On 22 May, Aberhart's kidneys failed – a side-effect of cirrhosis of the liver – and the public was told that his doctors had given up all hope for his recovery. Ernest Manning and W.A. Fallow, minister of Public Works, rushed from Edmonton to Aberhart's bedside,[76] but he died early Sunday morning, 23 May, before they arrived. He was sixty-four.

Albertans were shocked to hear of Aberhart's passing. Tributes poured in from many quarters.[77] Both Edmonton dailies were very kind in their comments about Aberhart. The Edmonton *Bulletin* was most eulogistic:

> Whatever his obsessions, whatever his political acts, whatever his economic creed, that will be his final tribute – that he loved his fellow man. Everything in his life pointed to it.[78]

Mackenzie King's public comments on Aberhart's death were full of sympathy, but his diary revealed his true feelings about the man who had been the greatest challenge to his leadership of the country:

> Was unexpectedly drawn into a word of appreciation regarding Aberhart.... Found it difficult to say much about Aberhart. Was determined not to be insincere in my remarks.[79]

Aberhart's life had been marked by contradictions since he had first adopted Social Credit in 1932; he had created a quasi-social gospel, but continued to preach his dispensational apocalypticism at the same time. The contradictions in Aberhart's thoughts and behaviour were present even at his funeral, which was conducted by the Reverend G. Harrison Villett, minister of the liberal Canadian Memorial United Church and a family friend of long standing. Ministers of Aberhart's own sect were not represented. The Alberta government had proposed a state funeral be held in Edmonton, but the Aberhart family's decision to hold the semi-private funeral in Vancouver may have been due to Jessie Aberhart's illness and her plans to remain at the West Coast with her daughters. On that rainy Wednesday, 26 May 1943, Aberhart's interment followed at the Forest Lawn Cemetery in Burnaby.[80] He was buried there because members of the family felt that Aberhart's efforts in Alberta had not been appreciated.

CHAPTER TWENTY-ONE

WILLIAM ABERHART: AN ASSESSMENT

I N THIS *hour of his*
death, it is not important to consider the fine social
legislation he gave this province. But it is important
to remember that that Social legislation was the
product of a burning sympathy for the aged
and the sick and the helpless.
That will be his epitaph, whatever one may
think of his politics, that he was the champion
of the oppressed.

— Editorial *Edmonton Bulletin*, 24 May 1943

William Aberhart fits into a long tradition of political unrest in Western Canada. As a farmer's son Aberhart identified with agrarian needs and aspirations, and was able to articulate them for the average Albertan. As John A. Irving pointed out, Aberhart's movement was effective at least partly because he was able to lift people out of their emotional doldrums during the Great Depression by giving them hope that they could bring in a new social order by their collective effort for Social Credit.[1] Politically, Aberhart's government brought in needed reforms in education, labour relations, social welfare, and debt legislation. In ideology and practice his administration was the most radical of any Canadian provincial government before or since. However, his inability to effect the promised economic cure drove some people to renewed discouragement.

The good pieces of legislation that Aberhart introduced in Alberta – those affecting health care, labour, education, oil and gas conservation, and moratoriums on foreclosures – were unrelated to Social Credit ideology. Almost every economic scheme he tried ended in failure – the dividends, the Prosperity Certificates, the purchase of the *Albertan* – and for a long time the Treasury Branches were a drain on the public purse. He was economicaly naïve; he was like another religious leader he had described in 1906:

> there are to be found in all communities erratic people, who get hold of an idea and without stopping to get all the bearing of the case, jump at conclusions and then make everything bend to their opinions. In some cases these men are men of influence and personal magnetism and therefore they soon gain a following.[2]

In his efforts to ameliorate economic problems in Alberta, Aberhart had unfortunately adopted the "cure all" of the eccentric and anti-Semitic Major Douglas. Aberhart has been heavily criticized for his Social Credit failures, which was somewhat unjust for Aberhart was a product of his times and many of the intellectual leaders of Alberta – William Irvine, J. Larkham Collins, W. Norman Smith, leaders in the U.F.A., and even the Calgary *Herald* – were at one time or another disciples of Douglas. Those men and groups opposed Aberhart by playing him off against the "orthodox" Douglas, even after they themselves had dropped Douglas when they found no substance behind his vague theories. Had Aberhart's critics been more honest with him, he might not have rushed into some of the impractical stances which he took.

In this book a number of issues have been addressed. In the earlier studies by S.D. Clark, John A. Irving, and W.E. Mann,[3] Aberhart's political activities were seen as an extension of his religious sectarianism. We have argued that they were not. The Great Depression forced Aberhart out of his other-worldly approach to life, derived from dispensational pre-millennialism. His political involvement was a time of personal growth reflected in his switch from the apocalyptic eschatology of Daniel, Paul, and John to the prophetic social passion of Amos and Jesus. Aberhart's political activities had more to do with his earlier involvement with the Presbyterians and Methodists than it had to do with the Baptist sects with which he was associated after the First World War. Yet, this theological transition was not complete, for we find him in his final years still clinging to his pre-millennial eschatological rhetoric, even while he implied that the implementation of Social Credit would bring the Millennium. This contradiction can be explained by the fact that Aberhart demonstrably pushed himself so hard that he did not have the time to work out contradictions in his thinking and behaviour. While his compartmentalized thought can be criticized, he must be credited with not sitting still when people were losing their homes to mortgage companies and banks, when children were starving while good food was being destroyed to keep prices up. In many ways Aberhart's political involvement had more to do with his career as a highschool principal training children to be citizens of this world than it had to do with his dispensational preaching relating mostly to the next world.

At the same time, however, there was a strange connection between Aberhart's theology and his political ideology; both were dominated by conspiracy theories. The devil and the fascist machinations of the Antichrist played inordinately important roles in Aberhart's theology. It was not too difficult for him to move from these fantasies to fantasies about the "international Jewish conspiracy" as taught by Major Douglas. The political system that Aberhart envisioned under Social Credit had ironic parallels to the totalitarian system he feared the Antichrist would implement.[4]

Aberhart was involved in more religious controversy, strife, and schism than any other person in western Canada. He had attracted people because of his strong personality and his innovations in Christian education: his radio broadcasts, dramatic performances and a Radio Sunday School which had over 9,000 children enrolled in 1938-1939.

However, it is a mistake to see Aberhart's Social Credit movement as typical of religious fundamentalism. Aberhart's unique theology and his political ideology brought him opposition from Pentecostals, Plymouth Brethren, Regular Baptists, Prairie Bible Institute, and even from within his own sect. Most of his political support seems not to have come from members of other religious sects, but from people who belonged to mainline churches or who had only marginal religious commitment.

Aberhart's theology was very eclectic, moving from the worlds of John Calvin, John Wesley, and John Bunyan into those of the Plymouth Brethren, Pentecostalism, the social gospel, and British-Israelism. The final result was the creation of his own sect, built around his own personality – but his sectarianism operated on different levels. After Aberhart adopted Social Credit in 1932 his radio broadcasts and public statements were quite "ecumenical," even as the theology within the Calgary Prophetic Bible Institute and the Bible Institute Baptist Church remained rigidly sectarian. This nuance was missed in Harry Hiller's sociological study of Aberhart's movement.[5]

Most of the authors of the series on Social Credit edited by S.D. Clark interpreted Aberhart's movement as right-wing, if not fascist. This assessment, largely influenced by sociological methodology, failed to note ideological differences between Douglas and Aberhart and between Aberhart and Manning. This series assumed that the Social Credit government of Alberta during the late 1940s and early 1950s, when the basic research was done, reflected Aberhart's ideology. We have argued that his political ideology was in fact leftist; his Yellow Pamphlet was assembled with the help of a communist, and Aberhart had early dealings with members of the C.C.F. After he was in power Aberhart received support from the Communists. Yet even C.B. Macpherson, a Marxist who focused on Alberta's class structure (or lack of it), failed to note the leftist tendency in Aberhart's political ideology.[6] Recent scholarship is, however, gradually reversing the image of Aberhart as right-wing.[7]

It is possible to classify Aberhart as a left-wing fascist because he was a charismatic leader, he used propaganda effectively, his theory of the State was very authoritarian. He obliterated the distinction between party and government, issued much order-in-council legislation, used repressive legislation and boycotts against the press and dissenters, employed anti-capitalistic rhetoric, and promoted financial conspiracy theories that were laden with anti-Semitic overtones. Only the violent element of fascism was missing; Douglas advocated a military *coup* but Aberhart refused that option.

Because of the mixture of right- and left-wing elements in Aberhart's thought and behaviour some scholars have classified him as a populist, since populism borrowed from both sides of the political spectrum. However, in several important ideological aspects, Aberhart's ideas differed from populism – in his theory of the state, and in his proposal of rule by "experts" – not the rule by the common man that was the characteristic of populism. In terms of Richard Hofstadter's definitions of populism and progressivism, Aberhart would fall into the latter category.[8] The federal government alone prevented Aberhart from establishing an authoritarian state, and he never did find those "experts."

Aberhart was a complex man; like most people he was torn between altruism and egotism. He began both his preaching and his political career out of love and concern for the spiritual and physical welfare of his fellow man. However, as he gained power his ego overtook his altruism, and megalomania reigned. This process was reflected in Aberhart's "apostleship," the power struggles in the various churches with which he was associated, and his deliberate lying from the pulpit while attempting to defend his political errors and economic failures.

Aberhart was succeeded as premier of Alberta by thirty-five-year-old Ernest C. Manning, his protégé and intimate friend. From 1943 until 1968 Manning ruled the province with little or no opposition. While Manning continued Aberhart's *Back-to-the-Bible Hour* and directed the affairs of the Calgary Prophetic Bible Institute, he differed from Aberhart in maintaining a separation between church and state. He also did his best to purge his party of anti-Semitic elements. During Manning's régime Alberta became prosperous without the help of Social Credit theories. The war had stimulated the economy, and the discovery of oil at Leduc in 1947 brought the province into the realm of economic prosperity.

NOTES

■

MAJOR COLLECTIONS USED

Aberhart Family Papers, in the possession of Khona Cooper, Half Moon Bay, B.C.

Aberhart Papers, deposited by Ola MacNutt, Provincial Archives of Alberta, Edmonton, Alberta.

Irene (née Eberhardt) Barrett Papers, in the possession of Irene Barrett, Burlington, Ontario.

Bible Institute Baptist Church Papers, Glenbow-Alberta Institute, Calgary, Alberta.

J.C. Bowen Papers, Provincial Archives of Alberta.

Brantford Public Library, Brantford, Ontario.

Calgary Herald Papers, Glenbow-Alberta Institute.

Calgary Prophetic Bible Conference Minutes, copied by Iris Miller, but present location of originals is unknown.

Calgary Prophetic Bible Institute Financial Records, found in the basement of the Calgary Prophetic Bible Institute building by David R. Elliott and turned over to Canada's National Back-to-the-Bible Hour, Edmonton.

Calgary Prophetic Bible Institute Papers, Glenbow-Alberta Institute.

Calgary School Board Minutes, Calgary School Board.

Stewart Cameron Cartoon Collection, Provincial Archives of Alberta.

Chancellors' Correspondence, Canadian Baptist Archives, McMaster University, Hamilton, Ontario.

Crescent Heights High School Library, Calgary.

Hugh W. Dobson Papers, United Church of Canada Archives, Vancouver School of Theology, University of British Columbia.

David R. Elliott Collection, to be deposited in appropriate archives at a later date.

Grace Presbyterian Church Records, Calgary.

Ernest G. Hansell Papers, Glenbow-Alberta Institute.

H.B. Hill Collection, Devonian Foundation Papers, Glenbow-Alberta Institute.
Hillhurst Baptist Church Records, Glenbow-Alberta Institute.
John W. Hugill Papers, Glenbow-Alberta Institute.
Huron County Registry, Goderich, Ontario.
Huron Expositor, Seaforth, Ontario.
William Irvine Papers, Provincial Archives of Alberta.
John A. Irving Papers, Thomas Fisher Rare Book Library, University of Toronto.
Rev. George Kerby Papers, United Church Archives, St. Stephen's College, Edmonton.
William Lyon Mackenzie King Diaries, Public Archives of Canada, Ottawa.
Ola MacNutt Papers, Glenbow-Alberta Institute.
Iris Miller Collection, to be deposited in appropriate archives at a later date.
Land Titles Office, Calgary.
Solon Low Papers, Glenbow-Alberta Institute.
Charles R. Pearce Papers, Glenbow-Alberta Institute.
Prairie Bible Institute Library, Three Hills, Alberta.
Premiers' Papers, Provincial Archives of Alberta.
Presbyterian Archives, Knox College, Toronto.
Norman F. Priestly Papers, Glenbow-Alberta Institute.
Registry of Companies, Victoria, B.C.
Social Credit Papers from the Alberta Dept. of Agriculture, Glenbow-Alberta Institute.
W. Norman Smith Papers, Glenbow-Alberta Institute.
Fred Stone Diary Tapes, Glenbow-Alberta Institute.
Trinity Methodist Church Records, Trinity United Church, Calgary.
United Church of Canada Archives, Toronto.
United Church Collection, Provincial Archives of Alberta.
Westbourne Baptist Church Records, Calgary.
Woman's Canadian Club Papers, Glenbow-Alberta Institute.
Women's Christian Temperance Union Papers, Glenbow-Alberta Institute.
Zion Presbyterian Church Records, Zion United Church, Brantford.
J.J. Zubick Papers, Glenbow-Alberta Institute.

CHAPTER I – THE FORMATIVE YEARS

1. Elliott's telephone interview with Thelma Dale, Seaforth, 22 Feb. 1977.
2. Elliott's telephone interviews with George Aberhart, London, Ont., 9 and 10 March, 1 June 1977.
3. *Canada West Census* 1861, Huron County, Tuckersmith Township, ward 1, p.4; *Huron Expositor*, 9 April 1915, p.8; Isabella Campbell, *A Hibbert Review: County of Perth* (Seaforth: Huron Expositor, 1953), p.12.
4. *Canada Census* 1871, Huron County, Tuckersmith Township, ward 3, p.33.
5. Irving's interview with George Chesney, Calgary, 25 Aug. 1946, Irving Papers.
6. Miller's interview with Charles Aberhart, London, Ont., 16 Nov. 1954.
7. Campbell, *A Hibbert Review*, p.12.
8. Elliott's interview with Irene Barrett, Burlington, Ont., 15 Feb. 1977.
9. *Huron Expositor*, 30 Aug. 1935, p.3.
10. Miller's interview with Charles Aberhart, 16 Nov. 1954.
11. *Huron Expositor*, 17 Sept. 1897, p.8.
12. Aberhart's sermon, "Bible Reading #28," Premiers' Papers, box 99, file 1049.
13. Miller's interview with Irene Barrett, 8 July 1956, and Elliott's interview with Khona Cooper, Half Moon Bay, B.C., 19 Dec. 1973.
14. Miller's interview with Charles Aberhart, 16 Nov. 1954.
15. Miller's interview with Jessie Aberhart, Vancouver, 11 April 1954.
16. Aberhart's speech, "Horse Sense and Machinery," Aberhart Papers, box 1, and Miller's interview with Charles Aberhart, 16 Nov. 1954.

17. Miller's interview with Jessie Aberhart, 29 March 1954.
18. Irving's interview with George Chesney, 25 Aug. 1946, Irving Papers.
19. Elliott's interview with George Aberhart, 9 March 1977.
20. Elliott's interview with Irene Barrett, 1 April 1977.
21. Miller's interview with Charles Aberhart, 16 Nov. 1954.
22. Irving's interview with George Chesney, 25 Aug. 1946; Miller's interview with Alec Bethune, Seaforth, n.d.
23. Miller's interview with Mr. Sills, Seaforth, 7 July 1956.
24. Elliott's interview with George Aberhart, 9 March 1977.
25. Edmonton *Journal*, 11 Aug. 1939, p.2.
26. *Huron Expositor*, 11 Sept. 1896, p.8.
27. Cited in Charles E. Phillips, *The Development of Education in Canada* (Toronto: W.J. Gage and Company, 1957), p.577.
28. *Huron Expositor*, 8 Jan. 1897, pp.1 and 8.
29. D. McLachlan, Principal of Chatham Business College, to whom it may concern, 8 Aug. 1899, Aberhart Family Papers.
30. A.E. Galbraith, Chatham Business College, to whom it may concern, 14 July 1899, Aberhart Family Papers, and *Huron Expositor*, 27 Aug. 1897, p.1.
31. *Huron Expositor*, 19 Aug. 1898, p.1.
32. *Ibid.*, 8 Oct. 1897, p.8.
33. *Ibid.*, 19 Nov. 1897, p.8 and 3 Dec. 1897, p.8.
34. *Ibid.*, 20 Sept. 1935, pp.1-2.
35. *Ibid.*, 13 June 1898, p.8.
36. William James, *The Varieties of Religious Experience* (London: Collins, 1960), p.203.
37. *Canada West Census* 1861, Huron County, Tuckersmith Township, ward 1, p.4, and Miller's interview with Mr. Sills, 7 July 1956.
38. *Canada West Census* 1851, Perth County, Fullerton Township, p.57.
39. *Canada Census*, 1871, Huron County, Tuckersmith Township, ward 3, p.33; Aberhart's speech, "Horse Sense and Machinery," Aberhart Papers, box 1.
40. Miller's interview with Charles Aberhart, 16 Nov. 1954.
41. Irving's interview with Norman Priestly, U.F.A. leader, 11 July 1947, Irving Papers. Priestly had heard the story from a C.C.F. worker who claimed to have been present when Aberhart related the incident. As an interesting aside, one of Aberhart's contemporaries, who also became a great orator, eleven-year-old Adolf Hitler, spent many hours out in the forest speaking to trees in order to develop his powers of oratory. See Robert G.L. Waite, *Hitler: The Psychopathic God* (New York: Mentor Books, 1975), p.188.
42. E.C. Manning to David R. Elliott, 4 Feb. 1977.
43. *Huron Expositor*, 21 Oct. 1898, p.8.
44. W.M. Martin to Iris Miller, 4 April 1954.
45. William Aberhart, "God's Great Divisions of the World's History," Lecture 2 in his *God's Great Prophecies* (Calgary: Calgary Prophetic Bible Conference, *circa* 1922), pp.27-28. Aberhart was probably referring to his classes at Normal School. As far as we know, he never actually attended university. Later he took a degree from Queen's University by correspondence, but he could not have been referring to those studies because the chronology will not fit.
46. *Ibid.*, pp. 28-30
47. *Prophetic Voice*, Aug. 1942, p. 1.
48. *Huron Expositor*, 2 Feb. 1900, p.1.
49. Aberhart's speech, "Horse Sense and Machinery," Aberhart Papers, box 1.
50. Certificate #16340, Aberhart Family Papers, and copy of unaddressed letter by D. Robb, June 1901, Irving Papers.

CHAPTER II – VOCATION OR AVOCATION?

1. Brantford *Daily Courier*, 6 Sept. 1901, p.5.
2. Aberhart, "God's Great Divisions of the World's History," Lecture 2 in his *God's Great Prophecies*, pp.28-30.
3. See Leroy Edwin Froom, *The Prophetic Faith of Our Fathers* 4 Volumes (Washington: Review and Herald, 1946-1954).
4. Aberhart, p.25.
5. John Nelson Darby, *The Faith Once Delivered to the Saints and Various Papers* (London: Stow Hill Bible and Tract Depot, n.d.), reprinted 1943.
6. See William Blair Neatby, *A History of the Plymouth Brethren* (London: Hodder and Stoughton, 1902); Henry Allen Ironside, *A Historical Sketch of the Brethren Movement* (Grand Rapids: Zondervan Publishing House, 1942); Clarence C. Bass, *Backgrounds to Dispensationalism* (Grand Rapids: Wm. B. Eerdmans Publishing Co., 1960); and Elmer William Powell, "Plymouth Brethrenism," *Crozier Quarterly* 16 (1939), pp.32-40.
7. C.A. Briggs, "Origins and History of Premillenarianism," *Lutheran Quarterly* 9 (1879), pp.207-244.
8. See C. Norman Kraus, *Dispensationalism in America* (Richmond: John Knox Press, 1958) and Ernest R. Sandeen, *The Roots of Fundamentalism: British and American Millenarianism 1800-1930* (Chicago: University of Chicago Press, 1970), pp.132-161.
9. John Calvin, the founder of Presbyterianism, was especially critical of millenarianism. See his *Institutes of the Christian Religion* Book 3:25:5.
10. Samuel H. Kellogg, "Premillennialism: Its Relations to Doctrine and Practice," *Bibliotheca Sacra* 45 (1888), pp.253-254.
11. Ernest R. Sandeen, "Towards a Historical Interpretation of the Origins of Fundamentalism," *Church History* 36 (1967), pp.66-83.
12. Kraus, pp.102-104.
13. James E. Bear, "Historic Premillennialism," *Union Seminary Review* 55 (1944), pp.193-221.
14. John Wick Bowman, "The Bible and Modern Religions: II. Dispensationalism," *Interpretation* 10 (1956), p.172.
15. Kraus, pp.31-33, 95. Cyrus I. Scofield, *The Scofield Reference Bible* (New York: Oxford University Press, 1909), p.i. See also Charles M. Johnston, *McMaster University: Vol. 1. The Toronto Years* (Toronto: University of Toronto Press, 1976), p.28.
16. Aberhart's sermon, "Bible Reading #10," Premiers' Papers, box 98, file #1048.
17. Brantford *Daily Courier*, 10 May 1902, p.4 and 20 May 1902, p.4.
18. *Ibid.*, 19 Sept. 1903, p.6 and 21 Sept. 1903, p.4.
19. Elliott's interview with Khona Cooper, 19 Dec. 1973.
20. Brantford *Daily Courier*, 1 Aug. 1902, p.4.
21. Elliott's telephone interview with George Aberhart, 10 March 1977.
22. Unaddressed letters from William Wilkinson, June 1902, Irving Papers, and M.J. Kelly, 7 Feb. 1903, Aberhart Family Papers.
23. Miller copied Aberhart's essay from his notebook, which was in the possession of Charles R. Pearce, secretary-treasurer of the Calgary Prophetic Bible Institute.
24. Miller's interviews with Mrs. J.B. Walden, 11 Jan. 1955 and Clayton S. Moyer, Brantford, 28 Dec. 1954.
25. See a typewritten history of Central Public School, Brantford, in the principal's office of that school.
26. Miller's interview with A.C. Burt, Brantford, n.d.
27. Brantford *Daily Courier*, 6 Feb. 1905, p.4; 9 Feb. 1905, p.2; 7 April 1905, p.1; 2 June 1905, p.5; 11 July 1905, p.1. Aberhart's Commercial Specialists Diploma (#2238) is in the Aberhart Family Papers.

28. Miller's interviews with Mr. Batson, Brantford, 28 Dec. 1954 and the Rev. Harold Vaugh, Zion United Church, Brantford, 28 Dec. 1954.

29. Norman Camp to Aberhart, 18 Feb. 1937, Premiers' Papers, box 112, file #1182; Brantford *Daily Courier*, 13 Nov. 1903, p.4 and 15 Dec. 1903, p.5; George H. Pember, *Earth's Earliest Ages* (New York: Fleming H. Revell Co., c.1890).

30. Brantford *Daily Courier*, 6 April 1904, p.4 and 17 Oct. 1906, p.6; Aberhart's notes of Riley's 1906 meeting are in the Aberhart Papers.

31. *Ibid.*, 14 Oct. 1905, p.4.

32. *Ibid.*, 6 Jan. 1906, p.8 and 17 Jan. 1906, p.1; see Aberhart's sermon, "Dr. Wilbur Chapman," Premiers' Papers, box 98, file #1048.

33. J. Wilbur Chapman, *The Life and Work of Dwight L. Moody* (Toronto and Brantford: The Bradley-Garretson Co., 1900), pp.102-103.

34. Brantford *Daily Courier*, 25 April 1907, p.4; Jean Royce, Registrar of Queen's University to Harold J. Schultz, 4 Sept. 1958, cited in his "William Aberhart and the Social Credit Party: A Political Biography" (unpublished Ph.D. dissertation, Duke University, 1959), p.8, and G.C. Leech, Registrar of Queen's University to David R. Elliott, 12 June 1974.

35. Brantford *Daily Courier*, 10 Dec. 1906, p.4.

36. Aberhart's sermon ledger can be found in the Aberhart Papers, item #70.239/27.

37. Aberhart's sermon, "The Second Coming of Christ," Aberhart papers, box 1, item #70.239/51a.

38. Samuel P. Tregelles, *The Hope of Christ's Second Coming* (London: Sovereign Grace Advent Testimony, 1864), reprinted in 1964, p.35.

39. "Watchman" to the editor, *Christian Guardian*, 2 May, 1888, p.276.

40. See a critique of the social views of premillennialism by Walter Rauschenbush, *A Theology For the Social Gospel* (New York: The Macmillan Company, 1917), pp.210-211.

41. Cyrus I. Scofield, *Addresses on Prophecy* (New York: A.C. Gabelein, 1910), p.41.

42. Neatby, pp.40, 267-275.

43. Aberhart's sermon, "The Second Coming of Christ," 1907.

44. Aberhart's sermon, "Church Ministry and Govt.," Aberhart Papers, box 1, item #70.239/51a.

45. Aberhart's sermon, "The Second Coming of Christ"; see also Tregelles, p.69.

46. Brantford *Daily Courier*, 16 June 1908, p.4; 23 March 1909, p.4; 7 April 1909, p.4; 29 Oct. 1909, p.5; 2 Nov. 1909, p.5; 10 Feb. 1910, p.4.

47. Minute Book of the Paris Presbytery 1901-1923, 11 May 1909, p.276; 13 July 1909, p.280 in the United Church of Canada Archives; Minutes of the General Assembly, Presbyterian Church in Canada, 1910, p.59, Knox College.

48. Minutes Book of the Paris Presbytery, 12 July 1910, p.314.

49. Brantford *Daily Courier*, 15 Jan. 1910, p.1.

50. Miller's interview with Jessie Aberhart, 26 March 1954.

51. Brantford *Daily Courier*, 20 Jan. 1910, p.5 and 4 Feb. 1910, p.6.

52. *Ibid.*, 4 March 1910, pp.1 and 4; Miller's interviews with Mrs. J.B. Walden, 11 Jan. 1955, Frank Culbeck, Brantford, 16 Nov. 1954, and Sam Stedman, Brantford, 8 July 1956.

53. Brantford *Daily Courier*, 4 March 1910, p.4.

54. *Ibid.*, 9 March 1910, p.6.

55. Aberhart to the editor, Brantford *Daily Courier*, 10 March 1910, p.4.

56. William B. Wood to Aberhart, 1910, Irving Papers.

CHAPTER III – PREACHER ON THE PRAIRIES

1. Irving's interview with Dr. John H. Garden, Mount Royal College, 29 Aug. 1946, Irving Papers.
2. Calgary *Herald*, 16 April 1910, p.7.
3. *Huron Expositor*, 22 July 1910, p.8.
4. Cited in James H. Gray, *Red Lights on the Prairies* (New York: Signet Books, 1971), p.150.
5. Miller's interview with Jessie Aberhart, 26 March 1954.
6. Elliott's interview with Khona Cooper, 4 July 1974.
7. Calgary *Herald*, 26 Nov. 1910, p.21.
8. *Ibid.*, 10 Dec. 1910, p.17.
9. *Ibid.*, 9 April 1910, p.7; 1 Oct. 1910, p.7; see also Aberhart's sermon ledger.
10. Quarterly Official Board Minutes, Trinity Methodist Church, 29 Aug. 1915, p.151.
11. Calgary *Herald*, 3 July 1909, special section.
12. Miller's interview with John McLellan, 1955.
13. *Ibid.*
14. *Ibid.*
15. *Ibid.*
16. *Seventh Annual Report*, Grace Presbyterian Church, 31 Dec. 1911, pp.3-4, 12-13, 17, 21-22.
17. *Albertan*, 13 May 1911, p.9.
18. *Ibid.*, 22 July 1911, p.11.
19. Miller's interview with Hugh Fraser, 24 Aug. 1954.
20. Aberhart's sermon ledger, p.16.
21. For background on the business, social and political life of Calgary see Max Foran, *Calgary: An Illustrated History* (Toronto: James Lorimer and Company, Publishers, 1978).
22. Miller's interview with Hugh Fraser, 24 Aug. 1954.
23. Elliott's interview with Ola MacNutt, 1 Dec. 1973.
24. Calgary Presbytery Minutes, 1904-1915, 10 Sept. 1912, pp.295-296; 10 Dec. 1912, pp.303-307, United Church Collection, Provincial Archives of Alberta.
25. John A. Irving, *The Social Credit Movement in Alberta* (Toronto: University of Toronto Press, 1959), pp.24-25; L.P.V. Johnson and Ola MacNutt, *Aberhart of Alberta*, (Edmonton: Institute of Applied Art, Ltd., 1970), pp.50-51.
26. Calgary *Herald*, 5 April 1919, p.13.
27. *Ibid.*, 22 Jan. 1916, p.14; 19 Feb. 1916, p.11; 5 Oct. 1918, p.24.
28. Aberhart's sermon ledger, p.17 and Calgary *Herald*, 15 April 1922, p.7.
29. Aberhart's sermon ledger, pp.16-17 and Calgary *Herald*, 15 June 1912, p.9; 22 June 1912, p.22.
30. Wesley Methodist Quarterly Official Board Minutes, 1906-1915, 23 Sept. 1913, p.153; 17 Feb. 1914, p.158; 10 Sept. 1914, p.171; 12 Nov. 1914, p.176; 6 Dec. 1913, p.155.
31. Miller's interview with John E. Brownlee, 21 April 1954; *Albertan*, 26 Sept. 1914, p.2.
32. Miller's interview with George Ferguson, Montreal, 2 April 1956.
33. *Albertan*, 4 April 1914, p.7.
34. Trinity Methodist Church Quarterly Official Board Minutes, 1907-1916, 7 Oct. 1913, p.117.
35. *Ibid.*, 16 March 1915, p.139; 24 March 1915, p.141.
36. *Albertan*, 4 Sept. 1915, p.3 and 4 Dec. 1915, p.8.
37. Wesley Methodist Church Quarterly Official Board Minutes, 3 April 1916.
38. Calgary *Herald*, 13 Nov. 1915, p.14 and *Albertan*, 20 Nov. 1915, p.5.
39. Aberhart's sermon ledger, pp.18-20.
40. Minutes of Westbourne Baptist Church, 19 Jan. 1916, p.122.

41. *Ibid.*, 19 April 1916, p.123. The illuminated address is in the Aberhart Family Papers.
42. Trinity Methodist Church Quarterly Official Board Minutes, 11 Feb. 1916, p.153; Minutes of the East-End Bible Class, 28 May 1916. The latter document was in the possession of C.R. Pearce, but its whereabouts is now a mystery.
43. Minutes of the East-End Bible Class, 28 May 1916 and 4 June 1916; Trinity Methodist Church Quarterly Official Board Minutes, 13 June 1916, pp.170-171.
44. Mrs. A. Perkins to Aberhart, [Sept. or Oct.] 1916, Aberhart Papers, box 1, item #70.239/51a.
45. Minutes of Westbourne Baptist Church, 14 March 1917, p.130.
46. Dave Gamble, Okanagan Publishing, to David R. Elliott, 16 Aug. 1974.
47. *Henderson's Directory*, 1911, p.307; 1914, pp.253 and 916; and Principal's Report, 3 June 1912, Board of Governors' Minutes, Mount Royal College, 1910-1925, Mount Royal College; *Albertan*, 3 Oct. 1914, p.5 and Calgary *Herald*, 4 Nov. 1916, p.7.
48. Miller's interview with E. Geehan, 6 March 1954 and Irving's interview with Dr. John Garden, 29 Aug. 1946, Irving Papers.
49. Calgary *Herald*, 31 Aug. 1918, p.7 and 27 Sept., 1919, p.7.
50. Minutes of Westbourne Baptist Church, 7 Nov. 1917, p.131.
51. *Ibid.*, 5 Dec. 1917, p.132.
52. *Ibid.*, 16 Jan. 1918, p.132.
53. Miller's interview with H.B. Scrimgeour, 18 Oct. 1954.
54. Elliott's interview with Mabel Giles, Calgary, 27 April 1978.
55. Miller's interview with H.B. Scrimgeour, 19 Oct. 1954.
56. Minutes of Westbourne Baptist Church, 16 Jan. 1918, p.132.
57. Calgary *Herald*, 4 Jan. 1919, p.16; Miller's interview with Lem Fowler, 11 Oct. 1954; Minutes of Westbourne Baptist Church, 29 Jan. 1919, p.143.
58. Minutes of Westbourne Baptist Church, 16 April 1919, p.145 and 23 April 1919, p.146.
59. G. Hannah to Executive Board, Alberta Provincial Baptist Convention, 4 June 1920. Copied by Miller from the original, whereabouts now unknown.
60. Minutes of Westbourne Baptist Church, 23 April 1919, p.146.
61. *Ibid.*, 27 May 1919, p.146; 3 June 1919, p.150; 24 June 1919, p.151; 10 July 1919, p.153; Instrument 5031 CH, 18 July 1919, Land Titles Office, Calgary.
62. G. Hannah to Executive Board, Alberta Provincial Baptist Convention, 4 June 1920.
63. Miller's interview with Mrs. W.P. Harvey, Detroit, 13 Nov. 1954.

CHAPTER IV – ABERHART'S THEOLOGY

1. Miller's interview with J.U. Dick, Calgary, April 1954.
2. William Aberhart, "Is Christ's Coming Again a Reality or a mere Fancy?" Lecture 3 in his *God's Great Prophecies*. That series of booklets, based on his prophetic lectures, formed the corpus of his theological thought. Although printed in 1922, those lectures had been given much earlier. Hereafter we will cite them as *G.G.P*, lecture #. Aberhart gave two lectures the number 4, so we will distinguish them as 4a and 4b.
3. See Harry Emerson Fosdick, *The Modern Use of the Bible* (New York: The Macmillan Company, 1924).
4. For critiques of dispensationalism and fundamentalism, see Oswald T. Allis, *Prophecy and the Church* (Philadelphia: The Presbyterian and Reformed Publishing Company, 1945) and James Barr, *Fundamentalism* (Philadelphia: Westminster Press, 1978).

5. Aberhart, "The Basic Question of Every True Religion — What Happens After Death?" *G.G.P.*, lecture 1, pp.15-18.
6. Aberhart, *An Introduction to the Study of Revelation* (Calgary: Calgary Prophetic Bible Conference, c.1925), p.12; Aberhart to J.H. Coldwell, 2 Feb. 1933, W. Norman Smith Papers; Aberhart's sermon, "New Testament Prophecy #10," Premiers' Papers, box 99, file 1049; *Prophetic Voice*, Sept. 1942, p.1; an unsigned letter to Aberhart, received June 22, 1937, commenting on his radio broadcast, Premiers' Papers, box 112, file 1182; Aberhart to J.J. Reid, 9 Sept. 1942, Premiers' Papers, box 111, file 1178.
7. *Prophetic Voice*, Feb. 1943, p.1.
8. Aberhart, "The Latest of Modern Movements or What About the Revised Version of the Bible," *G.G.P.*, lecture 12, pp.5-6.
9. *Ibid.*, p.10.
10. Aberhart, "The Present Eastern Question in the Light of Prophecy or What the Bible Says About Turkey," *G.G.P.*, lecture 11, p.7.
11. *G.G.P.*, lecture 1, p.13.
12. See C.I. Scofield, *The Scofield Bible Correspondence Course* Vol. II. (Chicago: Moody Bible Institute, 1907), p.329; R.A. Torrey, *What the Bible Teaches* (New York: Fleming H. Revell Co., 1898); and W.B. Riley, *The Menace of Modernism* (New York: Christian Alliance Publishing Co., 1917), p.13.
13. Irving's interview with Dr. John H. Garden, 29 Aug. 1946, Irving Papers; Miller's interview with the Rev. Ernest G. Hansell, 24 Sept. 1954 and H.B. Scrimgeour, Aug. 1954.
14. Irving's interview with the Rev. H.H. Bingham, 14 Sept. 1948, Irving Papers.
15. Aberhart's eschatology has been further elaborated by David R. Elliott, "The Devil and William Aberhart: The nature and function of his eschatology," *Studies in Religion* 9:3 (summer 1980), pp.325-337.
16. Aberhart, "God's Great Divisions of the World's History", *G.G.P.*, lecture 2, p.33.
17. Aberhart, "Sign-Posts on the Way to the Millennium, or the period-Divisions of Daniel's Seventieth Week," *G.G.P.*, lecture 6, p.16.
18. Aberhart, "Armageddon: The Climax of Battles," *G.G.P.*, lecture 9, p.12.
19. *Ibid.*, p.15.
20. Aberhart, "The Anti-Christ: Individual or System?", *G.G.P.*, lecture 7, p.4 and "The Anti-Christ: Man or Demon?", *G.G.P.*, lecture 8, p.9. See also Aberhart to Albert Scheerschmidt, 20 Dec. 1941, Premiers' Papers, box 121, file 1183.
21. Daniel 7:8, 21; II Thessalonians 2:3-4; Revelation 13-24 and I John 2:18.
22. See Norman Cohn, *Warrant for Genocide* (London: Eyre and Spottiswoode, 1967), p.57; Robert Anderson, *The Coming Prince: The Last Great Monarch of Christendom* (London: Hodder and Stoughton, 1881).
23. Sydney Watson, *In the Twinkling of an Eye* (Old Tappen, N.J.: Fleming H. Revell, 1904) and *The Mark of the Beast* (London: W. Nicholson and Sons, 1911). See also *Prophetic Voice*, Dec. 1926, p.4.
24. *G.G.P.*, lecture 7, p.1.
25. *G.G.P.*, lecture 9, p.15.
26. *G.G.P.*, lecture 7, p.4.
27. *G.G.P.*, lecture 8, p.7.
28. Aberhart, "The Zionist Movement, or the Restoration of the Hebrews," *G.G.P.*, lecture 5, p.13 and lecture 9, p.15.
29. *G.G.P.*, lecture 7, p.13 and lecture 9, p.15.
30. *G.G.P.*, lecture 7, p.2.
31. Aberhart, "The Future Metropolis of the World's Commerce," *G.G.P.*, lecture 13.
32. *G.G.P.*, lecture 9, p.16.

33. *G.G.P.*, lecture 7, p.2.
34. Aberhart, "The Signs and the Shadows of the Coming of Christ," *G.G.P.*, lecture 4b, p.8.
35. *G.G.P.*, lecture 5, p.15.
36. *G.G.P.*, lecture 9, p.16.
37. *G.G.P.*, lecture 5, p.13. See Aberhart's *Systematic Theology* Vol. 3 (Calgary: Calgary Prophetic Bible Institute, *c.*1927), pp.44-46 for his description of the Millennium.
38. *G.G.P.*, lecture 6, p.19 and lecture 9, p.11.
39. *G.G.P.*, lecture 9, p.15 and lecture 11, pp.9-11.
40. *G.G.P.*, lecture 11, p.7.
41. Calgary *Herald*, 1 Nov. 1924, p.20 and Aberhart, "The Signs of the Times, or Is Christ's Coming at Hand?" *G.G.P.*, lecture 4a, pp.13-15.
42. *G.G.P.*, lecture 4a, p.18 and lecture 9, p.14.
43. *G.G.P.*, lecture 8, p.9.
44. *G.G.P.*, lecture 4b, p.8 and lecture 4a, p.17.
45. *G.G.P.*, lecture 7, p.2.
46. *Ibid.*
47. See the end of each lecture in his *G.G.P.*
48. Elliott's interview with J. Fergus Kirk, President Emeritus, Prairie Bible Institute, Three Hills, Alta., 27 April 1974.
49. *G.G.P.*, lecture 2, p.26.
50. *G.G.P.*, lecture 8, p.9.
51. Aberhart based his idea that angels could impregnate women on Gen. 6:4 and I Corinthians 11:10. He departed from Scofield on this matter. The idea and practice of head covering for women is still prevalent in the churches that Aberhart founded.
52. Irving's interview with the Rev. H.H. Bingham, 14 Sept. 1948, Irving Papers.

CHAPTER V – THE PRINCIPAL OF
CRESCENT HEIGHTS HIGH SCHOOL

1. Miller's interview with H.D. Cartwright, 1 April 1954.
2. Irving's interview with Paul Brechen, 5 July 1946, Irving Papers.
3. Miller's interview with H.D. Cartwright, 1 April 1954.
4. Elliott's interview with Mrs. J.J. Sergeant, Calgary, 10 May 1972 and Miller's interviews with Mr. Watts and Mr. Gell, no dates.
5. See tape recording by N. Pickard, one of Aberhart's staff members, Aberhart Papers, box 2, item #70.239/77 and Miller's interview with Ethel Hopkins, Edmonton, n.d.
6. Miller's interview with Gladys Bennett, n.d. and Irving's interviews with F.C. Buchanan, 27 June 1946 and Margaret Wylie, 2 July 1946, Irving Papers.
7. Miller's interview with Ethel Hopkins, n.d.
8. *Ibid.*
9. Irving's interview with H.G. Beacom, 27 June 1946, Irving Papers. For Aberhart's position on dances, see Calgary School Board Minutes, 22 Nov. 1921, p.323.
10. Miller's interviews with James D. Ferguson, n.d. and Mabel Giles, Calgary, 20 Aug. 1954.
11. Miller's interviews with H.D. Cartwright, 1 April 1954, Fred Spooner, 20 April 1954, and Mr. Gell, n.d.
12. Miller's interview with H.D. Cartwright, 1 April 1954.
13. Elliott's interview with Mabel Giles, 27 April 1978.
14. Miller's interview with H.D. Cartwright, 1 April 1954.
15. Calgary School Board Minutes, 23 and 24 June 1919, pp.185, 195.

16. Irving's interview with H.G. Beacom, 27 June 1946, Irving Papers.
17. Miller's interviews with H.G. Beacom, 5 April 1954 and Paul Brechen, 8 Oct. 1954.
18. A.M. Scott to Aberhart, 9 Feb. 1921, which enclosed the report of the School Inspector, Aberhart Papers, box 2, item #70.239/69.
19. For Aberhart's chess manual, see item #70.33, Provincial Archives of Alberta.
20. Elliott's interview with R.L. Bittle, Red Deer, 26 May 1972.
21. Irving's interview with Jessie Aberhart, 30 Aug. 1946, Irving Papers.
22. Miller's interview with Jessie Aberhart, May 1954.
23. *Henderson's Directory*, 1912, p.325 and Elliott's interview with Khona Cooper, 19 Dec. 1973.
24. Aberhart's letters to Irene (née Eberhardt) Barrett are in the possession of Irene Barrett, who graciously gave us access to them.
25. E.H. Rivers to Iris Miller, 20 Dec. 1954.
26. For the anti-masonic attitudes of fundamentalists, see Charles A. Blanchard, *Modern Secret Societies* (Chicago: National Christian Association, 1903).
27. Miller's interview with Ralph Barnett, A.T.A., n.d.
28. Miller's interview with H.D. Cartwright, 1 April 1954.
29. Miller's interview with John McLellan, n.d.
30. Calgary *Herald*, 30 Nov. 1918, p.17. Aberhart's Big Chart can be found in the Aberhart Papers, box 2, item #70.239/32.
31. Miller's interview with Mrs. W.P. Harvey, 13 Nov. 1954.
32. Membership #310, Membership List, 1911-1916, Woman's Canadian Club Papers, box 6, file 18; Calgary *Herald*, 14 Jan. 1966, p.25.
33. Johnson and MacNutt, p.74.
34. Miller's interview with Jessie Aberhart, 11 April 1954 and Elliott's telephone interview with Ola MacNutt, 12 Nov. 1974.
35. Elliott's interview with Mabel Giles, 27 April 1978.
36. H.B. Hill Memoirs, p.2, Devonian Foundation Papers. We agree that intense activity can often be a substitute for sexual gratification. Political activity can sometimes be an expression of intense sexual drive. See Sam Janus and Barbara Bess, *A Sexual Profile of Men in Power* (Englewood, N.J.: Prentice-Hall, 1977).
37. Elliott's interview with Mabel Giles, 12 Nov. 1973 and Miller's interview with Mrs. W.P. Harvey, 13 Nov. 1954.
38. Calgary School Board Minutes, 23 Feb. 1920, p.70; Miller's interview with Harry Scrimgeour, n.d.
39. Miller's interview with Jessie Aberhart, 26 March 1954.
40. Elliott's telephone interviews with Bill Phillips, Calgary, 12 Jan. 1974; Mr. Summers, Vancouver, 5 July 1974; R.S. Twitty, Calgary, 10 Jan. 1974; and Jim Main to David R. Elliott, n.d.

CHAPTER VI – THE BIRTH OF A SECT

1. For an uncritical history of Pentecostalism in Canada, see Gloria G. Kulbeck, *What God Hath Wrought* (Toronto: Pentecostal Assemblies of Canada, 1958).
2. Robert A. Larden, *Our Apostolic Heritage* (Calary: Apostolic Church of Pentecost of Canada, Inc., 1971), pp.32 and 86.
3. *Ibid.*, p.118 and Elliott's telephone interview with the Rev. Walter McAlister, Hemet, California, 24 July 1978.
4. Calgary *Herald*, 28 Feb. 1920, p.28.
5. *Ibid.*, 1 May 1920, p.18.
6. *Ibid.*, 24 April 1920, p.22.
7. *Ibid.*, 15 May 1920, p.16. *cf.* 1 May 1920, p.18.
8. As early as 1864, some dispensationalists had advocated the "Jesus only" baptismal formula. See Tregelles, *The Hope of Christ's Second Coming*, p. 96. In

Elliott's interview with the Reverend Walter McAlister, the latter said that Pentecostals had been influenced by dispensationalism and that may have been one of the sources for their use of the new baptismal formula.

9. Miller's interviews with Mrs. Splane, Jr., Desson's daughter, 9 Sept. 1954 and Lem Fowler, 11 Oct. 1954. Aberhart recorded baptismal dates of various members of Westbourne Church in a little notebook, which is in the Bible Institute Baptist Church Records. His date of baptism was 9 May 1920.

10. Elliott's interview with the Reverend Theo. Gibson, Ancaster, Ont., 15 Oct. 1975. Gibson's parents and sister had witnessed Aberhart's baptism.

11. Elliott's interview with Dr. Murray Ford, McMaster Divinity College, 8 Oct. 1975.

12. Aberhart to Mrs. A. Perkins, 4 Oct. 1916, Aberhart Papers, item #70.239/51A.

13. Chapman, *The Life and Work of Dwight L. Moody*, pp.412-413; R.A.Torrey, *The Person and Work of the Holy Spirit* (Grand Rapids: Zondervan Publishing House, 1910).

14. Miller's interview with Mrs. W.P. Harvey, 13 Nov. 1954.

15. Elliott's interview with the Rev. Cyril Hutchinson, 20 June 1972.

16. *Ibid.*

17. Calgary Prophetic Bible Conference Minutes, April 1920. Miller copied them, but the whereabouts of the originals is now a mystery.

18. Elliott's interview with Dr. L.P.V. Johnson, Mill Bay, B.C., 27 Nov.1980. Aberhart's contemporary Adolf Hitler, another master-orator, seems to have used public speaking as a sexual release. He described an audience as being like a woman who had to be verbally seduced. Descriptions of both men's public speaking techniques are almost identical. See Waite, *Hitler: The Psychopathic God*, pp.61-62.

19. Miller's interview with the Reverend Cyril Hutchinson, 22 April 1954.

20. Miller's interview with Noel Hutchinson, 9 and 10 June 1954.

21. Minutes of the Calgary Prophetic Bible Conference, Sept. 1921; Miller's interview with H.B. Scrimgeour, n.d.

22. Irving's interview with R.W. Scrimgeour, 13 Aug. 1946, Irving Papers; Miller's interview with Lem Fowler, 11 Oct. 1954; and Elliott's telephone interview with Lem Fowler, 24 Aug. 1978.

23. Calgary *Herald*, 30 Oct. 1920, p.16; 29 Jan. 1921, p.6; 25 March 1922, p.18.

24. *Ibid.*, 23 Sept. 1922, p.14.

25. Bryan Wilson, *Religious Sects* (New York: McGraw Hill, 1970), p.29.

26. Calgary *Herald*, 17 April 1920, p.23 and 24 April 1920, p.22.

27. *Ibid.*, 9 April 1921, p.27.

28. *Ibid.*, 2 Oct. 1920, p.13 and 24 Sept. 1921, p.5.

29. *Ibid.*, 15 April 1922, p.7; 29 April 1922, p.6; 25 Nov. 1922, p.6; 7 April 1923, p.17; 14 April 1923, p.17; and 21 April 1923, p.15.

30. *Ibid.*, 19 March 1921, p.14; 25 Feb. 1922, p.14; and 10 June 1922, p.16.

31. W.E. Mann, *Sect, Cult and Church in Alberta* (Toronto: University of Toronto Press, 1955), pp.30-31, 156.

32. Aberhart, *G.G.P.*, lectures 1, p.10 and 2, p.27.

33. Calgary *Herald*, 6 Nov. 1920, p.6.

34. Elliott's interview with J. Fergus Kirk, 27 April 1974.

35. Irving's interview with the Reverend H.H. Bingham, 14 Sept. 1948, Irving Papers.

36. Miller's interview with the Reverend E.G. Hansell, 24 Sept. 1954.

37. Calgary *Herald*, 21 Oct. 1922, p.6 and 4 Nov. 1922, p.6.

38. Irving's interview with R.W. Scrimgeour, 15 Aug. 1946, Irving Papers.

39. Minutes of the Calgary Prophetic Bible Conference, 18 Jan. 1923; Calgary *Herald*, 3 Feb. 1923, p.15.

40. Calgary *Herald*, 31 Dec. 1920, p.14.

41. For an uncritical history see W. Phillip Keller, *Expendable!: The Story of Prairie Bible Institute* (Three Hills: Prairie Press, 1966).
42. Mann, p.50 and Calgary *Herald*, 16 June 1922, p.16.
43. *Bulletin* of the Calgary Bible Institute, *c.* 1923. An original copy was in the possession of the late Rev. Cyril Hutchinson.
44. Miller's interview with the Reverend E.G. Hansell, 24 Sept. 1954.
45. Irving's interview with the Reverend E.G. Hansell, 28 Oct. 1957, Irving Papers.
46. Calgary *Herald*, 28 April 1923, p.19.
47. Declaration of Incorporation for Westbourne Baptist Church, registered 21 June 1923. Original at Westbourne Baptist Church.
48. Calgary *Herald*, 11 Oct. 1923, p.4 and 29 Dec. 1923, p.17.
49. See Charles S. Price, *And Signs Followed: The Story of Charles S. Price* (Plainfield, N.J.: Logos International, 1972). For Aimee Semple McPherson see Lately Thomas, *Storming Heaven* (New York: William Morrow and Company, 1970) and Aimee's edited autobiography *Aimee: The Life Story of Aimee Semple McPherson* (Los Angeles: Foursquare Publications, 1979).
50. Calgary *Herald*, 8 Sept. 1923, p.15.
51. *Ibid.*, 1 Sept. 1923, p.21 and 10 Sept. 1923, p.11.
52. *Ibid.*, 15 Sept. 1923, p.14 and 22 Sept. 1923, p.15.
53. *Ibid.*, 8 Sept. 1923, p.15; 10 Sept. 1923, p.9; 12 Sept. 1923, p.10; and 22 Sept. 1923, p.12.
54. A copy of the investigation of Price's "cures" in Vancouver can be found in the Hugh W. Dobson Papers, box A2, file G. For a description of Price's methods see Ernest Thomas to Hugh Dobson, 4 June 1923, Dobson Papers, box A7-2, file T.
55. Calgary *Herald*, 12 Sept. 1923, p.11 and 14 Sept. 1923, p.15.
56. *Ibid.*, 13 Oct. 1923, p.5 and *Albertan*, 15 Oct. 1923, p.2 and 17 Oct.1923, p.4.
57. Elliott's interview with Mabel Giles, 31 Aug. 1978.
58. Calgary *Herald*, 29 Sept. 1923, p.20; 13 Oct. 1923, p.4; and 6 Oct.1923, p.16.
59. *Ibid.*, 21 Sept. 1923, p.15; Acts 19:1-6.
60. See Edward Miller, *The History and Doctrines of the Irvingites* 2 vols. (London: K. Paul and Company, 1878).
61. John Thomas Nichol, *Pentecostalism* (New York: Harper and Row, 1966), pp.102-103, 116-117, and 181.
62. Calgary *Herald*, 8 May 1920, p.8.
63. *Ibid.*, 13 Oct. 1923, p.5; 3 Nov. 1923, p.20 and 10 Nov. 1923, p.18.
64. Minutes of the Calgary Prophetic Bible Conference, 13 Nov. 1923.
65. Elliott's telephone interview with the Rev. L.H. Fowler, Port Hope, Ont., 30 Aug. 1978.
66. Elliott's telephone interview with Lem Fowler, Calgary, 26 Nov. 1973.
67. Minutes of the Calgary Prophetic Bible Conference, 18 March 1924 and Calgary *Herald*, 8 March 1924, p.16.
68. Miller's interview with the Rev. E.G. Hansell, 24 Sept. 1954.
69. The Minutes for Westbourne Baptist Church for the period 1919 to 1925 are lost and repeated searches have not found them.
70. Miller's interview with the Rev. E.G. Hansell, 24 Sept. 1954.
71. Elliott's interviews with C.R. Pearce, Vancouver, 17 Dec. 1973 and Mrs. H.B. Scrimgeour, Calgary, 7 Jan. 1975.
72. Elliott's interview with the Rev. Cyril Hutchinson, 22 Aug. 1978.
73. Acts 21:10-12.
74. Elliott's telephone interview with Ronald Ross, Leduc, Alta., 16 Jan. 1974.

CHAPTER VII – AN EXPANDING INFLUENCE

1. *Prophetic Voice*, Oct. 1924, p.14.
2. Aberhart to R.A. McKay, 2 July 1924, Aberhart Papers, box 1, item #70.239/30; Los Angeles *Times*, 26 July 1924, part 2, p.3.
3. Irving's interview with H.B. Scrimgeour, n.d.; Ethelbert W. Bullinger, *The Witness of the Stars* (London: Eyre and Spottiswoode Ltd., 1893); Joseph A. Seiss, *The Gospel in the Stars* (Grand Rapids: Kregel Publications, 1972), reprint of 1882 edition; Sydney Watson, *What the Stars Held? or the Secret of the Sphinx* (London: W. Nicholson and Sons, Ltd., n.d.).
4. Calgary *Herald*, 21 Feb. 1925, p.10; *Prophetic Voice*, Jan. 1925, pp.26-29; Elliott's interview with Mr. and Mrs. J.U. Dick, 18 Jan. 1974.
5. Minutes of Westbourne Baptist Church, 13 Jan. 1925.
6. Calgary *Herald*, 31 March 1923, p.15; Miller's interview with H.B. Scrimgeour, 18 Oct 1954.
7. Instrument 2425 D.H., 3 April 1924, Land Titles Office, Calgary.
8. For the historical background on the formation of the United Church of Canada see John Webster Grant, *The Canadian Experience of Church Union* (Richmond, Va.: John Knox Press, 1967).
9. For Aberhart's identification of the seven churches of Revelation see his sermon notes in the Aberhart Papers, box 1, item #70.239/51c and Aberhart to George Seeger, 17 July 1936, Premiers' Papers, file 1180.
10. Calgary *Herald*, 2 May 1925, p.30.
11. For more on the fundamentalist-modernist controversy see Fosdick, *The Modern Use of the Bible*; J. Gresham Machen, *Christianity and Liberalism* (New York: The Macmillan Company, 1925); Stewart G. Cole, *The History of Fundamentalism* (New York: Richard R. Smith, Inc., 1931), and Norman F. Furniss, *The Fundamentalist Controversy 1918-1931* (Hamden, Conn.: Archon Books, 1963); and George M. Marsden, *Fundamentalism and American Culture* (New York: Oxford University Press, 1980).
12. Full coverage was given to the trial in the New York *Times*, July 1925. See also Ray Ginger, *Six Days or Forever* (Boston: Beacon Press, 1958) and L. Sprague de Camp, *The Great Monkey Trial* (Garden City: Doubleday and Company, 1968).
13. W. Arnold Bennett, "Facts Concerning Brandon College," Vancouver, 28 Jan. 1922 and "Jesuit Methods Used by Baptist Union of Western Canada," Vancouver, March 1922. Original copies are in the Canadian Baptist Archives, McMaster University.
14. See Charles M. Johnston, *McMaster University: The Toronto Years*.
15. For an uncritical biography of Shields see Leslie K. Tarr, *Shields of Canada* (Grand Rapids: Baker Book House, 1967). For more critical accounts see D.E. Duzois, "Dr. Thomas Todhunter Shields (1873-1955): In the Stream of Fundamentalism" (unpublished B.D. thesis, McMaster University, 1963) and W.G. Carder, "Controversy in the Baptist Convention of Ontario and Quebec, 1908-1929" (unpublished B.D. thesis, McMaster University, 1950).
16. Calgary *Herald*, 26 Sept. 1925, p.8 and 3 Oct. 1925, p.9.
17. *Gospel Witness*, Autumn 1925.
18. Minutes of the Calgary Prophetic Bible Conference, 25 Sept. 1925.
19. *Ibid.*, 5 Nov. 1925, and Calgary *Herald*, 7 Nov. 1925, p.5.
20. Minutes of the Calgary Prophetic Bible Conference, 8 Jan. 1926 and Nov. 1926.
21. Cited in the Reverend R.S. Stevens to Aberhart, 14 Jan. 1936, Premiers' Papers, file 1161.
22. George Hilton to Dr. H.P. Whidden, 18 Dec. 1925, Chancellors' Correspondence, McMaster University, Canadian Baptist Archives.
23. Minutes of Westbourne Baptist Church, 1 Feb. 1926, and Calgary *Herald*, 20 March 1926, p.10.

24. Calgary *Herald*, 11 Sept. 1926, p.22.
25. Elliott's interview with C.R. Pearce, 18 Dec. 1973.
26. Minutes of Westbourne Baptist Church, 17 March 1926. See also "The Need of the West," a pamphlet advertising the scheme, Calgary Prophetic Bible Institute Papers.
27. Minutes of Westbourne Baptist Church, 24 March 1926 and 9 June 1926.
28. Miller's interview with Mabel Giles, 16 Oct. 1954.
29. Minutes of the Calgary Prophetic Bible Conference, date uncertain. In Miller's notes this entry followed immediately after one for 8 June 1926. Since the original minutes are lost or unavailable, we cannot check further.
30. Our information comes from a signed deposition by H.B. Scrimgeour, 10 Aug. 1946, Irving Papers, and Miller's interview with Scrimgeour.
31. A.L. Box to Aberhart, 1 Feb. 1929, Irving Papers; Minutes of the Calgary Prophetic Bible Conference, Aug. 1926.
32. Elliott's interview with C.R. Pearce, 18 Dec. 1973. Mr. Pearce was one who lost his money in the scheme.
33. Aberhart to William Taverner, 19 Jan. 1927, Irving Papers.
34. Aberhart to A.L. Box, 6 Feb. 1929, Irving Papers.
35. Calgary *Herald*, 2 Jan. 1926, p.19.
36. *Ibid.*, 11 Oct. 1926, p.4; Minutes of Westbourne Baptist Church, 13 Oct. 1926.
37. Aberhart to W.C. Smith, 22 Oct. 1926, Irving Papers, and *Gospel Witness*, 16 Dec. 1926.
38. Calgary *Herald*, 16 Oct. 1926, p.22; Minutes of Westbourne Baptist Church, 20 Oct. 1926.
39. *Covenant, Confession of Faith and Duties of Members* (Calgary: Westbourne Baptist Church, 1927), p.10.
40. Minutes of Westbourne Baptist Church, 1 and 8 Dec. 1926.
41. Aberhart's correspondence concerning the law course can be found in the Irving Papers.
42. Calgary *Herald*, 6 Nov. 1926, p.30.
43. From a pamphlet entitled, "Why not Have a Share in This," n.d.
44. Whether Aberhart conceived the sods, bricks, mortar, and rafter campaign himself is a matter of question. Aimee Semple McPherson had earlier used a similar scheme in the building of her Angelus Temple and Bible Institute in Los Angeles. At that time, her name and activities were very much in the news after she was accused of faking her own kidnapping. See Lately Thomas, *Storming Heaven*, p.25; Calgary *Herald*, 14 Oct. 1926, p.1.
45. Elliott's interview with C.R. Pearce, 18 Dec. 1973.
46. E.H. Rivers, Grand Secretary, to Iris Miller, 20 Dec. 1954 and Calgary *Herald*, 12 March 1927, p.16.
47. Minutes of Westbourne Baptist Church, 2 and 27 Feb. 1927.
48. Calgary *Herald*, 4 June 1927, p.16.
49. Instruments 2125 D.Q. and 2126 D.Q., Land Titles Office, Calgary.
50. "Declaration of Incorporation" for the Calgary Prophetic Bible Institute Church, Premiers' Papers, file 1861.
51. Minutes of Westbourne Baptist Church, 18 Oct. 1927 and 20 June 1928.
52. *Bulletin* of the Calgary Prophetic Bible Institute, 1927, p.18.

CHAPTER VIII – HE WAS LOVED. HE WAS HATED

1. Minutes of Westbourne Baptist Church, 20 June 1928.
2. The original copy of that address is in the Aberhart Papers, item #70.239/33.
3. Declaration of Incorporation of the Calgary Prophetic Bible Institute Church, articles 1c, 3e, and 4b.
4. Irving's interview with H.B. Scrimgeour, n.d., Irving Papers.

5. Elliott's interviews with Ronald Ross, 16 Jan. 1974 and the Rev. Cyril Hutchinson, 8 July 1974.
6. Calgary *Herald*, 30 June 1928, p.13.
7. *Ibid*, 25 Aug. 1928, p.13 and 15 Sept. 1928, p.13.
8. Irving's interview with H.B. Scrimgeour, n.d., Irving Papers.
9. Miller's interviews with Fred Spooner, 2 April 1954 and J.D. McAra, 15 Sept. 1954. Both men were members of the Calgary School Board.
10. Calgary *Herald*, 6 Oct. 1928, p.25.
11. *Ibid.*, 7 May 1927, p.34.
12. *The Crescent Bugle*, Crescent Heights High School, 1929, p.19.
13. Calgary *Herald*, 16 Jan. 1929, p.26. There were rumours that Thomas Underwood was behind the School Board's action against Aberhart.
14. Minutes of the Calgary School Board, 9 Jan. 1929, p.9.
15. *Ibid.*, 15 Jan. 1929, p.17.
16. Miller's interview with Fred Spooner, 2 April 1954.
17. Minutes of the Calgary School Board, 20 Feb. 1929, p.58.
18. *Ibid.*, 12 March 1929, pp.83-84.
19. Minutes of Westbourne Baptist Church, 9 Jan. 1929, p.8 and Calgary *Herald*, 19 Jan. 1929, p.26.
20. Minutes of Westbourne Baptist Church, 30 March 1927.
21. Elliott's interview with Mabel Giles, 31 Aug. 1978.
22. Minutes of Westbourne Baptist Church, 20 March 1929, pp.13-14.
23. *Ibid.*, 9 Jan. 1929, p.9.
24. *Ibid.*, 27 March 1929, p.15.
25. Aberhart, *G.G.P.*, lecture 11, p.7.
26. Minutes of Westbourne Baptist Church, 10 April 1929, pp.16-17. See also Irving's interviews with Robert and H.B. Scrimgeour, Irving Papers and Miller's interview with H.B. Scrimgeour.
27. Calgary *Herald*, 20 April 1929, p.39; 10 Aug. 1929, p.21; 14 Sept.1929, p.16; and 2 Nov. 1929, p.14.
28. Minutes of Westbourne Baptist Church, 8 Jan. 1930, p.36.
29. *Ibid.*, Jan. 1934, p.100, Sept. 1934, p.101, and 3 Aug. 1940, p.126. The Bulletin of the Western Baptist Bible College can be found in the Premiers' Papers.
30. Minutes of Bible Institute Baptist Church, 11 April 1929, p.3; 18 April 1929, p.5.
31. *Ibid.*, 11 April 1929, p.4.
32. Calgary *Herald*, 20 April 1929, p.39.
33. *Ibid.*, 23 Nov. 1929, p.2.
34. Miller's interview with E.C. Manning, 5 and 6 May 1954.
35. Miller's interview with Mrs. W.P. Harvey, 13 Nov. 1954.
36. When Calgary *Herald* reporter Fred Kennedy first met Manning he was sweeping the floor, and Kennedy mistook him for the janitor; Elliott's interview with Fred Kennedy, 8 June 1972.
37. Miller's interview with John Mavor, Aberhart's lawyer, 12 Oct. 1954 and Elliott's interview with the Rev. W.J. Laing, 9 Dec. 1973.
38. Miller's interview with C.R. Pearce, 26 April 1954.
39. In the 1927 *Bulletin* of the Calgary Prophetic Bible Institute "William Aberhart, B.A." appeared six times.
40. *The Crescent Bugle*, 1931, p.17.
41. The annual income of the Calgary Prophetic Bible Institute based on that organization's financial records has been compiled by David R. Elliott, "The Dispensational Theology and Political Ideology of William Aberhart" (unpublished M.A. thesis, University of Calgary, 1975), p.137.

CHAPTER IX – BACKGROUND TO SOCIAL CREDIT

1. For the political background on Alberta see L.G. Thomas, *The Liberal Party in Alberta* (Toronto: University of Toronto Press, 1959).
2. Irving's interview with George Bevington, Edmonton, 21 Aug. 1949.
3. William Irvine, *Farmers in Politics* (Toronto: McClelland and Stewart, 1976), reprinted from 1920. For a broader picture of the Progressives see W.L. Morton, *The Progressive Party in Canada* (Toronto: University of Toronto Press, 1950).
4. For Woodsworth's involvement in social reform see his works: *Strangers Within Our Gates* (Toronto: University of Toronto Press, reprint of 1909 edition), *My Neighbour* (Toronto: The Missionary Society of the Methodist Church, 1911). For his life see Kenneth McNaught, *A Prophet in Politics* (Toronto: University of Toronto Press, 1959). The wider context of Woodsworth's activities can be found in Richard Allen, *The Social Passion* (Toronto: University of Toronto Press, 1971).
5. Irvine's career has been treated by Anthony Mardiros, *William Irvine: The Life of a Prairie Radical* (Toronto: James Lorimer and Company, 1979).
6. *Alberta Labour News*, 25 March 1922, p.5.
7. C.H. Douglas to W. Norman Smith, 9 Dec. 1922, W. Norman Smith Papers.
8. Douglas reprinted his speech to the Standing Committee on Banking and Commerce in *Canada's Bankers and Canada's Credit: The Evidence of Major C.H. Douglas before the Select Standing Committee on Banking and Commerce* (London: The Credit Research Library, 1923).
9. Biographical details on Douglas are scant and confusing. See John Finlay, *Social Credit: The English Origins* (Montreal: McGill-Queen's University Press, 1972).
10. Douglas's anti-Semitism has been explored by David R. Elliott, "Anti-Semitism and the Social Credit Movement: The Intellectual Roots of the Keegstra Affair," *Canadian Ethnic Studies* 17:1 (1985), pp.78-89.
11. Some of Douglas's works included: *Economic Democracy* (London: Cecil Palmer, 1920); *Credit-Power and Democracy* (London: Cecil Palmer, 1921); *The Control and Distribution of Production* (London: Cecil Palmer, 1922); *Social Credit* (London: Eyre and Spottiswoode, 1924); and *Warning Democracy* (London: Stanley Nott, 1934). Besides his books, Douglas circulated his ideas mainly through *The New Age*, edited by A.R. Orage. For their relationship see Philip Mairet, *A.R. Orage: A Memoir* (New York: University Books, 1966).
12. Miller's interview with John Mitchell, 1955.
13. Douglas, *Canada's Bankers*, p.50.
14. Douglas, *The Alberta Experiment* (London: Eyre and Spottiswoode, 1937), p.17. John Kenneth Galbraith attributes the crash of the stockmarket to the speculative orgy that preceeded it. See his *Great Crash* (Boston: Houghton Mifflin Company, 1961).
15. Unless otherwise stated wheat prices quoted in this study are average prices of wheat grown in Canada as given in the *Canada Year Book* for 1935 and 1940.
16. Annual Report of the Alberta Department of Agriculture, 1931, *Sessional Papers*, vol. 26, 1931-1932, p.15.
17. For a series of interviews with survivors of the Depression see Barry Broadfoot, *Ten Lost Years 1929-1939* (Toronto: Doubleday Canada Ltd., 1973). James H. Gray also provided first-hand observations of the Depression in the prairie provinces: *The Winter Years* (Toronto: MacMillan of Canada, 1966). For a more scholarly treatment of the effects of the depression on society, see James Struthers, *No Fault of Their Own: Unemployment in Canada, 1914-1941* (Toronto: University of Toronto Press, 1983).
18. For pre-Depression life in the west see James H. Gray, *The Roar of the*

Twenties (Toronto: MacMillan of Canada, 1975). Jean Burnett's study, *Next-Year Country* (Toronto: University of Toronto Press, 1951) described conditions of a rural area in east-central Alberta during the Depression and the farmers' recurring hopes that next year's crop would be their salvation.

19. J. Fergus Kirk, "Social Credit and the Word of God," mimeographed letter, Three Hills, Alta., 1935. See also Samuel C. Kincheloe, *Research Memorandum on Religion in the Depression* (New York: Arno Press, 1937), reprinted 1971.

20. See Sydney Watson, *The New Europe* (London: William Nicholson and Sons, Ltd., n.d.). One of Aberhart's supply preachers who later dropped that idea was Harry Rimmer, *The Coming League and the Roman Dream* (Grand Rapids: Wm. B. Eerdmans Publishing Company, 1943).

21. See Oswald J. Smith, *The Antichrist is at Hand* (Toronto: Tabernacle Publishers, 1926) and *When Antichrist Reigns* (New York: The Christian Alliance Publishing Co., 1927); A. Sims, *The World's Desperate Cry for a Superman: An Unveiling of the Satanic Forces Behind the Screen. The Universal Commotion Explained* (Toronto: A. Sims, Publisher, c.1930); and L. Sale-Harrison, *Ethiopia in the Light of Prophecy* (London: Pickering and Inglis, 1935).

22. Aberhart, *G.G.P.*, lecture 4a, p.18.

23. *Ibid.*, lecture 8, p.9.

24. Calgary *Herald*, 3 Feb. 1934, p.8; CFCN broadcast, 21 April 1935, W. Norman Smith Papers; *The Rebel*, 30 July 1937, p.4.

25. Calgary *Herald*, 6 Feb. 1926, p.14; 27 Oct. 1928, p.34; 10 Jan.,1931, p.8; 27 June 1931, p.18; and 29 Aug. 1931, p.18.

26. Some of those dispensationalists who interpreted prophecy and history in that manner and who spoke at the Calgary Prophetic Bible Institute were L. Sale-Harrison, Harry Rimmer, and Rev. E.R. Hooper.

27. Calgary *Herald*, 5 Sept. 1931, p.18. The text of the play can be found in Johnson and MacNutt, pp.231—239.

28. Aberhart, *G.G.P.*, lecture 5, p.15.

29. Irving's interview with Mrs. R.D. Murray, 25 Aug. 1946 and Elliott's interview with Dr. Murray Ford, 7 March 1977.

30. Elliott's interview with Mrs. C.R. Elliott, n.d.

31. Aberhart to Aaron Patterson, 26 Nov. 1931, Irving Papers.

32. See Florence Todd, "The Rise of Social Credit in Alberta," university essay, 6 Aug. 1947, p.11, Irving Papers, box 15.

33. Rev. Hugh Dobson to Aberhart, 11 Oct. 1929 and Aberhart to Dobson, 14 Oct. 1929, Irving Papers.

CHAPTER X – THE DIVIDING OF THE WATERS

1. Miller's interview with Mrs. Charles Scarborough, n.d.

2. J.M. Swain, "A Vision of Mr. Aberhart in 1928," an unpublished manuscript sent by Swain to Aberhart, 15 Jan. 1936, Premiers' Papers, file 1053.

3. Maurice Colbourne, *Unemployment or War* (New York: Coward-McCann Inc., 1928).

4. Miller's interview with Mabel Giles, 20 Aug. 1954 and Elliott's interview with Miss Giles, 12 Nov. 1973. See also Aberhart to Maurice Colbourne, 5 Nov. 1935, Premiers' Papers, file 1053.

5. Miller's interview with Charles R. Pearce, 10 March 1954.

6. Calgary *Herald*, 20 Aug. 1932, p.6; 3 Sept. 1932, p.10.

7. See Michiel Horn, *The League for Social Reconstruction: Intellectual Origins of the Democratic Left in Canada 1930-1942* (Toronto: University of Toronto Press, 1980).

8. See Walter D. Young, *The Anatomy of a Party: The National C.C.F.Party 1932-61* (Toronto: University of Toronto Press, 1969).
9. Aberhart to J.H. Coldwell, 14 Sept. 1932, W. Norman Smith Papers. Coldwell forwarded his correspondence with Aberhart to W. Norman Smith, who was editor of the *United Farmer*.
10. Aberhart to J.H. Coldwell, 15 Oct. 1932, W. Norman Smith Papers.
11. Edmonton *Journal*, 16 Sept. 1935, p.2.
12. Edmonton *Bulletin*, 16 Sept. 1935, p.8.
13. Aberhart to his son-in-law, Charles MacNutt, 7 Dec. 1932, Irving Papers.
14. Lethbridge *Herald*, 23 Sept. 1935, p.7.
15. From the unpublished memoirs of H.B. Hill, pp.7-10, in the Devonian Foundation Papers.
16. [W. Aberhart], *The Douglas System of Economics*, n.p., n.d. This document can be dated from February 1933 when references concerning it first appeared in Aberhart's correspondence and the press.
17. Irving's interview with H.B. Scrimgeour, n.d., Irving Papers.
18. Calgary *Herald*, 18 Feb. 1933, p.3.
19. *Ibid.*, 25 March 1933, p.8.
20. *Ibid.*, 15 April 1933, p.4 and 10 June 1933, p.8.
21. Elliott was told about this incident by the niece of the man in question.
22. For more on the relief camps see Stuart Marshall Jamieson, *Times of Trouble: Labour Unrest and Industrial Conflict in Canada, 1900-66* (Ottawa: Study #22, Task Force on Labour Relations, 1968), pp.236-275 and James Eayrs, *In Defence of Canada: From the Great War to the Great Depression* (Toronto: University of Toronto Press, 1964), pp.124-148; see also Struthers, *op. cit.*
23. Calgary *Herald*, 25 April 1933, p.9.
24. *Ibid.*, 9 May 1933, p.1.
25. Aberhart to Coldwell, 29 March 1933, W. Norman Smith Papers.
26. Coldwell to Aberhart, 2 May 1933, W. Norman Smith Papers.
27. Aberhart to C.M. Scarborough, 23 Feb. 1933, Irving Papers.
28. Aberhart to Coldwell, 29 March 1933, W. Norman Smith Papers.
29. Coldwell to Aberhart, 2 May 1933, W. Norman Smith Papers.
30. William Irvine to W. Norman Smith, 1 June 1933, W. Norman Smith Papers.
31. Aberhart to W.J.C. Madden, 23 Feb. 1933, Irving Papers.
32. Douglas, *Social Credit*, 1933 edition, p.10.
33. Aberhart to Irene Eberhardt, 31 July 1933, Barrett Papers.
34. W. Norman Smith to William Irvine, 22 Aug. 1933 and Smith to Aberhart, 22 Aug. 1933, W. Norman Smith Papers, file 22.
35. William Irvine to W. Norman Smith, 29 Aug. 1933, W. Norman Smith Papers, file 22.
36. Elliott's interviews with Charles R. Pearce, 18 Dec. 1973 and Mrs. Andrew Imrie, 19 Dec. 1973 and 5 July 1974.
37. Minutes of the Bible Institute Baptist Church, 12 Feb. 1930, p.27 and 26 April 1933, p.129.
38. Minutes of the Calgary Prophetic Bible Institute, 17 March 1933, cited by Johnson and McNutt, pp.106-107 and Elliott's interviews with Mrs. Andrew Imrie, 19 Dec. 1973 and 5 July 1974.
39. Irving's interview with R.W. Scrimgeour, 15 Aug. 1946.
40. Minutes of the Bible Institute Baptist Church, 6 Sept. 1933, pp.136-139.
41. *Ibid.*, 29 Nov. 1933, p.153 and 23 Jan. 1934, p.163.
42. Elliott's interview with the Reverend Cyril Hutchinson, 8 July 1974.
43. *Ibid.*
44. Calgary *Herald*, 9 Sept. 1933, p.5.
45. Aberhart to Coldwell, 15 Oct. 1932, W. Norman Smith Papers.
46. Aberhart to Coldwell, 2 Feb. 1933, W. Norman Smith Papers.

47. Aberhart to Coldwell, 29 March 1933, W. Norman Smith Papers.
48. Douglas, *Credit Power and Democracy*, p.8; Douglas, *Social Credit*, 1933, p.70; Colbourne, *Unemployment or War*, p.4; and Colbourne, *Economic Nationalism* (London: Figurehead, 1933), p.72.
49. Douglas, "Those Who Are Not For Us Are Against Us," *The Fig Tree*, Dec. 1937, p.611.
50. Calgary *Herald*, 9 Sept. 1933, p.5 and Aberhart to Norman Camp, 24 Feb. 1937, Premiers' Papers, file 1182. *cf.* Colbourne, *Economic Nationalism*, pp.58-61.
51. Aberhart to Coldwell, 2 Feb. 1933, W. Norman Smith Papers.
52. For a full report on his sermon see Barak, "Peregrinations of a Church Tramp," Calgary *Herald*, 19 Nov. 1932, p.9.
53. *Ibid.*, 14 Oct. 1933, p.8.
54. N.J. Noble to the editor, Calgary *Herald*, 22 Feb. 1933, p.4.
55. A.H. Cook to the editor, Calgary *Herald*, 3 June 1933, p.4.
56. Aberhart's sermon, "The Second Coming of Christ," Aberhart Papers, box 1, item #70.239/51a.
57. Aberhart, *G.G.P.*, lecture 2, pp. 25 and 31.
58. *Ibid.*, lecture 14, p.20.
59. L.E. Maxwell, "Christians and World Reform," *The Prairie Pastor*, May-June 1933, pp.1-2.
60. See C.I. Scofield, *The Scofield Bible Correspondence Course* Vol. 1, p.25 and Lewis Sperry Chafer, *Systematic Theology* Vol. 4. (Dallas: Dallas Theological Seminary, 1948), pp.144 and 205-207.
61. See Ralph Lord Roy, *Apostles of Discord* (Boston: Beacon Press, 1953); John Harold Redekop, *The American Far Right* (Grand Rapids: Wm. B. Eerdmans Publishing Co., 1968); Erling Jorstad, *The Politics of Doomsday* (Nashville: Abingdon Press, 1970); and Carl F.H. Henry, *The Uneasy Conscience of Modern Fundamentalism* (Grand Rapids: Wm. B. Eerdman's Publishing Co., 1948). A recent spokesman for militant fundamentalism continues to view with pride their negative position. See George W. Dollar, *A History of Fundamentalism in America* (Greenville: Bob Jones University Press, 1973).
62. Miller's interview with Mrs. W.P. Harvey, 13 Nov. 1954.
63. Miller's interview with Jessie Aberhart, May 1954.
64. Calgary *Herald*, 6 Oct. 1923, p.15. Copies of Aberhart's correspondence for the League of Nations Society can be found in the Irving Papers.
65. Fraus Pia to the editor, Calgary *Herald*, 18 Jan. 1926, p.3.
66. For earlier religious social reform movements see Timothy L. Smith, *Revivalism and Social Reform* (New York: Abingdon Press, 1957); Norris Magnuson, *Salvation in the Slums: Evangelical Social Work, 1865-1920* (Metuchen, N.J.: The Scarecrow Press, Inc., 1977); and Ernest R. Sandeen, ed. *The Bible and Social Reform* (Philadelphia: Fortress Press, 1982. The shift away from evangelical social concern in North America came after D.L. Moody espoused dispensationalism. See David Moberg, *The Great Reversal: Evangelism versus Social Concern* (Philadelphia: J.B. Lippincott Company, 1972).
67. From a signed deposition by H.B. Scrimgeour, 10 Aug. 1946, Irving Papers.
68. Aberhart to W.R. Vines and Son, 6 May 1937, Premiers' Papers, file 1061.

CHAPTER XI – THE MUSHROOMING MOVEMENT

1. Miller's interview with Charles Palmer, 23 Sept. 1954.
2. Miller's interview with Dr. Tudor Jones, 4 June 1955 and W.L. Bardsley, 2 April 1955.
3. Douglas's speech in Sydney, Australia, 25 Jan. 1934, cited by Aberhart in *The Douglas System of Social Credit: Evidence Taken by the Agricultural*

Committee of the Alberta Legislature, Session 1934 (Edmonton: King's Printer, 1934), p.12. (Hereafter cited as *Evidence*).

4. Aberhart to C.M. Scarborough, 23 Feb. 1933, Irving Papers and Aberhart to Coldwell, 23 Sept. 1933, W. Norman Smith Papers.
5. Note Aberhart's letter to Scarborough, 23 Feb. 1933, Irving Papers.
6. Miller's interviews with W. Norman Smith, Oct. 1954 and J. Larkham Collins, 12 Sept. 1954.
7. Collins to W. Norman Smith, 2 June 1933, W. Norman Smith Papers, file 32.
8. Collins to Douglas, 19 July 1933; Kerslake to Collins, 1 Aug. 1933 and Douglas to Collins, 17 Aug. 1933, W. Norman Smith Papers, file 21.
9. For background on the constitutional question see J.R. Mallory, *Social Credit and the Federal Power in Canada* (Toronto: University of Toronto Press, 1954).
10. Smith to Irvine, 22 Aug. 1933, W. Norman Smith Papers, file 22.
11. Irvine to Smith, 29 Aug. 1933, W. Norman Smith Papers, file 22.
12. Cited by Aberhart in *Evidence*, p.65.
13. The copy of Aberhart's "Yellow Pamphlet" autographed by Major Douglas is in the Aberhart Papers.
14. Cited by Aberhart in *Evidence*, pp.20, 62, 65, 123-4.
15. Coldwell to Smith, 13 Oct. 1933, W. Norman Smith Papers.
16. Douglas to J.G. McKay, n.d., cited by Aberhart in *Evidence*, p.65.
17. Miller's interview with Charles Palmer, 23 Sept. 1954.
18. A copy of the petition was received in the Premier's Office, 3 Nov. 1933, Premiers' Papers, file 624. The petition was submitted to the government in Feb. 1934, Premiers' Papers, file 71.
19. John H. Cope to George Hoadly, 11 July 1933, Social Credit Papers from the Alberta Dept. of Agriculture, file 1.
20. R.G. Reid to J.E. Brownlee, 31 Oct. 1933, Premiers' Papers, file 624.
21. Calgary *Herald*, 13 Nov. 1933, p.1.
22. Kerslake to Brownlee, 8 Sept. 1933; Brownlee to Kerslake, 1 Nov. 1933, Premiers' Papers, file 624.
23. Collins to Douglas, 2 Sept. 1933, W. Norman Smith Papers, file 21.
24. Douglas to Collins, 11 Oct. 1933, W. Norman Smith Papers, file 21.
25. Douglas to N.V. Fearnehough, 12 Oct. 1933, W. Norman Smith Papers, file 21.
26. Kerslake to Brownlee, 11 Nov. 1933, Premiers' Papers, file 624.
27. Brownlee to George E. Church, 22 Nov. 1933, Premiers' Papers, file 624.
28. Calgary *Herald*, 9 May 1933, p.1 and 10 May 1933, p.2.
29. *Ibid.*, 22 Sept. 1933, p.1; 23 Sept. 1933, p.17; 14 Nov. 1933, p.2; and 27 April 1934, p.1.
30. Coldwell to W. Norman Smith, 27 Sept. 1933, W. Norman Smith papers, file 30; Irving's interview with the Rev. Harrison Villett, 31 Aug. 1946, Irving Papers.
31. W.L. Bardsley to Collins, presumably 29 Nov. 1933, copy in the W. Norman Smith Papers, file 21. The same information was contained in a letter from Kerslake to Brownlee, 13 Dec. 1933, Premiers' Papers, file 624.
32. Collins to Brownlee, 22 Dec. 1933 and Brownlee to Collins, 26 Dec. 1933, Premiers' Papers, file 624.
33. W.H. Eraut to the editor, Calgary *Herald*, 26 Oct. 1933, p.4 and "A Citizen" to the editor, Calgary *Herald*, 16 Nov. 1933, p.4.
34. James Gaule to the editor, Calgary *Herald*, 11 Dec. 1933, p.4.
35. Aberhart to the editor, Calgary *Herald*, 15 Dec. 1933, p.4.
36. Gaule to the editor, Calgary *Herald*, 18 Dec. 1933, p.8.
37. Gaule to the editor, Calgary *Herald*, 27 Dec. 1933, p.4.
38. *Albertan*, 8 Jan. 1934, p.3.

39. Miller's interview with Amelia Turner Smith, 1 Sept. 1954; Calgary *Herald*, 9 Jan. 1934, p.3, 10 Jan. 1934, p.9, 12 Jan. 1934, p.13.
40. Calgary *Herald*, 12 Jan. 1934, p.3.
41. *Ibid.*, 15 Jan. 1934, p.3.
42. R.G. Reid to Brownlee, 31 Oct. 1933, Premiers' Papers, file 624; Miller's interviews with Charles Palmer and W. Norman Smith, Oct. 1954.
43. Miller's interview with Charles Palmer, Oct. 1954.
44. Calgary *Herald*, 20 Jan. 1934, p.2.
45. *Ibid.*, 18 Jan. 1934, p.18.
46. Miller's interview with J.J. Bowlen, April 16, 1954.
47. Calgary *Herald*, 10 Feb. 1934, p.11.
48. Brownlee to J. Showalter, 21 Dec. 1933, Premiers' Papers, file 624.
49. Douglas to James G. McKay, 7 Dec. 1933, Premiers' Papers, file 624.
50. Douglas to Collins, 8 Dec. 1933, Premiers' Papers, file 624.
51. Aberhart to C.M. Scarborough, 7 Feb. 1934, Irving Papers.
52. Telegrams, Brownlee to Douglas, 15 Feb. 1934; Douglas to Brownlee, 19 Feb. 1934, Premiers' Papers, file 624.
53. Telegrams, Brownlee to Kerslake, 22 Feb. 1934; Kerslake to Brownlee, 25 Feb. 1934, Premiers' Papers, file 624.
54. Calgary *Herald*, 24 Feb. 1934, p.8.
55. *Albertan*, 28 Feb. 1934, p.9.
56. A hostile source, *The Rebel*, 25 June 1937, p.3, cited a story, probably apocryphal, which claimed that the young man cried out, ''Arise and worship William Aberhart, the Son of God!''
57. *Albertan*, 28 Feb. 1934, p.8.
58. Bardsley to Palmer, date uncertain. The letter was seen and copied by Iris Miller.
59. Miller's interviews with Charles Palmer, 23 Sept. 1954 and Oct. 1954; Calgary *Herald*, 16 Feb. 1934, p.21.
60. Miller's interview with Charles Palmer, Oct. 1934.
61. Palmer to P. Neish, 18 July 1934. A copy of the letter was given by Palmer to Iris Miller.
62. Financial Records of the Calgary Prophetic Bible Institute.
63. Calgary *Herald*, 2 March 1934, p.23.
64. Aberhart to Irvine, 14 March 1934, Irving Papers.
65. Irvine to Smith, 14 March 1934, W. Norman Smith Papers, file 22.
66. Aberhart to A.B. Claypool, 14 March 1934, Irving Papers.

CHAPTER XII – ABERHART VERSUS DOUGLAS

1. *Evidence*, p.11.
2. *Ibid.*, p.18.
3. *Ibid.*, pp. 19-20, 62, 65.
4. *Ibid.*, pp.25-26. For more details on the motion picture projector episode see a tape by Norman Pickard, 1965, in the Aberhart Papers, item #70.239/77.
5. Collins' critique of the ''Yellow Pamphlet'' can be found in the Premiers' Papers, file 624.
6. *Evidence*, p.37.
7. Collins to Douglas, 6 March 1934, W. Norman Smith Papers, file 21.
8. *Evidence*, p.45.
9. *Ibid.*, pp.55-57.
10. *Ibid.*, pp.58-59.
11. *Ibid.*, p.60.
12. *Ibid.*, p.62.
13. *Ibid.*, pp.72-73.
14. *Ibid.*, p.73.

15. *Ibid.*
16. *Ibid.*, p.62.
17. *Ibid.*, p.75.
18. H.M. Lussier to the editor, Calgary *Herald*, 22 March 1934, p.4.
19. Minutes of the Calgary School Board, 14 March 1934, p.103.
20. Miller's interview with W.L. Bardsley, April 1955.
21. For coverage of Douglas's visit to Australia see *The New Era*, 18 Jan. 1934.
22. Collins to Douglas, 6 March 1934, W. Norman Smith Papers, file 21.
23. Calgary *Herald*, 29 March 1934, p.2.
24. Aberhart to F.E. Livingstone, 28 March 1934, Irving Papers.
25. Calgary *Herald*, 4 April 1934, p.1.
26. Miller's interview with J. Larkham Collins, 12 Sept., 1954.
27. *Evidence*, p.78.
28. *Ibid.*, pp.82-83.
29. *Ibid.*, p.97.
30. *Ibid.*, p.82.
31. *Ibid.*, p.83.
32. *Ibid.*, p.103.
33. *Ibid.*, p.95.
34. Douglas, *Warning Democracy*, p.163.
35. *Evidence*, p.95.
36. New York *Times*, 29 Jan. 1942, p.15.
37. C.B. Macpherson, "The Political Theory of Social Credit," *Canadian Journal of Economics and Political Science* 14 (1949), p.380.
38. *Evidence*, p.122.
39. *Ibid*, p.98.
40. Calgary *Herald*, 6 April 1934, p.1.
41. *Ibid.*, 9 April 1934, p.15.
42. Douglas, *The Monopoly of Credit*, pp.72 and 84.
43. Miller's interview with Charles Palmer, Oct. 1954.
44. Collins to Douglas, 16 April 1934, W. Norman Smith Papers, file 21.
45. Irving's interview with I.F. Fitch, 1 Aug. 1946, Irving Papers.
46. C.B.C. interview with Joe Unwin, in the documentary radio program, "Profiles in Politics: William Aberhart," aired 4 Oct. 1961.
47. *Evidence*, p.106.
48. *Evidence*, pp.123-124.
49. Calgary *Herald*, 18 April 1934, p.1. For a account of Douglas' performance in Ottawa written by William Irvine, see *The United Farmer*, 25 May 1934, pp.7-8.
50. Collins to Douglas, 16 April 1934, W. Norman Smith Papers, file 21.
51. Douglas to Collins, 20 April 1934, Premiers' Papers, file 624.
52. Douglas to Brownlee, 5 May 1934, Premiers' Papers, file 624 and Miller's interview with Dr. Tudor Jones, 4 June 1955.
53. Kerslake to Brownlee, 9 June 1934, Premiers' Papers, file 624.
54. Calgary *Herald*, 11 April 1934, p.3.
55. *Ibid.*, 20 April 1934, p.4 and Collins to Brownlee, 23 April 1934, Premiers' Papers, file 624.
56. Calgary *Herald*, 8 May 1934, p.9.
57. Charles A. Bowman, *Ottawa Editor* (Sidney: Gray's Publishing Ltd., 1966), p.189.
58. Calgary *Herald*, 12 May 1934, p.3.
59. *Evidence*, introduction.
60. F.W. Gershaw to Aberhart, 12 May 1934 and Aberhart to Gershaw, 16 May 1934, Irving Papers.
61. Aberhart to John C. Buckley, 23 May 1934, Irving Papers.

62. [W. Aberhart], "The B.N.A. Act and Social Credit" (Calgary: Calgary Prophetic Bible Institute, [1934], pp.6-7.
63. Miller's interview with Charles Palmer, Oct. 1954.
64. Full coverage of Brownlee's trial was given in *The United Farmer*, 6 July 1934.
65. D.M. Duggan to W. Norman Smith, 19 July 1934, W. Norman Smith Papers, file 8.

CHAPTER XIII – WHERE WILL ALL THE MONEY COME FROM?

1. Elliott's interview with Eva Reid, 6 June 1972.
2. *Alberta Social Credit Chronicle*, 3 Aug. 1934, p.3.
3. William Aberhart, "Social Credit: History and Character," (pamphlet), *c.*1934, pp.5-6.
4. Collins to Douglas, 17 Aug. 1934, W. Norman Smith Papers, file 32.
5. Douglas to Norman F. Priestly, 18 Sept. 1934, W. Norman Smith Papers, file 21.
6. Douglas to Priestly, 21 Sept. 1934, W. Norman Smith Papers, file 21.
7. Priestly to Douglas, 3 Oct. 1934, W. Norman Smith Papers, file 21.
8. William Irvine to Smith, 31 Oct. 1934, W. Norman Smith Papers, file 22.
9. Smith to Irvine, 9 Nov. 1934, W. Norman Smith Papers, file 22.
10. Maurice Colbourne, *Economic Nationalism*, pp.91-92.
11. *Man from Mars* script, 27 Nov. 1934. The scripts, which were in the possession of Clifford Willmott in 1954, were copied by Iris Miller. The whereabouts of the originals are now unknown.
12. *Ibid.*, 20 Nov. 1934.
13. *Ibid.*, 4 Dec. 1934.
14. *Ibid.*, 8 Jan. 1935.
15. *Ibid.*, 24 Oct. 1934.
16. It should be noted, however, that Aberhart's conception of Social Credit was far more concrete that Douglas's.
17. Aberhart used this example at the 1935 U.F.A. Convention. See the transcript of Aberhart's speech, p.12, W. Norman Smith Papers, file 90.
18. Douglas, *Canada's Bankers and Canada's Credit*, pp.111-116. Douglas used almost the same example when he testified before the Macmillan Committee on Finance and Industry in 1930.
19. See *Albertan*, 16 Nov. 1934, p.4.
20. See H.T.N. Gaitskell, "Four Monetary Heretics," in G.D.H. Cole, ed. *What Everybody Wants to Know About Money: A Planned Outline of Monetary Problems* (London: Victor Gollancz, Ltd., 1933), pp.346 ff.
21. *Man from Mars* script, 8 Jan. 1935.
22. Stephen Leacock, "Alberta's Fairy Story," *The Commentator*, date unknown, p.70.
23. See *Alberta Social Credit Chronicle*, 4 Jan. 1935, p.1.
24. *Man from Mars* script, 13 Nov. 1934.
25. *Ibid.*, 4 Dec. 1934.
26. *Ibid.*, 30 Oct. 1934.
27. *Ibid.*, 13 Nov. 1934. See *Albertan*, 9 Nov. 1934, p.4.
28. *Man from Mars* script, 6 Nov. 1934.
29. *Ibid.*
30. *Ibid.*, 18 Dec. 1934.
31. *Ibid.*
32. *Ibid.*, 25 Dec. 1934.
33. *Ibid.*, 22 Jan. 1935.
34. Aberhart to Irene Eberhardt, Christmas 1934, Irene Barrett Papers.
35. *Man from Mars* script, 1 Jan. 1935.
36. *Alberta Social Credit Chronicle*, 18 Jan. 1935, p.4.

37. Aberhart's speech, U.F.A. 1935 Convention transcript, p.2, W. Norman Smith Papers, file 90.
38. *Ibid.*, p.6.
39. *Ibid.*, p.46.
40. Irvine's speech, U.F.A. 1935 Convention transcript, p.62.
41. Miller's interview with Norman F. Priestly, 29 April 1954.
42. *Alberta Social Credit Chronicle*, 25 Jan. 1935, p.1.
43. Henry E. Spencer to Smith, 19 Jan. 1935, W. Norman Smith Papers, file 24.
44. H.B. Hill's unpublished memoirs, p.18.

CHAPTER XIV – ALBERTA'S MESSIAH

1. *Man from Mars* script, 13 Nov. 1934.
2. *Alberta Social Credit Chronicle*, 5 Oct. 1934, p.2.
3. Aberhart's CFCN broadcast, 9 April 1935, W. Norman Smith Papers.
4. *Ibid.*, 26 March 1935.
5. Miller's interview with E.C. Manning, 5 and 6 May 1954.
6. Miller's interview with C.M. Willmott, 24 Feb. 1954. See also the *Alberta Social Credit Chronicle*, 12 April 1935, p.3.
7. Smith to Henry E. Spencer, 29 Jan. 1935, W. Norman Smith Papers, file 24.
8. Aberhart's CFCN broadcast, 24 Feb. 1935.
9. Copies of the U.F.A. broadcasts can also be found in the W. Norman Smith Papers.
10. *Alberta Social Credit Chronicle*, 14 March 1935, pp.1-2.
11. *Albertan*, 13 May 1935, p.2.
12. C.H. Douglas, *Brief for the Prosecution* (Liverpool: K.R.P. Publications Ltd., 1945), p.15.
13. Arthur Brenton to Smith, 15 Feb. 1935, W. Norman Smith Papers, file 9.
14. Calgary *Herald*, 6 March 1935, pp.1 and 3.
15. *Alberta Social Credit Chronicle*, 1 March 1935, p.1.
16. *The United Farmer*, 8 March 1935, pp.1 and 4.
17. R.G. Reid to Aberhart, 7 March 1935, Premiers' Papers, file 1070.
18. Aberhart to Reid, 11 March 1935; Reid to Aberhart, 18 March 1935; Aberhart to Reid, 25 March 1935; and Reid to Aberhart, 30 March 1935, Premiers' Papers, file 1070.
19. Calgary *Herald*, 11 May 1935, p.5.
20. Douglas's speech at Buxton, England, 9 June 1934, published under the title, *The Nature of Democracy* (Stratford-on Avon: K.R.P. Publications Ltd.) *c*.1934, pp. 10 and 12.
21. *Ibid.*
22. *Alberta Social Credit Chronicle*, 5 April 1935, p.4.
23. See John S. Conway, *The Nazi Persecution of the Christian Churches, 1933-45* (Toronto: Ryerson Press, 1968), p.155.
24. Calgary *Herald*, 5 April 1935, p.5.
25. Charles A. Grant to the editor, Calgary *Herald*, 27 April 1935, p.5 and Elliott's telephone interview with Archie Key, 11 May 1979.
26. Calgary *Herald*, 6 April 1935, p.5.
27. *Alberta Social Credit Chronicle*, 12 April 1935, p.3 and Aberhart to Reid, 9 April 1935, Premiers' Papers, file 1070.
28. Miller's interview with C.M. Willmott, May 1954.
29. Calgary *Herald*, 6 April 1935, p.6.
30. Aberhart's CFCN broadcast, 3 Feb. 1935.
31. *Ibid.*, 24 March 1935 and 24 May 1935.
32. Harry Humble's broadcast on CFAC., 24 March 1935, W. Norman Smith Papers, file 42. See also his *Social Credit for Alberta?* (Calgary: W.D. Stovel, 1935), p.8.

33. Norman F. Priestly's broadcast, n.d., W. Norman Smith Papers, file 42.
34. Aberhart's CFCN broadcast, 9 April 1935.
35. *Ibid.*, 19 April 1935.
36. *Ibid.*, 30 April 1935, file 81.
37. J. Fergus Kirk, "Social Credit and the Word of God," open letter, [1935]. We are indebted to Mary Macomber of Berean Bible College who had saved a copy of that letter.
38. Aberhart's CFCN broadcasts, 21 and 28 April 1935.
39. Aberhart received a lot of mail criticizing him for his attack on Prairie Bible Institute and he read those letters over the air. Information on Prairie Bible Institute's loss of support was gained by Elliott's interview with the Rev. L.E. Maxwell, 16 April 1979.
40. Aberhart's CFCN broadcast, 21 April 1935.
41. *Ibid.*, 7 May 1935.
42. *Ibid.*, 21 April 1935.
43. W.E. Mann, *Sect, Cult and Church in Alberta.*
44. Roger P. Kirk to Aberhart, 11 April 1936, Premiers' Papers, file 637.
45. Elliott's interview with the Rev. W.J. Laing, n.d. Isaac McCune, who was an elder in a Brethren Assembly, was a successful Social Credit candidate in 1935. See *Canadian Parliamentary Guide*, 1936, pp.389-90.
46. Cardston *News*, 20 Aug. 1935, p.2.
47. Aberhart referred to Seventh-Day Adventist fears in his broadcast, 11 Aug. 1935. See also telegram from Alfred Rawlins to Aberhart, 18 Nov. 1936, Premiers' Papers, file 1126.
48. H.L. Malliah, "A Socio-Historical Study of the Legislators of Alberta, 1905-1967" (unpublished Ph.D. dissertation, University of Alberta, 1970), p.69.
49. Owen A. Anderson, "The Alberta Social Credit Party: An Empirical Analysis of Membership, Characteristics, Participation and Opinions" (unpublished Ph.D. dissertation, University of Alberta, 1972), pp. 215-219.
50. *Ibid.*, p.218a.
51. Calgary *Herald*, 20 April 1935, p.5.
52. "No Sig." to editor, *ibid.*, 6 April 1935, p.6.
53. A.E. Todd to editor, *ibid.*
54. "Fairplay" to editor, *ibid.*
55. Harry Humble, "Just Another Party," CFAC broadcast, 7 April 1935, reprinted in his booklet, *Social Credit: Democracy vs. Dictatorship* (Calgary: W.D. Stovel, 1935), pp.4-5.
56. *Alberta Social Credit Chronicle*, 8 March 1935, p.4.
57. *Ibid.*, 12 April 1935, p.4.
58. *Ibid.*, 19 April 1935, pp.1 and 5; Elliott's telephone interview with Archie Key, 11 May 1979.
59. Harry Humble, *Social Credit*, p.3.
60. Aberhart's CFCN broadcast, 14 April 1935.
61. Instrument 2485 D.Q., Land Titles Office, Calgary.
62. Instrument 2463 E.N., Land Titles Office, Calgary.
63. Harry Humble, *Social Credit*, p.3.
64. Calgary *Herald*, 23 April 1935, p.1.
65. *Alberta Social Credit Chronicle*, 3 May 1935, p.1.
66. Calgary *Herald*, 29 April 1935, p.11.
67. *Ibid.*, p.4.
68. Elliott's telephone interview with Archie Key, 14 Jan. 1978.
69. Calgary *Herald*, 11 May 1935, p.5.
70. J.J. Zubick to the editor, Calgary *Herald*, 27 April 1935, p.5.
71. Aberhart's CFCN broadcast, 7 April 1935.
72. *Ibid.*, 5 May 1935.

73. *Ibid.*, 7 April 1935.
74. *Ibid.*, 14 April 1935.
75. Calgary School Board Minutes, 3 May 1935, p.139.
76. Aberhart's CFCN broadcast, 9 April 1935.
77. *Ibid.*, 9 June 1935.
78. Hewlett Johnson, *The Soviet Power* (New York: International Publishers, 1941).
79. John, Duke of Bedford. *Silver Plated Spoon* (London: Cassell and Company, 1959), p.161.
80. Ezra Pound, *Social Credit: An Impact* (London: Stanley Nott Ltd., 1935), p.5.
81. Hugh Dalton's introduction to W.R. Hiskett, *Social Credits or Socialism* (London: Victor Gollancz Ltd., 1935), p.8.
82. Aberhart's CFCN broadcast, 9 April 1935.
83. Calgary *Herald*, 11 May 1935, p.1.
84. *Alberta Social Credit Chronicle*, 31 May 1935, pp.1, 4 and 5.
85. Douglas, *Social Credit*, p.199.
86. C.H. Douglas, *First Interim Report on the Possibilities of the Application of Social Credit Principles to the Province of Alberta* (Edmonton: King's Printer, 1935).
87. *Ibid.*, pp.7-8.
88. Douglas to R.G. Reid, 23 May 1935, included in the above, p.10.
89. Douglas to J.R. Lymburn, 1 June 1935, included in the above, pp.14-15.
90. Alberta, *The Constitutionality and Economic Aspects of Social Credit: Evidence of Dean Weir and Professor Elliott before the Agricultural Committee of the Alberta Legislature, 1935* (Edmonton: King's Printer, 1935).
91. Larry Hannant, "The Calgary Working Class and the Social Credit Movement in Alberta, 1932-35," *Labour/Le Travail* 16 (Fall 1985), p.109.
92. W. Aberhart, *Social Credit Manual: Social Credit as Applied to the Province of Alberta* (Calgary: Western Printing, 1935), pp.7 and 15.
93. *Ibid.*, pp.21, 33, and 47.
94. *Ibid.*, p.33. See Edward Bellamy, *Equality* (New York: D. Appleton and Company, 1897), p.41.
95. Aberhart, *Social Credit Manual*, p.55.
96. *Ibid.*, pp.51 and 61.
97. *Ibid.*, pp.51-53.
98. *Ibid.*, p.57.
99. *Ibid.*, pp.19-21.
100. *Ibid.*, p.27.
101. *Ibid.*, p.62.
102. Calgary *Herald*, 2 July 1935, p.1; C.W. Gordon, *et al*, "The Trekkers: A Statement — A Protest — An Appeal," 1935, from the W. Norman Smith Papers, file 139.
103. *Alberta Social Credit Chronicle*, 12 July 1935, pp.1 and 6.
104. Miller's interview with Dr. Victor Wright, 1 Oct. 1954.
105. Calgary *Herald*, 27 July 1935, p.5.
106. Reported in *The Rebel*, 7 Jan. 1938, p.3.
107. Aberhart's CFCN broadcast, 7 July 1935.
108. *Ibid.*, 3 May 1935 and 12 Aug. 1935.
109. John A. Irving, "Psychological Aspects of Social Credit in Alberta," *Canadian Journal of Psychology* 1 (1947), p.85.
110. Irving's interviews with J.J. MacLellan, 12 July 1947 and W.R. Howson, n.d., Irving Papers. See also Miller's interview with J.E. Brownlee, 21 April 1954.
111. Edmonton *Journal*, 6 July 1935, p.1 and *The United Farmer*, 12 July 1935, p.9.
112. Reported in the *Albertan*, 22 July 1935, p.2.

113. Aberhart's CFCN broadcast, 11 Aug. 1935.
114. *Alberta Social Credit Chronicle*, 7 Dec. 1934, p.2.
115. *Ibid.*, 16 Aug. 1935, p.8.
116. Miller's interview with Dr. Victor Wright, 1 Oct. 1954.
117. *Alberta Social Credit Chronicle*, 16 Aug. 1935 (Supplement), p.4.
118. Calgary *Herald*, 8 Aug. 1935, p.3.
119. Miller's interview with J.E. Brownlee, 21 April 1954.
120. Miller's interview with Norman F. Priestly, 29 April 1954.
121. Aberhart's CFCN broadcast, 11 Aug. 1935.
122. H.B. Hill's diary, 20 Aug. 1935.
123. Calgary *Herald*, 21 Aug. 1935, p.9.
124. Aberhart's CFCN broadcast, 21 Aug. 1935.
125. Calgary *Herald*, 21 Aug. 1935, p.9.
126. *Alberta Social Credit Chronicle*, 23 Aug. 1935, p.8.
127. I.F. Fitch to Aberhart, 29 Nov. 1935, Premiers' Papers, file 1053. All of the profits from the sale of the "Blue Manual" were exhausted paying for Roger's bills and the legal expenses. Later Aberhart had Rogers and his family shipped to another province where they would no longer be an embarrassment to him. See I.F. Fitch to Aberhart, 27 Feb. 1936, Premiers' Papers, file 1053.
128. Calgary *Herald*, 16 Aug. 1935, p.13. According to "Hilly" Hill's diary, this was going to be the practice on election day also. See his entry for 20 Aug. 1935.
129. Irving, *Social Credit Movement in Alberta*, p.253.
130. *Alberta Social Credit Chronicle*, 30 Aug. 1935, pp.1-2.
131. Hannant, p.116.

CHAPTER XV – "VICTORIOUS! WHEN COULD YOU COME?"

1. Calgary *Herald*, 26 Aug. 1935, p.1.
2. Mackenzie King Diary, 23 Aug. 1935, Public Archives of Canada.
3. Reported in the *Literary Digest*, 7 Sept. 1935, p.15.
4. Reprinted in the Calgary *Herald*, 28 Aug. 1935, p.4.
5. *The Pentecostal Testimony*, Sept. 1935.
6. Ottawa *Citizen*, 24 Aug. 1935, editorial page.
7. Hanna *Herald*, 22 Aug. 1935, p.2.
8. *Alberta Labour News*, 24 Aug. 1935, p.4.
9. Calgary *Herald*, 23 Aug. 1935, p.4.
10. *Albertan*, 23 Aug. 1935, p.1.
11. *Alberta Social Credit Chronicle*, 23 Aug. 1935, p.7.
12. *Ibid.*, 13 Sept. 1935, p.6.
13. *Ibid.*, 30 Aug. 1935, p.1.
14. *Huron Expositor*, 30 Aug. 1935, p.3.
15. Douglas to Aberhart, 23 Aug. 1923, Premiers' Papers, file 646.
16. Hewlett Johnson to Aberhart, 27 Aug. 1935, Premiers' Papers, file 646.
17. Aberhart to Douglas, 24 Aug. 1935, reprinted in Douglas, *The Alberta Experiment*, p.125.
18. Douglas to Aberhart, 26 Aug. 1935, *ibid.*
19. Aberhart to Douglas, 27 Nov. 1935, *ibid.*, p.152.
20. Calgary *Herald*, 7 Aug. 1935, p.9.
21. *Ibid.*, 28 Aug. 1935, p.2.
22. *Ibid.*, pp.1-2.
23. Miller's interview with Dr. Victor Wright, 1 Oct. 1954.
24. *Alberta Social Credit Chronicle*, 16 Aug. 1935, p.1.
25. Miller's interview with J.W. Hugill, 8 and 9 June 1954.
26. Calgary *Herald*, 31 Aug. 1935, p.1.
27. *Alberta Social Credit Chronicle*, 6 Sept. 1935, p.4.

28. Fred Stone Diary, 19 May 1935.
29. Calgary School Board to Aberhart, 16 Sept. 1935, Premiers' Papers, file 1458.
30. Aberhart to Douglas, 4 Sept. 1935, reprinted in Douglas, *The Alberta Experiment*, p.126.
31. Aberhart to R.B. Bennett, 4 Sept. 1935, Premiers' Papers, file 1441.
32. Douglas to Aberhart, 5 Sept. 1935, Premiers' Papers, file 1081.
33. Douglas to Aberhart, 6 Sept. 1935, Premiers' Papers, file 1081.
34. Calgary *Herald*, 12 Sept. 1935, p.1.
35. *Ibid.*, 11 Sept. 1935, p.3.
36. R.B. Bennett to Aberhart, 4 Sept. 1935, Premiers' Papers, file 1458.
37. Bowman, *Ottawa Editor*, pp.185-186.
38. *Alberta Social Credit Chronicle*, 6 Sept. 1935, p.8.
39. Edmonton *Bulletin*, 4 Oct. 1935, p.2.
40. Douglas to Aberhart, 11 Sept. 1935, Premiers' Papers, file 1081. Mackenzie King's diary confirms Douglas's belief that Montagu Norman had tried to persuade R.B. Bennett not to help Alberta. See the entry for 3 January 1936.
41. Bowman, *Ottawa Editor*, p.193.
42. Miller's interview with John Hugill, 8 and 9 June 1954.
43. H.B. Brougham to Rev. Michael James Gallagher, Bishop of Detroit, 10 Sept. 1935, copy in Premiers' Papers, file 1084.
44. Calgary *Herald*, 18 Sept. 1935, p.1.
45. *Ibid.*, 28 Nov. 1935, p.1.
46. *Huron Expositor*, 30 Aug. 1935, p.3.
47. Edmonton *Journal*, 16 Sept. 1935, p.2.
48. Calgary *Herald* 16 Sept. 1935, p.1. See also *Huron Expositor*, 20 Sept. 1935, pp.1 and 4.
49. Aberhart to Douglas, 24 Sept. 1935, first letter of that date, Premiers' Papers, file 1082.
50. Aberhart to Douglas, 24 Sept. 1935, third letter of that date, Premiers' Papers, file 1082.
51. Aberhart to Douglas, 24 Sept. 1935, first letter of that date, Premiers' Papers, file 1082.
52. Aberhart to Douglas, 24 Sept. 1935, second letter of that date, Premiers' Papers, file 1082.
53. Miller's interview with John Hugill, 8 June 1954.
54. Miller's intervew with Dr. Victor Wright, 1 Oct. 1954.
55. Calgary *Herald*, 25 Sept. 1935, p.2.
56. *Ibid.*, 27 Sept. 1935, p.15.
57. *Alberta Social Credit Chronicle*, 20 Sept. 1935, p.1.
58. *Ibid.*, 27 Sept. 1935, p.1.
59. Aberhart's broadcast, 21 Aug. 1935, W. Norman Smith papers, file 83.
60. Douglas to Aberhart, 5 Sept. 1935, Premiers' Papers, file 1081.
61. Douglas to Aberhart, 28 Aug. 1935, reprinted in Douglas, *The Alberta Experiment*, pp.125-126.
62. Douglas to Aberhart, 5 Sept. 1935, Premiers' Papers, file 1081.
63. R.G. Williams to Aberhart, 18 Sept. 1935, Premiers' Papers, file 1071 and Aberhart to Douglas, 24 Sept. 1935, first letter of that date, Premiers' Papers, file 1082.
64. Elliott's interview with Charles R. Pearce, 18 Dec. 1973.
65. Edmonton *Bulletin*, 1 Oct. 1935, p.2.
66. Mackenzie King Diary, 25 Sept. 1935.
67. Reported in H. Napier Moore, "What of Social Credit?" *Maclean's Magazine*, 15 Jan. 1936, p.15.
68. J.W. Hugill to R.J. Magor, 30 Sept. 1935 and Magor to Hugill, 5 Oct. 1935, Premiers' Papers, file 988.

69. Aberhart to Edith Armstrong, 5 Oct. 1935, Premiers' Papers, file 1137a.
70. *Alberta Social Credit Chronicle*, 15 Nov. 1935, p.1.
71. Mackenzie King Diary, 14 [sic] Oct. 1935.
72. Douglas to Aberhart, 15 Oct. 1935, Premiers' Papers, file 1081.
73. H.B. Hill to Aberhart, 23 Oct. 1935, Premiers' Papers, file 1059.
74. *Alberta Social Credit Chronicle*, 8 Nov. 1935, p.1.
75. O.S. Longman's interview with John Hugill, n.d., Hugill Papers, file 44.
76. Aberhart to Mrs. J.N. Culshaw, 13 May 1937, Premiers' Papers, file 1053. Aberhart may have lived in the hotels in deliberate imitation of his friend R.B. Bennett, who lived in the Palliser Hotel and Château Laurier.
77. Miller's interview with Dr. Victor Wright, 1 Oct. 1954.
78. Calgary *Herald*, 21 Oct. 1935, p.11 and *Alberta Social Credit Chronicle*, 25 Oct. 1935, p.1.
79. Douglas to Aberhart, 29 Oct. 1935, Premiers' Papers, file 1081.
80. Calgary *Herald*, 1 Nov. 1935, p.1.
81. *Alberta Social Credit Chronicle*, 29 Nov. 1935, p.1.
82. *Ibid.*, 8 Nov. 1935, p.1.
83. *Ibid.*, 22 Nov. 1935, p.1.
84. *Ibid.*, 15 Nov. 1935, p.1.
85. See Premiers' Papers, file 1134.
86. *Alberta Social Credit Chronicle*, 15 Nov. 1935, p.5.
87. Brougham to Aberhart, 3 Oct. 1935; Brougham to Aberhart, 8 Oct. 1935, Premiers' Papers, file 1084.
88. See Brougham's press release, 26 Nov. 1935, W. Norman Smith Papers, file 89.
89. Calgary *Herald*, 27 Nov. 1935, p.1.
90. *Ibid.*, 28 Nov. 1935, p.1 and Brougham to Aberhart, 28 Nov. 1935, Premiers' Papers, file 1084.
91. Charles A. Bowman to Brougham, 2 Dec. 1935, Premiers' Papers, file 1084.
92. *Albertan*, 27 Nov. 1935, pp.1-2.
93. Calgary *Herald*, 28 Nov. 1935, p.1.
94. Aberhart to Douglas, 27 Nov. 1935, reprinted in Douglas, *The Alberta Experiment*, pp.153-154. See Brougham to Aberhart, 8 Oct. 1935, Premiers' Papers, file 1084.
95. *Alberta Social Credit Chronicle*, 6 Dec. 1935, p.1.
96. Douglas to Aberhart, 5 Dec. 1935, reprinted in Douglas, *The Alberta Experiment*, p.158.
97. Aberhart to Douglas, 6 Dec. 1935, *ibid.*, p.158.
98. Magor to Aberhart, 29 Nov. 1935, Premiers' Papers, file 987 and a brief, presumably prepared by Magor, Aberhart Papers, item #70.239/6.
99. *Albertan*, 6 Dec 1935, p.2.
100. Calgary *Herald*, 9 Dec. 1935, p.16.
101. *Ibid.*, 10 Dec. 1935, p.4.
102. Mackenzie King Diary, 11 Dec. 1935.
103. Douglas to Aberhart, 11 Dec. 1935, reprinted in Douglas, *The Alberta Experiment*, pp.160-161.
104. Aberhart to Douglas, 19 Dec. 1935, *ibid.*, p.161.
105. Aberhart to Douglas, 23 Dec. 1935, *ibid.*, pp.162-163.
106. Douglas to Aberhart, 27 Dec. 1935, *ibid.*, pp.163-164.
107. Executive Council to Douglas, 31 Dec. 1935, *ibid.*, p.164.
108. Douglas to Executive Council, 31 Dec. 1935, *ibid.*, pp. 164-167.
109. Aberhart to C.A. Bowman, 11 Jan. 1936, Premiers' Papers, file 1053.
110. Aberhart to Douglas, 24 Jan. 1936, reprinted in Douglas, *The Alberta Experiment*, p.169.
111. Douglas to Aberhart, 6 Feb. 1936 and 13 Feb. 1936, *ibid.*, pp.171-175.
112. Aberhart to Douglas, 6 Feb. 1936, *ibid.*, pp.172-174.

113. Douglas to Aberhart, 18 Feb. 1936, *ibid.*, pp.178-181.
114. Douglas to Aberhart, 24 Feb. 1936, *ibid.*, pp.184-189.
115. Aberhart to Douglas, cable, 12 March 1936, Premiers' Papers, file 1081. Douglas incorrectly dated the cable 13 March 1936 in his *Alberta Experiment*, pp.190-191.
116. Douglas to Aberhart, 13 March 1936, *ibid.*, pp. 191-194. See also the contract between Douglas and the Alberta government, 29 March 1935, Premier's Papers, file 1081.
117. Douglas to Aberhart, cable, 13 March 1936, *ibid.*, p.194.
118. Douglas to Aberhart, 24 March 1936, *ibid.*, pp.197-198.
119. See transcript of Douglas's evidence in Hiskett, *Social Credits or Socialism*, pp.33 and 52.
120. Douglas to Collins, 11 Oct. 1933, W. Norman Smith Papers, file 21 and Calgary *Herald*, 9 April 1934, p.15.

CHAPTER XVI – "I AM GLAD THERE WILL BE NO NEWSPAPERS IN HEAVEN"

1. H. Napier Moore, "What of Social Credit?: Impartial notes on the progress of Alberta's New Prophet," *Maclean's Magazine*, 1 Jan. 1936, pp.14-15, 35-36; and 15 Jan. 1936, pp.15, 40-41.
2. *Alberta Social Credit Chronicle*, 10 Jan. 1936, p.1.
3. Moore, "What of Social Credit?" *Maclean's Magazine*, 15 Jan. 1936, pp.40-41.
4. Walter Davenport, "Milk and Honey, Ltd., or Another Paradise Lost," *Collier's Magazine*, 25 Jan. 1936, p.11.
5. *Ibid.*, p.54.
6. *Ibid.*, p.56.
7. Aberhart to Ralph V. Blake, 30 Jan. 1936, Premiers' Papers, file 1153.
8. *Albertan*, 15 Jan. 1936, p.1.
9. *Alberta Social Credit Chronicle*, 17 Jan. 1936, p.1.
10. *Ibid.*, and Calgary *Herald*, 18 Jan. 1936, p.16; Aberhart to Dr. William Spankie, 6 Jan. 1936, Premiers' Papers, file 1038.
11. C.R. Pearce to Aberhart, 21 March 1936, Premiers' Papers, file 1059; Elliott's interview with C.R. Pearce, 18 Dec. 1973; C.R. Pearce Papers, files 6-7. See also H.B. Hill Collection in the Devonian Foundation Papers.
12. Edmonton *Journal*, 27 Jan. 1936, p.9.
13. Aberhart to the Rev. Hewlett Johnson, 29 Jan. 1936, Premiers' Papers, file 1071.
14. *The United Farmer*, 25 Jan. 1936, pp.1, 6-7.
15. William Irvine to Aberhart, *People's Weekly*, 25 Jan. 1936, p.4.
16. William Irvine to Aberhart, *People's Weekly*, 1 Feb. 1936, p.4.
17. Calgary *Herald*, 18 Jan. 1936, p.16. Petitions had already been circulating to get Aberhart off the air before that incident. See *Alberta Social Credit Chronicle*, 10 Jan. 1936, p.1.
18. John J. Barr, *The Dynasty: The Rise and Fall of Social Credit in Alberta* (Toronto: McClelland and Stewart Ltd., 1974), pp.90-91.
19. Bruce Hutchison, *Far Side of the Street* (Toronto: Macmillan of Canada, 1976), p.105.
20. *The United Farmer* 28 Feb. 1936, p.12.
21. Douglas to Aberhart, 13 March 1936, reprinted in Douglas, *The Alberta Experiment*, pp.191-194.
22. *Statutes of Alberta*, I Edward VIII, 1936, chapter 76.
23. *Ibid.*, chapter 69.
24. *Ibid.*, chapter 50.
25. *Ibid.*, chapter 82. The Progressives earlier had proposed a recall act, but

Aberhart's recall act required a much higher percentage of votes to become effective.

26. *Ibid.*, chapter 88.
27. *Ibid.*, chapter 85. See Calgary *Herald*, 15 April 1936, p.16.
28. See Aberhart to editor, Brantford *Daily Courier*, 10 March 1910, p.4. Aberhart's plan for consolidating the school districts was actually borrowed from the previous U.F.A. administration, which had been unable to implement it. For more details on Aberhart's career as minister of Education see Barry C. Oviatt, "The Papers of William Aberhart as Minister of Education, 1935-1943" (unpublished M.Ed. thesis, University of Alberta, 1971).
29. Calgary *Herald*, 18 Dec. 1935, p.1.
30. *Alberta Social Credit Chronicle*, 10 Jan. 1936, p.1.
31. *Statutes of Alberta*, I Edward VIII, 1936, chapter 66.
32. *Ibid.*, chapter 67.
33. See Premiers' Papers, file 922.
34. Edmonton *Journal*, 27 Jan. 1936, p.10.
35. *Statutes of Alberta*, I Edward VIII, 1936, chapter 3.
36. *Alberta Social Credit Chronicle*, 17 Jan. 1936, p.1. The *Alberta Temperance Review*, May 1940, criticized Aberhart's government for making a profit on liquor.
37. W.L. Walsh to Aberhart, 21 March 1936, Premiers' Papers, file 1038.
38. Calgary *Herald*, 10 March 1936, p.4.
39. *Ibid.*, 1 April 1936, p.3.
40. *Statutes of Alberta*, I Edward VIII, 1936, chapter 5.
41. Douglas to Aberhart, 24 Feb. 1936, reprinted in Douglas, *The Alberta Experiment*, pp.184-189.
42. Aberhart to Douglas, 6 Feb. 1936, *ibid.*, p.173.
43. Calgary *Herald*, 1 April 1936, p.1. The defaulted bonds were not refunded until 1945 by Manning's government. See Hugh J. Whalen, "The Distinctive Legislation of the Government of Alberta (1935-1950)" (Unpublished M.A. thesis, University of Alberta, 1951), pp.154-158.
44. *Statutes of Alberta*, I Edward VIII, 1936, chapter 8.
45. Fred Kennedy, *Alberta Was My Beat* (Calgary: the *Albertan,* 1975), p.232.
46. Protest poem found in the Premiers' Papers, file 1247a.
47. Calgary *Herald*, 15 April 1936, p.20.
48. Edmonton *Journal*, 27 Jan. 1936, p.10
49. J.D. Adam to Aberhart, 13 March 1936, Premiers' Papers, file 1231.
50. *Record of Proceedings of the Twelfth Meeting of the Alberta Conference of the United Church of Canada.* 26 May to 1 June 1936, Robertson United Church, Edmonton, Alberta, pp.11-13.
51. Aberhart to James Cooper, 21 Jan. 1936, Premiers' Papers, file 1458.
52. *Statutes of Alberta*, I Edward VIII, 1936, chapter 5.
53. Robert G.L. Waite, *Vanguard of Nazism: The Free Corps Movement in Postwar Germany, 1918-1923* (New York: W.W. Norton and Company, Inc., 1952), pp.82-83.
54. See the Alberta government's Agricultural Committee's hearing on the scrip program at Raymond, Alberta, 8 April 1935, W. Norman Smith Papers, file 140.
55. Aberhart to Magor, 29 April 1936, Premiers' Papers, file 988.
56. Hewlett Johnson to Aberhart, 24 Feb. 1936; Aberhart to Johnson, 11 March 1936; Johnson to Aberhart, 27 March 1936, Premiers' Papers, file 1071; and Aberhart to L.A. Haire, 19 March 1936, Premiers' Papers, file 1247a.
57. Magor to Aberhart, 5 May 1936, Premiers' Papers, file 988.
58. Victoria *Daily Times*, 14 Dec. 1923, p.12; 28 Feb. 1925, p.12; and Bulletin, Victoria City Temple, 9 Aug. 1931, in the Victoria City Temple documents, Registry of Companies, Victoria.

59. E.S. Woodward to Aberhart, 26 Aug. 1935, Premiers' Papers, file 1085. Aberhart frequently received unsolicited advice from British-Israelites who had their own economic schemes.
60. Aberhart to E.S. Woodward, 24 March 1936; Woodward to Aberhart, 28 March 1936, Premiers' Papers, file 1085.
61. Woodward to Aberhart, 4 May 1936, Premiers' Papers, file 1085.
62. Aberhart to Woodward, 11 May 1936, Premiers' Papers, file 1085.
63. H.B. Hill to Aberhart, 11 May 1936, Premiers' Papers, file 1038.
64. Miller's interview with Stewart Cameron, 8 Aug. 1954.
65. Woodward to Aberhart, 13 and 14 July 1936, Premiers' Papers, file 1085.
66. Aberhart to Woodward, 15 July 1936, Premiers' Papers, file 1085.
67. Edmonton *Journal*, 5 Aug. 1936, p.1.
68. *Ibid.*, 8 Aug. 1936, pp.1-2.
69. *Ibid.*, 5 Aug. 1936, p.9 and 6 Aug. 1936, p.9.
70. Alberta Provincial Douglas Social Credit Association to Aberhart, 9 July 1936, Premiers' Papers, file 1066.
71. Edmonton *Journal*, 5 Aug. 1936, p.10.
72. Edmonton *Bulletin*, 20 July 1936, p.1.
73. Edmonton *Journal*, 4 Aug. 1936, p.1.
74. *Ibid.*, 3 Aug. 1936, p.10.
75. *Albertan*, 31 July 1936, p.2. For a copy of the Citizens' Registration Covenant see Premiers' Papers, file 1138.
76. Edmonton *Journal*, 31 July 1936, pp.1-2.
77. *Ibid.*, 1 Aug. 1936, pp.1 and 3; 5 Aug. 1936, p.9.
78. Miller's interview with Mrs. W.P. Harvey, 13 Nov. 1954.
79. *Albertan*, 22 Aug. 1936, p.1.
80. Edmonton *Journal*, 10 Aug. 1936, p.5.
81. Hill Diary, 12 Aug. 1936, Devonian Foundation Papers.
82. *Ibid.*, and entry for 15 Aug. 1936.
83. *Ibid.*, 22 Aug. 1936.
84. Calgary *Herald*, 24 Aug. 1936, p.1.
85. *Albertan*, 24 Aug. 1936, pp.1-2.
86. *Statutes of Alberta*, I Edward VIII, Session 2, 1936, chapter 1.
87. W.L. Walsh to Aberhart, 31 Aug. 1936, Premiers' Papers, file 1038.
88. *Statutes of Alberta*, I Edward VIII, Session 2, chapter 2.
89. *Ibid.*, chapter 3.
90. *Ibid.*, chapter 4.
91. *Ibid.*, chapter 11.
92. *Ibid.*, chapter 16.
93. H.B. Hill to Aberhart, 19 Oct. 1936, Premiers' Papers, file 1059.
94. Aberhart to Charles McNutt [sic], 3 Nov. 1936, Premiers' Papers, file 1458.
95. N.E. Tanner to Aberhart, 27 April 1936; Aberhart to Tanner, 2 May 1936, Premiers' Papers, file 1059.
96. O.C. Arnott to H.B. Hill, 20 July 1936, Hill Collection, Devonian Foundation Papers.
97. Hill Diary, 22 July 1936, 10 Aug. 1936, and 12 Aug. 1936.
98. *Today and Tomorrow*, 22 Oct. 1936, p.1.
99. *Ibid.*, p.2.
100. W.W. Grant to C.R. Pearce, n.d., C.R. Pearce Papers, file 7.
101. Aberhart to Charles McNutt [sic], 3 Nov. 1926, Premiers' Papers, file 1458.
102. Kennedy, *Alberta Was My Beat*, p.251.
103. Aberhart to Cyril Hutchinson, 17 Nov. 1936, Premiers' Papers, file 1156; Aberhart to E.G. Hansell, 20 Nov. 1936, Premiers' Papers, file 1180; Aberhart to N.B. James, 30 Nov. 1936, Premiers' Papers, file 1180.

104. Hill Diary, 8 Aug. 1936; Aberhart to J.W. Hugill, 20 Dec. 1936, Hugill Papers, file 49.
105. Whalen, p.178.
106. Protest poem, n.d., found in the Premiers' Papers, file 1247a.

CHAPTER XVII – THE REBELLION

1. Cited in John Hargrave, *Official Report — Alberta: A Documented Record of Mr. John Hargrave's Visit to the Province of Alberta, Canada, December 8, 1936 to January 25, 1937* (London: The Social Credit Party of Great Britain and Northern Ireland, 1937), p.43.
2. *Ibid.*, p.1.
3. *Ibid.*, p.2.
4. Calgary *Herald*, 13 May 1935, p.4.
5. Hargrave, p.4.
6. *Ibid.*, p.14.
7. *Ibid.*, p.25.
8. *Ibid.*, pp.25-26.
9. *Ibid.*, p.32.
10. *Ibid.*, p.34. See also Calgary *Herald*, 26 Jan. 1937, p.2.
11. Charles Cockroft to his constituents, 12 April 1937, Premiers' Papers, file 1057; Miller's interviews with Charles Cockroft, 12 June 1954 and William N. Chant, 10 June 1954.
12. Calgary *Herald*, 1 March 1937, p.1.
13. *Ibid.*, p.4.
14. *Ibid.*, 3 March 1937, p.4.
15. Miller's interview with Earl Ansley, May 1954.
16. Calgary *Herald*, 5 March 1937, p.1.
17. Aberhart to C.A. Bowman, 16 Feb. 1937; Bowman to Aberhart, 22 Feb. 1937, Premiers' Papers, file 1458.
18. Douglas to Aberhart, 25 Feb. 1937, Premiers' Papers, file 1458.
19. Calgary *Herald*, 6 April 1937, p.5.
20. Aberhart to Mitchell, 26 Feb. 1937, Premiers' Papers, file 1066.
21. Percy Hawkins to Aberhart, 15 March 1937, Premiers' Papers, file 1053.
22. Aberhart to Gladstone Murray, 22 March 1937, Premiers' Papers, file 1018.
23. Calgary *Herald*, 27 March 1937, p.3.
24. Those who supported the insurgents seemed to think also that Aberhart would not risk his leadership over the budget. See J.H. Galbraith to Edith Rogers, 25 March 1937, Irving Papers.
25. Calgary *Herald*, 31 March 1937, p.17.
26. *Ibid.*, 1 April 1937, p.1.
27. *Ibid.*, 5 April 1937, p.1; 6 April 1937, p.1.
28. Aberhart to Elizabeth O. Moss, 6 May 1937, Premiers' Papers, file 1057; Aberhart to H. Meeres, 4 June 1937, Premiers' Papers, file 645.
29. *Statutes of Alberta*, I George VI, 1937, chapter 10.
30. *Ibid.*, chapter 9, sections 27, 29, and 30.
31. *Ibid.*, chapter 11.
32. *Ibid.*, chapters 12-13.
33. *Ibid.*, chapter 30.
34. *Ibid.*, chapter 10; Miller's interview with Earl Ansley, May 1954.
35. Miller's interview with Dr. Victor Wright, 1 Oct. 1954.
36. Mrs. E.M. Court to Aberhart, 19 May 1937 and Aberhart to Mrs. Court, 25 May 1937, Premiers' Papers, file 643.
37. *Albertan*, 5 April 1937, p.1.
38. Calgary *Herald*, 16 April 1937, p.4.
39. G.L. MacLachlan to Douglas, 14 April 1937, reprinted in G.L. MacLachlan,

Report of the Chairman of the Social Credit Board, 1937, p.2, Premiers' Papers, file 1079.
40. Douglas to MacLachlan, n.d., reprinted in *ibid.*
41. Aberhart to W. Ironfield, 14 April 1937, Premiers' Papers, file 1053.
42. For MacLachlan's contract with Douglas see Memorandum of Agreement, 18 May 1937, Premiers' Papers, file 1079.
43. Hargrave, p.19.
44. Aberhart to W.N. Chant, 28 April 1937; Chant to Aberhart, 30 April 1937; Aberhart to Chant, 30 April 1937, Premiers' Papers, file 1038.
45. Miller's interview with W.N. Chant, 10 June 1954.
46. Hans Wight to Aberhart, 7 May 1937; Aberhart to Wight, 11 May 1937, Premiers' Papers, file 1057. Another insurgent, Earl Ansley, also thought that Chant was an ineffective minister of the government and needed to be fired; Miller's interview with Earl Ansley, May 1954. However, two cabinet colleagues, John Hugill and Charles Cockroft backed Chant's contention that his fight with Aberhart had been over patronage. See Miller's interview with John Hugill, 8 and 9 June 1954 and Charles Cockroft 12 June 1954; Calgary *Herald*, 23 Sept. 1937, p.2.
47. *The Rebel*, 24 April 1937, pp.1-2.
48. *Ibid.*, 28 May 1937, p.2.
49. *Ibid.*, 11 June 1937, p.2.
50. Douglas, *The Alberta Experiment*, pp.90ff.
51. Miller's interview with L.D. Byrne, 26 Jan. 1954.
52. *Ibid.*

CHAPTER XVIII – ABERHART VERSUS THE CONSTITUTION

1. *Statutes of Alberta*, I George VI, Session II, 1937, chapter 1.
2. *Ibid.*, chapter 2.
3. *Ibid.*, chapter 5.
4. Calgary *Herald*, 7 Aug. 1937, p.4.
5. Lethbridge Board of Trade to J.C. Bowen, 6 Aug. 1937, J.C. Bowen Papers, file 4.
6. John W. Hugill, "Constitutional Principle #1, in *re* the office of His Majesty's Attorney General," pamphlet edition of Hugill's speech in the Alberta Legislature, 28 Feb. 1939.
7. Hugill to Aberhart, 6 Aug. 1937, Hugill Papers, file 34.
8. Calgary *Herald*, 17 Aug. 1937, p.1.
9. *Ibid.*, 18 Aug. 1937, p.3.
10. For the history and implications of disallowance see J.R. Mallory, *Social Credit and Federal Power in Canada* (Toronto: University of Toronto Press, 1954).
11. Douglas to Powell and Byrne, 18 Aug. 1937, Premiers' Papers, file 1083.
12. See Premiers' Papers, file 708. The U.F.A. Convention of 1936 had urged Aberhart's government to get rid of the R.C.M.P. because it represented undue centralization of police power. The motion had been made by Henry Spencer, a Douglasite. See *The United Farmer*, 24 Jan. 1936, p.1.
13. *The Rebel*, 30 July 1937, p.4.
14. G.L. MacLachlan to L.D. Byrne, 23 Aug. 1937, Premiers' Papers, file 1083.
15. *Social Credit*, 23 Sept. 1938.
16. Aberhart to Mackenzie King, 26 Aug. 1937, Premiers' Papers, file 1257a.
17. Calgary *Herald*, 28 Aug. 1937, p.4.
18. *Ibid.*, 9 Sept. 1937, pp.1 and 7.
19. *Ibid.*, 22 Sept. 1937, pp.1-2.
20. Hugill Papers, file 34; Irving's interview with John Hugill and Miller's interview with Hugill, 8 and 9 June 1954.

21. Calgary *Herald*, 23 Sept. 1937, p.4 and J. McKinley Cameron to Hugill, 22 Sept. 1937, Hugill Papers, file 37.
22. O.S. Longman's memo, 24 Feb. 1964, Hugill Papers, file 44. Hugill's unfinished manuscript can be found in his papers.
23. Hugill, "Constitutional Principle #1," p.14.
24. J.C. Bowen to Aberhart, 1 Oct. 1937; Aberhart to Bowen, 1 Oct. 1937, Premiers' Papers, file 774.
25. Reported in *The Rebel*, 13 May 1937, p.4.
26. *Ibid.*, 27 Aug. 1937, p.1. See Ivan Avakumovic, *The Communist Party in Canada: A History* (Toronto: McClelland and Stewart Limited, 1975), p.109.
27. Open letter from Lawrence Anderson, secretary, Communist Party of Canada, Alberta Provincial Committee, to Aberhart, Sept. 1937, Premiers' Papers.
28. Aberhart to Armand Turpin, 13 Sept. 1937, Premiers' Papers, file 1117; W. Norman Smith to the Rev. Herbert Higginbotham, 10 Sept. 1937, W. Norman Smith Papers, file 11.
29. Reported in *The Rebel*, 17 Sept. 1937, p.1.
30. *Ibid.*, 8 Oct. 1937, p.2.
31. R.M. Johnstone to J.J. Zubick, 22 Oct. 1937, Zubick Papers, file 1.
32. *Financial Post* 11 Sept. 1937, p.1.
33. For various kinds of fascisms see Seymour M. Lipset, *Political Man* (Garden City: Doubleday, 1960), pp.131-176. His definition depicts the political spectrum as a circle with communism and fascism meeting at the bottom. Lipset, himself, did only a cursory examination of Aberhart's movement when he studied the C.C.F. in Saskatchewan, and did not reach the same conclusion we did. He based his remarks primarily on Manning's administration in the late 1940s.
34. R. Thomas to Aberhart, 1 April 1937, Premiers' Papers, file 643; J. McKinley Cameron to Hugill, 22 Sept. 1937, Hugill Papers, file 37; C.W. Peterson, *Social Credit: A Critical Analysis* (Calgary, 1937), p.30.
35. *Financial Post*, 11 Sept. 1937, p.1.
36. Aberhart broadcast tape obtained from CFCN by Dr. A.W. Rasporich, History Dept., University of Calgary.
37. *Statutes of Alberta*, I George VI, Session III, 1937, bill 9.
38. *Ibid.*, bill 1.
39. *Ibid.*, bill 8.
40. J.C. Bowen to Ernest Lapointe, 9 Oct. 1937, Bowen Papers.
41. *Statutes of Alberta*, I George VI, Session III, chapter 1.
42. Calgary *Herald*, 28 Sept. 1937, p.4.
43. *Statutes of Alberta*, I George VI, Session III, chapter 7.
44. Aberhart to J.J. Baker, 2 Nov. 1937, Premiers' Papers, file 1111.
45. Calgary *Herald*, 25 Sept. 1937, p.3.
46. *Albertan*, 4 Oct. 1937, p.4.
47. Calgary *Herald*, 5 Oct. 1937, p.1; 6 Oct. 1937, p.1.
48. *Ibid.*, 13 Nov. 1937, pp.1-2, 11-12.
49. *Ibid.*, 15 Nov. 1937, p.1; 16 Nov. 1937, p.1.
50. Douglas to Mackenzie King, 10 Dec. 1937, quoted in the Edmonton *Journal*, 10 March 1938, pp.1 and 3.
51. Aberhart to Mackenzie King, 10 Feb. 1938, Premiers' Papers, file 1080.
52. Joseph T. Shaw to Aberhart, 15 Feb. 1938 and Shaw to Mackenzie King, 15 Feb. 1938, Premiers' Papers, file 1080.
53. Mackenzie King to Aberhart, 11 Feb. 1938, Premiers' Papers, file 1080.
54. Edmonton *Journal*, 22 March 1938, pp.1-2.
55. E.H. Coleman, Under-Secretary of State, to Aberhart, 29 April 1938, Premiers' Papers, file 1080.
56. Calgary *Herald*, 23 May 1938, p.1. Upon arriving in England Powell's had

more difficulties. When he attempted to present his report on Alberta at a Social Credit rally, the meeting was broken up by John Hargrave and his Green Shirts. (Calgary Herald, 21 July 1938, pp.1-2). Hargrave had repudiated Douglas's leadership and had proclaimed himself head of the Social Credit movement. Most of the Secretariat had also left Douglas.

57. Edmonton *Bulletin*, 5 Feb. 1938, p.2.
58. Calgary *Herald*, 4 March 1938, pp.1-2.
59. Edmonton *Journal*, 4 March 1938, p.1.
60. Fred Kennedy, *Alberta Was My Beat*, pp.289-290.
61. Edmonton *Journal*, 2 May 1938, pp.1-2.
62. Mackenzie King to Aberhart, 6 May 1938; Aberhart to Mackenzie King, 14 May 1938; Aberhart to J.C. Bowen, 14 May 1938, Premiers' Papers, file 774.
63. Calgary *Herald*, 11 Jan. 1934, p.1 and 16 March 1934, p.4. Ontario and Saskatchewan also closed their Government Houses for economic reasons. See L.H. Thomas, ed. *The Making of a Socialist: The Recollections of T.C. Douglas* (Edmonton: University of Alberta Press), pp.198-199.
64. See Premiers' Papers, file 774.
65. Thomas, ed. *The Making of a Socialist*, pp.199-200.
66. *Statutes of Alberta*, II George VI, 1938, chapter 3.
67. *Ibid.*, chapter 8.
68. *Ibid.*, chapter 22.
69. *Ibid.*, chapter 7.
70. *Ibid.*, chapter 28.
71. *Ibid.*, chapter 16.
72. *Ibid.*, chapter 6.
73. *Ibid.*, chapter 18.
74. Calgary *Herald*, 5 June 1938, p.1.
75. *Ibid.*, 15 June 1938, p.1 and 16 June 1938, p.4.
76. For details on the election results see John C. Courtney and David E. Smith, "Saskatchewan: Parties in a Politically Sensitive Province," in Martin Robin, ed. *Canadian Provincial Politics*, second ed. (Scarborough: Prentice-Hall of Canada Ltd., 1978), p.307. Ken Andrews, "'Progressive' Counterparts of the C.C.F.: Social Credit and the Conservative Party in Saskatchewan, 1935-1938," *Journal of Canadian Studies* 17:3 (Fall 1982), pp.58-74, has a good discussion Aberhart's political efforts in Saskatchewan.
77. Kennedy, *Alberta Was My Beat*, p.292-296, 300.
78. *Ibid.*, 297-298.
79. Edmonton *Journal*, 26 Aug. 1938, pp.1 and 9.
80. Calgary *Herald*, 24 Sept. 1938, pp.1-2.
81. Aberhart to Mackenzie King, 3 June 1938, Premiers' Papers, file 1184.
82. *Statutes of Alberta*, II George VI, Session II, 1938, chapter 3.
83. Alberta, "How to Use Your Treasury Branches" (Edmonton: King's Printer, 1938). For a more complete discussion of the Treasury Branches see Bruce Allen Powe, "The Social Credit Interim Program and the Alberta Treasury Branches" (unpublishd M.A. thesis, University of Alberta, 1951).
84. See James Barr, *The Dynasty: The Rise and Fall of Social Credit in Alberta* (Toronto: McClelland and Stewart Ltd., 1974), p.115.
85. *Statutes of Alberta*, II George VI, 1938, chapter 15.
86. Aberhart, *Let's Look at the Record* (Edmonton: King's Printer, 1939).
87. *Statutes of Alberta*, III George VI, 1939, chapter 3.
88. *South Side Advertiser*, 8 May 1939, pp.1-2.
89. King's Diary, 2 June 1939.
90. Aberhart to the Reverend H.D. Linnen, 16 Nov. 1939, Premiers' Papers, file 1181.
91. Calgary *Herald*, 15 May 1939, p.18.

92. Alberta, *The Records Tell the Story* (Edmonton: The Social Credit Board, 1939), p.33.
93. See Alvin Finkel, "Social Credit and the Unemployed," *Alberta History* 31:2 (Spring 1983), pp.24-32.
94. Aberhart's salary as premier was slightly higher than he would have been getting as a high school principal, but he was also able to carry on much of his religious work (i.e. stenographic services, mailing, long-distance telephone calls, and travel) at government expense.

CHAPTER XIX – THE WAR YEARS

1. Aberhart repeatedly claimed that the Second World War was not the Tribulation and Hitler was not the Antichrist. See Aberhart to O.B. Prosser, 6 Dec. 1939, Premiers' Papers, file 1181; Aberhart to B.L. Murray, 15 July 1940, Premiers' Papers, file 1183.
2. Calgary *Herald*, 26 Sept. 1938, p.1.
3. Edmonton *Journal*, 26 Sept. 1938, p.2.
4. Calgary *Herald*, 28 Sept. 1938, p.4.
5. Aberhart's sermon, "Prophecy #21: The Lesson of Germany," n.d., Premiers' Papers, file 1048.
6. Aberhart to Arthur Dowling, 10 Oct. 1940, Premiers' Papers, file 1458 and *Prophetic Voice*, Aug. 1942, p.4.
7. From a signed deposition of J.S. McGowan, T.O.F. Herzer, and E.H. Gurton, C.N.R. Records, R.G. 30, Volume 8349, Public Archives of Canada. This material was brought to our attention by Professor Howard Palmer of the University of Calgary.
8. *Statutes of Alberta*, IV George VI, 1940, chapter 5.
9. *Prophetic Voice*, July 1942, p.4.
10. *Ibid.*, July 1942, p.2.
11. E. Wagstaff to Aberhart, 13 July 1940, Premiers' Papers, file 1190.
12. *Statutes of Alberta*, VI George VI, 1942, chapter 16; VII George VI, 1943, chapter 30.
13. Aberhart to Mrs. C. McGregor, 26 Sept. 1940. A copy of the original letter was given to us by Professor M.J. Penton, University of Lethbridge. The authoritarian tone of Aberhart's letter and his failure to understand her anxiety caused that mother great stress, which eventually resulted in a nervous breakdown. She lived in fear of having her children taken from her, and because of it disassociated herself from the Jehovah's Witnesses for some time. (Elliott's interview with Professor M.J. Penton, Lethbridge, 1 Aug. 1980).
14. H.N. Stovin to E.H. McGuire, 9 Feb. 1940; McGuire to Aberhart, 12 Feb. 1940; Stovin to McGuire, 13 Feb. 1940; McGuire to Aberhart, 14 Feb. 1940, Premiers' Papers, file 1157.
15. McGuire to Aberhart, 5 March 1941; Aberhart to McGuire, 6 March 1941; Aberhart to C.R. Pearce, 20 March 1941, Premiers' Papers, file 1157.
16. Aberhart to H.B. Love, 18 July 1941; McGuire to Aberhart, 22 July 1941, Premiers' Papers, file 1157.
17. The fullest treatment of New Democracy and its involvement with Social Credit is Mary Hallett, "The Social Credit Party and the New Democracy Movement: 1939-1940," *Canadian Historical Review* 47 (1966), pp.301-325.
18. Calgary *Herald*, 27 July 1939, p.3.
19. *Today and Tomorrow*, 7 Sept. 1939, p.5. See also Aberhart, "Conscription of the Monetary System!", pamphlet *circa* 15 Aug. 1941, Premiers' Papers, file 1243.
20. Aberhart to C.A. Bowman, 8 Sept. 1939, Premiers' Papers, file 1238b.
21. Bowman to Aberhart, 15 Nov. 1939, Premiers' Papers, file 1238b.

22. Aberhart to Bowman, 17 Nov. 1939 and Aberhart to W.D. Herridge, 18 Nov. 1939, Premiers' Papers, file 1238b.
23. Calgary *Herald*, 17 Jan. 1940, p.2.
24. *Ibid.*, p.1.
25. Mrs. George Smith to Aberhart, 31 Jan. 1938; Aberhart to Mrs. Smith, 9 Feb. 1938; Mrs. Smith to Aberhart, 22 Feb. 1938; Aberhart to Mrs. Smith, 19 March 1938; George Smith to Aberhart, 25 July 1941; Aberhart to George Smith, 28 July 1941, Premiers' Papers, file 1266.
26. Reported in *The Rebel*, 2 Jan. 1939, p.2.
27. Calgary *Herald*, 19 Jan. 1940, p.2.
28. *Ibid.*, 8 Feb. 1940, p.1.
29. *Ibid.*, p.10.
30. Douglas, *The Big Idea*, p.45.
31. Calgary *Herald*, 10 Feb. 1940, pp.1 and 5; 16 Feb. 1940, p.3; 18 May 1940, pp.9 and 11.
32. *Ibid.*, 16 Feb. 1940, pp.1-2.
33. *Ibid.*, 10 Feb. 1940, pp.1-2; 16 Feb. 1940, pp.1-2.
34. Edmonton *Bulletin*, 7 March 1940, p.2.
35. Calgary *Herald*, 9 March 1940, p.1.
36. Unity Council of Alberta, *The Truth About the Records* Vol. 1. (Calgary, [1940]), p.10.
37. *Ibid.*, p.31.
38. *Ibid.*, pp.15 and 19.
39. William Irvine, *The Trail of a Truth Twister: An Answer to "The Records Tell the Story"* (Edmonton: Commercial Printers Ltd., 1939).
40. Calgary *Herald*, 11 March 1940, p.1.
41. *Ibid.*, 2 March 1940, pp.1-3; 5 March 1940, p.8.
42. *The Truth About the Records*, p.28.
43. Aberhart to Charles Aberhart, 11 Jan. 1940, Premiers' Papers, file 1458.
44. See Aberhart's plays, "The Great God Gold" and "A Popular Loan," Premiers' Papers, file 1051.
45. Calgary *Herald*, 1 March 1940, p.13.
46. *Ibid.*, 5 March 1940, p.1.
47. Aberhart to Mrs. E. Boydell, 30 Sept. 1940, Premiers' Papers, file 1458.
48. Elliott's interview with Mrs. J. Cooper, 29 Nov. 1980.
49. *Alberta Social Credit Platform* [1940], Iris Miller Collection.
50. See Meir Serfaty, "The Unity Movement in Alberta," *Alberta Historical Review* 21:2 (spring 1973), pp.1-9.
51. Calgary *Herald*, 22 March 1940, p.1.
52. *Today and Tomorrow*, 4 April 1940, p.1.
53. Aberhart to Herridge, 1 April 1940, Premiers' Papers, file 1238b.
54. Calgary *Herald*, 20 June 1940, pp.1-2.
55. *Ibid.*, 24 July 1940, p.1.
56. *Ibid.*, p.4.
57. *Ibid.*, p.2.
58. *Ibid.*, 28 Nov. 1940, p.11.
59. From the Trochu *Tribune*, reprinted in the *Calgary Herald*, 4 Dec. 1940, p.4.
60. Calgary *Herald*, 12 Dec. 1940, p.4. For a thorough discussion of the Commission see W.A. Mackintosh, *The Economic Background of Dominion-Provincial Relations* (Toronto:McClelland and Stewart Limited, 1964) and Donald V. Smiley, ed. The Rowell-Sirois report, Book 1. (Toronto: McClelland and Stewart Limited, 1963).
61. Calgary *Herald*, 18 Dec. 1940, p.9.
62. *Ibid.*, 14 Jan. 1941, pp.1-3.
63. *Ibid.*, 16 Jan. 1941, p.5.

64. *Ibid.*, 15 Jan. 1941, p.1.
65. King's Diary, 16-17 Jan. 1941; Calgary *Herald*, 16 Jan. 1941, p.1.
66. Calgary *Herald*, 20 Feb. 1941, p.4.
67. *Ibid.*, 15 Jan. 1941, pp.2 and 5; 16 Jan. 1941, p.2.
68. King's Diary, 14 Jan. 1941.
69. Calgary *Herald*, 16 Jan. 1941, p.4; 17 Jan. 1941, p.4.
70. *Ibid.*, 20 Feb. 1941, pp.1-2.
71. *Ibid.*, 24 Feb. 1941, pp.1-2.
72. *Ibid.*, 5 May 1941, pp.1-2.
73. Aberhart's undelivered convocation address, Premiers' Papers, file 1048.
74. Calgary *Herald*, 13 May 1941, pp.1-2.
75. John W. Barnett for the Alberta Teachers' Association to Aberhart, 20 May 1941, Premiers' Papers, file 1460.
76. Edmonton *Bulletin*, 14 May 1941, p.1.
77. Aberhart to Mrs. Dorothy Antonio, 11 June 1941, Premiers' Papers, file 1460.
78. *Statutes of Alberta*, VI George VI, 1942, chapter 4.
79. Calgary *Herald*, 23 Oct. 1940, p.4.
80. *Ibid.*, 19 Nov. 1940, p.4; 25 Nov. 1940, p.4.
81. Aberhart broadcast, 23 July 1935, W. Norman Smith Papers, file 83.
82. The shape of modern dispensational eschatology developed at about the same time as the *Protocols* appeared, and some issues of the *Protocols* were published by fundamentalists and included premillennial eschatological schemes. The connection between the two requires more investigation.
83. Aberhart to the editor, *Western Jewish Press*, 24 Aug. 1936, Premiers' Papers, file 1263; A.I. Shumiatcher to Aberhart, 16 March 1937; Aberhart to Shumiatcher, 22 March 1937, Premiers' Papers, file 1042; F. Fingerate to Aberhart, 12 Aug. 1938, Premiers' Papers, file 1262.
84. Edmonton *Journal*, 21 Sept. 1938, p.4. Douglas's comments were originally published in *Social Credit*, 26 Aug. 1938 and were reprinted in the Edmonton *Journal*, 26 Sept. 1938, p.4.
85. *Ibid.*, 22 Sept. 1938, p.1.
86. *Ibid.*, 23 Sept. 1938, p.4.
87. Reported in *The People's Weekly*, 10 Feb. 1945, p.2
88. *New English Weekly*, 27 July 1933, p.359.
89. C.H. Douglas, *The Big Idea* (Stratford-on-Avon: K.R.P. Publications Ltd., 1942), p.50.
90. C.H. Douglas, *Programme for the Third World War* (Stratford-on-Avon: K.R.P. Publications Ltd., 1943), pp.27-28.
91. C.H. Douglas, *The "Land for the (Chosen) People" Racket* (Liverpool: K.R.P. Publications Ltd., 1943), p.24.
92. Vancouver *News Herald*, 29 Jan. 1942, p.13.
93. I. Miller to Aberhart, 22 Feb. 1942; Aberhart to I. Miller, 11 March 1942, Premiers' Papers, file 1250. For a fuller treatment of anti-Semitism see David R. Elliott, "Anti-Semitism and the Social Credit Movement: The Intellectual Roots of the Keegstra Affair," *Canadian Ethnic Studies* 17:1 (1985), pp.78-89.
94. *Prophetic Voice*, Sept. 1942, pp.2-3.
95. Calgary *Herald*, 27 Oct. 1941, p.11.
96. *Ibid.*, 28 Oct. 1941, p.3.
97. "Principles for Association, or: For What Do We Stand?" Democratic Monetary Reform Association, Premiers' Papers, file 1174.
98. Calgary *Herald*, 29 Oct. 1941, p.3.
99. *Ibid.*, 11 Sept. 1941, p.3. "Union Now" was the creation of a journalist Clarence K. Streit. See his *Union Now: A Proposal for a Federal Union of the Democracies of the North Atlantic* (London: Jonathan Cape, 1939).
100. W. Aberhart and L.D. Byrne, *National Monetary Reform: Canada's Urgent*

□ ▬▬▬▬▬▬▬▬▬▬▬▬▬▬▬▬▬▬▬▬▬▬▬▬▬▬ □

Need (Edmonton: Today and Tomorrow, 1941, p. 30.

101. *Ibid.*, p.32. The anti-Semitic nature of the opposition to the "Union Now" movement can be clearly seen in *The Annual Report of the Social Credit Board*, 1942.

102. Calgary *Herald*, 11 Sept. 1941, p.3.

103. *Ibid.*, 29 Oct. 1941, p.9.

104. *Ibid.*, 30 Oct. 1941, p.3.

105. Aberhart to Major A.H. Jukes, 17 Dec. 1941, Premiers' Papers, file 1130; *Constitution and By-laws of the Democratic Monetary Reform Organization of Canada*, 1941.

106. Calgary *Herald*, 8 Nov. 1941, p.9.

107. *Programme* of the Seventh Annual Convention of the Alberta Social Credit League, 3-4 Dec. 1941, Premiers' Papers, file 1117.

108. Calgary *Herald*, 16 Jan. 1942, p.11; Democratic Victory League pamphlet, Premiers' Papers, file 1130.

109. Aberhart to the editor, Glastonbury *News*, 6 July 1939; Aberhart to G.A. Morton Sr., 10 July 1939, Premiers' Papers, file 1181; Aberhart to Mrs. H. Fareh, 12 Nov. 1941, Premiers' Papers, file 1183.

110. *Today and Tomorrow*, 28 Sept. 1939, p.1 and Aberhart to J.E. Paynter, 6 Oct. 1939, Premiers' Papers, file 1181.

111. Aberhart to Stanley Dowling, 15 Feb. 1941, Premiers' Papers, file 1183.

112. Copies of Aberhart's pamphlets on the British Coat of Arms can be found in the Calgary Prophetic Bible Institute papers and in the *Prophetic Voice*, July 1942 and following; also Aberhart to Charles Aberhart, 11 July 1940, Premiers' Papers, file 1458.

113. Aberhart to Paul Prince, 25 Nov. 1942, Premiers' Papers, file 1166.

114. Paul Prince to Aberhart, 17 Nov. 1942 and Aberhart to Prince, 25 Nov. 1942, Premiers' Papers, file 1166.

115. William Aberhart, *Post-War Reconstruction* (Edmonton: Today and Tomorrow, 1942-1943), Series 2, p.24; Series 3, p.62.

116. Social Credit Board, *Prepare Now: A Suggested Policy for Post-War Reconstruction* (Edmonton: Social Credit Board, 1943), pp.12, 35.

117. *Statutes of Alberta*, VII George VI, 1943, chapters 3,8, and 9. The Post-War Reconstruction program was abolished in 1954. See *Statutes of Alberta*, 1954, chapter 79.

118. Aberhart, *Post-War Reconstruction*, Series 3, pp.21-30.

119. Calgary *Herald*, 1 Feb. 1943, p.1.

120. Aberhart broadcast, 4 Feb. 1943, transcript in Hansell Papers, file 4.

121. Aberhart to C.H. Baird, 17 Feb. 1943, Premiers' Papers, file 1171.

122. Aberhart to A.H. Jukes, 19 Feb. 1943, Premiers' Papers, file 1166b.

CHAPTER XX – THE PREACHING PREMIER

1. E. Gardiner to Aberhart, 25 Jan. 1936, Premiers' Papers, file 1180.

2. Aberhart to Cyril Hutchinson, 6 Jan. 1936; M.L. Burget to Aberhart, 10 Aug. 1936, Premiers' Papers, file 1180.

3. Bible Institute Baptist Church Minutes, 28 Oct. 1936, pp.265-266.

4. Elliott's telephone interview with Mrs. M.L. Burget, Denver, 12 Jan. 1974; Bible Institute Baptist Church Minutes, 31 Aug. 1937, pp.19-20.

5. Hughes may have studied at Cliff College in England, but that fact is far from certain; Elliott's interview with the Reverend Cyril Hutchinson, 1 Feb. 1974.

6. Elliott's interview with Mrs. Fred Capocci, Vancouver, 18 Dec. 1973.

7. Bible Institute Baptist Church Minutes, 19 Jan. 1938, p.32; 20 April 1938, p.39; 8 May 1938, p.40; 9 Oct. 1938, p.47.

8. *Ibid.*, 20 April 1939, p.72.

9. Calgary *Herald*, 7 June 1939, p.11.

10. Bible Institute Baptist Church Minutes, 14 May 1939, pp.74-75.
11. Calgary *Herald*, 8 June 1939, p.9.
12. Bible Institute Baptist Church Minutes, 12 April 1939, pp.68-71; 29 May 1939, pp.5-9.
13. Aberhart to Mrs. A. Perkins, 6 June 1939, Premiers' Papers, file 1181.
14. Calgary *Herald*, 3 June 1939, p.10.
15. Elliott's interview with Mr. and Mrs. J.U. Dick, 18 Jan. 1974.
16. Bible Institute Baptist Church Minutes, 12 Oct. 1937, p.23 and 16 Nov. 1938, p.55.
17. Aberhart to Dr. W.P. Harvey, 30 July 1940, Premiers' Papers, file 1068.
18. Irving's interview with H.B. Scrimgeour, n.d., Irving Papers.
19. Calgary *Herald*, 12 June 1939, pp.9 and 18.
20. F.G. Harbidge to Aberhart, 14 Aug. 1939 and Aberhart to Harbidge, 16 Aug. 1939, Premiers' Papers, file 1181.
21. Calgary *Herald*, 12 June 1939, p.18; Bible Institute Baptist Church Minutes, 13 Nov. 1939, p.84.
22. The schism between the Bible Institute Baptist Church and the Calgary Prophetic Bible Institute in 1948-1949 has been covered in David R. Elliott and Iris Miller, "Aberhart and the Calgary Prophetic Bible Institute," *Prairie Forum* 9:1 (Spring 1984), pp.61-77.
23. John Armstrong to Aberhart, 12 Oct. 1936, Premiers' Papers, file 1133.
24. Oscar Morck to Aberhart, 27 March 1938, Premiers' Papers, file 1133.
25. Calgary *Herald*, 26 April 1938, p.1 and 27 April 1938, p.1.
26. Phoebe E. Owen to Aberhart, 8 May 1937, Premiers' Papers, file 1247.
27. Mrs. W.P. Doyle to Aberhart, 22 Nov. 1938, Premiers' Papers, file 1182.
28. A. Keeler to Aberhart, 20 Nov. 1936, Premiers' Papers, file 1180 and I.I. Penner to Aberhart, 23 June 1938, Premiers' Papers, file 1182.
29. Aberhart to I.I. Penner, 30 June 1938, Premiers' Papers, file 1182; Aberhart to E.W. Davies, 10 Feb. 1939, Premiers' Papers, file 1055; Aberhart to Miss K.M. Rowley, 23 May 1941, Premiers' Papers, file 1183.
30. Miller's interview with Mrs. W.P. Harvey, 13 Nov. 1954.
31. Aberhart to Norman H. Camp, 24 Feb. 1937, Premiers' Papers, file 1182.
32. Aberhart to Mr. and Mrs. W.P. Doyle, 24 Nov. 1938, Premiers' Papers, file 1182.
33. G.M. Trygstad to Aberhart, 6 April 1939; A.D. Stewart to Aberhart, 26 April 1939; Aberhart to A.D. Stewart, 28 April 1939, Premiers' Papers, file 1181.
34. Jean Thurston to Aberhart, 9 Dec. 1941., Premiers' Papers, file 1183.
35. Aberhart to Jean Thurston, 10 Dec. 1941, Premiers' Papers, file 1183.
36. Cyril Hutchinson to Aberhart, 19 Dec. 1941, Premiers' Papers, file 1183.
37. Cyril Hutchinson to Aberhart, 3 July 1942 and Jean Thurston to Aberhart, 4 July 1942; Aberhart to C.R. Pearce, 4 July 1942; Aberhart to Jean Thurston, 6 July 1942, Premiers' Papers, file 1178.
38. Elliott's interview with Mrs. F. Capocci, 18 Dec. 1973.
39. *The Gospel Witness*, 2 Sept. 1937, pp.9-10.
40. *Ibid.*, 7 July 1938, p.1.
41. A.H. Booth to Aberhart, 28 July 1936, Premiers' Papers, file 1137; A.F. Auclair to Aberhart, 19 Oct. 1936, Premiers' Papers, file 641; Thomas A. Rodger to Aberhart, 14 Feb. 1941, Premiers' Papers, file 1183.
42. Calgary *Herald*, 1 March 1941, p.15 and John Burns to Aberhart, 15 Feb. 1941; Aberhart to Burns, 17 Feb. 1941; Rabbi J.J. Eisen to Aberhart, 27 Feb. 1941; Aberhart to Rabbi Eisen, 28 Feb. 1941, Premiers' Papers, file 1183.
43. Irving's interview with the Reverend G.H. Villett, 31 Aug. 1946, Irving Papers; Miller's interview with the Reverend Herb Ashford, 3 May 1954.
44. Compare *Prophetic Voice*, Dec. 1926, p.6 and Sept. 1942, pp.1-2.
45. Aberhart to Miss N.J. Fisher, 8 May 1942, Premiers' Papers, file 1129; Aberhart

to W. Bollen, 12 March 1943, Premiers' Papers, file 1178; and Aberhart to Mrs. B.G. Marshall, 16 April 1943, Premiers' Papers, file 1178.

46. Charles Kirby to Aberhart, 19 Oct. 1941 and 24 Oct. 1941, Premiers' Papers, file 1157.

47. Aberhart to Charles Kirby, 22 Oct. 1941, Premiers' Papers, file 1157.

48. *Prophetic Voice*, July 1942, p.4.

49. Melvin V. Donald to Aberhart, 23 June 1942; Aberhart to Dr. G.F. McNally, 7 July 1942; Aberhart to Donald, 9 July 1942, Premiers' Papers, file 709.

50. G.F. McNally to Aberhart, 14 July 1942, Premiers' Papers, file 709.

51. Aberhart to Mabel Giles, 25 July 1942; Giles to Aberhart, 28 July 1942; Aberhart to Giles, 29 July 1942; Melvin V. Donald to Aberhart, 12 Nov. 1942; Aberhart to Donald, 19 Nov. 1942, Premiers' Papers, file 709.

52. Calgary *Herald*, 24 Feb. 1943, p.12.

53. *Ibid.*, 27 Feb. 1943, p.5.

54. W. Kent Power to the editor, Calgary *Herald*, 2 March 1943, p.2.

55. Aberhart to Ella Deadmarsh, 21 Jan. 1936, Premiers' Papers, file 1180.

56. Aberhart's palmistry notes can be found in the Aberhart Papers.

57. T.E. Hughes to Aberhart, 14 May 1940 and Aberhart to T.E. Hughes, 20 May 1940, Premiers' Papers, file 1458.

58. Aberhart's horoscope can be found in the Aberhart Papers.

59. Aberhart to Murial Jury, 27 July 1942, Premiers' Papers, file 1051.

60. Miller's interview with Charles Aberhart, 16 Nov. 1954.

61. Miller's interview with Jessie Aberhart, 19 Oct. 1954.

62. Aberhart to Charles R. Pearce, 8 July 1942.

63. Aberhart to the Reverend Palmer Peterson, 8 Jan. 1943, Premiers' Papers, file 1178.

64. Miller's interview with Jessie Aberhart, May 1954.

65. Aberhart to Cyril Hutchinson, 12 April 1943, Premiers' Papers, file 1178.

66. Aberhart to Cyril Hutchinson, 15 April 1943, Premiers' Papers, file 1178.

67. A.J. Hooke, *30 + 5: I Know I Was There* (Edmonton: Institute of Applied Art, Ltd.), p.165

68. Elliott's interview with Khona Cooper, 18 Dec. 1973.

69. Miller's interview with Jessie Aberhart, May 1954.

70. Calgary *Herald*, 17 May 1943, p.1.

71. Aberhart to May Crowell, 23 March 1942, Premiers' Papers, 1178.

72. Calgary *Herald*, 19 May 1943, p.1.

73. *Ibid.*, 20 May 1943, pp.1 and 8.

74. Press release, 21 May 1943, Premiers' Papers, file 1260.

75. Elliott's interview with Khona Cooper, 18 Dec. 1973.

76. Calgary *Herald*, 22 May 1943, p.1.

77. Edmonton *Journal*, 24 May 1943, p.2; *Calgary Herald*, 25 May 1943, p.9.

78. Edmonton *Bulletin*, 24 May 1943, p.4.

79. King's Diary, 24 May 1943, p.395 and King to Jessie Aberhart, 24 May 1943, Irving Papers, box 1.

80. Calgary *Herald*, 25 May 1943, p.1.

CHAPTER XXI – WILLIAM ABERHART: AN ASSESSMENT

1. John A. Irving, "The Psychological Aspects of the Social Credit Movement in Alberta," *Canadian Journal of Psychology* 1 (1947), pp.17-27, 75-86, 127-140.

2. Aberhart's sermon, "The Second Coming of Christ," Aberhart papers, box 1, #70.239/51A.

3. S.D. Clark, "The Religious Sect in Canadian Politics," *American Journal of Sociology* 51 (1945), pp.207-216; Irving, *op. cit.*; and W.E. Mann, *Sect, Cult and Church in Alberta*.

4. See David R. Elliott, "The Devil and William Aberhart: The nature and function of his eschatology," *Studies in Religion* 9 (summer 1980), pp.325-337.

5. Harry H. Hiller, "A Critical Analysis of the Role of Religion in a Canadian Populist Movement: The Emergence and Dominance of the Social Credit Party in Alberta" (unpublished Ph.D. dissertation, McMaster University, Hamilton, 1972).

6. C.B. Macpherson, *Democracy in Alberta: Social Credit and the Party System* (Toronto: University of Toronto Press, 1962).

7. See David R. Elliott, "William Aberhart: Right or Left?" in D. Francis and H. Ganzevoort, *The Dirty Thirties in Prairie Canada* (Vancouver: Tantalus Research Limited, 1980), pp.11-31; Myron Johnson, "The Failure of the CCF in Alberta: An Accident of History," in Carlo Caldarola, ed. *Society and Politics in Alberta: Research Papers* (Toronto: Methuen, 1979), pp.87-107; and Alvin Finkel, "Alberta Social Credit Reappraised: The Radical Character of the Early Social Credit Movement," *Prairie Forum* 11 (Spring 1986), pp.69-86.

8. Richard Hofstadter, *The Age of Reform* (New York: Vintage Books, 1955), p.62.

BIBLIOGRAPHICAL ESSAY

■

William Aberhart has been the subject of many articles, theses, and books, most of which have been cited in the Notes section of this book. Because of the massive bibliography available, only the more important works are discussed below.

The first major book on Aberhart's political activities was C.H. Douglas's *Alberta Experiment* (London: 1937). That work is important for Douglas's assessment of Aberhart's personality and selected portions of their correspondence which Douglas published.

Considerable academic attention was paid to Aberhart and Social Credit in the late 1940s, attention that resulted in the multi-volume series on Social Credit, edited by S.D. Clark for the Social Science Research Council of Canada and published by the University of Toronto. Those books explored the social, political, economic, and religious background to Aberhart's victory in Alberta. S.D. Clark's *Church and Sect in Canada* (Toronto: 1948) mentioned Aberhart by way of comparison but did not deal with him directly. Clark's earlier article, "The Religious Sect in Canadian Politics" in the *American Journal of Sociology* (1945) contained a number of factual errors that weaken his interpretation of Aberhart. Clark's suggestion that Aberhart attacked the mainline churches because of their wealth or their Eastern leadership is highly questionable.

W.L. Morton's *The Progressive Party in Canada* (Toronto: 1950) saw Aberhart's movement as a continuation of the Progressive movement's protest because of economic and political alienation. Jean Burnett's *Next-Year Country* (Toronto: 1951) examined rural life in east-central Alberta during the 1920s and 1930s.

C.B. Macpherson's *Democracy in Alberta* (Toronto: 1953, revised 1962) analyzed the political and economic ideology of Social Credit from a Marxist perspective. Only cursory attention was given to Aberhart. Macpherson interpreted Social Credit as essentially a fascist movement. His preliminary research first appeared in the *Canadian Journal of Economics and Political Science* (1949).

J.R. Mallory's *Social Credit and Federal Power in Canada* (Toronto: 1954) was the best documented book in the series. He explored Aberhart's years in office and his difficulties with the federal government over the disallowance of his radical legislation.

W. E. Mann's *Sect, Cult and Church in Alberta* (Toronto: 1955) sketched Aberhart's religious career; but his synthesis of Aberhart's activities with the diversity of religious sects and cults in Alberta is not convincing. Mann focused much of his attention on the Prairie Bible Institute at Three Hills, which opposed Aberhart's political activites. Some of the other sects, like the Plymouth Brethren and other dispensationalists, also opposed Aberhart. Mann's work did not indicate their religious opposition to Aberhart.

Unfortunately that series did not contain a complete biography of Aberhart. Working independently of S.D. Clark's research group, Iris Miller wrote a short character-sketch of Aberhart for the *Alberta Jubilee Anthology* of 1955. Her unfinished biography, based on extensive oral history, Aberhart documents, and records from the various religious organizations with which Aberhart had been involved, was available to John A. Irving whose semi-biography of Aberhart, *The Social Credit Movement in Alberta* (Toronto: 1959), dealt with Aberhart's life until the election victory in 1935. Irving's early research was published in the *Canadian Journal of Psychology* (1947) and the *Canadian Journal of Economics and Political Science* (1948). Irving's book was also influenced by Malcolm Gordon Taylor's M.A. thesis, "The Social Credit Movement in Alberta," done for the University of California in 1946. Taylor dealt with the history of Social Credit in Britain and the United States, and with Aberhart's political career until the election victory in 1935. Irving also used his own oral sources, newspaper accounts, the U.F.A. papers in the possession of W. Norman Smith and some Aberhart correspondence obtained from Aberhart's widow. Unfortunately Irving, a professor of philosophy and ethics, was misled on important factual details by his oral sources and did not make the best use of the Aberhart documents he had available. He even plagiarized from an essay written by one of his summer-school students, Florence Todd, who had been on Aberhart's staff at Crescent Heights High School (note Irving, p.42, paragraph 2; Todd's essay is in Irving's papers at the University of Toronto Library). In spite of these weaknesses, the main thrust of Irving's study – that the Social Credit movement was a phenomenon of mass psychology and collective behaviour – has been a valuable contribution.

While few scholarly monographs have been published on Aberhart's years in office, his legislation, and the economic history of the province under his administration, there are several unpublished theses available. Rose P. Madsen's M.A. thesis "The Fiscal Development of Alberta" (University of Alberta, 1949) covered the period well, as did Hugh J. Whalen's M.A. thesis "The Distinctive Legislation of the Government of Alberta (1935-1950)" (University of Alberta, 1951). See also Bruce Allen Powe, "The Social Credit Interim Program and the Alberta Treasury Branches" (unpublished M.A. thesis, University of Alberta, 1951). The above works relied heavily on newspaper reports and the *Statutes of Alberta*.

In 1959 Harold J. Schultz completed a Ph.D. dissertation at Duke University entitled, "William Aberhart and the Social Credit Party: A Political Biography."

Had it been published, it would have become the standard biography of Aberhart until the Premiers' Papers were opened. Schultz's heavily documented manuscript made exhaustive use of newspapers and oral history. However, he did not use any of Aberhart's vast correspondence; he did not know that such correspondence existed. Portions of Schultz's dissertation appeared in *The Canadian Historical Review* (1960, 1964) and *The Alberta Historical Review* (1959, 1962).

A professor of agricultural genetics, L.P.V. Johnson, working with Aberhart's daughter Ola MacNutt, produced *Aberhart of Alberta* (Edmonton: 1970). Following Irving and Schultz quite closely, their book added little to our understanding of Aberhart.

Few of the Social Credit members of the Legislature have written about their experiences in office. Norman B. James, *The Autobiography of a Nobody* (Toronto: 1947) is worth little. A.J. Hooke's *30 + 5: I Know, I Was There* (Edmonton: 1971) is the recollection of a former cabinet minister and member of the Social Credit Board angry with Aberhart's political successors Manning and Strom.

Fred Kennedy who covered Aberhart's political activities for the Calgary *Herald* has provided interesting details of his experiences with Aberhart in his memoir, *Alberta was my Beat* (Calgary: 1975).

With the opening of the Premiers' Papers of Alberta, research on Aberhart's career was made more fruitful. Aberhart's career as Minister of Education was explored in Barry C. Oviatt's M.Ed. thesis, "The Papers of William Aberhart as Minister of Education" (University of Alberta, 1971).

Harry Hiller's Ph.D. dissertation "A Critical Analysis of the Role of Religion in a Canadian Populist Movement: The Emergence and Dominance of the Social Credit Party in Alberta" (McMaster University, 1972) also used the Premiers' Papers to examine religious sectarianism. His study challenged aspects of W.E. Mann's thesis, but was weak historically because his sociological methodology did not allow for examination of historical change and nuances in Aberhart's thought and behaviour.

In response to the weaknesses of the sociological approach, particularly those of Clark and Mann, David R. Elliott's M.A. thesis "The Dispensational Theology and Political Ideology" (University of Calgary, 1975) made extensive use of the Premiers' Papers and church records not previously used by other scholars. Portions of that thesis have already appeared in the *Canadian Historical Review* (1978), *Studies in Religion* (1980), *Prairie Forum* (1984), *Canadian Ethnic Studies* (1985), and D. Francis and H. Ganzevoort, eds. *The Dirty Thirties in Prairie Canada* (Vancouver: 1980). This book is an enlargement of that thesis and Iris Miller's unfinished manuscript after a co-authorship contract was signed in 1977.

John L. Finlay's *Social Credit: The English Origins* (Montreal: 1972) has delved into the intellectual underworld of British Social Credit, but did not deal with Aberhart in any significant way. Additional material on Douglas's activities in England can be found in Francis Richard Swann, "Progressive Social Credit in Alberta, 1935-1940" (unpublished Ph.D. dissertation, University of Cincinnati, 1971).

John J. Barr's *The Dynasty: The Rise and Fall of Social Credit in Alberta* (Toronto: 1974) is good on the administrations of Manning and Strom, but added little new on Aberhart. Barr was a member of the Alberta Social Credit Party's "think tank" during its final years in office and offers some interesting insights into the demise of the party.

Joseph A. Bourdreau has edited a collection of newspaper editorials on

Aberhart in *Alberta, Aberhart and Social Credit* (Toronto: 1975). His work would have been more balanced had he also examined letters to the editors of those newspapers. Aberhart's relationship with the press has also been explored by Robert C. Hill's M.A. thesis "Social Credit and the Press: The Early Years" (University of Alberta, 1977), which noted the totalitarian aspects of the 1937 legislation concerning the press.

Lewis H. Thomas's *William Aberhart and Social Credit in Alberta* (Toronto: 1977) is a collection of primary and secondary sources relating to Aberhart's tripartite career. Some of the more important documents, like the "Yellow" Pamphlet, were unfortunately omitted. Thomas interpreted Aberhart's political career as part of the social-reform tradition.

Ernest Watkins' *The Golden Province: A Political History of Alberta* (Calgary: 1980) has six chapters devoted to Aberhart. A number of minor factual errors mar the text, but Watkins obtained some important behind-the-scene details from tape-recorded excerpts from the diary of Aberhart's former executive secretary, Fred Stone. Those tapes are now in the Glenbow-Alberta Institute.

As more research has been done on Aberhart, Marxist scholarship has also seen Aberhart in new light. Older Marxists such as C.B. Macpherson saw Aberhart's political support coming from farmers and the *petite bourgeoisie*. The urban working-class support of Social Credit has been examined in Alvin Finkel's article "Populism and the Proletariat: Social Credit and the Alberta Working Class," *Studies in Political Economy* 13 (Spring 1984), pp. 109-135. Also important is Larry Hannant's piece "The Calgary Working Class and the Social Credit Movement in Alberta, 1932-35", *Labour/Le Travail* 16 (Fall 1985), pp. 97-116. Finkel has also shown how working-class support for Aberhart fell as he was unable to reverse the economic depression. See Alvin Finkel, "Social Credit and the Unemployed," *Alberta History* 31 (Spring 1983), pp. 24-32. In another study Finkel has expanded on Elliott's "William Aberhart: Right or Left?" (1980), by noting that the Social Credit Party's ideology and support changed during Manning's administration and the party deliberately rewrote its own history. See Alvin Finkel, "Alberta Social Credit Reappraised: The Radical Character of the Early Social Credit Movement," *Prairie Forum* 11 (Spring 1986), pp. 69-86.

Aberhart has received passing comment in prairie fiction. Edward A. McCourt made a brief reference to him in *Music at the Close* (Toronto: 1947). Aberhart was parodied in Robert Kroetsch's *The Words of My Roaring* (Markham, Ont.: 1977), as "Applecart." By far the best piece of fiction that captures the period is Bruce Powe's *Aberhart Summer* (Toronto: 1983), which was been built around Aberhart's election campaign of 1935.

The richest source of primary source material on Aberhart's life and career is found in the Premiers' Papers in the Provincial Archives of Alberta at Edmonton. Since Aberhart died in office, his papers where quickly put into storage and appear to be intact. The archives of the Glenbow-Alberta Institute are another important source for material on Aberhart. The collections used in this study are listed in the introduction to the Notes.

INDEX

■

PHOTO CREDITS

■

Cover photo, courtesy Public Archives of Canada, Ottawa.
pp. 4, 7, 14, 19, 49, 80, 193, 197, 206, 208, 210, 212, 218, 220, 241, 242, 248, 251, 254, 257, 260, 265, 267, 275, 276, 277, 279, 282, 283, 284, 285, 288, 293, 298, courtesy Provincial Archives of Alberta, Edmonton
p. 82, courtesy Clarence Otterbein
pp. 81, 103, 159, 192, 246, courtesy Glenbow Museum Archives
pp. 222, 291, courtesy *MacLean's* Magazine
p. 244, courtesy the Edmonton *Journal*
pp. 39, 41, 69, 72, 99, 194, courtesy the Calgary *Herald*
Images on pp. 112, 156, 184, 314, were reproduced from the authors' collections.